CONTEMPORARY ISSUES IN MARKETING

Sara Miller McCune founded SAGE Publishing in 1965 to support the dissemination of usable knowledge and educate a global community. SAGE publishes more than 1000 journals and over 800 new books each year, spanning a wide range of subject areas. Our growing selection of library products includes archives, data, case studies and video. SAGE remains majority owned by our founder and after her lifetime will become owned by a charitable trust that secures the company's continued independence.

Los Angeles | London | New Delhi | Singapore | Washington DC | Melbourne

Edited by
Ayantunji Gbadamosi

CONTEMPORARY ISSUES IN MARKETING

PRINCIPLES & PRACTICE

Los Angeles | London | New Delhi
Singapore | Washington DC | Melbourne

Los Angeles | London | New Delhi
Singapore | Washington DC | Melbourne

SAGE Publications Ltd
1 Oliver's Yard
55 City Road
London EC1Y 1SP

SAGE Publications Inc.
2455 Teller Road
Thousand Oaks, California 91320

SAGE Publications India Pvt Ltd
B 1/I 1 Mohan Cooperative Industrial Area
Mathura Road
New Delhi 110 044

SAGE Publications Asia-Pacific Pte Ltd
3 Church Street
#10-04 Samsung Hub
Singapore 049483

Editor: Matthew Waters
Assistant editor: Jasleen Kaur
Production editor: Sarah Cooke
Marketing manager: Lucia Sweet
Cover design: Francis Kenney
Typeset by: C&M Digitals (P) Ltd, Chennai, India
Printed in the UK

Library of Congress Control Number: 2019932562

British Library Cataloguing in Publication data

A catalogue record for this book is available from
the British Library

ISBN 978-1-5264-7886-3
ISBN 978-1-5264-7888-7 (pbk)

At SAGE we take sustainability seriously. Most of our products are printed in the UK using responsibly sourced
papers and boards. When we print overseas we ensure sustainable papers are used as measured by the PREPS
grading system. We undertake an annual audit to monitor our sustainability.

CONTENTS

PREFACE

A plethora of evidence all around us indicates that the landscape of marketing knowledge has changed from what it was several decades ago. Contemporary marketing now revolves around the notions of value creation, value delivery and value co-creation between businesses and consumers. The pattern of events all over the world as they unfold, which could be explicated by unprecedented changes in the dimensions of the marketing environment, indicates that marketers, irrespective of the sector in which they operate, and whether they are multinationals with relatively considerable resources or SMEs that are not so well endowed, are now confronted with a whole new level of challenge as they operate to address consumer needs in the marketplace. For example, consumers' needs, tastes and aspirations are changing vis-à-vis what constitutes value in their various transactions, and they are now more informed as is evident in the various ways they explore meeting these copious needs. This is a remarkable development. Similarly, new business opportunities continue to emerge in various forms, ranging from explosive developments in the world of technology, to an unprecedented depth of branding activities in various ways, and the changing roles of different consumer groups in society – not only in terms of the market offerings that might be offered in the marketplace, or the various means by which their values are communicated to their target audiences, but also in relation to other marketing mix elements. Evidently, there is an abundance of extant scholarship attention placed on marketing and this continues to increase, especially in the context of the usual mainstream marketing themes, linking consumption issues to marketing strategies. Nonetheless, there is a palpable gap in the extant literature concerning areas that pinpoint how the frontier of marketing knowledge on business-to-consumer (B2C) and business-to-business (B2B) has shifted. Accordingly, this book, which combines eclectic perspectives on contemporary issues in marketing, is introduced to address this lacuna.

SCOPE OF THE BOOK

Basically, this edited book is a comprehensive package of teaching and learning resources, put together with a clear target user group in mind. The book focuses on exploring contemporary issues in marketing. Hence, the chapters address different themes on how the frontier of marketing knowledge has changed and the implications of this both for theory and practice. The book takes readers through some contemporary and valuable but taken-for-granted topics which centre on consumers' aspirations and lifestyle, with a link to business and society. So, apart from postmodernism; green and sustainable marketing; brand, branding and brand culture; ethics and marketing research; and social marketing, the book also covers further thought-provoking issues including neuromarketing; religion and consumer behaviour; digital and social media marketing; entrepreneurial marketing; business-to-business (B2B) marketing; and contemporary issues in global marketing. By and large, it is hoped that the book should be able to:

- help students to develop a coherent understanding of contemporary issues in marketing as related to both the ultimate consumer and the organisational buyer
- provide students with an understanding of consumption issues beyond the underpinning of orthodox topics and the implications for their practical relevance.

OBJECTIVES

From the overarching aims, the following constitute the driving objectives of the book:

- To explore the paradigm shift in marketing in such a way that this clearly shows the development in thoughts around this discipline and explicates the similarities/overlaps in these perspectives while using appropriate illustrations to contextually delineate the boundaries.
- To develop an understanding of consumer behaviour, paying special attention to postmodernism, shifts in consumption patterns and the associated discourse, and to examine the roles of religion in consumer behaviour.
- To identify, understand and critique the issues around arts marketing; social marketing; and brands, branding and brand culture.
- To articulate a coherent framework for the emerging issues in marketing research; neuromarketing; and digital and social media marketing.
- To explore the emerging issues in entrepreneurial marketing, business-to-business marketing, and to examine contemporary global marketing.

THE TARGET AUDIENCE

The book is intended to be comprehensive and 'direct and to the point' pedagogical material for students, instructors and practitioners in the field. The primary target audience includes both undergraduate and postgraduate students studying contemporary issues in marketing. The secondary target audience of the book consists of practitioners who will find the book an invaluable reference guide and a source of information for operating within the complexities of the prevailing marketing environment.

FEATURES OF THE BOOK

The following are the distinctive features of the book.

Summary of key ideas

At the beginning of every chapter, key learning objectives of the chapter are outlined to give readers a feel of what the chapter contains, and each of the chapters ends with a summary of key ideas discussed in the chapter. This serves as a means of gauging the extent to which the objectives set at the beginning of the chapter have been achieved as well as recapping the learning outcomes.

Style of writing

A clear and interesting communication style has been consciously adopted throughout the book without jeopardising the need to uphold academic excellence. This is meant to ensure the achievement of the prime aim of writing the book which is to produce a comprehensive guide and easy-to-read material with a fulfilling learning experience on the subject of contemporary issues in marketing.

Illustrations, diagrams and case studies

In addition to setting out the key issues both at the beginning and at the end of the chapters, each chapter of the book is supported by various 'real-life' illustrations and exercises to facilitate and enrich students' learning. These provide further explication of the issues discussed in the chapter. Further, many of the chapters feature contemporary case studies that primarily focus on problem solving vis-à-vis the content of the chapter.

Discussion questions

The chapters end with discussion questions that relate directly to the topic discussed in the chapter. This will allow readers to assess themselves on the level of understanding attained on the topic covered and might prove handy for assessments on related modules.

Vignettes

Each of the 14 chapters of this book features vignettes on the relevance of technological advancement, ethics and practitioners' viewpoints on the content of the chapter, entitled

'Digital Focus', 'Ethical Focus' and 'Practitioner's Perspective'. To allow readers optimum engagement with these materials, they are followed by discussion questions relating to the content.

Web resources

In view of the positioning of the book, it is accompanied by valuable online resources: PowerPoint slides, journal articles, instructor's manual, end of chapter discussion questions & answers and video links to provide further context and serve as valuable teaching aids vis-à-vis the topics covered in the text.

Visit https://study.sagepub.com/cim

ACKNOWLEDGMENTS

As the editor of this book, I have received tremendous support and generosity from many people in various ways. Most notably, the contributions, enthusiasm and strong commitment of the chapter contributors of this book are invaluable as they constitute the bones, tendons and ligaments of the book. These colleagues are great scholars to work with. Similarly, I would like to specially appreciate the contributions of the practitioners whose views are presented in the practitioners' perspective vignettes. Their time and effort have contributed towards making this book a reality. To them I say many thanks. In the same vein, I owe many thanks to the team at SAGE who have supported the project from proposal to final stage: Sarah Turpie, Matthew Waters, Jasleen Kaur, Sarah Cooke and Carina Uchida. Evidently, their expertise and commitment to the project are noteworthy and significant to the successful completion of this work. Their professional contributions to the text are warmly appreciated.

I am greatly indebted to my family – my wife, Sarah Remilekun Gbadamosi and children (Miracle, Favour and Joy) – for their understanding and encouragement. Their support is much appreciated. Indeed, there are many others who have contributed in various other ways towards making this book a reality, such as those authors whose publications are cited, our students whose enthusiasm and interest in marketing prompted some of the ideas discussed in the book, and others whom I have not explicitly mentioned – I think of you and thank you also. By and large, it is noteworthy that the inspiration and empowerment for this book come from God, for which I am perpetually grateful.

Ayantunji Gbadamosi
University of East London, UK

ABOUT THE EDITOR AND CONTRIBUTORS

Ayantunji Gbadamosi (Bsc Hons, Msc, PhD, FHEA, FCIM, FCMI) is the Research Coordinator and The Chair of the Research and Knowledge Exchange Committee at Royal Docks School of Business and Law, University of East London, UK. He received his PhD from the University of Salford, UK and has taught marketing courses at various institutions, including the University of Lagos (Nigeria), the University of Salford (UK), Manchester Metropolitan University (UK), Liverpool Hope University (UK) and various professional bodies. 'Tunji Gbadamosi has several research outputs – journal articles, chapters in edited books, edited books, monographs, conference papers and case studies. His articles have appeared in numerous journals including the *Journal of Strategic Marketing; Journal of Brand Management; Thunderbird International Business Review; International Journal of Market Research; International Journal of Retail and Distribution Management; Marketing intelligence and Planning; Social Marketing Quarterly; Nutrition and Food Science; Young Consumers; Journal of Fashion Marketing and Management; Society and Business Review; International Journal of Consumer Studies; The Marketing Review; International Journal of Small Business and Enterprise Development; Entrepreneurship and Regional Development; International Journal of Entrepreneurship and Innovation; Journal of Place Branding and Public Diplomacy; Journal of Management Development* and *Industry and Higher Education*. He is the author of the book *Low-income Consumer Behaviour* and the editor of *Young Consumer Behaviour* (Routledge, 2018), *The Handbook of Research on Consumerism and Buying Behaviour in Developing Nations* (IGI Global, 2016) and *Exploring the Dynamics of Consumerism in Developing Nations* (IGI Global, 2019). His co-edited books are *Principles of Marketing: A Value-Based Approach* (Palgrave, 2013) and *Entrepreneurship Marketing: Principles and Practice of SME Marketing* (Routledge, 2011). Dr Gbadamosi is an editorial board member of several academic journals. He has supervised several undergraduate and postgraduate students, including PhD students, to successful completion and served as an examiner for several doctorate degree examinations. He is the current Programme Chair of the International Academy of African Business Development (IAABD). His research interests lie in Consumer Behaviour, SME Marketing, Marketing to Children, and Marketing Communications. He won the Emerald Best Paper Award at the International Academy of African Business Development (IAABD) conference in 2014. He is listed in *Who's Who in the World*.

Adya Sharma is a dedicated professional with more than 20 years of experience. She brings with her rich practical experience from the corporate world that perfectly blends with theory and enhances academics. She has also been connected to the industry as a corporate trainer at the Goldman Sachs Women Entrepreneurship program, the Tata Motors Development Centre, Amdocs, McDonalds, Wipro, Coca Cola, CPHR Services Pvt Ltd, Konnet Solutions Pvt Ltd, Yazaki, Sigatul Mazaraat and Al Vazaratus Saifiyah, among others. She brings with her a missionary zeal to keep the learning environment vibrant and energised. An avid researcher, she has a number of case studies to her credit which are based on real-time events. She has also written research papers in reputed journals, including Scopus-indexed journals, and has authored chapters in books. She is also the editor of the book *Marketing Techniques for Financial Inclusion and Development* by IGI Global. She visited the A4+ Consortium universities in Spain through the University of Pompeu Fabra (UPF) Mobility Programme under an Erasmus grant. She has also been the second supervisor for Master's students at the Berlin School of Economics and Law, Germany. Under her leadership, the Symbiosis Centre for Management was ranked the best institute in India in 2015, 2016, 2017 and 2018 (India today AC Nielson ranking and Times of India ranking).

Aidan Kelly is a Senior Lecturer in Marketing at Royal Docks School of Business and Law, University of East London. His research interests are broadly in the areas of advertising, brand management and consumer research and his work has been published in international journals, edited books and at global conferences. His current research project explores consumer collecting practices in the context of analogue music.

Angela Lawrence is a Chartered Marketer and a Senior Lecturer in Marketing at Staffordshire University, where she specialises in digital marketing strategy. She was awarded a Teaching Excellence Fellowship at Staffordshire University in 2017 and champions the use of digital tools in teaching practice, notably sharing best practice in online delivery. Her academic status is underpinned by extensive industry experience as a B2B marketer within industrial manufacturing organisations in the North West of England. She has also worked in fully integrated marketing agencies and ran her own consultancy business before moving into the Higher Education (HE) sector. Angela is currently studying for a Doctorate in Education, with her research exploring the use of social media within HE and its perceived impact on academic identity.

Christopher John Bamber has been a Research Fellow in Agile Manufacturing at the University of Salford. He is currently Managing Director of OLC (Europe) Ltd. He has worked at Higher Education colleges in Manchester and Bolton and studied Mechanical Engineering at the University of Central Lancashire. Bamber is enthusiastic about management systems and in particular integrated management systems. As a professional and experienced change agent, he is familiar with modern management techniques related to continual improvement, six sigma, managerial breakthrough, agile manufacturing and project management. He has successfully led organisations to achieve ISO 9001, ISO 14001, OHSAS 18001 and ISO 27001.

David James Bamber is Director of PhD Studies at Bolton Business School (University of Bolton). He has worked as Research Fellow in Organizational Learning at the University of Salford, as Senior Lecturer in International Marketing at Liverpool Hope University, and is External Examiner in International Marketing and Business at several UK universities. He is a founding member of the Chartered College of Teaching. He has been track co-chair for Organisational Studies with the British Academy of Management for 15 years and has presented academic papers at 40 international peer-reviewed conferences. He is a reviewer for the *International Journal of Contemporary Hospitality Management*.

Ejindu Iwelu MacDonald Morah, BSc (Hons), MA, PhD, ACIM, FHEA, is a Lecturer in Marketing at the School of Management and Marketing, Westminster Business School, University of Westminster, London. He received his PhD in Marketing and International Business from Anglia Ruskin University, Cambridge, and has taught Marketing and Research Methodology courses at various universities, including Anglia Ruskin University and the University of Wales. He has presented papers at several academic conferences, including the Academy of Marketing Conference, British Academy of Management (BAM) and European Conference on Research Methodology for Business Studies. His research interests, consulting works and publications are in the field of Marketing Science (Marketing Metrics and Marketing Analytics), Business-to-Business Marketing, Marketing Strategy, Change Management and Innovation. He reviews for and is a member of the editorial and scientific boards of several international journals, including *The Service Industries Journal* (UK), *International Business Research* (Canada), *International Journal of Business and Management* (Canada), *International Journal of Marketing Studies* (Canada) and *International Journal of Arts and Sciences* (USA). Ejindu has supervised undergraduate and postgraduate student dissertations and serves as an external examiner for several doctorate examinations for universities in the UK and South Africa. Before joining academia, Ejindu had extensive industry experience traversing banking and finance (investment and commercial banking) and the oil and gas sectors. He is a member of the Chartered Institute of Marketing, a fellow of the Higher Education Academy and a football coach (licensed by the English Football Association (the FA)).

Geraint Evans is an award-winning international chief marketing officer, board advisor, author and academic researcher. He has held a variety of global marketing leadership roles and delivered work for brands such as ODEON Cinemas Group, Virgin Media, Tesco, Boots and Whitbread. Geraint also consults with a wide variety of clients from SMEs to global blue-chip companies on marketing, digital and strategic growth. He has a PhD in Marketing and Entrepreneurship, is a Visiting Fellow at St Mary's University, and is a Fellow and Board Member of the Chartered Institute of Marketing.

Gift Donga is a PhD candidate in the Department of Business Management at the University of Venda. Gift is registered for a PhD in Business Management and his thesis is in the area of consumer behaviour, specialising in the adoption of mobile commerce among young consumers. His research interests are in the areas of e-commerce, technology and culture.

Hsiao-Pei (Sophie) Yang, Senior Lecturer in Marketing, Coventry University, held several marketing posts in industry prior to joining academia. Her research interests are in the marketing of Higher Education, the consumption of services and Entrepreneurial Marketing. Since acquiring her doctorate, Sophie has published in a number of journals, including the *Journal of General Management*. In addition, she has written book chapters and case studies in the areas of services marketing and consumer behaviour.

Nashaat H. Hussein is Assistant Professor of Childhood Sociology in the Alsun and Mass Communication Department of Misr International University in Cairo. He has published extensively in *Cairo Papers in Social Sciences* of the American University in Cairo, the *Journal of the History of Childhood and Youth* of the Johns Hopkins University Press, and the *International Journal of Sociology and Social Policy* (Emerald Publications). He is the author of 'Egyptian Families' in the *Encyclopedia of Family Studies* (Wiley Blackwell, 2016), and 'Children's Consumer Perception' in *Young Consumer Behaviour: A Research Companion* (Routledge, 2017).

Nayyer Samad is a Senior Lecturer in Marketing at the University of Northampton. He has over 25 years of industry experience in pharmaceutical and healthcare marketing with multinational firms like Sandoz, SmithKline Beecham and Roche at senior positions, and over 10 years of teaching experience at undergraduate and postgraduate levels in the UK, the Middle East and South Asia. He holds a PhD in Social Marketing from the University of East London and an MBA from the Institute of Business Administration, Karachi. He is research active and has presented papers at international marketing conferences and has publications to his credit in peer-reviewed journals. His research interests include social marketing models, behaviour change communications and obesity prevention strategy.

Nnamdi O. Madichie, PhD, is Director of the Centre for Research & Enterprise at the Bloomsbury Institute London. His research interests encompass marketing (consumer behaviour, sports, entertainment, film and media marketing) and entrepreneurship (corporate, diasporic, ethnic minority, gender and social entrepreneurship). Madichie is a Fellow of the Chartered Institute of Marketing. He is also a Fellow of the Higher Education Academy for

England & Wales. He has published papers in mainstream journals such as the *International Marketing Review, International Journal of Entrepreneurship and Innovation, International Journal of Entrepreneurial Behaviour & Research, Marketing Intelligence & Planning* and the *Thunderbird International Business Review*, among others. He is author of 'Marketing Senegal through hip-hop: A discourse analysis of Akon's music and lyrics', published in the *Journal of Place Management and Development* (2011), and of 'The Nigerian movie industry "Nollywood": A nearly perfect marketing case study', published in *Marketing Intelligence & Planning* (2010).

Paul Dobson is a Senior Lecturer at Staffordshire Business School (SBS) in digital and strategic marketing, including search engine optimisation, conversion rate optimisation, growth hacking, inbound and outbound marketing, mobile and social media marketing. He has been lecturing and undertaking consultancy at SBS for eight years. Paul is actively involved in giving hands-on demonstrations of making Digital Marketing effective in various European businesses environments, which includes: changing a loss-making pub into a profit-making one by marketing on Facebook, improving hotels and restaurants' search engine ranking with inbound marketing and SEO, enabling restaurants to increase sales during off-peak times using chatbots, and increasing B2C sales using geolocation. Paul has three postgraduate degrees and is undertaking a PhD in Social Enterprise Marketing Strategies. He is a Fellow of the Higher Education Academy, Fellow of the Chartered Management Institute, member of the Academy of Marketing and member of the Association of Internet Researchers. Prior to SBS, Paul worked for over 25 years in various internal and external consultancies, including in the UK, France and Germany. As a hobby, he helps local charities, social enterprises and businesses with their digital and strategic marketing.

Rebecca Fakoussa is a Senior Lecturer at the University of Northampton, UK, where she enthusiastically teaches and publishes. She is an international family business consultant and mediator working with small to multinational businesses on issues ranging from succession to strategy. Rebecca has particular expertise in start-up, nextGen, marketing, consumer behaviour, international business, cross-cultural management, decision making and women on boards. She has started and run several of her own companies and gained her PhD in Family Business Governance from Kingston University in Surrey, UK.

Richard Shambare is an Associate Professor in the School of Business & Finance at the University of the Western Cape. He teaches entrepreneurship and marketing in the Department of Business Management, where he also supervises postgraduate students. Shambare's research interests are in consumer behaviour, technology acceptance, microfinance and the entrepreneurship–marketing interface. He has published extensively in peer-reviewed journals, book chapters, and presented at international conferences.

Rula M. Al Abdulrazak is a branding and global marketing specialist with diverse experience in the oil industry, business consultancy and higher education. She spent over a decade working with multicultural organisations, mainly Royal Dutch Shell and the European Commission, before joining academia at Royal Holloway, University of London and University of East London. She was awarded senior fellowship status by the Academy of Higher Education. Rula trained as an accountant and holds a BSc in Economics and Management, Accounting Major, and a postgraduate degree in Finance Management from Damascus University, from which she also received a postgraduate degree in Psychology and Education. At Royal Holloway, Rula completed an MBA in International Management and Marketing, and a PhD in Marketing ('The Branded Nation: A comparative review with reference to Syria and the United Arab Emirates'), in addition to a postgraduate degree in Inspiring Skills in Teaching and Learning. She researches in branding, nation and place marketing, cross-cultural and Islamic marketing. Her interests include the examination of cultural diplomacy and art with reference to the United Arab Emirates, Arab Spring and nation image, nation-brand state and public diplomacy, trust, religiosity and branding in Islamic contexts. Rula is an editor and international and interdisciplinary conference organiser. She champions research income generation, research ethics, knowledge exchange and business consultancy.

Vishwas Maheshwari is Associate Dean with student experience responsibility at Staffordshire Business School. Also, as Professor of Marketing, Vish leads research development in the broader area of Marketing but specifically within Brand Management, in collaboration with peers nationally and globally. His research and practice-led projects have been supported by the European Regional Development Fund, British Academy's Newton Fund and Santander Bank's International Research Excellence Scheme. Vish is a Co-founding Chair for Place Marketing and Branding track and Special Interest Research group (SIG) at the Academy of Marketing. He is a Fellow of the Chartered Institute of Marketing; Senior Fellow of the Higher Education Academy and serves as visiting professor at the University of Sao Paulo. Vish is an active member of the Academy of Marketing Science and the American Marketing Association. He serves as a member of the editorial board for two emerald journals and as an active reviewer for several reputed publication outlets. Vish has published a number of journal articles and book chapters in branding and marketing management, including digital marketing. He is also a Senior Examiner at the Chartered Institute of Marketing.

Yiwen (Evie) Hong (Bsc, Msc, PhD) is researcher in Marketing at Coventry University. She specialises in the areas of entrepreneurship and entrepreneurial marketing. Yiwen has a particular research interest in the interaction between entrepreneurship and the online environment, focusing on the exploitation and development of entrepreneurial marketing in an online business context. She is interested in understanding how entrepreneurial marketing strategies are being re-shaped by the evolving online landscape. More specifically, her recent research has examined decision-making and practices in China's rapidly expanding and large e-commerce market from an entrepreneurial perspective.

Zubin Sethna is a Reader in Entrepreneurial Marketing & Consumer Behaviour at Regent's University London. He has worked in a variety of universities in the UK and, as an Associate Professor of Marketing, Zubin has been responsible for managing a postgraduate portfolio with approximately 1500 students and an income of over £15m. He has successfully launched five businesses (one of which won a UK National Award). In his capacity as Managing Consultant at Baresman Consulting (www.baresman.com), he has integrated marketing strategy/ communications with management consultancy and training for numerous organisations both in the UK and internationally, and across a variety of industry sectors (health care, professional services, music, travel, manufacturing, retail, IT, education and 'cottage' industries). He has written the books *Entrepreneurial Marketing: Global Perspectives* (Emerald, 2013) and *Consumer Behaviour* (Sage, 4th edn, 2019, with Jim Blythe), the latter being the UK and Europe's most popular textbook on consumer behaviour and a bestseller! Zubin has conducted research all over the world and has raised external funding of over £570k for academic projects. He has delivered invited keynote lectures at HE institutions in the UK, EU, China and India. Sethna is also editor-in-chief of the prestigious *Journal of Research in Marketing and Entrepreneurship*.

PART I
Introducing Contemporary Marketing

1
MARKETING: THE PARADIGM SHIFT

Ayantunji Gbadamosi

Learning Objectives

At the end of this chapter, you should be able to understand and discuss:

- The meaning of marketing and how this has changed over the years
- Historical perspectives on marketing and various marketing orientations
- Customer value as the anchor of contemporary marketing and the notion of value co-creation in marketing
- Transactional and relationship marketing and their significance for contemporary marketing
- The notion of customer loyalty and internal marketing
- Demarketing and its relevance in contemporary marketing

INTRODUCTION

From all indications, marketing is not a new phenomenon. However, just as we humans experience change, grow and have new associations, it has undergone considerable changes over the years. This could be explained and justified in a number of ways. For example, we can simply examine these changes from the elements associated with it, such as consumer needs, wants, the nature of exchange, markets, market offerings and those other things that form part of the building blocks that define it. It is now crystal clear that the interaction between these concepts in the way marketing is being defined is in a state of flux. This is the case irrespective of the lens through which marketing is perceived, be it as an academic discipline, a practice or business philosophy. In view of this, this chapter sets the scene for others in this book by conceptually tracing the historical issues in marketing and linking it to the notions of value creation, value delivery and value co-creation; and discusses how these are linked to contemporary perspectives on the issues. The chapter takes us through areas of convergence among these views but also explores the tensions that persist among the contributions. The issue of relationship marketing (RM), customer loyalty, internal marketing, and demarketing are discussed in this chapter in such a way that anchors the fundamental discussion of the paradigm shift in marketing principles. The chapter also links this discourse to the emerging discussions on fundamental postulations of marketing-mix elements and the associated variants.

WHAT IS MARKETING? EXAMINING THE PERSPECTIVES

It is likely that readers of this book will ask the question: Why is the meaning of marketing required in a book on contemporary issues in marketing? The idea is that, for us to know how the landscape of marketing has changed over the years, it is important to know exactly what the term is and whether the way it is being defined has changed with the way it is being practised. Meanwhile, it is interesting to know that there are various misconceptions about the term *marketing*. The discrepancy in the way the term is defined or explained is due to a number of reasons. Essentially, these revolve around how people have practised the profession or seen others use it in the past. Some simply call it public relations (PR), market research, advertising, branding, and many other things based on their knowledge of how marketing is used. While these are relevant to marketing in one form or another, it would be very limiting to restrict the meaning to each of these in that marketing covers more in terms of scope and significance. Meanwhile, as noted by Brodie et al. (1997), one of the very popular definitions of marketing among academics is that provided by the American Marketing Association (AMA) in 1985, which states that 'marketing involves the integrated analysis, planning, and control of the "marketing mix" variables (product, price, promotion, and distribution) to create exchange and satisfy both individual and organisational objectives' (AMA, 2013).

This definition highlights some useful points that are noteworthy. We can infer from this perspective that marketing involves the notion of exchange; it is a process and considers the traditional marketing mix as salient. It also recognises the need for businesses to satisfy the objectives of organisations and individuals. However, it is short of perfect and has attracted criticism on many grounds, as argued by authors such as Gummesson (1987) and Grönroos (1989). Overall, these criticisms could be summarised into the fact that the focus of the definition is not contemporary enough and does not adequately cover the emerging issues in the marketing of today. Meanwhile, a more recent definition approved by the Board of Directors of the American Marketing Association has fine-tuned this old definition and added a number of new elements. It presents marketing as 'the activity, set of institutions, and processes for creating, communicating, delivering, and exchanging offerings that have value for customers, clients, partners, and society at large' (July 2013).

If examined closely, we can see that this definition extends our understanding of what marketing stands for by emphasising the notion of *value*. To put this discussion in the right perspective, it will be useful to define the term value, which stands as a dominant element in contemporary marketing. As noted by Solomon et al. (2013), value can be defined as the perceived benefits minus the perceived costs in relation to money, time or emotion. This is a very useful definition in the sense that it indicates that the value of a transaction is not necessarily in money alone. Imagine you urgently need a bottle of water just before your class and this is available in a vending machine just at the entrance of the class for 30 pence more than you could get it from a supermarket. Considering the time and the emotional input involved, the value of getting it just at the entrance of the room will probably be higher than going all the way to the supermarket to get the same product at a relatively cheaper price. So, we can see that the definition of value may not be as straightforward as it seems. To reiterate this point, an exploratory study by Zeithaml (1988: 13) revealed that respondents who were customers defined value in four different ways:

1. Value is low price.
2. Value is whatever I want in a product.
3. Value is the quality I get for the price I pay.
4. Value is what I get for what I give.

Given the differences in what consumers perceive as value, Zeithaml (1988) suggests that perceived value could simply be defined as the consumer's overall assessment of the utility of a product based on perceptions of what is received and what is given.

Meanwhile, the notion of value varies in the way it relates to these various stakeholders. Some of the key stakeholders are:

- customers
- channel members
- suppliers

- producers
- society
- shareholders.

By and large, as shown in this latter definition of marketing, the focus of contemporary marketing is about value creation and delivery and involves various parties and institutions towards fulfilment of the marketing functions. This perspective has been reflected in some of the most recent definitions noted in the marketing literature, as indicated in Table 1.1.

Table 1.1   Some examples of contemporary definitions of marketing

Definitions/Perspectives	Authors
'Marketing is a social process and managerial process by which individuals and organisations obtain what they need and want through creating and exchanging value with others'	Kotler and Armstrong (2018: 29)
'It has become accepted that the co-creation of value, as perceived by the parties to a relationship, lies at the very heart of both marketing theory and practice and this notion has spread beyond simple commercial exchange to infuse all manner of human interactions'	Baker (2016: 20)
'Marketing is to establish, develop and commercialise long-term customer relationships, so that the objectives of the parties involved are met. This is done by a mutual exchange and keeping of promises'	Grönroos (1989: 57)

We can sketch out the elements associated with contemporary marketing in one form or another, as shown in Figure 1.1.

As Figure 1.1 shows, marketing has the customer at the centre of the system. Essentially, a marketing system is about satisfying consumers' needs through exchange. These needs refer to the discrepancy that occurs between the current state and the desired state of the consumer, but human wants are desires for specific market offerings to satisfy these needs. Since consumption is closely linked to the available resources, demand plays a pivotal role in this contemporary marketing system in that it is about consumers' wants being coupled with purchasing power. Ultimately, an effectively managed system will not only yield profit to the organisations but also create value for all stakeholders in one form or another.

HISTORICAL BACKGROUND OF MARKETING

It is reasonable to acknowledge that the discourse of marketing could be conceptualised along two dimensions – thought and practice. This will aid our understanding of the historical

Figure 1.1 The customer at the heart of marketing

knowledge around this important subject. More often than not, history has been a good link between the past and the future. Schmidt and Garcia (2010) put it in an interesting way by stating that people are 'backpackers' over time, in that they carry the remains of their experiences and those of others from one place to another for the purpose of assembling historical narratives by exploring documents. The historical account of marketing given by Tamilia (2009) pinpoints that commerce has existed from time immemorial in that men's survival has always been about trading and giving. This emphasises the notion of exchange, which was discussed by Bagozzi (1975) as being fundamental to marketing. It explains why any useful definition of marketing would have the term either directly stated or implicitly indicated. Apparently emphasising the same message echoed by Tamilia (2009), Baker (2016: 9) stresses that markets and marketing are as old as exchange itself. It is also shown by Cochoy (2014) in his article 'The American Marketing Association: A handrail for marketers and marketing history', about the first textbook on marketing, *The Marketing of Farm Products*, by L. D. H. Weld and published by Macmillan in 1919. This is good information for us to know in that it provides a platform for the contemporary marketing that is practised to this day. Meanwhile, Tamilia (2009) traced the roots of marketing to the thinking of the great philosophers Aristotle, Homer and Plato; Aristotelian economic philosophy was refined by scholars around the 12th and 13th centuries to result in a modern view of buying and selling (Tamilia, 2009). To add to the existing knowledge on how marketing thoughts evolve, Cochoy (2014) provides a very useful explanation which cannot be ignored towards having a good account of the development of marketing thoughts. Citing Bartels (1976: 22), he indicates that 'the first history of marketing was discontinuous [as] the first marketers were isolated figures without mutual knowledge of their respective initiatives' (Cochoy, 2014: 540). Nevertheless, there is acknowledgement of the work of Assistant Professor E. D. James who gave the first lecture on marketing in 1902 at the University of Michigan, and a recognition of the fact that marketing was explicitly introduced at Northwestern University in 1919 (Maynard, 1941; Ross and Richards, 2008; Cochoy, 2014). This seems to confirm the claim that marketing only became an academic discipline involving teaching, research and writing in North America around 1902–03 (Bartels, 1962; Witkowski, 2010). Overall, historically, it is indicated that marketing did not reach maturity until the mid-1930s (Witkowski, 2010).

There are also other interesting historical antecedents associated with marketing that are noteworthy. For example, it is documented that brand marketing was traced to the 1950s by historians, whereas the practice of modern brand marketing has been claimed to date back to the Industrial Revolution (Petty, 2012). Similarly, while market segmentation has been an important part of modern marketing, it is interesting to know that its practice has been in place throughout the 19th century, as demonstrated by Fullerton (2012) who explores the evolution of this practice over the period of 1800–1928. According to him, using the German book trade as an analytical case example, the transition of market segmentation from practice to thought may be traced to the publication of the publisher Host Kliemann's discussion of this phenomenon in 1928 (Fullerton, 2012). Also, the regulatory system in relation to advertising that is in place in the USA now has not always been like that. The detailed account of the historical development of modern US advertising regulation by Petty (2015) suggests that until the mid-19th century, when it was established that businesses' assertion claims should not be trusted, the maxim was that 'business could do no wrong' (Preston, 1996: 75; Petty, 2015: 526). More importantly, the post office has been credited as the first government agency to deal with blatant false advertisement through criminal prosecution, and it is noteworthy that in 1872 dealing directly with deceptive product advertising and mail fraud was authorised (Petty, 2015), while these efforts culminated in several developments around this issue, leading to this digital age.

Meanwhile, as many more authors become interested in critical marketing and marketing history, the literature is now replete with enriching details of how several aspects of marketing evolved, such as advertising, marketing research, PR and several other elements associated with marketing. However, since these aspects are beyond the scope of this chapter and nor are they the focus of this book, including such details here will be of minimal or no value. However, it is important to note that what we want to establish here is that marketing has come of age over the decades in several ways, and it will be particularly useful for our knowledge now to see what has changed along with the pattern of these changes.

MARKETING ORIENTATIONS

It is useful to start this discussion of marketing orientation with Schwarzkopf's claim (2015: 296) that in customer-centric marketing theory, the customer serves as the alpha and omega of all marketing activities and, increasingly, as the initiator of marketing innovations. This is reminiscent of the common saying 'he who pays the piper dictates the tune'. But as we have seen from the history of marketing, marketing thoughts and practices began a while ago. The notion of customer supremacy has not always been the case. Clearly, the customer is fundamentally interested in satisfaction over the years, but what constitutes value to business and to consumers has changed over time. The notion of various orientations of marketing presents a clear picture of these changes over the years, in phases. Specifically, it provides some understanding of the change in value perception over time, as demonstrated in Figure 1.2.

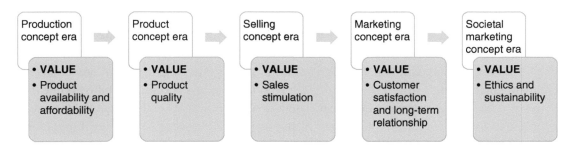

Figure 1.2   Phases of marketing

Production concept orientation to marketing is about focusing effort on attaining efficiency in production coupled with a wide distribution strategy. This is based on the assumption that value is defined by product availability and affordability. This orientation favours ensuring low prices, which are brought about by mass production and intensive distribution. Much as it sounds desirable to produce en masse as it lowers unit costs and ensures wide availability, this is of little benefit if the items produced are not needed by the target markets. This is the main flaw of this orientation. Meanwhile, unlike the production orientation, the main determinant of value in the product concept era is product quality. With this philosophy of marketing, the focus for the company is on producing the market offerings it considers to be of good quality. It does sound good to produce something of good quality. We often hear the word quality being used to describe market offerings: shoes, bags, clothes, cars, furniture and a host of other items. Nevertheless, the weakness of this orientation is that there could be a discrepancy between how the firm defines quality and the way the consumer perceives it. A seminal article by Theodore Levitt, entitled 'Marketing Myopia', gives an explanation of this issue, showing that firms in this scenario focus on the product and not the customer (Levitt, 1960). So, this orientation is not specifically in tune with contemporary marketing practice.

The selling concept is about sales stimulation as anchored by aggressive favourable mention of the products of the organisation to the target audience (Gbadamosi et al., 2013). The assumption is that if this is done, many people will buy and the firm will achieve profitability. However, this orientation ignores the key relevance of need satisfaction as an input to the firm's sales and profitability. So, again, the effort is misplaced as in the production and the product concepts. The firm is about focusing on making as many sales as possible without paying attention to the needs of customers and to how future relationships with them could be developed and maintained.

A marketing orientation is focused not only on satisfying the customer but also on ensuring the relationship is maintained. Following this philosophy of business entails identifying the needs and wants of the market, designing appropriate market offerings and strategies to help the firm satisfy those needs, and maintaining relationships with the customer. If effectively managed, these activities will lead the firm to profitability and the achievement of its other long-term goals in business.

The societal marketing concept orientation shares the points highlighted in other marketing orientations but with some extensions. It emphasises ethics and sustainability. While the societal marketing concept upholds satisfying the needs and wants of the target markets, and promises to be profitable to the business, it also emphasises the need to do these things in an ethical and sustainable way such that societal welfare is maintained and enhanced. Of what use is the satisfaction of the customer in the purchase of a product that will eventually harm the consumer and other societal members in the future? This is why the notion of ethics and sustainability discussed in Chapter 7 is now gradually becoming a point of competitive advantage in this day and age, as consumers are becoming more demanding and expecting businesses to be socially responsible.

VALUE AND VALUE CO-CREATION IN MARKETING

Having established that value occupies a focal point in contemporary marketing, it is noteworthy to examine the notion of value co-creation and how this shapes new thoughts around marketing these days. The central argument on the issue of value co-creation is that consumers' role in a marketing system is not that of a passive party whose concern in the system is simply to get the products and the associated value delivered to them by marketers, but rather is that of active members of the system who engage in co-production of value. One of the prominent publications on this topic that can enrich our understanding here is Vargo and Lusch's (2004) article 'Evolving to a New Dominant Logic in Marketing'. The authors' rich account of this important topic draws attention to the fact that being fixated on the notion of value delivery to the customer is built around the early marketing thought that revolves around physical products being the element in the marketing exchange. However, in their argument, the new dominant logic in marketing should see service provision rather than physical goods as being fundamental to economic exchange. On this perspective, the customer is continuously involved in thoughts around what kind of products and services are offered by the organisation. So, in a value co-creation system, the customer's perspective is paramount in new product development (NPD), including the development of new service offerings and the most effective way to make them available for consumption in such a way that satisfies the needs identified. Thoughts around the fundamental relevance of service provision have been expressed by many other authors such as Grönroos (2000) and Gummesson (1998). Their contributions stress that firms that provide services cannot produce something of value without the customer, and value is created through relationships between the two parties. A number of examples of value co-creation are noticeable around us these days. Various universities do not only consult students when developing programmes to gauge their views on the usefulness of such proposed provisions, but also consider employers' perspectives as significant inputs into the process. Some airlines and hotels have changed various parts of their business in response to the views and concerns of their customers, and continuously maintain such relationships for the survival of their business.

Digital Focus 1.1

The evolving digital economy

The business world has been transformed significantly in recent times. Invariably, astute businesses do not leave things to chance in relation to serving their various target markets in that the consumers of today are now more demanding, sophisticated and informed than ever before. An important part of this is the digital revolution that has brought businesses and consumers closer to one another. Consumers can now sit in the comfort of their own homes and order clothing, food and a host of other items. Several supermarkets, in the USA, the UK, Canada and in several other parts of the world, now make it possible for their customers to order items and have them delivered at the stated address on an agreed day, locally and internationally. In a recent write-up in the *Search Engine Journal* (SEJ), it is estimated, based on data from various sources, that content marketing will be worth around $313 billion by 2019 (McCoy, 2018). In addition to this, in reference to Shopify Plus (2018), the estimated global value of ecommerce sales for 2021 shown by HubSpot (2018) is at around $4.5 trillion. It is therefore not surprising that retailers of various product categories, such as Walmart, Amazon and Tesco, to mention but a few, are exploring this digital economy to create and deliver value to their customers. One of the key issues that constitute a hurdle to emarketing is that of trust. For instance, 84% of people would not make a purchase if their intended transaction involved an unsecured website (HubSpot, 2018). Nevertheless, businesses are now looking into this more closely, integrating it into their budget for digital marketing to ensure loyalty among their customers and improve traffic to their website.

Sources

HubSpot (2018) The Ultimate List of Marketing Statistics for 2018. Available at: www.hubspot.com/marketing-statistics (accessed 17 December 2018).

McCoy, J. (2018) What is internet marketing? Your guide to today's online marketing. *Search Engine Journal*, 8 January. Available at: www.searchenginejournal.com/internet-marketing/230047 (accessed 17 December 2018).

Questions

1. Visit a website of an organisation; make a note of its product categories, the prices, the organisation's policy around delivery, and the way the benefits of the products are communicated to visitors on the website. What are your evaluations of these details in relation to satisfying the needs and wants of customers in the contemporary business era?
2. To what extent would you agree that digital marketing will eventually totally replace conventional marketing practice?

TRANSACTIONAL VERSUS RELATIONSHIP MARKETING

The notion of profitability emphasised in the definition of marketing is crucial to the success of the organisation if the business is to continue to exist. This explains why business will have to put strategies in place to ensure that this goal is achieved. In an attempt to make profits, the focus of some businesses is on their own objective of maximising sales and they approach this by attracting customers without necessarily making efforts to retain them. This leads us to the crux of transactional marketing that is fundamentally based on use of the marketing mix elements, identified as product, price, place and promotions, towards achieving this objective. However, the changing frontier of marketing practice sounds a note of caution on how businesses should position this pursuit. Extensive studies have shown that pursuing relationship marketing (RM) is a key ingredient for success in contemporary marketing. The term was introduced by Berry (1983) but has become increasingly popular in the marketing literature. Authors like Grönroos (1997, 2017) and Gummesson (1998) have presented significant contributions around this phenomenon. Essentially, it is focused on marketing activities designed to attract, maintain and enhance customer relationships with the organisation. So, the focus of business in a relationship transcends what they could get from specific transactions with a customer or group of customers, to how these could be extended to future transactions in a mutually beneficial way. The justification for this viewpoint is that great value accrues to firms if they can retain their existing customers.

For customers to be served effectively, the scope of the relationship being pursued will have to be appropriate. The literature suggests that a more elaborate relationship involving all stakeholders will be more fruitful to yield the desired outcomes. Payne (1995) identified the following key markets to be focused on by the firm:

- customer markets
- internal markets
- seller markets
- recruitment markets
- influence markets
- referral markets.

The key message is that maintaining strong relationships with these several markets will contribute to ensuring a meaningful relationship with the customer and ultimately to achieving the profitability objective as well.

Several authors have made significant efforts to distinguish between transactional and relationship marketing. In most cases, these efforts are complementary. Meanwhile, to illustrate these two marketing approaches, ten key areas of differences between them have been teased out and fine-tuned from various sources, as shown in Table 1.2.

Table 1.2   Transactional marketing vs relationship marketing

Dimension		Transactional marketing	Relationship marketing
1	Objective	Each party involved is focused on achieving what is best for her	Objectives are shared among parties and they are mutually beneficial
2	Primary focus	High sales volume and attracting new customers towards achieving profitability	Retaining existing customers, satisfying customers, increasing loyalty, increasing profit
3	Time horizon	Short-term	Long-term
4	Emphasis	Economic transaction predominantly based on the marketing mix (4Ps)	Relationship-oriented, linking parties and stakeholders in the network, supported by the marketing mix
5	Price	Customers in these transactions tend to be more price-sensitive	The price-sensitivity of customers in relationship-oriented marketing tends to be low
6	The positioning of marketing in the establishment	Marketing is mainly handled by the marketing department	Marketing is a philosophy that drives the entire organisation. Hence, apart from the main marketing specialist, everyone is a part-time marketer
7	The relevance of internal marketing	No or limited importance for success	Substantial strategic importance to success
8	Measurement of customer satisfaction	Through indirect approach such as gauging the market share	Managing the customer base (direct approach)
9	Collaboration/ sharing	Sharing is limited by lack of trust and the arrangement is characterised by opportunistic behaviour	Mutual trust constitutes the basis for strong collaboration and working relationships. Also, the arrangement is characterised by the sharing of business plans and strategies
10	Customer feedback system	Ad hoc customer satisfaction surveys	Real-time customer feedback systems

Source: Adapted from Grönroos (1989, 1997); Payne (1995); Lindgreen et al. (2000); Zineldin (2000); Hollensen (2014)

The fact that you have decided to have breakfast in a particular restaurant on your very first visit to an airport could be for a number of reasons. It could be due to convenience, price, marketing communications messages around the place showing the type of food offered, and so on. Looking at this fundamentally and as shown in Table 1.1, a lot more is required for this experience to be regarded as what will lead to a long-lasting relationship in which you make this a place to be at every visit to the airport. It is logical for every customer to ask the questions, 'Has the organisation done enough to make me engage in repeat purchase? Can I be loyal to this organisation in relation to the fulfilment of my needs for this market offering?' So, for a seller–customer arrangement to be deemed relationship marketing, the focus will have to be a long-term one that transcends the immediate trans-action, and the parties involved in the relationship must see the arrangement as a win-win scenario in which *everyone is a winner*! For example, if the experience is not a particularly pleasant one, as expected at the restaurant, it is most likely you will not visit the same establishment on your next trip to the airport and a further relationship is unlikely to develop. Also, since the link between the parties is more robust and revolves around the value associated with the engagements, the customer is not particularly price-sensitive and both the customer and the business, as well as other related parties, are collaborators shar-ing plans and strategies regarding how the relationships will be sustained and improved over time.

TRUST, COMMITMENT AND RELATIONSHIP MARKETING

The seminal work of Morgan and Hunt (1994) presents a strong case for the significant rel-evance of trust and commitment to relationship marketing. They pinpoint ten forms of relational exchanges with other parties, as follows:

- goods suppliers
- services suppliers
- competitors
- non-profit organisations
- government
- ultimate customers
- immediate customers
- functional departments
- employees
- business units (strategic business units (SBU)).

So, apart from customers, firms have to keep and maintain relationships with several parties. Ultimately, how well they manage these relationships will determine how successful the busi-ness will be in achieving its objectives, including the satisfaction of customers' needs.

For a good explanation of trust, we can turn our attention to a very useful perspective from Rotter (1967) in which it is explained as a generalised expectancy that is held by someone that the 'word of another person can be relied upon'. For example, the promise of a car dealer to a customer that the car to be bought is fuel efficient and reliable should hold true for the dealer to be deemed as a party to be trusted. Similarly, the clients of a lawyer would expect the standard of service that was promised before their involvement with the organisation. To help understand the term further, we can look more closely at elements of trust which are listed as credibility, integrity and benevolence (Heffernan et al., 2008). According to these authors, for the transacting party to be deemed credible, she should be capable of executing the task involved while the integrity component relates to whether the partner keeps the terms of the agreement. As presented, the third component, benevolence, is about the extent to which the partner can act with equity when new conditions that relate to the business issue in question develop (Nicholson et al., 2001; Heffernan et al., 2008). Meanwhile, while drawing from a body of literature, Morgan and Hunt (1994: 23) define relationship commitment as 'an exchange partner believing that an on-going relationship with another is so important as to warrant maximum effort at maintaining it, that is, the committed party believes the relationship is worth working on to ensure that it endures indefinitely'. Reiterating the claim of Morgan and Hunt, it is logical for us to hold that trust and relationship are central to relationship marketing. From this work, the authors identify the antecedents to commitment and trust as:

- relationship termination costs
- shared value
- relationship benefits
- communication
- opportunistic behaviour (the tendency to take undue advantage of another party).

The outcomes of having trust and commitment in a relationship are noted as follows:

- acquiescence and a propensity to leave: will the partner accept the specific request or policies of the other or leave the relationship?
- cooperation: working together to achieve mutual goals
- functional conflict: disagreements that are resolved amicably
- decision-making uncertainty: certainty or uncertainty around information, consequences and confidence that revolve around the decision to be made. (Achrol and Stern, 1988; Morgan and Hunt, 1994)

So, ultimately, the interplay of trust and relationship commitment is at the heart of any meaningful marketplace relationships for contemporary marketing. Meanwhile, have you ever wondered why you stay loyal to your hairdresser, maintain your financial transactions with the same bank, or always visit the same supermarket for your groceries? The answer could be as straightforward as being specifically linked to the notion of trust and commitment, but it could also be more complex than that. We will now look at this more closely in the next section.

Practitioner's Perspective 1.1

Who are the players and what role do they play?

'To survive and flourish organisations need to operate in and develop ecosystems. This is a portfolio of external relationships (formal and informal) in an area that enables the organisation to innovate, create and deliver value and service to customers.

To do this organisations, often led by marketers, must first decide on the relevant set of ecosystems. They should scan broadly and decide on which ecosystems offer the most valuable opportunities both short and long term. They should plot these ecosystems in a grid, rank their strategic importance and decide on their role. Organisations must understand who all the players are and what their different roles are.

Ideally they may want to try and lead these ecosystems but in some ecosystems, where there might for example be a digital giant, leadership may not be possible or desirable. Once the positioning is decided on it is important to understand the dynamics of the ecosystem, where the power lies, and to monitor and continually work on your positioning in the constantly evolving system.

It is important to acknowledge early that you may need to co-exist with a competitor in an ecosystem as together you may be stronger. You may also decide to recruit a new organisation into the ecosystem that may reposition you in the system and/or increase the value of the pie in your favour. Finally it is important to remember that over time ecosystems may die and others may start and flourish and it is as always important to move with the times.' (John Jeffcock, chief executive, Winmark Ltd)

Questions

1. As indicated by John, organisations must understand who all their players are and their respective roles. In view of this, select any two organisations operating in different sectors of the economy. Identify the various players in their relationship systems and highlight similarities and differences between these two establishments and the roles of the players.
2. Assuming you run an organisation that operates within the UK, in view of the UK Brexit arrangement, to what extent would you agree with John Jeffcock that you may decide to recruit a new organisation into the ecosystem that may reposition you in the system and/or increase the value of the pie in your favour?

CUSTOMER LOYALTY

As gathered from the discussion of relationship marketing, it is highly beneficial if business organisations can retain customers. It is strategically useful for having a competitive edge and profitability in a turbulent marketing environment. Besides, it also leads to positive word-of-mouth communications among customers. So, customer loyalty is very pertinent to contemporary marketing theory and practice. What exactly do we mean by loyalty and when can a customer be deemed to be loyal to an organisation, their offerings or brands? Looking at the early contribution of Oliver (1999), we can tease out a definition of customer loyalty as: 'a deeply held commitment to rebuy or repatronize a preferred product/service consistently in the future, thereby causing repetitive same-brand or same brand-set purchasing, despite situational influences and marketing efforts having the potential to cause switching behaviour' (Oliver, 1999: 34). This is a very useful definition in that it emphasises the fact that loyalty is a deeply held phenomenon. This brings in the relevance of the classification of customer loyalty into behavioural loyalty and attitudinal loyalty, as shown in Figure 1.3.

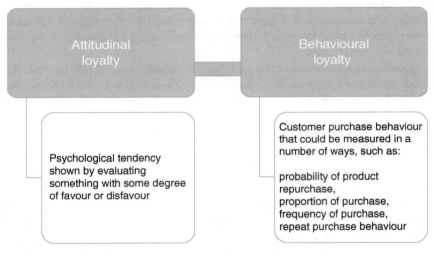

Figure 1.3 Customer loyalty

Source: Adapted from Baron et al. (2009)

It is important to note that a repetitive purchase from an organisation may not in itself necessarily indicate customer loyalty. For example, Gbadamosi (2009) studied the reactions of low-income consumers to low-involvement products and reported interesting findings about loyalty. The study showed that the women that participated in the study often buy the supermarket's own (no frill) brands of these products, which could suggest that they are loyal to these brands. However, the respondents reiterated that they also switch to manufacturers' brands when they are on special offer that makes them cheaper than the supermarket brands they buy frequently. This suggests that these consumers were merely interested in those retailers' brands because of the price, and do not have a deeply held commitment to the brands, as indicated in the definition above. At best, this action could be termed *spurious loyalty*.

It is relevant for us to examine the relevance of the seminal work of Dick and Basu (1994) entitled *Customer Loyalty: Toward an Integrated Conceptual Framework*. The authors provide a very useful framework which highlights various types of patronage behaviour as:

- no loyalty
- spurious loyalty
- latent loyalty
- loyalty (sustainable loyalty).

As the name suggests, the consumer has no loyalty to any particular brand or organisation in a *no loyalty* type, whereas consumers that have *spurious loyalty* in relation to a product service merely show high patronage behaviour but the relative attitude is low. Conversely, consumers that have *latent loyalty* type for a market offering would exhibit relative high attitude but low patronage. In this schema, *sustainable loyalty* (presented as loyalty in the study) shown for a product or service will involve exhibiting high loyalty both in attitude and in behaviour. This is deep-rooted and cannot easily be dissuaded by factors in the marketplace.

While sustainable loyalty is desirable for contemporary marketing practice, it has antecedents. The marketing literature indicates that customer loyalty will be preceded by service quality and customer satisfaction (Orel and Kara, 2014; Prentice and Loureiro, 2017). So, ultimately, the experience of the customer with the brand and the organisation will have to be value-oriented, which is the bedrock of contemporary marketing.

INTERNAL MARKETING

Business organisations are strategically in the marketplace to succeed both in terms of how they create value for their customers and achieve profitability to remain in business. Nonetheless, it is fundamentally essential to manage all resources effectively towards achieving these cardinal objectives. In most cases, these resources are identified as people, money, machines and materials. The notion of internal marketing is about practising marketing but the focus is on employees in this context. So, it is about identifying the needs and wants of employees, and designing appropriate strategies towards satisfying those needs effectively and efficiently in such a way that will make the firm sustainable. This relates to organisations with a focus on transactions involving both physical products and services. However, it has been stated that this is even more necessary in service-oriented organisations because of the nature of the offerings, which is basically and relatively intangible, perishable, variable and inseparable. The offerings are intangible because the transactions do not result in ownership of something physical or tangible that could be touched or felt, unlike a physical product like this book you are using. They are described as perishable as services that are not enjoyed at the time of production are lost forever and cannot be saved for later use, as can be the case with items like clothes and shoes. Services are described as variable in that they may vary by the people offering them or in terms of other circumstances associated with the transaction.

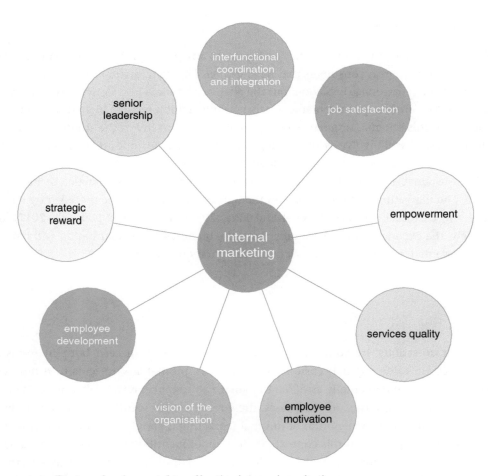

Figure 1.4 Factors fundamental to effective internal marketing

Source: Adapted from Kaurav et al. (2015)

The fact that those providing the services and the service offerings cannot be separated is why they are described as inseparable.

Generally, employees constitute a key part of the organisation as they relate to customers, and their demeanour and experience vis-à-vis the organisation will reflect in their interaction with those customers. So, just as it is discussed under relationship marketing in relation to customers, it is important for businesses to think about how to attract and retain the best employees.

There are many factors that are fundamental to effective internal marketing. Some of these are presented in Figure 1.4.

As an example, we are all aware that, in most cases, our first encounter on visits to banks, universities, hotels and other establishments is with a group of employees that may not be directly involved in the core services being provided by the organisation. However, the impressions given by these front-line employees may be very enduring as regards how we position the organisation in relation to the competition. To astute businesses, the investment and effort expended in ensuring effectiveness in these areas are worthwhile. Employees who are not well trained, who lack the required motivation and who are not empowered could make a firm lose lucrative business, especially as the consumer of today is now more informed, more demanding and dynamic in his tastes and preferences.

DEMARKETING

Up to now, this chapter's attention has been devoted to how organisations make the effort to attract and satisfy customers by meeting their needs in various ways. However, there will be situations or cases in which the firm may want to do something different from this. In this segment, we will be looking at the concept of demarketing and how it is used in the contemporary business world. There is agreement in the marketing literature that the term demarketing was first introduced by Kotler and Levy (1971) and it is defined as the practice of reducing demand. This will sound strange to someone who has been told that marketing is essentially about meeting needs and boosting demand towards profitability. However, there are instances where this approach is warranted. We will look at some of these in order to illustrate the relevance of this strategy to marketing systems.

There are different categories of demarketing as identified by Kotler and Levy (1971). Figure 1.5 has been adapted to show these categories. The first is general demarketing which relates to reducing the total demand for the product. Some of the reasons for this, as identified by these authors, are using it as a way of coping with chronic overpopularity, product shortages and product elimination. As the name sounds, selective demarketing is about reducing or discouraging demand for a product or service from particular groups of consumers so that others may be well served. A relevant example here could be in the policy of some hotels that stipulate that they can no longer accommodate guests with pets in that they know that encouraging this could be difficult to manage in relation to other guests who are not comfortable having pets around them. Ostensible demarketing is ironically aimed at ultimately increasing demand for the market offerings. However, the firm does this by creating an impression of being interested in reducing patronage.

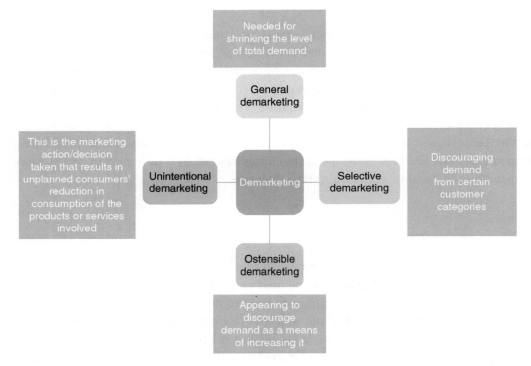

Figure 1.5 Types of demarketing

Source: Adapted from Kotler and Levy (1971)

We have heard at one time or another that due to the associated problems, efforts are being made to reduce consumption of certain products such as tobacco. The use of demarketing and social marketing has been adopted in some instances to address this problem. Due to pressure on public services, some patients have been encouraged to simply visit the local pharmacy to get medicines to address some minor ailments so that people with more serious medical conditions may have access to local doctors. Demarketing is now becoming increasingly popular in business circles for one reason or another. For instance, it has been applied to the marketing of places, where marketing effort is used to deter people from visiting a place (Medway et al., 2010). According to Medway et al., in their study which explored the rationale and strategies for demarketing places, these factors are:

- no marketing
- redirection to alternative places
- informational place demarketing
- restricting access
- pricing mechanisms.

It may also be used, for example, to reduce smoking, such as by tweaking the advertising messages through government policies, as in the cases discussed in the studies of Shiu et al. (2009) and Chauhan and Setia (2016). The case of green demarketing (GD) has also been mentioned in the literature, indicating that various marketing communication messages may be used to encourage consumers to reduce their consumption of certain products in the interest of protecting the environment (these issues are discussed in greater depth in Chapter 7).

What is important to note is that the approach to demarketing may be taken to revolve around any element of the marketing mix: product, price, place, promotion. This strategy is becoming popular as long as there are undesirable consumption practices to be curtailed. Meanwhile, it is interesting to see the statistics given by Lepthien et al. (2017) who quote, from the work of Ang and Taylor (2005), that 50% of some bank customers are unprofitable while 35% of customers who cross-buy are also unprofitable. This is an example of scenarios that make demarketing an attractive strategy. Meanwhile, these authors note that the negative effect of customer demarketing can be sustainable, so it would be useful if the firm could prevent attracting unprofitable customers in the first place by carefully monitoring its customer acquisitions strategy.

Figure 1.5 shows the fourth type of demarketing as unintentional demarketing. In this, while the firm engages in efforts to increase demand or patronage for its offerings, these efforts result in the opposite effect. Consumer behaviour is notably an intriguing phenomenon and, if not carefully and robustly approached, may result in unintentional demarketing. Consumers tend to interpret marketing stimuli differently. A reduction in the price of a product or service is conventionally expected to increase demand for a market offering, but such a step could be misinterpreted to indicate that the product or service is defective or inferior, and may lead to a reduction in demand. A change in packaging, colour, brand, labelling or another element, could trigger a dissenting behaviour pattern from some consumers, which could ultimately reduce demand for the item.

Ethical Focus 1.1

Paying more for pleasure: Demarketing with the sugar tax in the UK

Increasing evidence points at fizzy drinks, fatty products and the like when trying to unravel the causes of some of the most common diseases experienced in recent times. The World Health Organisation (WHO) indicates on its website that overweight and obesity are very much linked to chronic diseases such as cancer, diabetes and cardiovascular conditions. As an example, while in 1975 the number of children and adolescents (aged 5–19) who were overweight or obese was 4%, the proportion had risen to 18% in 2016. The WHO's claim puts the number of children and adolescents who were obese and overweight in 2016 at over 340 million. Clearly, this is one of the most difficult conundrums for a 21st century society, and it requires drastic action. It has reached an alarming stage such that action has been called for all over the world. Consequent upon this, as in other parts of the world, serious debates have emerged in the UK in the past couple of years, leading to the introduction of a sugar tax on 6 April 2018. With this, businesses are now taxed on the basis of the amount of sugar in their products. Products with a sugar content of more than 5g per 100ml attract a special tax, while those drinks with 8g per 100ml or more attract an even higher levy. These taxes are introduced at the point of production or importation, to be 18 pence per litre and 24 pence per litre respectively. Such taxing has been hailed by many as a welcome development in that similar measures have been introduced in France, Finland and Norway (the latter having a chocolate tax). Similarly, a 10% tax was introduced on sugary drinks in Mexico in 2014 with a considerable 12% reduction in consumption over the fiscal year. These examples stand as evidence to naysayers in the UK who think the attempt could be an exercise in futility. Although opinions may vary on the nitty-gritty of how the sugar tax will work in the long run, it seems clear that this step is an attempt to use price to discourage consumption of the affected products.

Sources

Birchall, B., Cambridge, E., Fruen, L. and De Vaal, D. (2018) Bittersweet: Sugar tax 2018 explained – what is it, when did it start, how much is the new fizzy drinks tax and is Coke now more expensive? *The Sun*, 9 July. Available at: www.thesun.co.uk/news/1619208/sugar-tax-uk-fizzy-drinks-coke-sugar-cost (accessed 10 September 2018).

Langley, E. (2018) Sugar tax 2018: How much is it and what does it mean for soft drinks? *Evening Standard*, 6 April. Available at: www.standard.co.uk/lifestyle/foodanddrink/sugar-tax-2018-when-does-it-start-and-what-will-it-mean-a3805971.html (accessed 10 September 2018).

WHO (2018) Obesity. Available at: www.who.int/topics/obesity/en (accessed 10 September 2018).

Questions

1. Using Kotler and Levy's (1971) classification of demarketing, assume that a friend of yours has argued that the UK sugar tax is a typical example of ostensible demarketing. To what extent would you agree or disagree with this viewpoint?

2. In view of this development (the sugar tax) in the UK business environment, what advice would you give a firm whose business is mainly the production and sale of chocolate products, in terms of embracing the social marketing concept?

Case Study 1.1

Marriott Hotels: Customer excellence for contemporary marketing

Hotels are big business in this day and age. Tourists, businesspeople and many other associated customer groups have made the likes of Marriot Hotels busier than usual. With over 6500 properties in 127 countries, Marriott Hotels has moved upward significantly compared to the days of its small start in 1927. Its links across the globe through owners and franchisees cut across several regions, including the USA, Europe, the Caribbean and Latin America and Canada. Nevertheless, the core values of the organisation have remained as the establishment has changed and grown over the years. These are about putting people first, embracing change and focusing on excellence. The hotel chain also prides itself on acting with integrity as it works closely with its various stakeholders. As shown in available records, not only did the organisation achieve over $22 billion revenue for the fiscal year 2017 but it also won several awards. Apart from those it had won in previous years, Marriott International has been recognised by the Ethisphere Institute with '2018 World's Most Ethical Company' and by Fast Company with '2018 Most Innovative Company'. Marriott was also recognised by the Alliance for Workplace Excellence with the '2018 Workplace Excellence Seal of Approval', in addition to being awarded the 'World's Most Admired Company' by Fortune. These are only examples of awards which show how well this group has been rated for creating and delivering value for all its stakeholders.

None of this is surprising in that the hotel's focus is on delivering value to its various stakeholders. The fundamental philosophy of the organisation is to position its customers at the centre of all its services by ensuring that their needs are met effectively. The hotel chain understands that keeping old customers often proves very rewarding, so apart from attracting

(Continued)

(Continued)

new customers through its services and marketing communication messages, it organises Marriot Rewards for its customers. These are in three forms – Silver, Gold and Platinum. The reward system works by earning customers points from various transactions on eligible hotel purchases like spa services, dining, rounds of golf, and so on, and involving both the organisation and its various partner organisations. The objective for doing this is very clear. It is about creating and managing relationships with customers which will ultimately lead to loyalty.

Marriott Hotels is closely connected to its numerous customers in various ways. Since the digital revolution in the world of today has widened customer options for connectivity, the Marriott presence on the internet is prompt, vibrant and robust. This means that customers and partners may be anywhere in the world with their internet access to connect to the organisation for transactions. Exploring the available options, reservations, cancellations and other hotel services is now aided by technology. The hotel chain is also on social media such as Facebook, YouTube, Twitter and Instagram, with thousands of followers. These media provide opportunities for the business to get to know its customers' viewpoints on its services, and serve as a platform for receiving feedback from customers in relation to the dynamics of their needs and wants. This helps to strengthen the competitive position of the organisation in the current turbulent business environment.

The organisation realises that serving its customers very well will also involve working closely with its employees. So, its philosophy of care permeates the entire organisation from customers to staff members by ensuring that the workplace is an environment where everyone feels valued. The emotional, financial and physical needs of employees are seen as paramount and are met. At Marriott, there is a strong motivation to make a difference in the firm's communities. This is called *Take Care* in the organisation. Having a career at Marriott is a stimulating experience, even in the way staff members are welcomed to the organisation. Prospects for career development are bright, even as the organisation embraces diversity in recruitment and staff management.

Marriott is not only concerned about its customers but also understands that, in contemporary marketing, customers are both interested in and how their needs are met in how well specific organisations relate to society. So, it is committed to being positioned as a socially responsible organisation as it focuses on improving the environment and society in general. For example, associates of the organisation have raised approximately $90 million over 30 years for Children's Miracle Network (CMN) hospitals for health care delivery in North America. Overall, Marriott's properties worldwide focus on key areas of the environment, shelter and food, empowering diversity, the vitality of children, and being ready for work, which is about training youth from disadvantaged backgrounds to gain skills for employment. Regarding the environment specifically, the organisation is keenly embracing sustainability in its many ramifications. Its target is to further reduce consumption of energy and water by 20% by the year 2020. Its green credentials are considerable but it also goes beyond what happens in the hotels to achieve this. It encourages its partners and associates to protect natural resources.

The organisation does not only display its environmental goals on its website, it also presents details of its achievements so far for the world to see. This includes over $2 million given to the Amazonas Sustainable Foundation, and nearly $300,000 raised through hotel guests, associates and partners to protect 1.4 million acres of rainforest in Brazil. While some would claim that Marriott is indeed typical of how contemporary marketing practice works, the organisation is not complacent about its achievements. It carries out constant research into how to keep delighting its customers.

Sources

About Marriot – Core values and culture: www.marriott.co.uk/culture-and-values/core-values.mi (accessed 21 December 2018).

About Marriot – Corporate responsibility: www.marriott.co.uk/corporate-social-responsibility/corporate-responsibility.mi (accessed 21 December 2018).

About Marriot – Corporate and career information: www.marriott.co.uk/marriott/about-marriott.mi (accessed 21 December 2018).

Marriot Careers: www.careers.marriott.co.uk/life-at-marriott (accessed 21 December 2018).

Questions for discussion

1. What are the key success factors that show Marriott as an organisation that creates value for its customers?
2. What is the marketing orientation being adopted by Marriott? Provide evidence from case study 1.1 to support your position.
3. Highlight specific points that show that Marriott hotels embrace internal marketing?
4. To what extent would you agree or disagree that Marriot adopts relationship marketing? What other recommendations would you give to the organisation in relation to the practice of this marketing approach?
5. Give an example of a scenario that could lead Marriot hotels to practise demarketing.

SUMMARY OF KEY IDEAS

- Marketing thought and practice have been in existence for some time but marketing thought did not reach maturity until the mid-1930s. Meanwhile, marketing has changed over the years.
- Contemporary marketing revolves around the notion of value co-creation between the firm and the customer, and places great emphasis on relationships rather than the product being offered.

- While transactional marketing is more focused on the short term, the orientation in relationship marketing is long term, and trust and commitment are fundamental to successful relationship marketing.
- Customer loyalty is significant to successful marketing practice. It could be in the form of various types, namely ranging from no loyalty to sustainable loyalty which involves showing high loyalty both in attitude and behaviour and cannot easily be dissuaded by factors in the marketplace.
- Internal marketing is about identifying the needs and wants of employees and putting appropriate measures in place towards addressing these needs.
- There are situations where businesses may have to use *demarketing* which involves reducing the demand for the products or services offered for sale which may take different forms, namely general demarketing, ostensible demarketing, selective demarketing and unintentional demarketing.

Chapter Discussion Questions

1. Looking at the marketing environment in your country, identify four specific examples that indicate that the landscape of marketing activities has changed in recent times. Compare these with four others provided by another student in your class.
2. Assuming that a friend of yours is proposing to start a business over the next summer and has approached you for advice, which of the competing marketing orientations would you recommend to her and why?
3. To what extent would you support the contention that contemporary marketing is anchored by customer value and value co-creation?
4. How would you react to an argument that relationship marketing could be very expensive and may be unnecessary during a volatile marketing environment due to financial constraints?
5. Choose two well-known organisations and compare and contrast the way they embrace these marketing issues:
   i   Internal marketing
   ii   Customer loyalty
   iii Demarketing.

REFERENCES

Achrol, R. and Stern, L. W. (1988) Environmental determinants of decision-making uncertainty in marketing channels. *Journal of Marketing Research*, 25(Feb.), 36–50.

AMA (2013) Definition of Marketing. American Marketing Association. Available at: www.ama.org/AboutAMA/Pages/Definition-of-Marketing.aspx (accessed 20 December 2018).

Ang, L. and Taylor, B. (2005) Managing customer profitability using portfolio matrices. *Journal of Database Marketing & Customer Strategy Management*, 12(4), 298–304.

Bagozzi, R. P. (1975) Marketing as exchange. *Journal of Marketing*, 32–9.

Baker, M. J. (2016) Marketing: Philosophy or function. In M. J. Baker and M. Saren (eds), *Marketing Theory: A Student Text*. London: Sage.

Baron, S., Harris, K. and Hilton, T. (2009) *Services Marketing: Text and Cases*, 3rd edn. Basingstoke: Palgrave.

Bartels, R. (1962) *The Development of Marketing Thought*. Homewood, IL: Richard D. Irwin.

Bartels, R. (1976) *The History of Marketing Thought*, 2nd edn. Columbus, OH: Grid.

Berry, L. L. (1983) Relationship marketing. In L. L. Berry, G. L. Shostack and G. D. Upah (eds), *Emerging Perspectives of Services Marketing*. Chicago, IL: American Marketing Association, pp. 25–8.

Brodie, R. J., Coviello, N. E., Brookes, R. W. and Little, V. (1997) Towards a paradigm shift in marketing? An examination of current marketing practices. *Journal of Marketing Management*, 13(5), 383–406.

Chauhan, H. and Setia, P. (2016) Discouraging cigarette smoking through de-marketing strategies. *Future Business Journal*, 2(1), 31–9.

Cochoy, F. (2014) The American Marketing Association: A handrail for marketers and marketing history. *Journal of Historical Research in Marketing*, 6(4), 538–47.

Dick, A. S. and Basu, K. (1994) Customer loyalty: Toward an integrated conceptual framework. *Journal of the Academy of Marketing Science*, 22(2), 99–113.

Fullerton, R. A. (2012) The historical development of segmentation: The example of the German book trade 1800–1928. *Journal of Historical Research in Marketing*, 4(1), 56–67.

Gbadamosi, A. (2009) Cognitive dissonance: The implicit explication in low-income consumers' shopping behaviour for 'low-involvement' grocery products. *International Journal of Retail & Distribution Management*, 37(12), 1077–95.

Gbadamosi, A., Bathgate, I. K. and Nwankwo, S. (2013) *Principles of Marketing: A Value-based Approach*. Basingstoke: Macmillan International Higher Education.

Grönroos, C. (1989) Defining marketing: A market-oriented approach. *European Journal of Marketing*, 23(1), 52–60.

Grönroos, C. (1997) Keynote paper: From marketing mix to relationship marketing – Towards a paradigm shift in marketing. *Management Decision*, 35(4), 322–39.

Grönroos, C. (2000) *Service Management and Marketing: A Customer Relationship Management Approach*. Chichester: John Wiley & Sons.

Grönroos, C. (2017) Christian Grönroos: I did it my way. *Journal of Historical Research in Marketing*, 9(3), 277–301.

Gummesson, E. (1987) The new marketing: Developing long-term interactive relationships. *Long Range Planning*, 20(4), 10–20.

Gummesson, E. (1998) Implementation requires a relationship marketing paradigm. *Academy of Marketing Science*, 26(3), 242–9.

Heffernan, T., O'Neill, G., Travaglione, T. and Droulers, M. (2008) Relationship marketing. *International Journal of Bank Marketing*, 26(3), 183–99.

Hollensen, S. (2014) *Marketing Management: A Relationship Approach*, 3rd edn. Harlow: Pearson.

Kaurav, R. P. S., Paul, J. and Chowdhary, N. (2015) Effect of internal marketing on hotels: Empirical evidence for internal customers. *International Journal of Hospitality & Tourism Administration*, 16(4), 311–30.

Kotler, P. and Armstrong, G. (2018) *Principles of Marketing*, 17th edn. Harlow: Pearson.

Kotler, P. and Levy, S. J. (1971) Demarketing, yes, demarketing. *Harvard Business Review*, 79, 74–80.

Lepthien, A., Papies, D., Clement, M. and Melnyk, V. (2017) The ugly side of customer management: Consumer reactions to firm-initiated contract terminations. *International Journal of Research in Marketing*, 34(4), 829–50.

Levitt, T. (1960) Marketing myopia. *Harvard Business Review*, 38(4), 45–56.

Lindgreen, A., Davis, R., Brodie, R. J. and Buchannan-Oliver, M. (2000) Pluralism in contemporary marketing practices. *International Journal of Bank Marketing*, 18(6), 294–308.

Maynard, H. H. (1941) Marketing courses prior to 1910. *Journal of Marketing*, 5(Apr.), 382–4.

Medway, D., Warnaby, G. and Dharni, S. (2010) Demarketing places: Rationales and strategies. *Journal of Marketing Management*, 27(1–2), 124–42.

Morgan, R. M. and Hunt, S. D. (1994) The commitment–trust theory of relationship marketing. *Journal of Marketing*, 20–38.

Nicholson, C. Y., Compeau, L. D. and Sethi, R. (2001) The role of interpersonal liking in building trust in long term channel relationships. *Journal of Academy of Marketing Science*, 29(1), 3–15.

Oliver, R. L. (1999) Whence consumer loyalty? *Journal of Marketing*, 63(4), 33–4.

Orel, F. D. and Kara, A. (2014) Supermarket self-checkout service quality, customer satisfaction, and loyalty: Empirical evidence from an emerging market. *J. Retail. Consum. Serv.*, 21(2), 118–29.

Payne, A. (ed.) (1995) *Advances in Relationship Marketing*. London: Kogan Page.

Petty, R. D. (2012) From label to trademark: The legal origins of the concept of brand identity in nineteenth century America. *Journal of Historical Research in Marketing*, 4(1), 129–53.

Petty, R. D. (2015) The historic development of modern US advertising regulation. *Journal of Historical Research in Marketing*, 7(4), 524–48.

Prentice, C. and Loureiro, S. M. C. (2017) An asymmetrical approach to understanding configurations of customer loyalty in the airline industry. *Journal of Retailing and Consumer Services*, 38, 96–107.

Preston, I. L. (1996) *The Great American Blowup: Puffery in Advertising and Selling*. Madison, WI: University of Wisconsin Press.

Ross, B. I. and Richards, J. I. (2008) A Century of Advertising Education. *American Academy of Advertising*. Available at: www.aaasite.org/assets/docs/a%20century%20of%20advertising%20education.pdf (accessed 2 April 2019).

Rotter, J. B. (1967) A new scale for the management of trust. *Journal of Personality*, 35, 651–65.

Schmidt, M. A. and Garcia, T. M. F. B. (2010) History from children's perspectives: Learning to read and write historical accounts using family sources. *Education*, 38(3), 289–99.

Schwarzkopf, S. (2015) Marketing history from below: Towards a paradigm shift in marketing historical research. *Journal of Historical Research in Marketing*, 7(3), 295–309.

Shiu, E., Hassan, L. M. and Walsh, G. (2009) Demarketing tobacco through governmental policies: The 4Ps revisited. *Journal of Business Research*, 62(2), 269–78.

Solomon, M. R., Marshall, G. W., Stuart, E. W. and Mitchell, V. (2013) *Marketing: Real People, Reach Choices*, 7th edn. Harlow: Pearson.

Tamilia, R. D. (2009) An overview of the history of marketing thought. *Journal of Historical Research in Marketing*, 1(2), 346–60.

Vargo, S. L. and Lusch, R. F. (2004) Evolving to a new dominant logic for marketing. *Journal of Marketing*, 68(1), 1–17.

Weld, L. D. H. (1919) *The Marketing of Farm Products*. New York: Macmillan.

Witkowski, T. H. (2010) The marketing discipline comes of age, 1934–1936. *Journal of Historical Research in Marketing*, 2(4), 370–96.

Zeithaml, V. (1988) Consumer perception of price, quality and value: A means–end model and synthesis of evidence. *Journal of Marketing*, 52(3), 2–22.

Zineldin, M. (2000) Beyond relationship marketing: Technologicalship marketing. *Marketing Intelligence & Planning*, 18(1), 9–23.

2
CONTEMPORARY GLOBAL MARKETING

Zubin Sethna, Rebecca Fakoussa and Geraint Evans

Learning Objectives

At the end of this chapter, you should be able to understand and discuss:

- Conceptual frameworks and models in order to gain meaningful insights for major international marketing decisions
- Different approaches for entering a global market
- The global marketing environment by analysing different environments
- Global marketing and the emerging market in the context of current and future directions
- The successes (and failures) of other companies in their development of their marketing strategies and campaigns

These objectives will be met through a unique combination of practitioner led-insight into the practical challenges of global marketing, case studies and academic research.

Digital Focus 2.1

Using technology in strategies and campaigns

The growth in digital technologies is exponential; disruptive digital technologies and the expectations of globally connected consumers are forcing firms to adjust and innovate. Using social media platforms such as Facebook, Twitter, Instagram, Weibo, Snapchat and Whatsapp means customers and companies are also more interconnected than ever, and the sharing of news, content and ideas has broken down the barriers (time or otherwise) between global and local marketing; platforms such as Amazon, eBay, Depop and ETSY provide an accessible global marketplace. As a result, companies have more opportunities than ever to calibrate local, regional and global multi-channel campaigns.

Questions

1. Do you think the use of digital technology means any small and medium-sized enterprises can aspire to be a 'global' company? If not, why not?
2. What other types of technology, e.g. artificial intelligence (AI), virtual reality (VR), would you use in your strategy and why?
3. How would you use social media to sell your company's products and services?

Ethical Focus 2.1

Self-reference criteria

All marketers interpret the potential effect of these environmental factors and adapt their marketing strategy accordingly. In doing so, marketers must be aware of their own frame of reference (or 'self-reference criteria'; Sethna and Blythe, 2016) that they are using when making decisions.

'Self-reference criteria' (SRC) is an unconscious reference to one's own cultural values, experiences, knowledge and ethical focus as a basis for decisions. It is about the individual's understanding of their own mental processes (Vazire and Solomon, 2015). People who understand their own strengths and weaknesses, as well as what they like and do not like, are in a better position to make realistic ethical purchasing decisions than people who are

(Continued)

(Continued)

not in touch with their own personalities (Sethna and Blythe, 2016). Market researchers employed by organisations know that self-referencing and self-knowledge are important because many of the decisions that organisations make are based on self-reports by consumers (Turk et al., 2015).

Numerous brands have experienced difficulties when not appreciating the differences in environmental factors – Hunt (2018) argues for scientific realism and the inductive realist models of theory status and generation as providing an appropriate philosophy of science foundation for marketing research. Thus, global marketers should use the principle of marketing relativism and not make judgements based on their own home country culture and experiences when considering strategies. It is often easier to highlight examples of unethical behaviour than it is to report on ethical behaviour. Examples include:

- **Horsemeat in the international supply chain for food products**: Three men conspired to sell horsemeat as beef over a 10-month period in 2012. In July 2017 they were found guilty of conspiracy to defraud and subsequently convicted. The convictions followed an investigation by the City of London Police alongside the Food Standards Agency. The investigation found that in 2012 Nielsen and Beech – owner and UK representative respectively of Danish meat trading company Flexi Foods – were buying horsemeat from Ireland and beef from Poland and delivering it to Tottenham-based company Dino's and Sons, which was owned by Sideras. Sideras would oversee the mixing of the two meats and apply false paperwork and labels to disguise the products before selling it on under the guise of pure beef. Mixing horsemeat into the beef like this increased profits on each consignment by about 40%, City of London Police said. The horsemeat scandal broke in 2013 when tests discovered horse DNA in a number of supermarket products both in the UK and across Europe, including burgers and ready meals.
- **Vaccination trials in Nepal**: In 1998, Glaxo Smith Kline (GSK) and the Walter Reed Institute, which conducts medical research for the US army, started cooperating to develop a Hepatitis E vaccine. Hepatitis E is a common disease in poor countries and there have been outbreaks in countries where US troops are deployed. Preparations for phase II trials were made in February 2000. Before launching the trials, GSK had already decided the vaccine would not be commercially developed for a travellers' market, while Walter Reed decided it would be unsuitable for US soldiers. Still, GSK and Walter Reed went ahead with phase II trials and wanted to test the candidate vaccine on 8,000 Nepalese volunteers in Lalitpur, without a plan to further develop the vaccine and make it available to the local population if the trials were successful. The Nepalese NGO Lumanti and municipal officers protested against the tests in Lalitpur because the majority of its population is illiterate and highly vulnerable. Walter Reed then decided to test the vaccine on 2,000 soldiers offered by the Royal Nepalese Army as volunteers (Andrews, 2005, 2006; Jack, 2006; Logan, 2006; Sarkar, 2006).

- **Indian shrimps win the race over Vietnamese shrimps**: The USA's move to introduce measures to prevent illegal, unreported and unregulated (IUU) fishing and misrepresented seafood from entering the country is likely to help Indian shrimp exports because new regulations will hurt exports from Vietnam, India's main competitor. The key market for global seafood producers, the USA, has introduced the Seafood Import Monitoring Programme (SIMP), covering 13 species, including shrimp. SIMP became applicable for shrimp on 31 December 2018. The programme mandates additional data requirements to trace the supply chain of seafood from the point of harvest to the point of entry into the USA. For the period ending March 2018, 2,433 aquaculture farms totalling 12,509 hectares of farmed area in India were registered under the Coastal Aquaculture Authority (CAA). Most Indian shrimp exports to the USA and the EU are from registered farms; however, shrimp exports to Vietnam (for forward shipping to America after value addition) come both from registered and unregistered farms, thereby hampering Vietnam's re-export prospects to the USA (owing to the lack of traceability). This is expected to support a shift in shrimp exports from Vietnam to India.

Questions

1. Why should companies pay careful attention to the varying attitudes to 'ethics' (marketing relativism) that exist around the world?
2. Under the guise of 'valid concerns over the ability to protect the larger civilian population against agents of bioterrorism', is it ethical to conduct human trials using vulnerable and, in many cases, illiterate people?
3. How important are the self-referencing criteria when judging the effects of various environmental factors?

Practitioner's Perspective 2.1

The practitioner interview

Quite often, learners benefit greatly from the wisdom and experience of a real-life practitioner. So, to get us started, we wanted to bring you these thoughts alongside our academic text. Hence, one of our team here (Geraint Evans), a highly experienced CMO who has launched multiple international campaigns and brands, was interviewed (Sethna, 2018) for his thoughts on global marketing in practice. The findings are interesting to say the least!

(Continued)

(Continued)

1. Can a company sell the same product using the same strategy all over the world?

    Delivering successful global marketing campaigns is a difficult, but hugely rewarding task for a marketer. Balancing global versus local marketing is often about managing things that are fairly opposite in nature. Building a recognisable global brand is typically a long-term strategy – and no matter how effective your planning and execution are, it is going to realistically take time. Local marketing in specific countries is often – and quite rightly – focused on the short term – delivering activity that is measured by daily, weekly and monthly results, hitting targets supporting the wider business' KPIs (the key performance indicators) as well as developing the brand. As such, I think global teams need to recognise the pressures different teams have, and aim to help them, rather than instruct them!

2. How is technology changing the way global marketing is conducted?

    Many aspects of managing teams in multiple countries are made so much quicker by technology now; web-based CMS (or content management systems) allow content, assets and branding to be shared so quickly over the 'cloud', and automation and work-flow software tools make collaboration so much easier. The counterpoint to this is dealing with the complexity of managing multiple social media platforms and websites in different languages and cultural norms!

3. Do you think there is always a role for 'local' marketing activities?

    I believe there is always going to be a role for local marketing – in my experience it's impossible to really get traction in a market without in-country assistance. While doing things on a global level definitely brings efficiency, it is often the insight and perspectives of the local team that ensure you do things that are relevant. Even more importantly, it is essential that the global teams learn from and share best practice from local markets. The relationship should always be a two-way process of collaboration and sharing – this ensures both innovation and alignment.

4. What happens when global marketing ideas fail to translate to the local level?

    There are a lot of ways that global-led marketing can fail; there have been numerous examples of brand, brand ID (such as logo, colours, icons), strap lines and campaign ideas failing to translate to local markets – and in some cases causing a lot of offence and damage in the process. For me, the key here, again, is balance; even if you are undertaking a globally led campaign, communication with local markets on how ideas translate in terms of language, cultural norms and political effects is key.

5.   How are key successes in global marketing defined?

Success in global marketing is predicated on the same items as any type of marketing – built on strong strategic direction and customer-focused campaign ideas that are suited, or can be adapted, to all the markets they are going to. Global teams need to focus on support to ensure flawless execution by local markets, and to recognise when and where engaging and relevant content can be used on a global level, or if careful consideration of risk mitigation is needed. Last (and I think the most important!) is TRUST! Trusting people to do their jobs is key here.

Questions

1.   To what extent do you agree with Geraint that 'insights and perspectives of the local team ensure that the organisation conducts activities that are relevant'?
2.   Geraint emphasises the relevance of social media in global marketing but makes reference to the complexities associated with multiple social media platforms. Assuming you are a marketing consultant, how would you advise an organisation that has a multinational operation in the retail sector to manage this situation?

INTRODUCTION

By now, we're really hoping that you're bursting with questions such as: What really is global marketing? How has it changed and developed? Where will it take us in the future? What are emerging markets going to look like? and How are consumers changing?

This chapter covers the most recent challenges facing companies expanding internationally, and looks at how the global marketing environment has experienced numerous changes which have resulted in significant transformation in how marketing activities are conducted (Eriksen, 2018; Gilpin, 2018; Leonidou et al., 2018). With innovations in technology and telecommunications (Aydalot and Keeble, 2018), companies view globalisation as both a challenge and an opportunity. It can be argued that the success of many of these firms, in fact, relies on them expanding out of their domestic (*or home*) market and finding new places to market and eventually sell their products and services. This global expansion strategy may be undertaken for a variety of reasons:

- to reduce risk based on over-reliance in one market, or intense competition within a highly competitive and possibly saturated domestic market
- to harness opportunities to make cost or efficiency savings based on achieving economies of scale and scope

- to follow competitors who are breaking into overseas markets
- to satisfy customer demand from overseas markets.

The phenomenon of 'international trade' between nations has been discussed extensively in the literature for centuries – *The Wealth of Nations* (Smith, 1776/2000), *The Principles of Political Economy and Taxation* (Ricardo, 1817), the economic theory of export (Heckscher and Ohlin, 1933/1991), the production and trade of high-quality goods (Linder, 1961), international investment and trade (Vernon, 1966) and, more recently, the role of services in international trade (Jones and Kierzkowski, 2018) and the Gravity Equation of International Trade (Chaney, 2018). With more established markets undertaking a process of liberalisation since the 1950s, through to the exponential growth of emerging markets from the 1990s, the world has seen more companies than ever (from small and medium-sized enterprises (SMEs) through to large multinational corporations) engaged in the practice of export activities.

According to the World Trade Organization, export merchandise trade has expanded dramatically from just over US$5 trillion in 1995 to US$17.20 trillion in 2017 (WTO, 2018). This not only confirms the importance of exporting goods and services but also ensures that there remains a global focus from both governments and businesses alike.

Table 2.1   Percentage revenues from outside of home country

Company	Global revenues (in $ billions)	Percentage revenues from outside the USA
Walmart	$446.9	26.1%
Ford	136.3	45.4
General Electric	147.3	52.6
CitiGroup	64.6	64.2
Hewlett-Packard	127.2	65.3
Boeing	68.7	50.0
Intel	54.0	84.4
Coca-Cola	46.5	59.8
Apple	108.3	61.0
Starbucks	11.7	22.1

Source: Compiled from annual reports of listed firms in Cateora et al. (2016)

The vast majority of industries – e.g. clothing, automotive and fast-moving consumer goods (FMCG) – are embracing the possibility of selling their products/services further afield, both to counteract the increased pressure of competition in their home market, and to compete with competitors through growth in international markets. Table 2.1 provides an indicative and interesting snapshot of American companies and their percentage revenues from outside of the USA.

While the advent of multinational platforms, such as Amazon, eBay, Depop and ETSY, has made many aspects of global marketing more accessible than ever, marketing products/services internationally or cross-border can be a daunting undertaking for many reasons:

- the need for local resources
- adapting to a new culture
- understanding ever-changing government regulation
- having a new in-market competitor set to contend with.

Companies rapidly appreciate that some customer needs will vary across markets, leading to considerations about whether they should customise for each market they are developing into or whether to standardise their offering. Companies such as Apple typically offer identical products in each country market, while companies with operations multinationally such as Procter and Gamble typically change product names (for example, their global product Mr Clean is translated into various languages including 'Maestro Limpio' in Mexico, 'Monsieur Propre' in France and 'Meister Proper' in Germany. It's the same product with the sailor mascot as it is in the USA. Colgate toothpaste is called Pinyin Gāolùjié in China which means 'high-quality cleaning gel'). Some companies, such as McDonalds, adopt a hybrid strategy of traditional lines such as The Big Mac (albeit renamed to suit the local language) and country specific offerings, for example, the Denali Mac (Alaska), the Maharaja Mac (India), the Giga Mac (Japan) and the Grand Mac (USA).

This chapter first examines some of the key theories and various conceptual frameworks/models that exist and which some companies use to provide meaningful insights for major international marketing decisions. Following this, we discuss the different approaches for entering global markets, where you will see various examples of who used which one and why! There are many ways to internationalise, ranging from franchising to acquisition. This chapter will consider the pitfalls and potential of each. Remember, the environment within which we work is constantly changing, and so what this chapter offers you is some structure (by way of models) with which you can analyse different environments.

If we briefly go around the world to see examples of how the marketing landscape at the global level has changed, there are many recent examples which have shaped marketing thinking: Britain's exit from Europe (aka Brexit), business takeovers in the USA, President Trump and his strategies to 'Make America Great Again', and the unfolding consumption patterns in various developing countries that challenge some of the extant assumptions on global marketing. Hence, only a flabby perspective would conclude that contemporary global marketing can still be viewed only through the lens of orthodox marketing. So there are a number of important questions that you may be asking yourself by now and which will constitute some of the issues to be addressed in this chapter:

- What are the changes in the discourses of global market entry strategies?
- How can the emerging global opportunities be fully explored with commensurate marketing toolkits?

The battle between technology as a force for globalisation and the changing political environment that is leading to a rise in protectionism and closed borders, both challenges changes in marketing and its trends and reinforces the localisation versus globalisation debate in decision making. It is a fact of life that because of social migration and mobility (the movement of individuals, families, households, or other categories of people within or between social strata in a society) we now live in more complex multicultural societies. This has resulted in a world struggling to strike a balance between consumption and spending growth; consumption and spirituality/inner peace; and to understand how to develop a sustainable consumption environment. Marketing decisions (let alone global marketing decisions) are becoming more problematic. All of these are subject to consumer centrism (the idea that customer service is central to a successful business model) and the personal and social struggle among ethnocentrism (the evaluation of other cultures according to preconceptions originating in the standards and customs of one's own culture), cosmopolitanism (the ideology that all human beings belong to a single community, based on a shared morality) and xenocentrism (a preference for the products, styles or ideas of someone else's culture rather than of one's own). Cultural distance and economic freedom exist not only among international markets but also among subcultures in the same international market.

Throughout this chapter, we will (hopefully!) inspire you with global examples of successes (and failures) of companies and the development of their marketing strategies and campaigns, in order to give you a real practical sense of global marketing environments.

OVERVIEW OF KEY CONCEPTUAL FRAMEWORKS AND MODELS FOR INTERNATIONAL MARKETING DECISIONS

Let's start with an overview of some conceptual frameworks and models in order to gain meaningful insights for major international marketing decisions and be crystal clear on the difference between internationalisation and global marketing.

As markets are becoming more global in nature, it is important for companies to be able to create and react to opportunities quickly and effectively. With all companies being able to access information assets and market intelligence, increased competition and dramatic changes to a market emerge more quickly than ever, leading to increased pressures at all levels of the organisation.

Globalisation can be described as a process in which the world appears to be converging across many dimensions – economically, politically and culturally. It is an evolutionary and complex process but by no means an irreversible or linear one. Cross-border movements of goods and people on a large scale date back to the Persian Empire circa 3000 BC (Sethna and Nightingale, 2017) and the more recent Roman Empire, and have continued to occur largely incrementally although with numerous discontinuities (Narula and Zanfei, 2005).

Economic globalisation, as defined by Narula and Zanfei (2005), implies 'the growing interdependence of locations and economic units across countries and regions'. In other words, globalisation is a process of increasing cross-border interdependence and integration of production and markets for goods, services and capital. From the international business perspective, there are two types of globalisation:

- globalisation of markets – a process of convergence upon a global, unified market with homogenised consumer preferences
- globalisation of industries – a process of increasing ability for businesses to configure and co-ordinate their productive activities globally.

These two types of globalisation are closely linked as they are driven by largely the same factors. Global industries tend to serve global markets. The main causal factors that have driven the globalisation process over the past 150 years are generally grouped into four broad-brush categories:

- political/economic factors
- the spread and intensity of multinational enterprise (MNE) activities
- technological factors.
- socio-cultural factors.

Both country-level and sectoral studies in recent years have found more evidence of regionalisation than globalisation of MNEs (Bitzenis, 2018). This builds on previous work by Delios and Beamish (2005) where, in a study of 1,229 Japanese MNEs, they presented evidence for the dominance of home-region-oriented strategy in the affiliate distribution of the analysed Japanese firms. Their findings indicated that only a few MNEs with strong standalone, non-location-bound, firm-specific advantages (achieved through high-intensity R&D, advertising and exporting) were able to execute a global strategy. Another country-level study found that 70% of the largest British MNEs (listed in the Fortune Global 500) had the majority of their sales in the home triad region of Europe (Rugman and Verbeke, 2007). In a study of British exporting SMEs, Beleska-Spasova and Glaister (2009) endorse these findings in the case of smaller international firms but also found them to be more globally diversified than is generally perceived. This is further corroborated by both Madsen and Moen (2018) and Stoian et al. (2018). China, other Asia-focused studies and regions in Latin America have also provided evidence for the prevalence of the home-region-oriented strategy (Cuervo-Cazurra et al., 2018; Enright, 2005; Yin and Choi, 2005).

At the sectoral level, research has found very little evidence of MNEs following global strategies in the automobile, pharmaceutical, retail and food and beverage industries (Caves, 2018; Filippaios and Rama, 2008; Hennart, 2018; Oh and Rugman, 2006; Schlie and Yip, 2000). The service sector, for example, has been found to have higher intra-regional sales than manufacturing firms have.

Global marketing usually begins as part of the process of internationalisation, where companies 'choose' (for a variety of reasons, as discussed earlier) a potential market and decide to enter using their chosen mechanisms (e.g. partnership, subsidiaries, satellite offices), then look to work in a local context by leveraging the acquired local knowledge and infrastructure. A variety of academic conceptual models, frameworks and theories have discussed the nature of strategy underpinning multinational enterprises moving into other markets at length. For example, Porter's single diamond (Porter, 1990), double diamond (Moon et al., 1995) and the integration-responsiveness framework (Bartlett and Ghoshal, 1989) all attempted to model the complex task of 'formalising institutions' for international business, with questions being asked about when, where and how to expand internationally. When companies seek to expand internationally, 'overcoming the liability of foreignness' in their choices and implementation is highly relevant. The subsequent application of traditional international business models to a contemporary context has seen the development of the CAGE model (Ghemawat, 2018) and the earlier Porter's Five Forces model (Porter, 1990), allowing analysis of the wider macro environment.

General theorem shows a clear, linear five-stage process when making decisions about global marketing:

1. Decide on whether to internationalise or not.
2. Decide on which markets to enter.
3. Decide on the market entry strategies to be used.
4. Design the global marketing programme.
5. Implement and coordinate the global marketing programme.

Global marketing is therefore a set of activities that a company (or brand) undertakes to sell its products and services. In order to be successful in the new target market or country, different global marketing strategies and tactics may then be applied as they need to choose per country. For example, companies are required to ask practical questions such as the following:

- Does the brand or its products and services 'fit' in that country?
- What is product positioning?
- What logo/design to use?
- What is it called?
- What channels to use?
- What pricing?
- What advertising?
- Which partners?

That said, however, a key contemporary issue here is that while it can be seen that global marketing is on the 'continuum' of internationalisation, in our opinion, it is not necessarily always executed in a linear fashion. It can be done first (in terms of exploration of possible 'fit'), or indeed sometimes opportunistically, and even with consumers demanding that a company begins to sell its products in their countries – as such, there is only sometimes a 'sequential' choice made by a company when entering a new market. So, is it time to redefine what global marketing is?

As mentioned earlier, the advent of a global market has also seen the threat of competition from companies in areas such as China, India, South East Asia and Brazil grow, threatening the dominance of traditional markets such as the USA, the UK and Europe. This has led to a global market context in which companies which had previously been able to rely on a relatively stable position in their home market, now need to defend their position from new entrants as well as others seeking new market opportunities. To further add to this challenge, these companies also need to continue to focus on innovation and on developing products that customers seek to buy.

This then begs the question - how much research is needed to make these decisions? You would be forgiven for thinking that when undertaking a global expansion, companies always undertake detailed research to develop a clear understanding of the new target market, and make decisions on how they will adapt their existing strategies, and confirm their capabilities and core competencies can also be leveraged in the new international market of their choosing. But we can see examples of failure in the Canadian food sector (Wade et al., 2018), in Russian manufacturing (Bykova and Lopez-Iturriaga, 2018) and in American life insurance moving into Australia (Keneley, 2018), to name but a handful. Thus, by researching answers to the above questions, this should then become part of a regular process of reassessment, learning and adapting as companies gain market share, and as presence and resource within a market grow to multiple countries. Companies are then required to think about their global marketing strategy more holistically, and consider evolving their strategy from a country-centered approach to one that seeks to leverage scale and deliver more integrated and centrally coordinated marketing and campaign activity across national markets through the utilisation of uniform elements of the marketing mix across the world.

DIFFERENT APPROACHES FOR ENTERING A GLOBAL MARKET

As we intimated earlier, there are a number of different approaches that may be identified for entering a global market.

Today, it is almost impossible to find a product or service that does not have an international aspect to it in at least one element of its supply or value chain; from the origins of the constituent raw materials or components, through the specialist equipment used to manufacture the products, to the international logistics of storage, packing and transit to the retailer and/or the final consumer. All supply chains are global in nature. These international supply chains include a number of different country operations, with the final goods likely to cross international borders several times during the end-to-end process, recording a customs clearance as an 'intermediate' good (Antràs et al., 2018; Gibson and Graciano, 2018). Some countries such as Taipei can have as much as two-thirds of their trade in intermediate goods (Meltzer, 2014). Detailed analysis of the countries involved and the trends of trade flows provide companies with valuable insight when internationalising; not only for identifying potential locations for future expansion but also for assessing the firm's position in relation to developments in its current markets. Karlsson et al. (2018), Marinova (2018) and Gaur et al. (2018) have written extensively on the drivers of globalisation being foreign direct investment (FDI) and international trade, creating multinational enterprises (MNEs).

FDI predominantly involves the ownership of a part (meaning joint ownership) or whole company in a foreign country (typically described as a foreign subsidiary), providing an opportunity to increase sales and profit by expanding into additional market(s) and not relying solely on domestic markets (see e.g. Paul and Benito, 2018; Tong et al., 2018) – also known as *market-seeking FDI* (Nielsen et al., 2018). In addition, some MNEs have an opportunity to reduce their cost base through producing their own product – also known as *efficiency-seeking FDI* (Ibeh et al., 2018). Some companies will then deliver their service in their home market as a result of factors such as a lower cost of labour, energy, materials and transportation in the new market country – also known as *resource-seeking FDI*. Additionally, MNEs also seek to protect their domestic markets through entering new international markets to reduce the threat of competitors potentially doing so, also known as *trade/import substituting FDI*. Finally, international expansion is also characterised by some companies using it as a route to acquire new technological and skills/management capabilities – also known as *strategic asset-seeking FDI* (Carneiro et al., 2018).

The rapid expansion of international business has led to many connected phenomena in global business value chains (Kolk et al., 2018), strategic alliances and global networks (Knoke, 2018) and the rise in outsourcing and offshoring (Drahokoupil and Fabo, 2019; Williams and Durst, 2018). International expansion is not just the preserve of major companies; the proliferation of the internet and communications technology, with its ability to share information, has enabled SMEs to also export for the first time, reaching customers around the world, with many embracing innovation and entrepreneurship at their heart as 'born global' firms (Moen and Rialp-Criado, 2018).

Table 2.2   Typology of multinational companies

		Local responsiveness	
		Low	High
Global integration	High	Global strategy	Transnational strategy
	Low	International strategy	Multidomestic strategy

Source: Bartlett and Ghoshal (1989)

While Edwards et al. (2012) suggest that there are three strategies (multidomestic, global and transnational), and Bartlett and Ghoshal (1989) suggest four (global, transnational, international and multidomestic) (Table 2.2), we suggest five! We have developed the framework and suggest companies adopt one of five strategies for implementing operations in other markets, all of which can directly inform their marketing strategy (Table 2.3).

Table 2.3   Five strategies for implementing operations in other markets

Strategy	Description	Why is this strategy undertaken?	Examples
Domestic-only strategy (Note: This is shown here for the purposes of context – in order to see what international strategies fit into)	Marketing activities employed on a national scale only	To cater to customers generally within the local limits of a country. It serves and influences the customers of a specific country only	Hakim group of companies (independent opticians)

(Continued)

Table 2.3   (Continued)

Strategy	Description	Why is this strategy undertaken?	Examples
Multinational corporation (MNC)	Has facilities and other assets in at least one country other than its home country. Such companies have offices and/or factories in different countries and usually have a centralised head office where they coordinate global management	To increase market share To secure cheaper labour, premises and resources To avoid tax or trade barriers To access government grants	Apple computers
Multi-domestic strategy	A strategy by which companies try to achieve maximum local responsiveness by customising both their product offering and marketing strategy to match different national conditions	Can often provide valuable insights into the nuances of the prevailing culture in an area, which leads to inspiration on how to present products to their best advantage	Starbucks
Global strategy	The organisation treats the world as largely one market and one source of supply with little local variation. Competitive advantage is developed largely on a global basis	Benefits include: Economies of scope Economies of scale Global brand recognition Global customer satisfaction Lowest labour and other input costs Recovery of research and development costs from across the maximum number of countries	INTEL
Transnational strategy	An international business structure where a company's global business activities are coordinated via cooperation and interdependence between its head office, operational divisions and internationally located subsidiaries or retail outlets	Helps the company in expanding its business because, once adopted, the whole world is the market for the company's products and its reach widens from home country to the whole world	P&G

When entering a new market, an organisation typically has the options seen in Table 2.4.

Table 2.4   Organisational options for entering new markets

Contract manufacturing	Contract manufacturing avoids the need for heavy investments and facilitates a quick entry with a lot of flexibility. A contract manufacturer is a manufacturer that contracts with a firm for components or products. It is a form of outsourcing	The medical sector has a directory devoted to it: www. medicaldevicedirectory.com/ category/contract-manufacturing
Franchising	An arrangement where one party (the franchisor) grants another party (the franchisee) the right to use its trademark or trade name as well as certain business systems and processes, to produce and market a good or service according to certain specifications.	Kumon Educational Centres – Kumon study helps children of any age and any ability to shine by undergoing programmes which establish strong foundations in Maths

	The franchisee usually pays a one-time franchise fee plus a percentage of sales revenue as royalty, and gains (1) immediate name recognition, (2) tried and tested products, (3) standard building design and décor, (4) detailed techniques in running and promoting the business, (5) training of employees, and (6) ongoing help in promoting and upgrading products	and English: www.kumon.co.uk/wembley-central
Licensing	A legal contract between two parties, known as the licensor and the licensee. In a typical licensing agreement, the licensor grants the licensee the right to produce and sell goods, apply a brand name or trademark, or use patented technology owned by the licensor	Coca Cola is a great example of this: www.licenseglobal.com/magazine-article/always-coca-cola
Joint ventures	Joint ventures can be defined as 'an enterprise in which two or more investors share ownership and control over property rights and operation'. A joint venture helps in spreading risk, minimises capital requirements and provides quick access to expertise and contacts in local markets	Caradigm is a joint venture between General Electric and Microsoft Corp. It is a health IT company working to improve the economics of the medical field guided by health and the betterment of patients: www.caradigm.com/en-us
Mergers and acquisitions (including wholly owned foreign investments)	Mergers and acquisitions are transactions in which the ownership of companies, other business organisations or their operating units are transferred or consolidated with other entities. An acquisition gives quick access to distribution channels, management talent and established brand names. However, the acquired company should have a strategic fit with the acquiring company, and the integration of the two companies, especially when there are major cultural differences, needs to be carefully managed	CVS (a pharmacy chain) acquired Aetna (a health insurer) in 2018 for the princely sum of $69bn: www.cnbc.com/2018/03/13/cvs-aetna-shareholders-approve-merger.html
Exporting	Exporting means sending goods or services to another country for sale or indeed spreading or introducing ideas and beliefs to another country	BAE systems (Aerospace and Defense)

It is perhaps in the embedded national institutions of 'culture, religion and language' in international business that the greatest gaps in usable frameworks can be seen as many are now considered significantly outdated in their narrative, language and approach.

For example, the often utilised Hofstede's Cultural Dimensions uses gender-based phraseology such as describing companies and countries as having 'feminine' or 'masculine' tendencies. Recently, Collinson and Rugman (2011) proposed a methodology for linking global strategies to country-specific factors – the FSA–CSA matrix. At the starting point of the formulation of the strategic options of an MNE seeking to market its products or services overseas, Collinson and Rugman (2011) propose that there are two primary sets of factors to consider: (1) their 'firm-specific advantages' (FSAs) which are factors that determine the competitive advantages of their organisation; and (2) the country-specific advantages (CSAs) or factors in the form of natural resources (e.g. energy and resources), human resources, relevant cultural factors, and formal and informal institutions. Figure 2.1 is the resulting FSA–CSA matrix which provides a useful framework for a further discussion on global marketing, as it allows businesses to map their relative strengths and weaknesses when formulating country-specific strategic options.

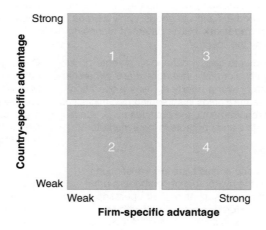

Figure 2.1   FSA–CSA matrix

Source: Adapted from Collinson and Rugman (2011)

In the matrix in Figure 2.1, the horizontal axis is used to place FSAs as either weak or strong, with the vertical axis for CSAs in the same manner. A strong FSA can imply that, under identical CSAs, a firm has a potentially strong competitive advantage over its rivals. Cells 1, 3 and 4 can incorporate broadly the three generic strategies suggested by Porter (1990): cost leadership, differentiation and focus. Table 2.5 summarises the key classifications.

Table 2.5   Key classifications of the FSA–CSA matrix

Cell 1	Represents a situation where only CSAs are important. The MNEs located in Cell 1 have a competitiveness that depends on natural endowments of their home country (minerals, oil wells, forest products, hydro-electric power and other natural resources). These MNEs could also have CSAs that are based on cheap labour (e.g. China) or cheap-skilled labour (e.g. India). Cell 1 firms are generally the cost leadership ones, producing a commodity-type product. Production FSAs flowing from the possession of intangible skills are less important than the CSAs of location and energy costs.

Cell 2   Here we have inefficient, floundering firms with neither consistent strategy, nor any intrinsic CSAs or FSAs. Here, neither CSAs nor FSAs are important. Firms in this cell need to restructure and move to either Cell 1 (building on CSAs) or Cell 4 (by developing FSAs).

Cell 3   Firms here can generally choose to follow any of the strategies listed above because of the strength of both their CSAs and FSAs. In this cell, both CSAs and FSAs matter. The FSAs of a firm are enhanced and facilitated through home country CSAs. In general, there may be internal managerial tensions in reconciling CSAs and FSAs. The better managed MNEs successfully combine FSAs and CSAs (Rugman, 1996).

Cell 4   These generally differentiated firms have strong FSAs in marketing and customisation, as well as strong brands. In this cell, the FSAs dominate, so, in world markets and the home country, CSAs are not essential in the long run. The FSAs stand alone and are not influenced by CSAs. The resource-based view of strategic management, where a firm has strong FSAs that are unique and proprietary, is what is key in Cell 4. There may also be 'entry barriers' that prevent rival firms from acquiring the FSA. These 'isolating mechanisms' may be entirely due to aspects of the organisational structure and the nature of the top management team.

Companies that expand internationally of course have to contend with cultural difference and with the 'distance' of the home office (domestic market) from the new markets that the company is working in. This is significant for global marketing in many ways; the company needs to understand the attitude, trends and norms of the new market both from the perspective of marketing its products/services to a new audience and from that of working with a new set of colleagues who, in the case of takeover or acquisition, will have already been performing a variety of marketing activities that may differ from the new strategy imposed by the acquiring company.

ANALYSING DIFFERENT CONTEMPORARY GLOBAL MARKETING ENVIRONMENTS

Let us now turn our attention to a consideration of how companies analyse the environments in which they find themselves and ultimately implement different global marketing strategies for these differing environments.

There are many ways in which you can analyse the environment. Some common frameworks include combinations of political, economic, socio-cultural, technological, environmental and media. For example, popular acronyms include PEST/SLEPT/PESTLE and MPESTLE. These frameworks, while broad, can be very useful for an initial analysis, although sometimes it is hard to decide which information goes into which part. For example, because the legal and the political environment are so interchangeable, this can be confusing at times.

However, one of the potential downfalls is that developed and under-developed countries might have different interpretations. For example, in some countries, there may be laws prohibiting something, however with a certain perceived status, the giving of bribes and/or particular social connections, these are sometimes circumnavigated. Further, while in some cultures this is socially acceptable and potentially even encouraged, for other cultures this is completely unacceptable (for instance, bribery in the UK contravenes the UK Bribery Act 2010) and individuals guilty of an offence under Sections 1, 2 or 6 of the Bribery Act 2010 are liable to a maximum of 10 years' imprisonment, an unlimited fine or both.

Another way of exploring and analysing the factors which influence the global marketing environment is by dissecting Jonathan Turner's (1997: 6) definition of social institutions:

> a complex of positions, roles, norms and values lodged in particular types of social structures and organizing relatively stable patterns of human activity with respect to fundamental problems in producing life-sustaining resources, in reproducing individuals, and in sustaining viable societal structures within a given environment.

Popular academic literature proffers eight social institutions which are present in societies regardless of how advanced or under-developed the society is:

- political: the system of transferring power
- economic: the method of wealth distribution
- legal: deciding right and wrong
- family: the unit of procreation
- religious: belief systems
- educational: passing on information for the preservation of society
- media: mass and individualised communication
- cultural: the way of life of a people
- technological: the influence of technology and innovation.

In real-life business contexts, companies would need to do a more in-depth analysis on each area (than shown below using the acronym LEEMSTEG: Legal, Economic, Environmental, Media, Socio-cultural, Technological, Education, Gender) and some areas might be more important than others. For example, the pharmaceutical industry needs to pay very close attention to the legal/political environment, while the technological environment of the country may not be as critical. Conversely, an internet start-up online is dependent on the new market having a technological environment which can support its services.

Legal/political environment

Internationalisation takes places across five continents with different legal and political environments, ranging from capitalism to communism. Trade agreements like NAFTA and the EU have collectively sought to influence the environment in which companies operate. The emergence of a global economy has also created unprecedented *juxtapositions* in how companies are owned and operate. According to Penrose (2017), firms involved in international business generally out-perform those not exporting, growing twice as fast as those who have not internationalised, and have much greater returns. For a long time (Buckley et al., 2018), the majority of foreign ownership involved US-owned companies owning foreign subsidiaries. This has changed – for example, many well-known 'household' US brand names are now foreign controlled (Pradhan, 2011).

Economic environment

At a time of unprecedented flux, many traditional global constructs are under challenge. In 2018, the majority of international trade was still conducted within the world triad – a group of three major trading and investment blocs:

- the European Union (the EU, consisting of 27 European countries)
- the North American Free Trade Agreement (NAFTA, consisting of the USA, Canada and Mexico)
- the Asia-Pacific region (including Japan).

According to the World Trade Organization (2018), these three regions account for more than 80% of world exports and imports of goods, with, at the time of writing, on the export side, North America, South and Central America and the Caribbean, Europe and Asia all recording stronger growth. Asia and North America saw steady year-on-year growth in imports throughout 2017, whereas import growth accelerated over the course of the year in Europe (1.4% in the first half, 4.1% in the second half) and South and Central America and the Caribbean (1.5% in the first half, 6.6% in the second half). Asia had the fastest trade volume growth of any region in 2017 on both the export side (6.7%) and the import side (9.6%) following two years of tepid expansion.

At a country level, the world's largest exporters (and importers) are China, Germany, the USA and Japan (World Trade Organization, 2018). China's economic rebalancing away from investment and toward consumption is continuing, with investment accounting for roughly 32% of GDP growth in 2017, down from 55% in 2013. This development may add some drag to world trade growth as China imports fewer capital goods, but the process has so far been gradual and not very disruptive to global trade. Less investment could also help reduce over-capacity in sensitive sectors such as steel and aluminium, thereby alleviating trade tensions.

The growth and/or breakdown stats of the free market system and the powerful emergence and evolution of significant large markets (e.g. BRICS [Brazil, Russia, India, China, South Africa] and MINT [Mexico, Indonesia, Nigeria, Turkey] countries), combined with disturbances to traditional home markets (e.g. Brexit in the UK), mean that companies are exporting in an era of greater uncertainty than ever. However, statistics around growth in the world economy (Wirtz et al., 2015) and the world system perspective (Shannon, 2018) confirm that companies as well as markets are seeking to grow.

Environmental issues

All companies need to demonstrate a high degree of awareness of the global impact that their business activity may have on the environment. This has resulted in companies increasing their focus on renewable energy, the reduction of carbon emissions and the use of sustainable materials. In addition, there has been an increase in companies supporting knowledge transfer (Watkins et al., 2015) within developing countries. These issues are not only linked to reputation management, but as companies increasingly aim to be 'good global citizens' they need to respect and abide by regulatory schemes such as the Paris Agreement (Oberthür and Groen, 2018). This is of course in addition to demonstrating an awareness of related trends and lifestyle choices such as mindfulness, veganism and reduced consumption.

Media

The media can be viewed as a central environmental factor. According to Legagneux et al. (2018), scientists, policy makers and journalists are three key, interconnected players involved in prioritising and implementing solutions to mitigate the consequences of anthropogenic pressures on the environment. In some countries, the media is tightly controlled with no freedom of speech. Countries such as North Korea and Russia have state-controlled media where both the content and the broadcasted angle are tightly controlled. In contrast, most of Europe has free press where governments, businesses as well as politicians and business people can be questioned for their actions and held accountable. This also means social media (bloggers, vloggers, influencers) or other types of self-publishing media do not face persecution for their views or opinions, whether politically or non-politically motivated/correct.

The media has the ability to change the environment within which it exists. A recent phenomenon is the idea of 'fake news', where a government, business, group or individual starts a campaign to disrupt or smear the other side (Doshi et al., 2018; Lazer et al., 2018; Pennycook and Rand, 2018). Similarly to the propaganda used during war, fake news has been linked to major political decisions internationally – for example, the Cambridge Analytica scandal (Schneble et al., 2018), the election of President Trump in the USA in 2016 (Allen et al., 2018), the Brexit vote in the UK in 2016 (Kim et al., 2018) and the violence in Myanmar in 2017 (Farid, 2018). The global digital landscape continues to grow rapidly. There are now 4.1 billion internet users, which is 52% of the world's population (Kujawski, 2018). With connectivity at an all-time high, people are quick to comment on social media or news items, meaning news spreads quickly and can be inflammatory. For example, when Shell had a gas leak in 2014, the CEO was pictured on holiday enjoying himself while millions of animals and thousands of people's lives lay in tatters because of 'his' oil spill. A Twitter campaign was started and he was removed from office soon after, all because of the 'media environment'.

Socio-cultural environment

Changes in the socio-cultural environmental context create an interesting paradox for companies growing globally. While multiple markets create challenges to do with how and where to internationalise, there has been increasing evidence over the past 30 years that consumer tastes are homogenising in terms of preferences and attitudes (from Appadurai, 1990 to Nguyen, 2018). For example, as we saw earlier, the majority (52%) of the global population now has access to the internet, and people are increasingly accessing it on mobile devices and through social media channels.

A good 50% of the population globally is under 30 but the purchasing power of the silver 'pound/dollar' is stronger (Mazur et al., 2018). The growth in 'digital natives' (Judd, 2018) is particularly obvious within Millennial age segments (Schneider et al., 2018), however recent studies (Cerna et al., 2018; Klimova et al., 2018; Mathur et al., 2018) demonstrate that an ageing portion of society is also extremely digitally literate, thus providing considerable opportunity for companies to grow their markets.

This is all in tandem with advances in the number of people having a secondary and tertiary education (Lee and Lee, 2016; World Bank, 2018), meaning that people are more educated, able to access and compare information quickly, and are aware of their rights. All of this leads to a more demanding public than we've ever had before.

Technological environment

Advances in technology mean that routes and channels to market have multiplied and brands are selling their products/services in a completely different way to how they did even five years ago. Consumers also have unprecedented access to 'information' – from pricing, production and delivery information to competitor information and alternative products. In a connected world of internet-enabled devices, mobile, artificial intelligence, voice and big data, all business activities are now operating in a global context. No longer solely orientated on export, even the smallest local business can be found by a global audience through a variety of search mechanisms. For example, technology has been the main driver for countries such as China and those in Africa leapfrogging over the analogue landline telephone or internet, straight to mobile and satellite devices. Mobile payments in Africa, through the M-Pesa platform, are considered the norm (Bounfour, 2018), while in the UK banks are using this as a USP (Kazan et al., 2018).

Education

Beechler and Woodward (2009) and Oseghale et al. (2018) have written at length on the global 'war' for talent, with companies increasingly finding it difficult to recruit skilled workers for key roles. As long-standing and experienced workers retire, the new millennial generation of workers has its own new approach to the workplace with its own expectations about tenure, location, mobility and loyalty (Brightenburg et al., 2018; Myers and Sadaghiani, 2010; Wootton and Grundy, 2018). The average job tenure for a millennial worker is only about three years (BBC, 2017; Cates, 2010) – about one-third the tenure of an older worker. Now that online talent platforms are making job markets more transparent, workers have more options. By 2025 these talent platforms could add $2.7 trillion to global GDP, and begin to ameliorate many of the persistent problems in the world's labour markets (McKinsey Consulting, 2015). Platforms such as LinkedIn, Glassdoor and monster.com give individuals more information about potential employers, job openings and the wages they could command. They then amass individual CVs with job postings from traditional employers, as well as those from the 'gig economy'. As a result, talented workers have many more options that could induce them to leave their current employer, further creating instability for companies as they seek to compete in a variety of markets.

Gender Inequality/Race/Religion

Understanding a country also means identifying the influences of gender inequality/race/ religion. Commentators have recently questioned the conditions under which ethnic diversity might become the foundation for a prosperous society (Mintchev and Moore, 2018). Gender inequality continues to be a pressing issue affecting global society (Healey et al., 2018) and is one that many global companies are seeking to tackle through diversity and equality initiatives, such as increasing the number of women, LGBT and multi-ethnic members represented on boards and in senior management roles (Colgan, 2018; Köllen et al., 2018). Connected to this is a need for companies to recognise that they must contribute to solving issues, such as increasing the provision of education for young girls and women (Singh, 2018) and ensuring they are providing opportunities for parents to learn skills to enter or re-enter the workforce (Renwick, 2018). Platforms such as Glassdoor are also offering greater visibility, transparency and disclosure, affecting reputation with both employees and consumers, and their consequent approach to global marketing.

The religious and cultural norms found in a new market need to also be carefully considered by the global marketer. For example, selling products that contain pork additives or beef extracts in Muslim countries or to Hindus is an obvious no-no (Alzeer et al., 2018). Gender issues (Hartsock, 2018) such as women having the final say over high-purchase items (Amirouche et al., 2017), or racial issues between castes in India or Muslim tribes in the Middle East, need to be carefully considered.

CURRENT AND FUTURE DIRECTIONS OF GLOBAL MARKETING

In this section, we will consider where we currently are, how history has influenced us and what this means for us going forward.

As discussed earlier, international trade has been around for many hundreds of years and, as such, global marketing can be seen as being an evolutionary phenomenon but one that has recently been revolutionised by the advances in digital and social media technology. While this has created unprecedented opportunities to reach consumers, it has also surfaced more challenges to get 'cut through' in their busy daily life. Recent studies from Saxon (2017) show that consumers receive over 10,000 messages a day. Statistics like this have instigated a shift in how companies are approaching the increasing number of markets they sell into around the world, with fewer relying on a 'domestic-only strategy' to cultivate growth. Any company which is developing a marketing strategy internationally/globally must seek to utilise its scale for efficiency, but also balance needs and resources in the individual local market.

Marketing started life by being restricted to the geo-political boundary of the home market country. This 'domestic marketing' activity meant that a company only had to consider its own market – in terms of customer and competition in a single geography. Fast-forward to today when we see that in the largest countries, companies often have regional offices, and major decisions are invariably taken by a central 'headquarters 'function. The local company's competition is likely to be from global companies who are exporting as part of their foreign market expansion strategy or using other forms of internationalisation strategy (as presented in Table 2.4). This may see innovative global marketing strategies and possibly greater 'scale' in terms of spending money on marketing communications and retail space, meaning that even domestic-only marketers need to look globally for inspiration, while also, crucially, utilising their local market knowledge and awareness of environmental conditions to maintain any competitive advantage.

A 'glocal' market orientation

As discussed, the key to successful global marketing can be seen as balancing a local and global marketing orientation: glocalisation. In fact, its roots stem from the Japanese economics term 'dochakuka' which first appeared in articles in the *Harvard Business Review* in the late 1980s. The term originally meant adapting farming techniques to one's own local condition. This was later adopted to refer to global-localisation (Sharma, 2009) – the tensions between doing all marketing activity on a global basis versus using local knowledge and execution. Marketers seek to use this approach to reconsider the drivers of firms' globalisation and global market performance (Bayraktar and Ndubisi, 2014; Oyedele, 2016) and to provide 'valuable' products, services and/ or solutions to customers (Kim, 2018) on a local, national, international or global basis.

Hollensen (2016) proposes a 'glocalisation framework' in which a company can balance standardisation and differentiation by adopting some activity on a global basis (such as research/development and production/selling) with local market penetration and flexible response mechanisms to local customer needs (see Figure 2.2).

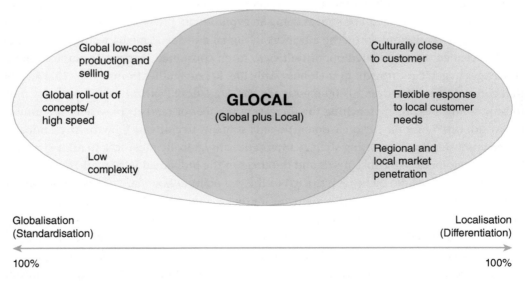

Figure 2.2   Global marketing model framework

Source: Adapted from Hollensen (2016)

Of course, this process is far from simple in practice. In reality, there are occasions (especially in developing markets) when because of the lack of market research, multinational firms find it very difficult to fully understand the needs and wants of potential customers. This, coupled with the fact that distribution networks are often quite scarce or under-developed in those markets, makes it very difficult for them to deliver products, even if there is customer demand. So, when a particular developing market opens up, local companies dominate the local market.

According to Bryan et al. (2006), 'a formal talent marketplace makes employees (rather than line managers or HR professionals) responsible for managing the greater part of their careers'. In talent markets, companies don't have enough knowledge about the local talent pool to design policies that will attract and motivate employees at the glocal, local and bottom-of-pyramid tiers. Therefore, when a developing country opens up, multinational companies rush into the global tier (as described by Khanna and Palepu, 2006), and local companies dominate the local tier. It stands to reason, therefore, that the bottom tier will thus provide plenty of opportunities for marketing managers who have to use their own particular talents and often 'radically different strategies to crack it open' (Khanna and Palepu, 2006). It is this glocal tier which, over time, becomes the hub of competition between local and foreign corporations.

Application of the traditional marketing mix

As discussed earlier in this chapter, global marketing is aligned to international expansion strategies such as export, franchising, joint ventures and/or direct entry into a new market.

According to the American Marketing Association (AMA), 'International marketing is the multinational process of planning and executing the conception, pricing, promotion and distribution of ideas, goods and services to create exchanges that satisfy individual and organisations goals'.

The development of McCarthy's (1960) original marketing mix model – the 4Ps (Product, Place, Price and Promotion) – will be relevant here, but it is clear that a myriad of additional factors needs to be taken into account in global marketing. The 'global' nature of domestic marketing, plus considerations around applying a unique set of approaches to each new market, mean the application of a company's marketing mix needs to evolve. A great deal of academic and practitioner discussion has covered an expansion of the 4Ps model. Grönroos (1997) notably wrote about a paradigm shift in marketing towards relationship marketing. Others have continued with the core model but sought to expand the overall *number* of Ps. Thus, we now have models with 8Ps (Goldsmith, 1999), 10Ps (Balmer, 1998) and 12Ps (Opitz,

2008; Zineldin and Philipson, 2007). Most recently, Salman et al. (2017) used their own adapted version of the 12P marketing mix model for the hospitality industry.

Several of the existing 'Ps' of marketing are hugely relevant to global marketing challenges.

Place

In this context, 'place' typically involves using techniques such as market research to understand local market conditions. While many multinational corporations believe this to be an essential global marketing activity, coordination with local market resources is key to facilitating effective sharing and knowledge transfer, as well as incorporating cultural differences across regions. Place, very often, implicitly refers to distribution: how to get your product/ service to customers. In practice, there are some markets where door-to-door distribution is still very popular, while in others people prefer channels such as shopping at retail stores. Telemarketing is also still quite popular in markets such as the USA but not so in many developing countries. However, opportunities to standardise approaches should not be ignored by companies in order to achieve efficiencies.

International distribution of products and services also has to take into account local factors. Strategies can vary from country to country owing to different buying habits. In some societies, small 'mom and pop' stores proliferate, while in others, large department stores carrying several items under one roof are popular. In some countries, intermediaries handle credit sales, while in others, cash transactions are the norm or indeed mobile payments dominate, as is the case in Kenya with the M-Pesa payments platform (Nair and Emozozo, 2018). Even within developed countries, significant differences exist in the channels of distribution. The rapid emergence of the internet is, however, changing the old paradigm. Many companies are seriously looking at the potential of the internet as a global distribution vehicle, an excellent example here being Amazon.com.

Product

The application of 'product' in the context of global marketing activities requires MNCs to make decisions regarding elements such as quality, range, design, brand name, features, packaging and support services. Some elements of 'product' can be seen as 'more global' than others. For example, technology such as smart phones (from companies like Apple, Samsung and HTC) can be identical in specification in many global markets, as can premium branded goods such as watches (e.g. Rolex, Breitling and Omega) and premium fashion goods (e.g. Tom

Ford, Gucci and Burberry). Other products such as automobiles are also increasingly aligned globally with common brands (Audi, Volkswagen, Jaguar, BMW and Mercedes Benz) being seen in multiple markets. However, specific technical features such as engine size, type and output, and accessories will often differ depending on the 'product functionality' demands of the consumer in the local market. As such, product development including decisions regarding when and where to 'tailor' (adapt the product offering) is a critical activity for all MNCs. While globally standardised products can harness more efficient production (excessive customisation for different market tastes can lead to higher costs), it is essential to recognise that individual markets and their differing consumer wants, needs and tastes may necessitate a certain level of investment in adaptation.

Promotion

Closely connected to 'product' is the necessary 'promotion' of those products and services within the target markets of the MNC. In some cases (such as the technology and premium brands discussed above), the distinction between 'home country' marketing and that implemented in other markets is rapidly diminishing, with brands, increasingly, using similar positioning strategies and marketing campaigns on a global basis. However, as with all other areas of the marketing mix, MNCs must carefully consider local nuances and cultural differences when deciding on and perhaps modifying their marketing strategies to meet the requirements of a specific country in the global marketplace (based on the specifics of local language, values, religion and customer need). As with product, there is great potential for companies to create globally aligned campaigns that allow for greater efficiency and consistency (using specific strategies both for offline and online promotions), however there needs to be the same recognition of local preferences (in terms of how consumers wish to receive communications). The most effective promotional channels to reach consumers will, therefore, differ greatly between countries. In addition, cultural difference could result in contradictory interpretations of the promotional strategy in different countries. This is in addition to influences from the macro environment and external factors such as 'government regulation'; for example, in the USA it is permissible and culturally acceptable to criticise competitors in advertisements, whereas this is generally not possible in markets such as the UK.

Price

As with product and promotion, pricing is sometimes adapted to both global and local markets depending on the specifics of the market. A uniform global pricing approach may be seen as challenging due to the differing levels of competition in different markets and the effects of exchange rates between the two countries involved: the home market and the target market. In addition, local market factors such as the channel(s) used to sell the product (i.e. online versus offline), as well as the degree to which discounts are applied (through the supply chain), and inter-company factors such as payment terms, credit periods, tax regimes, and incremental costs (e.g. shipping costs, insurance and tariffs), will all have a profound effect on the eventual price point. These effects may result in international markets having differing foreign retail prices, which will either make competing with existing offerings in the market difficult or create a price advantage. As with the other 'Ps', local market consumers' willingness to pay more for an item will likely be influenced by brand strength and perceived desirability as a 'premium' product. Although these are seemingly difficult issues to manage, if an MNC company can overcome these challenges they may be in a strong position to maintain long-term competitive advantage, as the same factors may create even higher barriers to entry for potential new, but smaller, competitors seeking to enter the same market.

People

The rise of the service industries sector has led to the development of strong customer loyalties (Sethna and Blythe, 2016). These loyalties are almost always based on loyalty to the people working in the industry. Thus, people become the element of the marketing mix concerned with employees and other consumers.

Process

This is the element of the marketing mix which is concerned with the overall delivery of a service. In services markets, consumers can sometimes be seen as a co-producer of the service (Sethna and Blythe, 2016). As with any other question in marketing, the starting point for developing a service process is the customer's needs. In some cases, the needs can be presented as a hierarchy. An example of this might be a cargo ship manufacturer who may not require new engines to be delivered urgently, but would probably need spare parts for a broken winch to be delivered quickly, as a docked and unproductive cargo ship is an expensive item! The marine engine manufacturer would therefore see the supply of engines as being less important than the supply of spare parts. These processes all involve human interaction, so they all provide opportunities to improve customer loyalty. Setting the right level of service can therefore be a source of competitive advantage.

Physical evidence

The element of the marketing mix concerned with the tangible aspects of products and services is physical evidence. The intangibility of most of the benefits of a service means that consumers do not have evidence that the service ever took place. The evidence might be useful to show other people (e.g. a certificate after a training course) or it might simply be something to act as a reminder of the pleasure the consumer obtained from the service (e.g. a souvenir). Physical evidence might also be used as a way of assessing the quality of a product before committing to a purchase.

Case Study 2.1

Dollar Shave Club launches in the UK

The Dollar Shave Club is a company headquartered in California, which delivers razors and other personal grooming products direct to customers by mail. It delivers razor blades on a monthly basis and offers additional grooming products for home delivery. It was founded by Mark Levine and Michael Dubin who first met at a party and spoke of their frustrations with the cost of razor blades.

An initial throwaway conversation turned into an idea, and with its own money (and investments from start-up incubator Science Inc.), the company started trading in January 2011. In March 2012, seed investors provided $1 million in funding. A year later, $9.8 million was raised in series A funding (the name typically given to a company's first significant round of venture capital financing) and a further $12 million was raised in series B funding. 2015 saw series D funding secure $75 million and on 19 July 2016, the Dollar Shave Club was acquired by Unilever for a reported $1 billion in cash. Michael Dubin continues to run the company as an independent, and the acquisition should help Dollar Shave Club

Image 2.1   Dollar Shave Club

(Continued)

(Continued)

expand faster into new geographies, and significantly improve its distribution abilities in existing markets.

There are three membership plans that are offered to currently over 3 million subscribers. The plans (named 'The Humble Twin', 'The 4X' and 'The Executive') are offered for $3, $6 and $9 per month respectively and each plan comes with a compatible handle. Other products in the range include shave butter, wet wipes, moisturiser, hair gel, hair cream and hair clay.

Having launched programmes in Canada and Australia back in 2012, February 2018 saw the launch of Dollar Shave Club in the UK.

To celebrate its UK launch, the company offered free shaves in its fully immersive barber shop set in London's Old Street Station. Other associated promotional events included comedy nights and free promotional items, and which were featured by the likes of *Time Out*.

Michael Dubin has the very tricky task of marketing the company in the UK like a start-up, while being owned by an FMCG giant with its own branding vision and with the knowledge that Unilever has helped the Dollar Shave Club to scale in the USA, Canada and Australia.

According to Euromonitor, the Dollar Shave Club brand now accounts for 54% of the US online shaving market and is torn between its original role as an irreverent challenger and now having to align its proposition to that of its parent company's corporate marketing strategy. This dichotomy also presents itself in the company's approach to research, development and innovation, where their natural test-and-learn approach is moderated by Unilever's more hard-nosed attitude.

So far, the approach taken in the UK is very different from the 2012 YouTube video entitled 'Our Blades Are F***ing Great', with the CEO delivering a very sarcastic speech about the company, but which prompted 12,000 orders over a two-day period after the video was released and, at August 2018, had received nearly 26 million views. Thus, the company stance now, when entering the UK, has basically been as a Unilever brand launching into the UK – not as some small start-up trying to find its way in the marketplace.

The company understood that it was not a simple case of 'slapping the US proposition into the UK market ... it is still run as a standalone [brand], we can use Unilever's capabilities but we stand alone. We still make our own decisions, but we confide in them a lot and discuss our ideas and plans. They have a boat load of great capabilities and access and scale and great quality people' (Stewart, 2018), and that the UK market needed to be assessed independently. The company now boasts a team of 300 people. All the creative elements of communications are handled in-house, and this, coupled with all the planning/buying of media on social platforms, means that the company has total control. There are of course some benefits to having a parent company like Unilever; Dollar Shave Club's wider media account still sits with Mindshare, the same shop that manages much of Unilever's media buying globally. So, continuing Unilever's 'unstereotype initiative', one presumes that a similar story, to that of sister brands Axe and Lynx, will be pursued where the focus will be on helping men to be the best version of themselves.

Right from the start, the company ensured that it was 'mobile-ready'; its app on Android devices has a conversion rate of over 125%, and it has plans to stay concurrent with developments in the 'voice space' such as with Amazon's Alexa, etc.; easing use for subscribers wanting to renew their subscriptions or check their delivery status.

The Dollar Shave Club has contributed to Unilever by teaching them about its direct-to-consumer model and how to apply it to other areas of Unilever's business. And Unilever is listening! It has launched two new direct brands: Skinsei (a skincare group of products) and Verve, in the UK (a monthly subscription of products that protects clothes from damage wash after wash).

Channels such as 'direct-to-consumer' continue to provide interesting opportunities for organisations as consumer expectations change continuously.

Questions for discussion

1. What are the differences between global and international marketing?
2. What factors should the company bear in mind when utilising direct-to-consumer channels?
3. Given that the company is 'mobile-ready', how can this channel be further utilised?
4. How do culture and subculture affect the company's marketing strategy in the UK?

SUMMARY OF KEY IDEAS

There are a variety of strategies and tactics that we have looked at in this chapter. Each of these, in global marketing, can also be viewed with potentially two broad strategic moves that could be adopted in relation to each of the marketing mix elements – standardisation or differentiation. *Standardisation* (the use of the same approach in all countries where the firm operates) is one option, while *differentiation* is about adapting the existing approach or introducing a new one completely. Furthermore, global marketing must carefully consider its 'positioning' of products relative to the other Ps discussed above (Place, Price, Promotion, Product, People, Process, Physical Evidence). Remember, a change in one P has a profound effect on the others. Effectively managing these factors will allow a company's brand to differentiate itself in the new international market it is seeking to enter and gain market share in. This may remain challenging for some brands who may not receive the same perception as in their home market. There is a complex variety of other factors affecting companies and the way that customers perceive them: the choice of partners, channels and operating sustainably under an ethos of corporate responsibility. Companies of course need to navigate the complexity of knowledge accumulation and execution on a local basis by tailoring existing and creating new marketing strategies, adapting marketing tools to realise the best brand localisation, develop tailored product offerings, investigate individual pricing strategies, develop distribution models and promote seamless campaign implementation. In some sense, it can be seen that there is no such thing as 'global' marketing – it is just 'marketing'. It sounds oversimplified, but is in fact the practical reality of how companies extend their brands and products – they always need to adapt (to a greater or lesser extent) to the local marketing context and also to remain globally aware. There are great benefits for those companies achieving effective global marketing strategies. Balancing the cost and quality efficiencies of standardisation in core products, research and development and brand strategy, combined with local customisation (and doing so flexibly), is compelling when executed well and, equally, extremely damaging when the local marketing dynamics and norms are not adhered to. The traditional market mix needs to be radically altered to cope with these opportunities and challenges. The rapidly evolving nature of the international marketplace is constantly transforming and has seen almost daily shifts in trading standards, policy, techniques and practices, and this, combined with an exponential growth in technology, means that there is more product being moved around the world than ever before as customers demand products when and where they want them – a global marketer's dream.

In this chapter, you have covered issues to do with the contemporary global marketing context. You have:

- developed an understanding of various conceptual frameworks and models and gained meaningful insights into why major international marketing decisions are made
- read and identified different approaches for entering a global market
- explored the global marketing context by analysing different environments using the PELFREC and LEEMSTEG frameworks
- had the opportunity to discuss global marketing in the context of current and future directions by looking at past, present and future trends
- gained inspiration from the successes of case companies such as the Dollar Shave Club in the development of their marketing strategies and campaigns.

Chapter Discussion Questions

You are the CEO of a Boston-based sports clothing company seeking to expand into multiple new markets:

1.   What information would you need in order to gain meaningful insights for major international marketing decisions?

2. Which of the different approaches for entering a global market is the right fit for your company?
3. What determines a firm's international marketing performance?
4. Are national markets converging? If so, how do we best compete effectively in the world?
5. What examples have you seen that you can gain inspiration from, in terms of the successes (and failures) of other companies in their development of their marketing strategies and campaigns?

REFERENCES

Allen, D. E., McAleer, M. and Reid, D. M. (2018) Fake news and indifference to scientific fact: President Trump's confused tweets on global warming. *Climate Change and Weather*. Working Paper No. 1817, Instituto Complutense de Análisis Económico.

Alzeer, J., Rieder, U. and Hadeed, K. A. (2018) Rational and practical aspects of Halal and Tayyib in the context of food safety. *Trends in Food Science and Technology*, 71, 264–7.

Amirouche, M., Arnault, F., Boyaval, F., Coste-Manière, I., Salomé, C. and van Holt, J. (2017) Luxury toys for men: When will women let us decide and buy on our own? *Procedia Computer Science*, 122, 548–55.

Andrews, J. (2005) US military sponsored vaccine trials and La Resistance in Nepal. *The American Journal of Bioethics*, 5(3), W1–W3.

Andrews, J. (2006) Research in the ranks: Vulnerable subjects, coercible collaboration and the Hepatitis E vaccine trial in Nepal. *Perspectives in Biology and Medicine*, 49(1), 35–51.

Antràs, P., Van Long, N., Benz, S., Carballo, J., Fernandes, A. P., Tang, H. and Bakhtiari, S. (2018) *Developments in Global Sourcing*. Cambridge, MA: MIT Press.

Appadurai, A. (1990) Disjuncture and difference in the global cultural economy. *Theory, Culture and Society*, 7(2–3), 295–310.

Aydalot, P. and Keeble, D. (2018) *High Technology Industry and Innovative Environments: The European Experience*. London: Routledge.

Balmer, J. M. (1998) Corporate identity and the advent of corporate marketing. *Journal of Marketing Management*, 14(8), 963–96.

Bartlett, C. A. and Ghoshal, S. (1989) *Managing across Borders: The Transnational Solution*. Boston, MA: Harvard Business School Press. Available at: www.business-to-you.com/international-business-strategy (accessed 31 July 2018).

Bayraktar, A. and Ndubisi, N. O. (2014) The role of organizational mindfulness in firms' globalization and global market performance. *Journal of Research in Marketing and Entrepreneurship*, 16(1), 26–46.

BBC (2017) How long should you stay in one job? Available at: www.bbc.co.uk/news/business-38828581 (accessed 1 August 2018).

Beechler, S. and Woodward, I. C. (2009) The global 'war for talent'. *Journal of International Management*, 15(3), 273–85.

Beleska-Spasova, E. and Glaister, K. W. (2009) The geography of British exports: Country-level versus firm-level evidence. *European Management Journal*, 27(5), 295–304.

Bitzenis, A. (2018) New industry policy in the post-communist countries: Globalization, regionalization, FDI and multinationals. In *Marketing Strategies for Central and Eastern Europe*. London: Routledge, pp. 1–19.

Bounfour, A. (2018) Africa: The next frontier for intellectual capital? *Journal of Intellectual Capital*, 19(3), 474–9.

Brightenburg, M. E., Francioli, S., Fu, N., Graßmann, C. and Tosti-Kharas, J. (2018) Millennials in the workplace. In *Academy of Management Proceedings*, *v1*: 14547. New York: Briarcliff Manor.

Bryan, L. L., Joyce, C. I. and Weiss, L. M. (2006) Making a market in talent. Book excerpt in *McKinsey Quarterly*. Available at: www.mckinsey.com/business-functions/organization/our-insights/making-a-market-in-talent (accessed 1 June 2018).

Buckley, P. J., Sutherland, D., Voss, H. and El-Gohari, A. (2018) The economic geography of offshore incorporation in tax havens and offshore financial centres: The case of Chinese MNEs – Networked multinational enterprises in the modern global economy. In *The Global Factory*. Cheltenham: Edward Elgar Publishing.

Bykova, A. and Lopez-Iturriaga, F. (2018) Exports-performance relationship in Russian manufacturing companies: Does foreign ownership play an enhancing role? *Baltic Journal of Management*, 13(1), 20–40.

Carneiro, J., Bamiatzi, V. and Cavusgil, S. T. (2018) Organizational slack as an enabler of internationalization: The case of large Brazilian firms. *International Business Review*, 27(5), 1057–64.

Cateora, P., Gilly, M. and Graham, J. (2016) *International Marketing*. New York: McGraw-Hill.

Cates, S. V. (2010) Generational management in corporate America: The differences and challenges in management of four generations of working adults. *Chinese Business Review*, 9(8), 46–54.

Caves, R. E. (2018) Growth and decline in multinational enterprises: From equilibrium models to turnover processes. In *Corporate Links and Foreign Direct Investment in Asia and the Pacific*. London: Routledge, pp. 9–28.

Cerna, M., Poulova, P. and Svobodova, L. (2018) The elderly in SMART cities. In *International KES Conference on Smart Education and Smart E-Learning*. Cham: Springer, pp. 224–33.

Chaney, T. (2018) The gravity equation in international trade: An explanation. *Journal of Political Economy*, 126(1), 150–77.

Colgan, F. (2018) Coming out of the closet? The implications of increasing visibility and voice for the career development of LGB employees in UK private sector organisations. In A. M. Broadbridge and S. L. Fielden (eds), *Research Handbook of Diversity and Careers*. Cheltenham: Edward Elgar Publishing.

Collinson, S. C. and Rugman, A. M. (2011) Relevance and rigor in international business teaching: Using the CSA-FSA matrix. *Journal of Teaching in International Business*, 22(1), 29–37.

Cuervo-Cazurra, A., Ciravegna, L., Melgarejo, M. and Lopez, L. (2018) Home country uncertainty and the internationalization–performance relationship: Building an uncertainty management capability. *Journal of World Business*, 53(2), 209–21.

Delios, A. and Beamish, P. W. (2005) Regional and global strategies of Japanese firms. *Management International Review*, 45(1), 19–36.

Doshi, A., Raghavan, S., Petitt, E. and Weiss, R. (2018) The economics of fake news: Consumer behavior during the 2016 election. In *Academy of Management Global Proceedings*, 61.

Drahokoupil, J. and Fabo, B. (2019) Outsourcing, offshoring and the deconstruction of employment: New and old challenges. In *The Deconstruction of Employment as a Political Question*. Cham: Palgrave Macmillan, pp. 33–61.

Edwards, J., Ketchen, D., Short, J. and Try, D. (2012) Mastering Strategic Management (1st Canadian edition). Available at: https://opentextbc.ca/strategicmanagement/chapter/types-of-international-strategies (accessed 1 June 2018).

Enright, M. J. (2005) Regional management centers in the Asia-Pacific. *Management International Review*, 45(1), 59–82.

Eriksen, T. H. (2018) Scales of environmental engagement in an industrial town: Glocal perspectives from Gladstone, Queensland. *Ethnos*, 83(3), 423–39.

Farid, H. (2018) Digital forensics in a post-truth age. *Forensic Science International*, 289, 268–9.

Filippaios, F. and Rama, R. (2008) Globalisation or regionalisation? The strategies of the world's largest food and beverage MNEs. *European Management Journal*, 26(1), 59–72.

Gaur, A. S., Ma, X. and Ding, Z. (2018) Home country supportiveness/unfavorableness and outward foreign direct investment from China. *Journal of International Business Studies*, 49(3), 324–45.

Ghemawat, P. (2018) CAGE Framework. Available at: https://ghemawat.com (accessed 3 June 2019).

Gibson, M. J. and Graciano, T. A. (2018) Using imported intermediate goods: Selection and technology effects. *Review of International Economics*, 26(2), 257–78.

Gilpin, R. (2018) *The Challenge of Global Capitalism: The World Economy in the 21st Century*. Princeton, NJ: Princeton University Press.

Goldsmith, R. E. (1999) The personalised marketplace: Beyond the 4Ps. *Marketing Intelligence and Planning*, 17(4), 178–85.

Grönroos, C. (1997) Keynote paper: From marketing mix to relationship marketing – Towards a paradigm shift in marketing. *Management Decision*, 35(4), 322–39.

Hartsock, N. C. (2018) Community/sexuality/gender: Rethinking power. In N. Hirschmann (ed.), *Revisioning the Political: Feminist Reconstructions of Traditional Concepts in Western Political Theory*. London: Routledge, pp. 27–49.

Healey, J. F., Stepnick, A. and O'Brien, E. (2018) *Race, Ethnicity, Gender, and Class: The Sociology of Group Conflict and Change*. London: Sage.

Heckscher, E. F. and Ohlin, B. (1933/1991) *Heckscher-Ohlin Trade Theory* (translated, edited and introduced by H. Flam and M. J. Flanders). Cambridge, MA: MIT Press.

Hennart, J.-F. (2018) Springing from where? How emerging market firms become multinational enterprises. *International Journal of Emerging Markets*, 13(3), 568–85.

Hollensen, S. (2016) *Global Marketing*, 7th edn. Harlow: Pearson.

Hunt, S. D. (2018) The philosophy of science foundations of marketing research: For scientific realism and the inductive realist models of theory status and generation. *Journal of Global Scholars of Marketing Science*, 28(1), 1–32.

Ibeh, K. I., Uduma, I. A., Makhmadshoev, D. and Madichie, N. O. (2018) Nascent multinationals from West Africa: Are their foreign direct investment motivations any different? *International Marketing Review*, 35(4), 683–708.

Jack, A. (2006) GSK is criticised for army drug test. *Financial Times*, 1 March.

Jones, R. W. and Kierzkowski, H. (2018) The role of services in production and international trade: A theoretical framework. *World Scientific Book Chapters: International Trade Theory and Competitive Models Features, Values, and Criticisms*, Chapter 14, pp. 233–53.

Judd, T. (2018) The rise and fall (?) of the digital natives. *Australasian Journal of Educational Technology*, 34(5), 99–119.

Karlsson, C., Cornett, A. P. and Wallin, T. (2018) Globalization, international spillovers and sectoral changes: An introduction. In *Globalization, International Spillovers and Sectoral Changes: Implications for Regions and Industries*. Cheltenham: Edward Elgar, pp. 1–22.

Kazan, E., Tan, C. W., Lim, E. T., Sørensen, C. and Damsgaard, J. (2018) Disentangling digital platform competition: The case of UK mobile payment platforms. *Journal of Management Information Systems*, 35(1), 180–219.

Keneley, M. J. (2018) The pitfalls of internationalization: The experience of American life insurers in Australia, 1885–1905. *Enterprise & Society*, 19(1), 31–57.

Khanna, T. and Palepu, K. G. (2006) Emerging giants: Building world-class companies in developing companies. *Harvard Business Review*, 84(10), 60–9. Available at: https://hbr.

org/2006/10/emerging-giants-building-world-class-companies-in-developing-countries (accessed 2 June 2018).

Kim, J. S. (2018) Measuring willingness-to-pay for mobile phone features: A multi-region study. *Journal of Research in Marketing and Entrepreneurship*, 20(2), 189–213.

Kim, J., Tabibian, B., Oh, A., Schölkopf, B. and Gomez-Rodriguez, M. (2018) *Leveraging the crowd to detect and reduce the spread of fake news and misinformation.* In Proceedings of the Eleventh ACM International Conference on Web Search and Data Mining (pp. 324–32).

Klimova, B., Maresova, P., Tomaskova, H., Mohelska, H., Novotny, M., Penhake, M. and Kuca, K. (2018) Are healthy older individuals ready to use smartphones? *Advanced Science Letters*, 24(4), 2870–2.

Knoke, D. (2018) *Changing Organizations: Business Networks in the New Political Economy.* London: Routledge.

Kolk, A., Rivera-Santos, M. and Rufín, C. (2018) Multinationals, international business, and poverty: A cross-disciplinary research overview and conceptual framework. *Journal of International Business Policy*, 1(1–2), 92–115.

Köllen, T., Kakkuri-Knuuttila, M. L. and Bendl, R. (2018) An indisputable 'holy trinity'? On the moral value of equality, diversity, and inclusion. *Equality, Diversity and Inclusion: An International Journal*, 37(5), 438–49.

Kujawski, M. (2018) Global Internet Statistics for 2018. Available at: www.mikekujawski. ca/2018/02/20/2018-global-internet-statistics-update (accessed 30 July 2018).

Lazer, D. M., Baum, M. A., Benkler, Y., Berinsky, A. J., Greenhill, K. M., Menczer, F. and Schudson, M. (2018) The science of fake news. *Science*, 359(6380), 1094–6.

Lee, J. W. and Lee, H. (2016) Human capital in the long run. *Journal of Development Economics*, 122, 147–69.

Lee, K. and Carter, S. (2011) Global marketing management. *Strategic Direction*, 27(1).

Legagneux, P., Casajus, N., Cazelles, K., Chevallier, C., Chevrinais, M., Guéry, L. and Ropars, P. (2018) Our house is burning: Discrepancy in climate change vs. biodiversity coverage in the media as compared to scientific literature. *Frontiers in Ecology and Evolution*, 5, 175.

Leonidou, L. C., Katsikeas, C. S., Samiee, S. and Aykol, B. (2018) International marketing research: A state-of-the-art review and the way forward. In *Advances in Global Marketing*. Cham: Springer, pp. 3–33.

Linder, S. (1961) *An Essay on Trade and Transformation.* Stockholm: Almqvist & Wiksell.

Logan, M. (2006) Nepal: Guinea pigs in Hepatitis E vaccine trials. IPS News Agency, 6 February. Available at: www.ipsnews.net/2006/02/nepal-guinea-pigs-in-hepatitis-e-vaccine-trials (accessed 2 April 2019).

Madsen, T. K. and Moen, Ø. (2018) Managerial assessments of export performance: What do they reflect? *International Business Review*, 27(2), 380–8.

Marinova, S. T. (ed.) (2018) *Foreign Direct Investment in Central and Eastern Europe*. London: Routledge.

Mathur, N., Karre, S. A., Mohan, L. S. and Reddy, Y. R. (2018) *Analysis of FinTech mobile app usability for geriatric users in India*. In *Proceedings of the 4th International Conference on Human–Computer Interaction and User Experience in Indonesia*, CHIuXiD'18 (pp. 1–11).

Mazur, E., Signorella, M. L. and Hough, M. (2018) The internet behavior of older adults. In *Encyclopedia of Information Science and Technology*, 4th edn. Hershey, PA: IGI Global, pp. 7026–35.

McCarthy, J. E. (1960) *Basic Marketing: A Managerial Approach*. Burr Ridge, IL: Irwin.

McKinsey Consulting (2015) Connecting Talent with Opportunity in the Digital Age. Available at: www.mckinsey.com/featured-insights/employment-and-growth/connecting-talent-with-opportunity-in-the-digital-age (accessed 1 July 2018).

Meltzer, J. P. (2014) Taiwan's Economic Opportunities and Challenges and the Importance of the Trans-Pacific Partnership. Available at: www.brookings.edu/research/taiwans-economic-opportunities-and-challenges-and-the-importance-of-the-trans-pacific-partnership (accessed 30 July 2018).

Mintchev, N. and Moore, H. L. (2018) Super-diversity and the prosperous society. *European Journal of Social Theory*, 21(1), 117–34.

Moen, Ø. and Rialp-Criado, A. (2018) European SMEs and the Born Global concept: Norwegian University of Science and Technology, Norway and Universitat Autònoma Barcelona, Spain. In *The Routledge Companion to European Business*. London: Routledge, pp. 99–110.

Moon, C. H., Rugman, A. M. and Verbeke, A. (1995) The generalized double diamond approach to international competitiveness. In *Beyond the Diamond*. Bingley: Emerald Group, pp. 97–114.

Myers, K. K. and Sadaghiani, K. (2010) Millennials in the workplace: A communication perspective on millennials' organizational relationships and performance. *Journal of Business and Psychology*, 25(2), 225–38.

Nair, M. and Emozozo, R. (2018) Electronic currency in Africa: M-Pesa as private inside money. *Economic Affairs*, 38(2), 197–206.

Narula, R. and Zanfei, A. (2005) The international dimension of innovation. In J. Fagerberg, D. Mowery and R. Nelson (eds), *Handbook of Innovation* (Chapter 12). Oxford: Oxford University Press.

Nguyen, Q. T. (2018) The regional MNE and coordination of MNE organizational structures. In G. Cook, J. Johns, F. McDonald, J. Beaverstock and N. Pandit (eds), *The Routledge Companion to the Geography of International Business*. London: Routledge, pp. 96–111.

Nielsen, B., Asmussen, C. and Goerzen, A. (2018) Toward a synthesis of micro and macro factors that influence foreign direct investment location choice. In G. Cook, J. Johns, F. McDonald, J. Beaverstock and N. Pandit (eds), *The Routledge Companion to the Geography of International Business* (Chapter 12). London: Routledge.

Oberthür, S. and Groen, L. (2018) Explaining goal achievement in international negotiations: The EU and the Paris Agreement on climate change. *Journal of European Public Policy*, 25(5), 708–27.

Oh, C. H. and Rugman, A. M. (2006) Regional sales of multinationals in the world cosmetics industry. *European Management Journal*, 24(2–3), 163–73.

Opitz, M. (2008) When innovating services, are 12 Ps enough? Towards a design oriented framework. *International Journal of Services Technology and Management*, 9(3–4), 320–33.

Oseghale, O. R., Mulyata, J. and Debrah, Y. A. (2018) Global talent management. In *Organizational Behaviour and Human Resource Management*. Cham: Springer, pp. 139–55.

Oyedele, A. (2016) Emerging market global business model innovation. *Journal of Research in Marketing and Entrepreneurship*, 18(1), 53–62.

Paul, J. and Benito, G. R. (2018) A review of research on outward foreign direct investment from emerging countries, including China: What do we know, how do we know and where should we be heading? *Asia Pacific Business Review*, 24(1), 90–115.

Penrose, E. T. (2017) Foreign investment and the growth of the firm 1. In P. Buckley (ed.), *International Business*. London: Routledge, pp. 33–48.

Pennycook, G. and Rand, D. G. (2018) Susceptibility to partisan fake news is explained more by a lack of deliberation than by willful ignorance. *Cognition*, doi: 10.1016/j.cognition. 2018.06.011, https://papers.ssrn.com/sol3/papers.cfm?abstract_id=3165567 (accessed 23 August 2018).

Porter, M. E. (1990) The competitive advantage of nations. *Competitive Intelligence Review*, 1, 14.

Pradhan, J. P. (2011) Emerging multinationals: A comparison of Chinese and Indian outward foreign direct investment. *International Journal of Institutions and Economies*, 3(1), 113–48.

Renwick, D. W. (2018) From green HRM towards workforce sustainability? In D. Renwick (ed.), *Contemporary Developments in Green Human Resource Management Research*. London: Routledge, in association with GSE Research, pp. 173–90.

Ricardo, D. (1817) *On the Principles of Political Economy and Taxation*. London: John Murray.

Rugman, A. M., and Verbeke, A. (1996) Foreign subsidiaries and multinational strategic management: An extension and correction of Porter's single diamond framework. *The Theory of Multinational Enterprises: The Selected Scientific Papers of Alan M. Rugman*, 1, 233. Cheltenham: Edward Elgar Publishing.

Rugman, A. M. and Verbeke, A. (2007) Liabilities of regional foreignness and the use of firm-level versus country-level data: A response to Dunning et al. *Journal of International Business Studies*, 38(1), 200–5.

Salman, D., Tawfik, Y., Samy, M. and Artal-Tur, A. (2017) A new marketing mix model to rescue the hospitality industry: Evidence from Egypt after the Arab Spring. *Future Business Journal*, 3(1), 47–69.

Sarkar, S. (2006) Nepal questions US army vaccine experiments. ISN Security Watch, 12 January.

Saxon, J. (2017) Why your customers' attention is the scarcest resource in 2017. IE School of Human Sciences and Technology, Spain. Available at: https://auth.ama.org/partners/content/Pages/why-customers-attention-scarcest-resources-2017.aspx (accessed 3 April 2019).

Schlie, E. and Yip, G. (2000) Regional follows global: Strategy mixes in the world automotive industry. *European Management Journal*, 18(4), 343–54.

Schneble, C. O., Elger, B. S. and Shaw, D. (2018) The Cambridge Analytica affair and Internet-mediated research. *EMBO Reports*, 19(8), e46579.

Schneider, B. C., Schröder, J., Berger, T., Hohagen, F., Meyer, B., Späth, C. and Vettorazzi, E. (2018) Bridging the 'digital divide': A comparison of use and effectiveness of an online intervention for depression between Baby Boomers and Millennials. *Journal of Affective Disorders*, 236, 243–51.

Sethna, Z. (2018) CEOs in practice: Narratives from those who've been there! A personal interview. Unpublished.

Sethna, Z. and Blythe, J. (2016) *Consumer Behaviour*, 3rd edn. London: Sage.

Sethna, Z. and Nightingale, K. (2017) Key elements of the 4S model. In *Refereed Proceedings of Global Research Symposium of Marketing and Entrepreneurship*. Babson College of Entrepreneurship, San Francisco, USA.

Shannon, T. R. (2018) *An Introduction to the World-System Perspective*. London: Routledge.

Sharma, C. K. (2009) Emerging dimensions of decentralisation debate in the age of globalisation. *Indian Journal of Federal Studies*, 1: 47–65.

Singh, M. (2018) Health and welfare of women and child survival: A key to nation building. *The Indian Journal of Pediatrics*, 1–5.

Smith, A. (1776/2000) *The Wealth of Nations*. (With an introduction by R. Reich; edited, with notes, marginal summary and enlarged index by E. Cannan.) New York: Modern Library.

Stewart, R. (2018) Unilever's influence looms large as Dollar Shave Club launches in the UK. *The Drum* (e-Magazine). Available at: www.thedrum.com/news/2018/01/29/unilevers-influence-looms-large-dollar-shave-club-launches-the-uk (accessed 1 June 2018).

Stoian, M. C., Dimitratos, P. and Plakoyiannaki, E. (2018) SME internationalization beyond exporting: A knowledge-based perspective across managers and advisers. *Journal of World Business*, 53(5), 768–79.

Tong, T., Singh, T. and Li, B. (2018) Country-level macro-corporate governance and the outward foreign direct investment: Evidence from China. *International Journal of Social Economics*, 45(1), 107–23.

Turk, D. J., Gillespie-Smith, K., Krigolson, O. E., Havard, C., Conway, M. A. and Cunningham, S. J. (2015) Selfish learning: The impact of self-referential encoding on children's literacy attainment. *Learning and Instruction*, 40(Dec.), 54–60.

Turner, J. (1997) *The Institutional Order*. New York: Longman.

Vazire, S. and Solomon, B. C. (2015) Self- and other-knowledge of personality. In M. Mikulincer, P. Shaver, M. L. Cooper and R. J. Larsen (eds), *APA Handbook of Personality and Social Psychology, Vol. 4: Personality Processes and Individual Differences*. Washington, DC: American Psychological Society, pp. 261–81.

Vernon, R. (1966) International investment and international trade in the product cycle. *The Quarterly Journal of Economics*, 80(2), 190–207.

Wade, R., Holmes, M. R. and Gibbs, C. (2018) The challenges of full-service restaurant brand internationalization: A United States/Canada perspective. *Journal of Foodservice Business Research*, 21(2), 139–53.

Watkins, A., Papaioannou, T., Mugwagwa, J. and Kale, D. (2015) National innovation systems and the intermediary role of industry associations in building institutional capacities for innovation in developing countries: A critical review of the literature. *Research Policy*, 44(8), 1407–18.

Williams, C. and Durst, S. (2018) Exploring the transition phase in offshore outsourcing: Decision making amidst knowledge at risk. *Journal of Business Research*. http://dx.doi.org/10.1016/j.jbusres.2018.01.013.

Wirtz, J., Tuzovic, S. and Ehret, M. (2015) Global business services: Increasing specialization and integration of the world economy as drivers of economic growth. *Journal of Service Management*, 26(4), 565–87.

Wootton, C. and Grundy, J. (2018) Millennials in the Workplace. A Poster Presentation at the Eastern Kentucky University. Available at: https://encompass.eku.edu/swps/2018/graduate/25 (accessed 1 July 2018).

World Bank (2018) World Development Report 2018: Learning to Realize Education's Promise. Available at: www.worldbank.org/en/publication/wdr2018 (accessed 28 July 2018).

World Trade Organization (WTO) (2018) Strong Trade Growth in 2018 Rests on Policy Choices. Available at: www.wto.org/english/news_e/pres18_e/pr820_e.htm (accessed 30 July 2018).

Yin, E. and Choi, C. J. (2005) The globalization myth: The case of China. *Management International Review*, 45, 103–20.

Zineldin, M. and Philipson, S. (2007) Kotler and Borden are not dead: Myth of relationship marketing and truth of the 4Ps. *Journal of Consumer Marketing*, 24(4), 229–41.

3

CONTEMPORARY MARKETING RESEARCH

David James Bamber and Christopher John Bamber

Learning Objectives

At the end of this chapter, you should be able to understand and discuss:

- How modern marketing professionals have adopted methods related to the psychology of individuals when eliciting insights into buyer behaviour and consumer marketing research, including neurosciences and psychonalytics
- The differences between traditional, modern and postmodern marketing research approaches with particular insights into the contemporary analysis of social media networks
- The importance of qualitative marketing research, qualitative marketing research and mixed methods marketing research
- Digital technologies and the emerging usage of fuzzy logic and artificial intelligence when analysing both digital big data, online netnographic data and online individuals' sensitive data
- The ethical dilemmas facing the contemporary marketing research professional and consulting marketing researchers

---

INTRODUCTION

This chapter explains to the student why marketing research is important and relevant in the modern world. The use of contemporary cases brings to life the world of the marketing research professional and highlights the ethical issues associated with handling personal and mass data. Important contemporary marketing research methods are described, highlighting the appropriate concepts, tools, techniques and marketing research methods.

At one time, the remit of contemporary marketing research might well have been within the realm of science fiction. There was a time when marketing research was limited to the use of questionnaires that assessed consumer perceptions and required self-reporting from convenient participants found on the street corners of city centres. Now, marketing research techniques stretch from those that focus on the individual to those using big data. However, the use of big data sets began in the 1920s when Deming (Census, 2018) used massive data sets but needed huge teams of individuals to process that data to allow him to radically improve the use of statistics in gathering census data. Later, George E. P. Box (1978) won the Shewhart Medal in 1968 for analysing big data in various ways to enable quality control in the chemical industry. Now, arguably at the other end of the data spectrum, magnetic resonance imaging techniques delve into the working of an individual's brain to show what is happening in real time at the electro-molecular level in relation to the differing consumer stimuli being presented.

The marketing process has traditionally been presented with various numbers of steps. Malhotra (2007) uses six steps: (1) problem definition, (2) development of an approach to the problem, (3) research design formulation, (4) fieldwork/data collection, (5) data preparation and analysis, and (6) report preparation and presentation. Wilson (2003) presents a seven-step approach, adding 'selection of the research provider/agency'. Masterson and Pickton (2010) suggest an 'eight steps with feedback' approach to the marketing research process, which is similar to that presented by McDaniel and Gates (2007): (a) recognise the marketing problem, (b) define the research problem, (c) set research objectives and a brief, (d) carry out the research, (e) analyse the data, (f) present and disseminate the results, (g) evaluate the data and research process, and (h) make marketing decisions and carry them out – then go back to (a). Computer software tools that may aid the marketing researcher continue to be developed and not all of the tools require big data: Lilien, Rangaswamy and De Bruyn (2007) have developed a series of eight software models with which 'marketing engineers' can 'score inexpensive victories' where sales might be increased by between 5% and 10% using relatively small amounts of data to develop marketing models where development costs are very low compared with potential gains. For example, Lilien et al. (2007) suggest the use of the Conjoint Analysis Model to measure, analyse and predict customers' responses to new products or to new features of existing products, and use perceptual mapping to help understand how customers view a product or service relative to competitors' products or services. However, wider reading from other academic fields shows that those fields have arguably progressed further in some specific directions: education makes use of 'reflective practice' (Dana and Yendol-Silva, 2003) and in the health field DePoy and Gitlin (1998) emphasise the philosophical foundations of research connected with thinking.

In the 1970s, one-megabyte computers were the size of large libraries that stocked hard copies of printed books. Modern mobile devices have thousands of times more memory and technical capabilities, and the operating systems on them collect a vast array of data that is gleaned from almost everyone's individual usage, location and preferences and resides with the data giants such as Chrome, Google, Facebook, Sino Web and Twitter, and retail and wholesale platforms such as Amazon and Alibaba. Not only that but the world-wide web has shrunk communication lead times, which were once held hostage to the vulnerabilities of 'snail mail' – letters and postage stamps are now superseded by a collective of collaborators who develop both quantitative and qualitative analytic software that is freely available in the public domain. Contemporary marketing research techniques, such as netnography, have been developed to probe new and profitable niche markets and diverse consumer bases. Artificial intelligence can now be used within the computer to perform quasi-experiments and fuzzy-logic studies that use a large complex mix of cultural, psycho-demographic and purchasing behaviour data sets and variables that were previously impossible to undertake. Not only does contemporary marketing research expand out into the global market thousands of billions of dollars but it also analyses the inner-most personal thoughts of the individual, using psychoanalytic techniques to reveal their motives, desires and drives that might well have been repressed deep in their psyche. Just as the one-megabyte computer that was once the size of a large library building is now a pocket-sized mobile device, so the capacity and capabilities of today's mobile devices will increase in the not so distant future to even go beyond what is now considered to be 'science fiction' to become the emergent reality.

Studies of the human brain are no longer the sole discipline of medical science; there are now extended applications into psychology, with relevance to the psychoanalyst and behavioural therapist, and extensive uses in the new discipline of neuromarketing. Advances in computational technologies have allowed the study of the human brain and its impact on consumer behaviour to take new directions. Consumers have been influenced by advertising and marketing campaigns presented on billboards, products, film footage in cinemas and in television advertising campaigns, leading to the television producers of the 1950s popularising the phrase television soaps. These TV programmes were intermittent with the popular advertising of products, both well-established and emerging new brands, hence soap being the popular product from TV sales. It was not long before psychoanalysts researched buyer behaviour and modified advertisements to target psycho-emotional, psycho-sexual and superego personas within their campaigns. The use of psychoanalysis in marketing research continues today but now utilising modern digital technologies.

Critical approaches to the findings and results of marketing research have been at the forefront of entrepreneurs' mindsets when innovatively introducing products into the market. This is seen as a postmodern approach to marketing research, where market activity is focused on consumers' acceptance and endorsement but uses advertising media that are as diverse, and often contradictory, as possible. The widespread magnetism of social media provides endless opportunities for the marketing researcher to access data, target social groups, attract followers, promote products and brands effectively and therefore increase sales. In this respect, the massive numbers of users (seen as unpredictable, yet marketing researchers want them to be predictable) of social media provide a platform for artificial intelligence and analysis techniques like fuzzy logic to direct computer robots to intervene in social conversations using 'chatbot' pursuers. Online discussions are analysed and interpreted to find out what is current and contemporary among social networks and social groups communicating online both locally and across continents. This allows the modern marketing researcher to adopt the study of human groups, ethnographic techniques, to social networks, hence netnography is now providing opportunities to research the needs of online communities.

NEUROMARKETING

When applied to the discipline of marketing, neuroscience is called 'neuromarketing'. Neuromarketing includes the direct use of neuroimaging, eye movement and other techniques to measure the response from 'consumers' to specific products, packaging, colours, advertising, tonality and other aspects of marketing. Many world-leading companies such as Daimler, EBay and PepsiCo are increasing their use of neuromarketing techniques. An overview of the methodologies of neuromarketing is presented by Gani et al. (2015), and Trabulsi et al. (2015) propose that consumer neuroscience can be used to optimise marketing communications, while Maxwell (2008) summarises how 'fair price' has been researched by behavioural economists, primate behaviour researchers and social neuroscientists. Luan et al. (2018) used the Tobii Eye-Tracker T120 (now superseded by the Tobii Pro Glasses 2; see www.tobiipro.com/product-listing/#Hardware) to study how the context congruity effects of online product recommendations influence consumers' attention to and memory of recommended products in an online shopping environment. (Some branches of neuroscience along with their possible relationships to marketing are given in the glossary at the end of the book.)

Pro Glasses 2 is a piece of relatively inexpensive eye-tracking equipment that detects and records the eyes with a broad spectrum of devices, including EEG, near-infrared spectroscopy (NIRS), galvanic skin response (GSR), motion detection, respiration rate and heart rate. Imotions (at https://imotions.com/blog/eeg-headset-prices) has details of EEG devices with prices that range from $99 to over $25,000. The Association for NeuroPsychoEconomics (ANPE, 2018) holds itself to be the premier scholarly organisation for scientists and professionals working at the interface of neuroscience, psychology, economics, organisational and consumer behaviour, and marketing, and the *Journal of Neuroscience, Psychology, and Economics* (JNPE, at www.neuropsychoeconomics.org/journal) presents interesting articles connecting those interrelated themes.

PSYCHOANALYSIS AND MARKETING RESEARCH

Following observations of, and using therapeutic techniques with, patients presenting with psycho-sexual problems, Sigmud Freud (1999) stated that early childhood experiences and innate drives lead to both normal and abnormal psychological development. Freud named and defined the ego, the id and the superego, proposing that they operate or are repressed in the individual's psyche. The id interacts with and encloses the pleasure-seeking libido, claiming urgent gratification of desires such as sex without concern for any consequences. The moral and ethical facet of the human psyche is the superego, which restricts the base drives of the id. The id and the superego are equalised by the ego. The ego is the part of the mind that mediates between the conscious and the unconscious and is responsible for reality testing and a sense of personal identity. Hence, a consideration between the costs and benefits of actions in terms of reality is made so that decisions are made either to act, to repress actions or to give up urges. Such processes are applicable to many aspects of contemporary marketing research (Parsons et al., 2017), including consumer desires (Mishra, 2013), consumption and repression (Cluley, 2015a), and advertising (Loose, 2014; Oswald, 2010), while Cluley (2015b) presents psychoanalysis as a marketing theory. Carl Jung (a Swiss psychiatrist) at times collaborated with, but at other times contradicted, Freud. Jung (1971) developed many psychological concepts, such as synchronicity, archetypal phenomena, the collective unconscious, the psychological complex, and extraversion and introversion. Both Jung and Freud adopted subjective approaches to their psychoanalytic work and psychoanalytic techniques have, by and large, been used in therapeutic settings. Hence, psychoanalytic marketing research techniques applied to consumer research are still in their infancy and have yet to flourish. However, Lambert et al. (2014) investigated the role of narcissism (self-importance) in relation to the consumer identity of young adults and further research could give insight into the role of consumption in the development of an adult identity, while Frosh (2010) reviews psychoanalysis outside the clinic, noting the importance of the inner and outer selves, which will have implications for marketing researchers who study consumer desires and behaviours that stem from either the inner self or the outer self.

POSTMODERN MARKETING RESEARCH

Postmodern marketing research is based on the philosophy of postmodernism which adopts an inbuilt culture of doubt towards a global cultural narrative and meta-narrative. Postmodern marketing research focuses on customised experiences and rejects the generality of the broad market. The postmodern marketing research method uses one-to-one communication between real humans based in the real world. The move towards postmodernism is widely seen in the use of terms such as 'my folder' on 'my computer'. Brown (1993) notes that postmodernism confronts the status quo of 'traditional' marketing theories with new notions of complex change (see Table 3.1). Lyotard (1984) rejects meta-narratives and grand theories as they discard the naturally existing chaos, disorder of the universe and power of individual events. Hence, if traditional theories are challenged, so too are the job roles associated with them and the postmodern marketing researcher advances marketing research through being a creative and thinking researcher focused on social engagement. Hirschman and Holbrook (1992) acknowledge that the Cartesian dualism between mind and matter leads to a variety of epistemological stances and validity concerns, and hence methodological orientations. At least two wide-ranging orientations are noted: 'sceptical post-modernism' and 'affirmative postmodernism' which promote redefinition and innovation (Rosenau, 1992). Postmodernism throws out epistemological assumptions, challenges methodological conventions and obscures all versions of truth, leading to an emergent politics where left wing and right wing no longer exist (Rosenau, 1992). Perhaps agreeing with

Table 3.1 Postmodern marketing contrasted with modern marketing

Modern marketing approach	Postmodern marketing approach
• Single universe	• Multidimensional universe
• Fixed	• Nimble
• Traditional media	• New media
• One to many	• One to one
• Static	• Interactive and immersive
• Brand endorsed	• Endorsed by consumer
• Broad	• Individually customised

Source: Brown (1993)

Brown (1995), postmodernist perspectives might lead the marketing researcher to the philosophy of ever-deepening quicksand: the postmodern approach may well profess to be nimble, but without direction it is not 'agile'. What the postmodernist approach does benefit from is the constant questioning of both assumptions and presumptions, and a critical perspective.

CONTRIBUTIONS OF SOCIAL MEDIA TO MARKETING RESEARCH

There is little doubt that social media platforms offer many, verging on unlimited, possibilities for analysts to collect information and to identify current, potential and future buyers and analyse consumer perceptions. Consequently, businesses can react to the research findings analysed from within social media domains. The likes of Twitter, LinkedIn, Facebook, Sino Web, Instagram, Qzone and other social media networks offer analysts informal snippets of information exchanged between consumers, and between a company and its customers, which have become data mines for marketing researchers. Just across those six social media networks of Twitter, LinkedIn, Facebook, Sino Web, Instagram and Qzone, there are in excess of 3.5 billion registered users and with under 8 billion people on earth, this potentially provides a massive consumer primary data set. Social media are mainly accessed by the 3 billion internet users or the 5 billion mobile phone users, for which providers often make secondary data sets available. Thus, as confirmed by Schwartz and Ungar (2015), using automated methods to access data-driven content analysis and discovery, from social media networks, is at an unprecedented level.

Social media provide the opportunity to know whether customers like something, because they may tweet about it, post a photo of themselves on Instagram, like it on Facebook, or do a YouTube video review. Marketing researchers may stratify the big data set accessible from social media users through sentiment analysis, as advocated by Bohlouli et al. (2015), but they must also respect the analysis of intimate feedback through studying the comments of loyal followers, as recommended by Liang and Shen (2017). Therefore, social media trend analysis, through big data analysis coupled with intimate feedback study, increases the analyst's understanding of how and why people are using products and services, when they are using them and in what context.

The benefits of using social media for marketing research stem from accessing instant feedback, which is essential when attempting to reduce market research time or when assessing the effectiveness of market campaigns or when following a product life cycle. Marketing research is able to follow product and service life cycles through trend analysis because when a consumer posts something, it's available to be read by anyone in real time. Since customer behaviour, tastes and needs can ebb and flow, this fast spread of information provides timely, up-to-date primary data that is accurate for following market trends.

A cornerstone of marketing research is the assessment of the effectiveness of marketing processes leading to product and service delivery. Social media provide an ideal opportunity for this. Being able to access consumers' and buyers' sharing of content, to interact with them, involve them and obtain their feedback, allows for an iterative process of primary data collection and analysis methods (Beig and Khan, 2018). Hence, social media allow relationship-based marketing research to a far larger extent than was previously possible.

DIGITAL MARKETING

Digital marketing campaigns are becoming commonplace, since shoppers are exploring the many suppliers growing their web presence. Products and services alike are being offered across the internet, through TV and on mobile phone devices, making the modern digital shopping experience more and more accessible. These multiple devices and shopping choices, referred to as 'online marketing', 'internet marketing' or 'web marketing', provide consumers and customers with worldwide digital purchasing options. This rapid advancement of digital media and greater access to digital devices provide opportunities for marketing research.

An analysis by O'Connor (2015) was concerned that 'digital marketers believe their companies are only 34 per cent proficient (effective) at digital marketing', while the International Chamber of Commerce (2018) reports that 'digital media growth is estimated at 4.5 trillion online advertisements served annually with digital media spend at 48% growth in 2010'. Likewise, researchers Taiminen and Karjaluoto (2015), when studying SMEs, pointed out that digital marketing campaigns, particularly among SMEs, are not keeping up with advancements in digital technology.

For marketing research, the implications are that there is a lot that practitioners are not doing to maximise their digital marketing potential, hence there is a need to study the opportunities available for value creation through improving such digital campaigns. The potential for both qualitative analysis and quantitative study of the impacts of digital marketing is almost limitless. The marketing researcher can utilise the mass of digital data available posted by companies in advertisements and advertising campaigns, and assess the success of such ventures in terms of market penetration, sales revenue, return on investment (ROI), brand image and other measures of the effectiveness of digital marketing. It is clear that research scholars and marketing research practitioners have noted the necessity for empirical investigation of the process of converting digital marketing into big data to enhance performance and create value (Bharadwaj et al., 2013; Zeng and Glaister, 2018).

THE USE OF DIGITAL MARKETING BIG DATA

The proliferation of online purchasing, social media and the accessibility of digital technologies mean that big data is available for marketing research purposes. In digital focus 3.1, we see that consumer- and customer-related big data has been available from several sources, but it also indicates that nowadays big data refers to the amount of data as well as to the complexity of data created at ever greater speeds.

Digital Focus 3.1

Sources of marketing research big data availability before 2008

A data set profile typically involved small to large data sets, mainly slow to access and analyse:

- marketing campaign analysis
- points of sale transactions
- response to direct mailing
- coupon redemption
- customer surveys
- loyalty programmes
- business created records
- focus groups.

Sources of marketing research big data predominantly available after 2008

A data set profile now typically consists of large data sets, with a high variety of uses and a fast speed of growth:

- social media interactions
- online purchase data
- websites analytics
- click-through rates
- browsing behaviour
- mobile device usage
- geo-location devices
- video, picture and audio streaming
- blogs and comments.

Traditional marketing analysis methods such as customer surveys and focus groups have aimed at obtaining customer perceptions and opinions, as they can be considered more important than reality, when predicting future buying trends. However, data analysts have said that the availability of big data will not prevent the need for traditional customer survey research. Moreover, big data allows a modern marketing researcher the opportunity to identify the changing perceptions of users of social media, using techniques of opinion mining such as semantic analysis (Abu-Salih et al., 2018; Cambria et al., 2013). Marketers can also detect buying signals, such as content shared by people, likes and dislikes, and questions posted online. An understanding of click-through rates, buying signals and online purchase data can help sales people target relevant prospects and direct marketers to run micro-targeted campaigns. Likewise, sentiment analysis has been employed in order to discover knowledge from social media interactions (Bohlouli et al., 2015). Thus, big data analysis of social media or online customer reviews and their perceptions and opinions is able to identify product and service improvement projects and marketing campaigns to further brand image, improve customer loyalty and increase sales. The rate at which big data can now be accessed and processed has led to the emergence of artificial intelligence in online user communications.

THE IMPORTANCE OF MARKETING RESEARCH METHODS

Goulding (2005) critiques qualitative methodologies including grounded theory, ethnography and phenomenology, whereas there is an increasing array of new quantitative methods, such as partial least squares (PLS), minimum condition analysis (MCA) and advanced analytics (ADAN, at www.mrs.org.uk/membership/advanced_analytics), which adopt procedures such as random forests and cluster ensemble analysis, looking for optimum approaches to analyse data from multiple sources. Usually, quantitative methods are deductive, using objectivity, seeking to measure causative effects, using pre-defined hypotheses, whereas qualitative methods tend to be inductive, using subjectivity while seeking meanings through open-ended processes. Importantly, rather than weighing the balance between qualitative and quantitative data, both approaches are important as each leads to different kinds of knowledge. However, a marketing research study may use multimethodologies and mixed research methods and not be based solely in a single qualitative or quantitative paradigm. Multimethodologies use more than one method of data collection or research methods originating from different theoretical perspectives (Brewer and Hunter, 2006) and, according to the *Journal of Mixed Methods Research*: 'Mixed methods research is defined as research in which the investigator collects and analyzes data, integrates the findings, and draws inferences using both qualitative and quantitative approaches or methods in a single study or program of inquiry' (taken from the description on the journal's home page, at https://us.sagepub.com/en-us/nam/journal-of-mixed-methods-research/journal201775#description).

THE EMERGENCE OF ARTIFICIAL INTELLIGENCE MARKETING RESEARCH

Artificial intelligence (AI) encompasses many types of technology that can simulate human intelligence; it uses computer algorithms to bring about machine learning. In the world of social media, AI teaches computers to categorise data in a contextual manner to provide the requested information, supply analysis or trigger an event based on their findings. In a keynote speech, aimed at marketing professionals and marketing researchers, Professor Malhotra (2012: 432) looked ahead at the possibilities artificial intelligence (AI) may bring: 'Quantitative data analysis will make greater use of artificial intelligence procedures such as artificial neural networks and genetic algorithms'.

In this regard, the professor anticipates that AI techniques will increasingly be applied to commercial marketing research. Even so, AI is already being adopted in commercial situations. For example, Quach and Thaichon (2018) tell us that Hong Kong customs has employed an AI system which robotically scans social networking sites to target sellers by using artificial intelligence to detect those selling counterfeit products. Also, anyone who uses Amazon to purchase things will realise the company has become very good at predicting just what they are interested in based on their online behaviour. The commercial success of these applications, in unique situations, can be adapted to marketing research to optimise sales within niche markets or mass markets too.

Although possibly still in its infancy, AI is currently present in social media networks, providing businesses with online advertisement optimisation based on learning customer preferences and learning from trend analysis about buyer behaviour to optimise online sales promotions. For example, a 'chatbot' on websites and on social media networks would use artificial intelligence when it provides a conversation. An example of a voice-responding 'chatbox' is Google Assistant or an example of both voice and a textual method is found within the Starbucks app, informing customers when their order is ready for pick-up. The inclusion of AI in marketing research activities may be in its infancy but the scope of usage in improving customer satisfaction is large. Further contributions of AI will come from its understanding of the application of netnography and fuzzy logic to marketing research.

APPLYING NETNOGRAPHY TO A SENSITIVE DATA SET

Netnography is the study of human and social interactions in a digital context. The method was popularised by the marketing professor Robert Kozinets who developed this research approach by applying many aspects of traditional ethnography to the internet and social networks (Kozinets, 1999). The online approach to understanding individuals in a social context offers scope for researching a large number of individuals (Kozinets, 2010). Because of this online approach to data gathering, netnography can provide anonymity to those individuals being studied and often the researcher is not known to the study group. Hence, a strength of anonymity is that it allows marketing analysts to study sensitive issues and provide a degree of privacy which often encourages the participants in a study to be honest about their situations and in their opinions. This approach also allows marketing researchers to explore consumer behaviour by understanding customers through listening to their frank, unadulterated comments.

The following practitioners' perspectives box mentions the use of sentiment analysis – sometimes this technique is referred to as opinion mining as it aims to analyse the opinions of survey respondents or bloggers, or consumers' feedback. This technique of analysing data is particularly useful in netnography in that the researcher uses methods of analysing feedback that is posted on various websites and social media sites by considering either positive or negative phrases or words used in the comments posted. Likewise, the practitioner also alludes to using semantic analysis as these efforts attempt to conduct an analysis of sentiment in posts' replies and therefore determine a level of trustworthiness. Amalgamating semantic analysis and sentiment analysis within social media research data analysis methods, allows the researcher to assess the trustworthiness of the opinions posted (Abu-Salih et al., 2018). Kozinets (2010) explains that there are five steps to netnography research: entrée, data collection, data analysis, data interpretation, and member checks. An example of the five steps is shown in the practitioners' perspectives box, providing at each step a practitioner's descriptor and an example from a potentially sensitive data set.

Practitioner's Perspective 3.1

Five steps of netnography research

Here we present the views and experiences of a marketing research consultant who followed their client's brief to investigate the possibility of expanding their cosmetic facial surgery business. The client is planning to operate in Poland, with a special focus on targeting UK citizens travelling to Poland for cosmetic procedures, thus taking advantage of the trend in medical tourism.

Step 1: Entrée

Selection and familiarisation with online communities

My first step was the identification of online cosmetic blog sites posted in the UK and in Poland for facial cosmetic surgery procedures. I recorded the search techniques and search engines that I used in my digital log book.

Step 2: Data collection

Collecting data from online communities

From my collection of cosmetic blog sites, I selected those that were most relevant and which provided views of consumer experiences. I excluded data sets such as blogs that were not relevant: in other words, those that were not from UK citizens experiencing facial surgery carried out in Poland.

Step 3: Data analysis

I then analysed the data using qualitative techniques such as semantic analysis and sentiment analysis and coded the group blogger posts using relevant selected words and phrases. These thematic groups included within the blogs both negative and positive consumer insights.

Step 4: Data interpretation

Interpreting the coded data

Based on the client's brief, I made sense of all the bloggers' coded data, and offered interpretations based on my knowledge of customer satisfaction theory, my years of experience and a literature review connected with the coded themes.

Step 5: Member checks

A component of validation in qualitative research

I then engaged with willing participant bloggers, from within the data set, to gain bloggers' feedback. This is when I presented my interpretations and findings to participating bloggers in order to elicit their opinions on my results. Their feedback validated my results of this netnographic study. I then pitched the report to the client at which time they commented that they would be keen to use the 'plan, do, check and act' project management approach to develop their market penetration.

Discussion Questions

1. How could the marketing researcher increase the number of relevant data sets, considering social media, similar consumer markets and geographical areas?
2. Which brand that you are familiar with could benefit from a netnography research study using the above five-step approach to research?
3. How could the marketing researcher have used social media to elicit further opinions and frank comments from relevant consumers?

These five steps have been shown by practitioners, academics and researchers to be appropriate for a wide range of setting and social groups, such as Wu and Pearce (2017) when they adopted netnography for a study concerned with the rise of the technology-empowered Chinese middle class and some features of their new overseas travel activities. Likewise, Hamilton and Hewer (2009) carried out an exploratory netnographic analysis of the salsa experience, also demonstrating the variety of situations the technique can be adapted to.

APPLICATIONS OF FUZZY LOGIC TO MARKETING RESEARCH

The study of human behaviour is complex; it is an art and at the same time a science, while often full of contradictions and misunderstandings among scholars, so analysis techniques must consider this confusion, based on a logic that is fuzzy. To begin with, let us answer the question, what is fuzzy logic? It is a:

Type of reasoning based on the recognition that logical statements are not only true or false (white or black areas of probability) but can also range from 'almost certain' to 'very unlikely' (gray areas of probability). Software based on application of fuzzy-logic (as compared with that based on Formal Logic) allows computers to mimic human reasoning more closely, so that decisions can be made with incomplete or uncertain data. (Technical term extracted from the Business Dictionary at www.businessdictionary.com/definition/fuzzy-logic.html)

Since the early theories of fuzzy logic emerged in the 1960s and, later, Zadeh (1974) applied theories of fuzzy logic, it has become a widely acceptable tool in decision making in a fuzzy environment, including marketing research. For example, the vagueness of sales planning using forecast systems, where forecasting is often seen as both an art and a science using truths, partial truths and completely false notions, has been explored using fuzzy logic for better planning and control (Kuo, 2001; Lin and Hong, 2008). Keyman (1997) likewise applied fuzzy logic to the complex marketing subject of segmentation. Similarly, the uncertainty within a retail environment of sales forecasts, market price and procurement is mitigated in a proposed model produced by Kumar et al. (2016), using fuzzy logic to understand a particular fuzzy marketing data set.

Given that fuzzy logic can be used to understand the concept of partial truth, where the truth value may range from completely true to completely false, it can also be used to handle the complexity of consumer feedback, the vagaries of customer delight and perceptions of product and service users. Hence, because of the fuzzy data set of human behaviour, fuzzy logic is predicted to be applied to many aspects of marketing research and customer relationship management.

ETHICAL ASPECTS FOR THE CONTEMPORARY MARKETING RESEARCH CONSULTANT

Contemporary marketing research is full of emerging data analysis techniques which are qualitative and quantitative, may use mixed research methods, and can be logical and also fuzzy, which includes both personal intimate data and big data. Marketers are presented at the same time with truths and untruths, opinions mixed with facts, perceptions intertwined with realities, among a virtual online and a real-world presence. This means that ethical boundaries become blurred. Nevertheless, Shaw (2012) explains marketing ethics as the systematic study of how moral standards are applied to marketing decisions, behaviours and institutions. For readers who need comprehensive information on many aspects of ethical conduct, Shaw's guide to marketing ethics would be a good place to gain an initial understanding. Therefore, rather than cover all aspects of ethics, this section will introduce ethics in a contemporary marketing research context. Contemporary marketing research incorporates the marketing researcher's methods of netnography, neuromarketing, fuzzy logic, psychoanalytic practices and also the use of digital marketing, big data, artificial intelligence and social media.

The code of ethics and conduct produced by the Ethics Committee of the British Psychological Society (BPS, 2018), which focuses on the four primary ethical principles of respect, competence, responsibility and integrity, is a good guide for marketing researchers to follow.

The manner in which these principles apply to the marketing researcher and to the contexts that they are applied in will inevitably change over time. Nevertheless, we can apply these categories to the dilemmas of contemporary marketing research and below is an example showing the perspective of a marketing research consultant based in the UK (see ethical focus 3.1). This represents the views of a Fellow of the Market Research Society (MRS) which is the world's leading research association. The information presented in the focus box is the result of discussion between researcher Dr Chris Bamber of OLC (Europe) Ltd and a Fellow of MRS (wishing to remain anonymous) during conference proceedings at Businet 2017. The discussion focused on the ethics and morals expected of a professional marketing researcher, and, as the Fellow was a veteran practitioner, he was able to consider not just the widely acknowledged aspects of market research, but also more recent concerns around ethical conduct, emerging trends in research practice and forthcoming regulatory frameworks affecting research involving human participants.

Ethical Focus 3.1

Ethical principles to guide the contemporary marketing researcher

Respect

Researchers need to demonstrate respect for the dignity of persons and individuals. Therefore, I shall ensure that:

- participation is based on voluntary informed consent
- confidentiality of information collected is maintained even for social media data
- all individuals' rights and well-being shall be respected
- the regulatory frameworks for data management such as the general Data Protection Act (GDPR 2018, at https://eugdpr.org) are complied with.

(Continued)

(Continued)

Competence

Researchers should not provide services that are outside their areas of knowledge, skill, training and experience. Therefore, I shall ensure that:

- I exercise independent professional judgement in the design, conduct and reporting of all my research activities
- I balance the needs of the individuals, groups and their professional activities, whether using intimate statements or big data sets
- all researchers including myself shall be competent through qualifications and experience.

Responsibility

Researchers should consider applying the values of responsibility. I shall therefore take responsibility to:

- take reasonable precautions to ensure participants are not harmed or adversely affected by my studies
- ensure the proper quality control of data management at every stage, across all communication methods, of the research including publication
- monitor my own and other researchers' approach to data collection.

Integrity

Researchers should always demonstrate the values of integrity. Therefore, my research activities will:

- ensure the integrity of the marketing research profession
- maintain integrity when presenting the results of research, unambiguously
- not purposely mislead the readers of market research, no matter in what form it is presented
- monitor the presentation of results across multi-media networks to ensure the findings are not degraded or delineated in any way.

Questions for discussion

1. What are some ethical problems associated with gathering personal marketing research data?
2. What ethical principles should guide a contemporary marketing researcher?
3. What skills are needed by the competent ethical marketing researcher?

Ethical focus 3.1 maps the responses of a consultant when asked about ethical dilemmas when carrying out marketing research to the framework of the BPS (2018), incorporating the principles of the MRS (2014) code of conduct. For the marketing and the contemporary market researcher who requires more guidance on ethical conduct, it is suggested that the Marketing Research Association code of marketing research standards and the Market Research Society code of conduct are considered (MRA, 2013 and MRS, 2014).

Case Study

Research in Cosmetic Facial Surgery business

This practitioner's descriptor box (above) is a contemporary case study. As shown on pages 86-87, it revolves around the views and experiences of a marketing research consultant and the brief of a client to investigate the possibility of expanding their cosmetic facial surgery business. Considering that context provide answers to the following questions:

1. Was the consultant practitioner narrow minded in their marketing research approach?
2. What other marketing research techniques could you, as a contemporary marketing researcher, have used?
3. The scope of the validation technique in the case study appeared to be limited, therefore what other validation techniques could be used to provide the client more confidence?

SUMMARY OF KEY IDEAS

The chapter has presented the following ideas and concepts of contemporary marketing research:

- methods related to the psychology of individuals when eliciting insights into buyer behaviour and consumer marketing research, including neurosciences and psychonalytics
- differences between traditional, modern and postmodern marketing research approaches, focusing on the contemporary analysis of social media networks
- qualitative marketing research, qualitative marketing research and mixed methods marketing research
- digital technologies, the emerging usage of fuzzy logic and artificial intelligence that use digital big data, online netnographic data and online individuals' sensitive data
- ethical dilemmas facing the contemporary marketing research professional and consulting marketing researchers.

Chapter Discussion Questions

1. Are there any marketing research project briefs that you as a marketing researcher would not accept from a client?
2. Does marketing research always gain consent to use participants' data?
3. In a contemporary world which widely uses social media and 'big data', are traditional marketing research methods still relevant?
4. How are psychoanalytic techniques different from neuroimaging techniques?
5. What are the main concerns of the ethical marketing researcher?

REFERENCES

Abu-Salih, B., Wongthongtham P., Yan, K. and Zhu, D. (2018) CredSaT: Credibility ranking of users in big social data incorporating semantic analysis and temporal factor. *Journal of Information Science*, 1–22.

ANPE (2019) Association for NeuroPsychoEconomics (www.neuropsychoeconomics.org).

Beig, F.A. and Khan, M.F. (2018) Impact of social media marketing on brand experience: A study of select apparel brands on Facebook. *Vision: The Journal of Business Perspective*, 22(3), 264–275

Bharadwaj, A.S., El Sawy, O.A., Pavlou, P. and Venkatraman, N. (2013), Digital business strategy: Toward a next generation of insights. *MIS Quarterly*, 37(2), 471–482.

Bohlouli, M., Dalter, J., Dornhöfer, M., Zenkert, J. and Fathi, M. (2015) Knowledge discovery from social media using big data-provided sentiment analysis (SoMABiT). *Journal of Information Science*, Special Issue on Big Social Data, 41(6), 779–98.

Box, J. F. (1978) *R. A. Fisher: The Life of a Scientist*. Hoboken, NJ: Wiley.

Brewer, J. and Hunter, A. (2006) *Foundations of Multimethod Research: Synthesizing Styles*. Thousand Oaks, CA: Sage.

British Psychological Society (BPS) (2018) Code of Ethics and Conduct 2018. *The British Psychological Society*, 18 April.

Brown, S. (1993) Postmodern marketing? *European Journal of Marketing*, 27(4), 19–34.

Brown, S. (1995) Postmodern marketing research: No representation without taxation. *Journal of the Marketing Research Society*, 37(3), 287–310.

Businet (2017) The 31st Annual Businet Conference, Vilamoura, Portugal, 8–11 November.

Cambria, E., Schuller, B., Xia, Y. and Havasi, C. (2013) New avenues in opinion mining and sentiment analysis. *IEEE Intelligent Systems*, 28(2), 15–21.

Census (2018) History of W. Edwards Deming 1900–1993 (www.census.gov/history/www/census_then_now/notable_alumni/w_edwards_deming.html).

Cluley, R. (2015a) Consumption and repression. *Marketing Theory*, 15(3), 365–79.

Cluley, R. (ed.) (2015b) Virtual Special Issue: Psychoanalysis as a marketing theory. *Marketing Theory*, 15(3).

Dana, N. F. and Yendol-Silva, D. (2003) *The Reflective Educator's Guide to Classroom Research: Learning to Teach and Teaching to Learn through Practitioner Inquiry*. Thousand Oaks, CA: Corwin Press.

DePoy, E. and Gitlin, L. N. (1998) *Introduction to Research: Understanding and Applying Multiple Strategies*. St Louis, MO: Mosby.

Freud, S. (1999) *The Standard Edition of the Complete Psychological Works of Sigmund Freud*, Vol. *XIX*. (Translated from the German under the general editorship of J. Strachey; in collaboration with A. Freud; and assisted by A. Strachey and A. Tyson.) London: Vintage/Hogarth Press.

Frosh, S. (2010) *Psychoanalysis Outside the Clinic: Interventions in Psychosocial Studies*. London: Palgrave.

Gani, M. O., Saleh-Reza, S. M., Rabi, M. R. I and Reza, S. (2015) *Neuromarketing: Methodologies of marketing science*. In *Proceedings of the Fourth International Conference on Advances in Economics, Management and Social Study (EMS)*. New York: Institute of Research Engineers and Doctors (IRED).

Goulding, C. (2005) Grounded theory, ethnography and phenomenology: A comparative analysis of three qualitative strategies for marketing research. *European Journal of Marketing*, 39(3/4), 294–308.

Hamilton, K. and Hewer, P. (2009) Salsa magic: An exploratory netnographic analysis of the salsa experience. *Advances in Consumer Research*, 36, 502–8.

Hirschman, E. C. and Holbrook, M. B. (1992) *Postmodern Consumer Research: The Study of Consumption as Text*. London: Sage.

International Chamber of Commerce (2018), International Chamber of Commerce (https://iccwbo.org/).

Jung, C. G. (1971) *Psychological Types: Collected Works of C.G. Jung 6*. Princeton, NJ: Princeton University Press.

Keyman, E. (1997) Fuzzy Segmentation: Everything is a Matter of Degree. ESOMAR World Research, Marketing Research, Edinburgh (www.warc.com/welcome).

Kozinets, R. V. (1999) E-tribalized marketing? The strategic implications of virtual communities of consumption. *European Management Journal*, 17, 252–64.

Kozinets, R. V. (2010) *Netnography: Doing Ethnographic Research Online*. Thousand Oaks, CA: Sage.

Kumar, A., Adlakha, A. and Mukherjee, K. (2016) Modeling of product sales promotion and price discounting strategy using fuzzy logic in a retail organization. *Industrial Management & Data Systems*, 116(8), 1418–44.

Kuo, R. (2001) A sales forecasting system based on fuzzy neural network with initial weights generated by genetic algorithm. *European Journal of Operational Research*, 129(3), 496–517.

Lambert, A., Desmond, J. and O'Donohoe, S. (2014) Narcissism and the consuming self: An exploration of consumer identity projects and narcissistic tendencies. *Consumer Culture Theory*, 16, 35–57.

Liang, Y. and Shen, W. (2017) Fan economy in the Chinese media and entertainment industry: How feedback from super fans can propel creative industries' revenue. *Global Media and China* 1(4), 331–349. Available at https://journals.sagepub.com/action/doSearch?content=articlesChapters&countTerms=true&target=default&field1=AllField&text1=fan+economy&field2=AllField&text2=&publication%5B%5D=gcha&Ppub=&Ppub=&AfterYear=&BeforeYear=&earlycite=on&access=

Lilien, G. L., Rangaswamy, A. and De Bruyn, A. (2007) *Principles of Marketing Engineering*. University Park, PA: Penn State Smeal College of Business/Decision Pro. Inc.

Lin, C. and Hong, C. (2008) Using customer knowledge in designing electronic catalog. *Expert Systems with Applications*, 34(1), 119–27.

Loose, R. (2014) The other side of marketing and advertising: Psychoanalysis, art and addiction. *Marketing Theory*, 15(1), 31–8.

Luan, J., Yao, Z., Shen, Y. and Xiao, J. (2018) Context congruity effects of online product recommendations: An eye-tracking study. *Online Information Review*, 42(6), 847–63.

Lyotard, J.-F. (1984) *The Postmodern Condition: A Report on Knowledge (Theory & History of Literature)*. Manchester: Manchester University Press.

McDaniel, C. and Gates, R. (2007) *Marketing Research Essentials*. New York: Wiley.

Malhotra, N. K. (2007) *Marketing Research: An Applied Orientation*. Upper Saddle River, NJ: Pearson.

Malhotra, N. K. (2012) A Key Note Address, by Professor Naresh Malhotra, Nanyang Business School, Nanyang Technological University, Singapore – Conference notes: 'Shaping the future of research in marketing in emerging economies: looking ahead', Indian Institute of Management (Lucknow), India, *International Journal of Market Research*, 54(3), 432.

Market Research Society (MRS) (2014) *Code of Conduct*. London: Market Research Society (www.mrs.org.uk).

Marketing Research Association (MRA) (2013) *Code of Marketing Research Standards*. Washington, DC: MRA (www.marketingresearch.org).

Masterson, R. and Pickton, D. (2010) *Marketing: An Introduction*. London: Sage.

Maxwell, S. (2008) Fair price: Research outside marketing. *Journal of Product & Brand Management*, 17(7), 497–503.

Mishra, A. A. (2013) Psychoanalytic accounts of consuming desire: Hearts of darkness. *Journal of Consumer Marketing*, 30(7), 608–9.

O'Connor, B. (2015) What Every CEO Needs to Know about Digital Marketing. *Journal of Creating Value*, 1(2), 214–220.

Oswald, L. R. (2010) Marketing hedonics: Toward a psychoanalysis of advertising response. *Journal of Marketing Communications*, 16(3), 107–31.

Parsons, E., Maclaran, P. and Chatzidakis, A. (2017) *Contemporary Issues in Marketing and Consumer Behaviour*. London: Taylor & Francis.

Quach, S. and Thaichon, P. (2018) Dark motives-counterfeit selling framework: An investigation on the supply side of the non-deceptive market. *Marketing Intelligence & Planning*, 36(2), 245–59.

Rosenau, P. M. (1992) *Post-Modernism and the Social Sciences: Insights, Inroads, and Intrusions*, Princeton: Princeton University Press.

Schwartz, H.A. and Ungar, L.H. (2015) Data-Driven Content Analysis of Social Media: A Systematic Overview of Automated Methods. *The ANNALS of the American Academy of Political and Social Science*, 659(1), 78–94.

Shaw, L. (2012) *SAGE Brief Guide to Marketing Ethics*. Beverly Hills, CA: Sage.

Taiminen, H. M. and Karjaluoto, H. (2015) The usage of digital marketing channels in SMEs. *Journal of Small Business and Enterprise Development*, 22(4), 633–651.

Trabulsi, J., Manuel, G. G. and Smith, M. (2015) Consumer neuroscience: A method for optimising marketing communication. *Journal of Cultural Marketing Strategy*, 1(1), 80–9.

Wilson, A. (2003) *Marketing Research: An Integrated Approach*. Harlow: Pearson.

Wu, M.-Y. and Pearce, J. (2017) Understanding Chinese overseas recreational vehicle tourists: A netnographic and comparative approach. *Journal of Hospitality & Tourism Research*, 41(6), 696–718.

Zadeh, L. A. (1974) *The Concept of a Linguistic Variable and its Application to Approximate Reasoning*. London: Springer.

Zeng, J. and Glaister, K.W. (2018) Value creation from big data: Looking inside the black box. *Strategic Organization*, 16(2) 105–140.

4
NEUROMARKETING

Nashaat H. Hussein

Learning Objectives

At the end of this chapter, you should be able to understand and discuss:

- The meaning of neuromarketing
- The importance of neuromarketing to the new digital market
- The techniques used to assess marketing stimuli
- The ethical problems related to neuromarketing and consumers' freedom of choice
- The limitations and problems associated with the global application of neuromarketing

INTRODUCTION

Recognising the needs of customers is the main concern of all organisations, since the basis of staying competitive lies in the capability to assess and develop products and services that can satisfy customers better than competitors. Traditional marketing methods and persuasion techniques (especially in light of technological advancements and digital marketing methods) have forced many organisations to reevaluate their ability to reach consumers. Many researchers argue that the methods of 'articulated answers' (Burgos-Campero and Vargas-Hernandez, 2013), such as market research, surveys and focus groups, are not enough to understand the way individuals feel about a product or service because it is difficult to describe exactly the emotions experienced by a person in response to a stimulus such as a product. They also question the validity of traditional methods in their analysis of consumer behaviour. For example, in the case of focus groups, participants' responses may be affected by the majority, in addition to being influenced by other factors such as incentives, time and pressure that may prejudice the final results. Surveys, in turn, require large samples and intricate design tools to be able to deal with variables that affect reliability such as language, education and cultural or subcultural variations.

Reconsidering traditional marketing methods, among other reasons, paved the way for the emergence of neuromarketing. Neuromarketing is the subfield of neuroscience research that attempts to better understand the consumer through his or her unconscious processes, explaining consumers' preferences, motivations and expectations, predicting behaviour and evaluating the needs and orientations of advertising messages (Fisher et al., 2010; Gatterer, 2012). Neuromarketing is an emerging interdisciplinary field that aims to investigate and understand consumer behaviour by studying the functions of the human brain. Neuroscience attempts to gather information on the structure and functions of the human brain and its subdomain called 'cognitive neuroscience' (Javor et al., 2013). It seeks to understand the neural mechanisms behind thoughts, reasoning, emotions, memory or decision making. One of the major techniques to measure marketing stimuli is neuroimaging. When used in marketing to comprehend consumer behaviour, these methods are called neuromarketing techniques. Thus, by using neuroimaging techniques, researchers can measure subjects' responses to marketing stimuli. Therefore, the development of this field depends on the advance of science, technology, computer science and neuroscience. The aim of neuromarketing is to study the physiological response of the brain to advertising and marketing strategies. In order to evaluate the effectiveness of these strategies, the resulting brain activity from this phenomenon is monitored and measured using neuroimaging techniques. Neuroscientists are now able to directly study the frequency, location and timing of neuronal activity in an exceptional way (Lee et al., 2007).

Neuromarketing involves the use of neuroscience research to form advertising and marketing strategies so that brands can easily target consumers in deeper and more lasting ways. It assumes that because consumers are usually unable to reveal their decision-making processes in purchasing goods and services, conventional market research methods, such as focus groups and surveys, are perceived by neuromarketers as being of limited value to marketers. Neuroscientists assert that consumers' inability to express their true feelings stems from the idea that some of the most significant influencers affecting their brand loyalty and purchase behaviour are unconscious brain processes beyond their calculations. By studying the effect of different marketing stimuli on the brain through advanced techniques, including functional magnetic resonance imaging (fMRI) and qualified electroencephalography (EEG), neuromarketers can create campaigns designed to develop more powerful and longer-lasting positive responses to advertising. As such, studies in the field of neuromarketing are considered as applicable to a better comprehension of human reasoning and for improving marketing techniques. Methods such as eye tracking or facial recognition can help to study human reactions when confronted with marketing stimuli. Understanding that the pressure to optimise advertising effectiveness and accountability is high, neuromarketing research can provide new ways to contribute to these goals as it enhances traditional marketing instruments by drawing on innovative ideas, applications and software. Supporters of neuromarketing expect that in the long term, findings reached from neuromarketing might change the interconnection between humans and machines and lead to the development of new brain–computer interfaces that facilitate direct communication between the human brain and an external device. Defenders of neuromarketing activities also assert that various benefits can be achieved from the technique for both consumers and companies, and that consumers would benefit from the creation of products and campaigns specifically targeting them since their decisions would be facilitated rather than manipulated, while companies would save large amounts of their budgets traditionally spent on marketing campaigns.

Nevertheless, the use of neuromarketing creates controversy. Many critics argue that the use of neuromarketing techniques affects consumers' ability to freely select not to consume certain marketed products, leaving individuals unable to struggle and making them easy targets for marketing campaigns. On the other hand, there is a certain scepticism around neuromarketing studies that use fMRI or EEG recordings to study customers' unconscious emotions and level of inclination towards products or trademarks. Critics also believe that neuromarketing still lacks sound and vigorous scientific methods, which negatively affect its credibility. It still lacks the scientific support that encourages neuromarketers to use meaningful methods. In order to avoid exaggeration of the power of neuromarketing methods, it should be acknowledged that the development of neuromarketing lies somewhere between academic research outcomes, which may result in studies ending without proving any correlation, and the business realm, which seeks rapid and profitable results. The critical view of neuromarketing relates to our neuro-culture. An increasing number of studies have been written on the subject of brain optimisation, meaning enhancements or threats to brain function that may optimise the functions of the brain (O'Connor et al., 2012). This implies that the brain is flexible and can be obstructed by outside sources, supporting the cultural theory that our brain may be manipulated and impacted by scientific forces such as neuromarketing.

This chapter aims to elucidate the meaning of neuromarketing and the way it combines neuroscience and marketing. It discusses the various techniques of neuromarketing, and highlights the importance and potential contributions of neuromarketing to marketing research. The chapter also tries to identify the ethical issues involved in neuromarketing research. The results obtained will allow for a comprehensive understanding of neuromarketing and the ways it might serve the marketing of various commodities.

WHAT IS NEUROMARKETING?

The application of neuroimaging to market research – what is called 'neuromarketing' – 'has caused considerable controversy within neuroscience circles in recent times' (Lee et al., 2007: 199). Neuromarketing emerged as an expanded field of research on neuro-economics. The term was first introduced by Ale Smitdts (Roebuck, 2011) as a reference to the application of neuroimaging techniques in market research. The main difference between neuromarketing research and traditional research methods lies in the fact that with the former the subjects are not asked to express their opinions regarding a particular topic. In other words, oral statements are not to be considered reliable, since the results are only obtained by recording the participants' brain activities. By getting into the human subconscious mind, neuromarketing research allows for the identification of subjects' direct reactions to the stimuli they are exposed to, such as packages, products, logos, visual or auditory elements characterising the goods that satisfy the needs of the consumers (Pop et al., 2014). Neuromarketing is the process that enables the knowledge and understanding of the mechanisms used by the human brain to process information. It is believed that neuromarketing is a way to describe the activity of the brain under the effect of marketing stimuli, which, by means of specific tools, correlates with the psychological reaction following subjects' exposure to certain advertisements and marketing stimuli. Therefore, neuromarketing helps entrepreneurs come up with basic ideas when making decisions about approaching the market and clients, and establishing communication with business partners. It is assumed that there are two main reasons for this trend: (1) the possibility that neuroimaging will become cheaper and faster than other marketing methods; and (2) the hope that neuroimaging will provide marketers with information that is not obtainable through conventional marketing methods. Although neuroimaging is unlikely to be cheaper than other tools in the near future, there is growing evidence that it may provide hidden information about the consumer experience. The most promising application of neuroimaging methods to marketing may come before a product is even released – when it is just an idea being developed.

Solomon and Rabolt (2004) assert that people buy products not for what they do but for what they mean, and here is where emotions come into play, underlying the notion that people feel first, think after and in the end they purchase or not (Solomon and Rabolt, 2004: 28). However, people usually consider many other aspects of a product or service before acquiring it, such as price, features, packaging, branding, origin of manufacture and brand culture. Since emotions interfere with how consumers process messages, understanding cognitive responses to selling messages has always been a methodological contest. For example, researchers have primarily depended on consumers' abilities to express how they feel about a particular piece of advertising, in a confidential setting such as a face-to-face interview, via a survey or in a focus group. These methods have significant boundaries. They emphasise that people are actually able to describe their own cognitive process, with its many limitations. Also, many factors may motivate research participants to manipulate the reporting of their feelings, including incentives, time or peer pressure. Therefore, the emergence of neuro-imaging techniques has offered stimulating methodological substitutes. Such techniques can allow marketers to probe consumers' brains to gain valuable insights into the subconscious processes and to explain the success or failure of messages. By referring to neuromarketing, they may remove an important issue facing conventional advertising research, which is to trust that people have both the motivation and the capacity to report how they are affected by advertising. Supporters of neuromarketing also believe that getting information through neuromarketing is more accurate because it takes into account not only the sociological and psychological profiles of customers, but also the cognitive.

It is obvious that the idea of evaluating the neurological correlates of consumer behaviour has caused considerable excitement within the marketing profession (Mucha, 2005), and also created confusion among marketers. For example, Hubert and Kenning (2008) view neuromarketing as a valuable means to carry out business. They propose that neuromarketing should be renamed 'consumer neuroscience'. Others believe that neuromarketing is a relatively novel and open-to-debate interdisciplinary research field, a component of marketing, by means of which one can properly understand the psychological and neuropsychological impulses behind customer behaviour and orientation. A third group proposes that the idea of neuromarketing needs further investigation and proper experimental techniques to assess its rationality within the marketing environment. Many scholars, such as Garcia and Saad (2008), believe that given its role as a young discipline, the theoretical, empirical and practical scope of neuromarketing is still being developed. Leon Zurawicki (2010) also thinks that there is an important opportunity for this field, as by better understanding the neural world of consumers, marketers can help them and the brands that serve them better adapt to an increasingly complex and overwhelming world. Allowing for the assumption in neuromarketing that the brain contains concealed information about preferences, it is reasonable to set aside, for the moment, the issue of 'concealment' and ask 'what relationships are known to exist between brain activity and expressed (that is, not hidden) preference' (Ariely and Berns, 2010: 284).

TECHNIQUES OF NEUROMARKETING

Neuroscientists use a number of tools in their methodological investigation of research problems. These research tools rely on recording the metabolic activities happening inside the consumer's brain or recording electrical-magnetic properties of the neurons in the brain or the other physiological activities of the human body. Tools working on the principle of recording these metabolic activities include functional magnetic resonance imaging (fMRI) and positron emission tomography (PET). Electrical activity recording tools consist of electroencephalography (EEG), event-related potential (ERP), magneto-encephalography (MEG), steady state topography (SST) and trans-cranial magnetic stimulation (TMS). Eye tracking, galvanic skin response, facial coding and facial electromyography are tools used to measure other human physiological activities. With fMRI, neuroscientists use a powerful magnet to track the blood flow in the brain as subjects respond to visual and audio cues to explore the pleasure centre, and let marketers assess the way people respond. Limitations concerning the mass use of fMRI include its cost and inconvenience, since the equipment is very expensive to operate and subjects must lie completely still in a large machine for a long period of time. Electroencephalography (EEG) is an electrophysiological monitoring method that records the electrical activity of the brain. It is much cheaper than fMRI, using a cap of electrodes attached to the sample's scalp to measure electrical waves produced by the brain to allow researchers to track emotions such as rage, pleasure, grief and desire through fluctuations of activity. Unlike fMRI, EEG does not grant access to deep parts of the brain where the 'pleasure centre' exists.

Eye tracking allows for the study of behaviour and cognition without measuring brain activity. It focuses on what the subject is looking at, for how long, the duration of time, the path of the subject's vision and changes in pupil dilation while the subject looks at certain stimuli. Zurawicki (2010) states that eye movements fall into two categories: fixations and saccades. Fixation is when the eye movement pauses in a certain position and saccade is a switch to another position. The resulting series of fixations and saccades is called a scan path, and these are used in analysing visual perception, cognitive intent, and interest. Measuring physiological responses to stimuli can give data on the subject's emotional states by monitoring heart rate, blood pressure, skin conductivity, stress hormone release from saliva, facial muscle contraction, and by inferring the emotional state for each moment of exposure to stimuli. Response-time measures give feedback on the time interval between a stimuli's appearance and its response, informing researchers as to the intricacy of a stimulus to an individual and how the subject relates to it, as Zurawicki (2010) states. This inexpensive technique can be utilised for measuring subjects' attitude towards certain stimuli.

To analyse data, researchers use different software packages to help analyse a consumer's data images, but the most widely used software for the analysis of brain-imaging data sequences is statistical parametric mapping, which aims to identify how well and how often the brain appoints areas for attention, emotion, memory and personal implication. Data can explicitly inform marketers about a consumer's thoughts while watching the experimental content. Correspondingly, marketers may recognise whether a participant is scared, sleepy, happy or interested by examining how the product or the commercial is affecting the consumer's brain. Ariely and Berns (2010) emphasise that brain-scanning techniques may provide clues concerning the basic preferences of an individual, which are more accurate than the data gathered by traditional market research, which may be looked at sceptically due to its subjectivity. If this is true, then the concepts and prototypes of the products could be quickly tested and those products which are not promising could be removed from the market. This would result in a more efficient allocation of resources that could be used only for promising products that may really attract consumers.

The major advantage, from the point of view of many scholars of all different methods and procedures for neurological investigation, is the reduction of method bias from traditional research methods. Neurological procedures can help overcome the practical issue of people which may include inability and being uncomfortable or unwilling to truthfully make a self-report (Dimoka et al., 2012). Neurophysiological data has the strength of offering real-time data while a subject is executing a task or responding to a specific stimulus (Dimoka et al., 2012). Dimoka et al. (2012) found that by permitting continuous real-time data collection and powerful time-series analysis, it is possible to capture the flow of either a single construct or many constructs simultaneously.

NEUROMARKETING AND MARKETING RESEARCH

The usefulness of neuromarketing depends on answering three fundamental questions. First, can neuromarketing reveal hidden information that is not apparent in other approaches? Second, can neuromarketing provide a more efficient cost–benefit trade-off than other marketing research approaches? Third, can neuromarketing provide early information about product design (Ariely and Berns, 2010: 284)? Many scholars believe that neuromarketing can be very useful as an alternative tool to traditional marketing studies. Among the reasons why marketers are excited about brain imaging is that they hope it will provide an accurate marketing research method that can be applied even before a product is made. The assumption is that neuroimaging data would give a more accurate suggestion of fundamental individual preferences than data gained from standard market research studies and would remain alert to the types of biases that are often present in the so-called 'subjective approaches' to valuations. From their perspective, product concepts can be tested rapidly, and those that are not promising can be eliminated at an early stage. This would allow for a more efficient allocation of resources to develop only promising products.

Other researchers are still sceptical about the efficacy of neuromarketing when compared to traditional marketing research methods. Among the various criticisms of neuromarketing is the idea that it rejects personal autonomy and choice in the consumer market. Under the pretext of manipulating consumer behaviour by exposing humans to various stimuli, there is an attack on autonomy. Murphy et al. (2008) sum up this by stating: 'Such stealth neuromarketing is not possible with current technology, but if developed would represent a major incursion on individual autonomy' (Murphy et al., 2008: 297).

Digital Focus 4.1

Neuromarketing data: Is it reliable?

The most significant requirement neuromarketing has not been able to meet is that of sampling sizes and generalisations. Neuromarketing studies usually depend on laboratories and expensive technologies (such as fMRI and EEG) which take a long time and represent a problem when obtaining data from large samples. On the other hand, neuromarketing researchers have also failed to collect large samples of statistically significant results that support their claims and prove their scientific validity. Although neuromarketing helps us understand the difference between what people say and what they do, the field still needs to be applied on a broader level in order to reveal human behaviour. The sampling problems of neuromarketing have caused an ongoing debate from the supporters of traditional research, who claim that neuromarketers use small sample sizes which are insufficient to draw valid conclusions that can be generalised.

Company X decided to use neuromarketing techniques to collect data on the best possible ways to increase its sales. The company needed to get a sample of people who could actually guide its production and sales strategies. It was able to get a sample of 15 people, particularly women since it sells cosmetics. After using the EEG technique, it was able to estimate what its customers wanted and began to develop its strategy accordingly. Surprisingly, the company's sales began to drop. It began to re-question the neuromarketing technique used as well as the nature of the sample of women reached.

Sources

Ariely, D. and Berns, G. (2010) Neuromarketing: The hope and hype of neuroimaging in business. *Nature Reviews Neuroscience*, 11(4), 284–92.

Calvert, G. and Thensen, T. (2004) Multisensory integration: Methodological approaches and emerging principles in the human brain. *Journal of Psychology*, 98(1–3), 191–205.

(Continued)

(Continued)

Fugate, D. (2007) Neuromarketing: A layman's look at neuroscience and its potential application to marketing practice. *Journal of Consumer Marketing*, 24(7), 385–94.

Maxwell, S. (2008) Fair price: Research outside marketing. *Journal of Product and Brand Management*, 17(7), 497–503.

Question

1. What went wrong with the company's strategy, and why do you think its sales dropped?

As part of the controversy over the issue, many researchers assume that numerous difficulties are usually associated with using fMRI machines. A safe and reliable medical environment, the large size of the machine and the space required to carry out experiments may all affect the validity of real-world marketing stimuli. Although many studies have to come up with special ideas and methods to ensure the accuracy of results, the results are still unsettled. For example, a Coke and Pepsi fMRI study used cooled plastic tubes held with plastic mouthpieces to enable participants to fully taste a sufficient volume of both sodas while lying inside the scanner. A computer-controlled syringe pump allowed for precise and accurate delivery of both sodas (McClure et al., 2004). Another study, conducted to examine the perceived trustworthiness of eBay offers, for example, found it hard to apply fMRI in a real-world experiment. The study recommended that online shoppers sit in front of their computers in a comfortable and calm environment to examine eBay offers, which is very difficult to implement in real life because of the size of the van as well as the requirement for a special room to control the safety of both subjects and researchers (Riedl et al., 2010).

These findings made many researchers and marketers claim that neuromarketing studies will become pure scientific projects rather than marketing ones, assuming that using these techniques will undermine the role of traditional marketing research techniques. Like traditional market research, there must be precise requirements for different control conditions. Yet, the difficulties of neurophysiological processes dictate a comprehensive understanding of the specific neuroscientific techniques in order to properly test a suggested hypothesis and evaluate the study's findings (Kenning et al., 2007). Hence, researchers may have trouble in testing all subjects to ensure that they are free from any medical or behavioural disorder, and in controlling the movements of the subject's body, mainly the head, which might affect the scanning pictures (Maxwell, 2008). The subject has to remain immovable while being surrounded by an acoustically noisy scanner for at least 45 minutes to an hour and a half, depending on the study in question, which may distress the subject (Riedl et al., 2010). These factors may all affect the reliability of the data provided by individuals under study.

On the other hand, neuromarketing represents a hard encounter for marketers and researchers because it endorses sophisticated experimental designs compared to the simple designs presented in traditional market research. Therefore, many still favour the use of conventional market research methods, assuming they will achieve similar results. For example, fMRI relies on a wide range of stimulus presentation repetitions as a way to reduce the noise in the fMRI signal through finding the average across a large number of trials that will definitely limit the effectiveness of complicated studies (Kenning et al., 2007). According to Kenning et al. (2007), processing and interpreting neuroimaging data is much more complex than that for general behavioural data or information-based data derived from questionnaires, since the brain itself is extremely intricate. The authors assert not only that the nature of the neuroimaging technique is sophisticated, but also that the relationship between performance and the underlying human physiology is considered a new issue for market researchers that requires further investigation.

Another question remains: who carries out neuromarketing experiments using fMRI machines, for example? In their research entitled 'Defining Neuromarketing: Practices and professional challenges', Carl Fisher and his colleagues (2010) argue that in particular relevance to psychiatry, neuromarketing may be seen as an extension of the search for quantification and certainty in previously indefinite aspects of human behaviour. They also claim that the issues raised by neuromarketing highlight important professional, ethical and scientific concerns. This new field exemplifies the complicated issue of professional ethics as applied to academic–industrial relationships. Furthermore, as a new application of neuroscience methods, neuromarketing raises important considerations for the responsible conduct of research and the public understanding of neuroscience (Fisher et al., 2010). Therefore, members of the medical professional community, such as psychiatry, who already rely on neuroscientific techniques need to be involved in defining human needs and cognitive processes.

CRITIQUE OF NEUROMARKETING

Assuming that neuroscience can be beneficial for marketing mix management practices, there are also some key shortcomings which must be taken into consideration. Alongside practical and theoretical issues, the privacy and ethical concerns of consumers must be reconsidered. People fear that neuromarketing might reveal deep insights into their unconscious minds and, therefore, manipulate their buying behaviour. Even though researchers state that finding a 'key to buy' in human brains is not possible, the picture of marketing used for techniques similar to brainwashing stays in people's minds. This requires robust regulation of neuro-ethics and laws to secure people's privacy rights. On the other hand, neuro-ethics covers topics like personal identity, autonomy and human dignity. In conclusion, the issues that neuro-ethics deals with, range from fundamental philosophical human concepts like free will to more practical issues like privacy and clinical practice. Neurotechnology offers possibilities which enable marketers to use information 'with the potential to trigger very positive affective responses in consumers' (Wilson et al., 2008; 404). Although insights from marketing will not find the 'buy button' in our brain, many argue that marketing will be used to sell people only what they want instead of encouraging people to buy what they really need (Wilson et al., 2008). But, as the 'application of neuroscience to marketing may form a basis for understanding how human beings create, store, recall, and relate to information such as brands in everyday life' (Lee et al., 2007: 203), neuroscience is only a tool that can be used to motivate or manipulate customers. While motivation is beneficial for both parties, manipulation is only beneficial for one.

Practitioner's Perspective 4.1

Pricing, neuromarketing and the willingness to buy

Advocates of neuromarketing techniques assume that it can be helpful to understand the interconnection between marketing activities and customer responses. It is expected that by doing so, next to subjective self-assessment methods, an objective perspective of brain activity may be assessed (Hubert and Kenning, 2008). Methods used in this field include body language, facial coding, empathic design, eye tracking, fMRI, EEG, MEG to galvanic skin conductance and heart rate (Calvert and Brammer, 2012). These methods are used to offer an internal view of the human brain. It is assumed that these methods may help capture data from the human brain without conscious manipulation by respondents, while at the same time being able to record the unconscious processes taking place in the human body. However, neuromarketing measurements mostly take place in an artificial environment instead of in familiar surroundings, which might bias the test results (Dimoka et al., 2012).

Related to this last point is pricing, represented in 'I like this product, but I can't afford it'. Price is an important factor in regard to the decision-making process because in a decision, mostly, costs are evaluated against benefits (Lee et al., 2007). In order to set the price of products appropriately, it is helpful to know the customer's willingness to pay, which means the maximum price that a consumer is ready to invest in exchange for a certain product or service (Simon and Dolan, 1998). Yet, there is a difficulty with the expression of willingness to pay. Consumers are often not in a position to retrieve the prices of certain products and not in a position to precisely determine how much they would be willing to pay for certain products. Therefore, one may contend that the application of neuromarketing techniques could prove helpful in determining consumers' willingness to pay, with marketers adjusting prices accordingly.

Roger Dooley, in his online article 'How to Set the Right Price Every Time' (n.d.), argues that various techniques can be utilised to do this. From his perspective, precise prices (involving odd numbers and decimals) are more believable. Both $4988 and $5012 caused subjects to estimate a higher real value for a product than for the same item priced at $5000. Following this guideline, a digital camera selling for $598.37 would appear to offer more value than a similar unit selling for $600. In conflict with this, however, is research showing that prices that are visually simpler seem lower (Dooley, 2012). The effect was found to be related to the number of syllables in the price. By conducting multiple experiments, scientists found that we humans 'sound out' prices in our mind (unconsciously, of course). More syllables translate into a higher perceived price. So, one might ask, which is better? A simple, rounded price that seems lower or a precise price that implies more value may psychologically achieve better results.

References

Calvert, G. and Brammer, M. (2012) Predicting consumer behaviour: Using novel mind-reading approaches. *Pulse: IEEE*, 3(3), 38–41.

Dimoka, A., Banker, R., Benbasat, I., Davis, F., Dennis, A., Gefen, D. and Weber, B. (2012) On the use of neurophysiological tools in IS research: Developing a research agenda for neuro IS. *MIS Quarterly*, 36, 1–24.

Dooley, R. (n.d.) How to Set the Right Price Every Time. Available at: www.neuroscience-marketing.com/blog/articles/round-pricing.htm (accessed 11 April 2019).

Dooley, R. (2012) *Brainfluence: 100 Ways to Persuade and Convince Consumers with Neuromarketing*. New Jersey: Wiley.

Hubert, M. and Kenning, P. (2008) A current overview of consumer neuroscience. *Journal of Consumer Behaviour*, 7(4–5), 272–92.

Lee, N., Broderick, A. and Chamberlain, L. (2007) What is 'neuromarketing'? A discussion and agenda for future research. *International Journal of Psychophysiology*, 63, 199–204.

Simon, H. and Dolan, R. (1998) 'Price Customization', *Marketing Management*, 7(3): 11 -17.

Question

1. If an individual wants to buy an item that he or she likes (based on neuromarketing methods) but cannot afford, would neuromarketing help?

The use of neuromarketing activities has caused controversy. On the one hand, critics of the subject believe that the use of such techniques might affect consumers' ability to choose not to consume marketed products, leaving the individual unable to resist such efforts and making them easy targets for the company's campaigns (Wilson et al., 2008). On the other hand, defenders of neuromarketing activities, such as Dooley (2011), discuss the benefits deriving from the technique for both consumers and organisations. According to these authors, consumers will benefit from the creation of products and campaigns directed at them and will have their decisions facilitated rather than manipulated, while organisations will save large portions of their budgets which are currently spent on inefficient and ineffective campaigns, ensuring greater competitiveness and improvements for customers. There is yet another segment of researchers who believe that neuromarketing is much more science fiction than reality because it is impossible to find people with identical thoughts in the world, as thought is changeable and varies according to personal experiences, values and character (Hubert, 2010).

Despite the great potential, the applications of neuro-imaging in relation to marketing initially focused primarily on brands and consumer behaviour, particularly using EEG to explore people's reactions. Also, they were used to assess individual preferences between brand familiarity and preference for the product, comparing familiar to unfamiliar brands. When a consumer sees a brand for the first time, he might feel a negative uncertainty compared with how he feels about a brand already familiar to him; a repetition of advertising messages at low levels increases their effectiveness and reduces uncertainty. Advertisers should be aware that repeated exposure to excess damages their advertising because it causes boredom in the consumer and must be balanced to be recognised by the customer while avoiding over-exposure of a product (Madan, 2010). With current advances, it might even be possible to know via eye tracking which aspects attract the customer's attention and what appears to be a distraction in the form of offering a product, thus obtaining a more detailed report that fills the gaps in the phenomena studied previously.

ETHICAL CONSIDERATIONS OF NEUROMARKETING

Neuromarketing is becoming much more complex under the pretext that it can access human brains and their unconscious minds. This is more likely to create disapproval among policymakers in different parts of the world since it can manipulate consumers' minds. Member states in the European Union, for example, have regulatory frameworks to control the mass use of such techniques through the EU's Unfair Commercial Practices Directive, which prohibits 'unfair commercial practices' which fall into two broad categories: practices that are 'misleading' and practices that are 'aggressive' (Solove, 2008). A practice may be considered 'aggressive' if it applies 'coercion' or 'undue influence' to impair the average consumer's freedom of choice to purchase. Therefore, neuromarketing's emphasis on targeting the subconscious impulses of consumers may be regarded as compromising their free will. Additionally, there is deep concern that advertisers may use neuromarketing to target vulnerable populations, such as children, the elderly, economically disadvantaged minorities, and persons suffering from, or vulnerable to, addiction or compulsive behaviour.

Ethical Focus 4.1

Is neuromarketing becoming unethical?

In the mid-1980s, Coke was losing the 'cola wars'. And science, it seemed, offered a stark explanation for what was going wrong. Countless blind taste tests showed that when people didn't know which cola they were drinking, they preferred the sweeter taste of Pepsi. So Coca-Cola embraced the science and developed a new, sweeter formula. As expected, focus groups preferred the new taste. The stage was set for a science-led comeback. Instead, the result was a marketing debacle of legendary proportions. New Coke debuted in April 1985. Positive initial reaction quickly gave way to an unprecedented consumer backlash. The company was swamped with hundreds of thousands of complaints. New Coke became the handle of late-night comedians' jokes, and the target of lawsuits. Within three months, Coke had announced it was going back to the old formula. Consumers were delighted, sales soared, and by year's end Pepsi was cemented back in second place. Some muttered that New Coke wasn't the spectacular own goal it appeared, but a cunning plan to revitalise the brand.

In fact, Coke was caught out by one of the most persistent problems in marketing psychology: asking us what we want when we don't always know ourselves. Our subjective reports are unreliable, and our self-assessments of why we choose the things we choose are even worse. Then, in 2004, Read Montague and his team at Baylor College did the same Coke/Pepsi blind tastings, but with a twist: scanning participants' brains at the same time. As in the 1980s, subjects preferred Pepsi if they didn't know what they were drinking, but preferred Coke if they did. However, the scans showed different activity in different parts of the brain in each case. When the subjects were tasting blind, one of the brain's reward centres (the ventromedial prefrontal cortex) responded more actively to Pepsi. But when they were told they were drinking Coke, there was more activity in the medial prefrontal cortex – a part of the brain dealing with higher cognitive processing and memory. In other words, positive brand associations could almost literally be seen overriding the basic pleasure response.

(Continued)

(Continued)

Sources

McClure, S., Li, J., Tomlin, D., Cypert, K., Montague, L. and Montague, R. (2004) Neural correlates of behavioural preference for culturally familiar drinks. *Neuron*, 44, 379–87.

Stokes, P. (2016) Is neuromarketing becoming unethical? *Acuity Magazine*, 1 December.

Question for discussion

1.   From an ethical perspective, should neuromarketing techniques be manipulated to promote commodities based on people's pleasure brand association and fMRI results?

Although neuromarketing provides new insights into physiological processes in decision making, applying methods from neuroscience is still controversial. Small and micro enterprises still do not have the opportunity to perform their own research by using neuromarketing. Therefore, they have to depend on the results obtained from large companies in other segments. Another issue is the availability of data gained from brain research. Neurological information results in a complex amount of data that requires complex analysis (Shaw and Tamilia, 2001; Nemorin and Gandy, 2017). Moreover, consumer free will can be challenging (Wilson et al., 2008). Consumer research can only be carried out when enough test persons are willing to take part in neuroscientific research. On the other hand, ethics and privacy concerns are important issues that have to be addressed when dealing with neuromarketing. Many people argue that consumers are afraid of data manipulation, especially in an era of spyware and other applications being used to gather private information. They assume that losing self-determination rights is a daily hazard. Many consumers are afraid that neuromarketing gives researchers a window into the human mind and offers possibilities to encode emotions and decision-making processes that they would and could not voluntarily provide to others. Therefore, to guarantee ethical guidelines and laws concerning marketing research, an international code on market and social research, based on key fundamentals that secure people's autonomy and privacy, should be developed globally, in which market researchers must conform to all national and international laws, behave ethically and act transparently. Issues such as honesty, data protection and professional responsibility would need to be covered therein (Gatterer, 2012; Pradeep, 2010).

As the use of neuroscience techniques has been expanding, there is a growing increase in concern among government regulators and consumer advocates that these new marketing tools will produce new types of consumer deception that obstruct privacy rights.

Although challenges of this kind are not new to the advertising industry, advances in consumer tracking due to the internet have increased consumer concerns, given advocacy groups more powerful opinions to support their enduring critique of industry practices, and stimulated government regulators and multilateral health standard-setting bodies to take notice. As neuromarketing techniques become ever more sophisticated, arguably producing more intrusive access to and manipulation of consumers' unconscious thought processes, the industry will likely face increasing opposition from regulators concerned that these techniques will result in advertising that is too persuasive and too powerful. Regulators may conclude that consumers are being misled into believing they want or need a product they have no use for, or deceived into thinking a purchase arises from their rational choice whereas in fact they are being induced to act based on subconscious impulses. To regulators, these techniques may cross the line from fair encouragement to unlawful coercion (Fisher et al., 2010).

Case Study 4.1

Effects of cigarette warnings on adolescents

In 2013, Nashaat H. Hussein carried out a research project entitled 'Pictorial Warnings on Cigarette Packets: Effectiveness and deterrence among Egyptian youth'. The research aimed to investigate the effectiveness of using pictorial warnings to change the attitudes and behaviour of smokers around smoking cigarettes, assuming that such images can be beneficial in raising awareness of the side-effects of using tobacco. Through semi-structured in-depth interviews with a sample of cigarette smokers, the research argued that various social, cultural and economic factors constrain the effectiveness of pictorial warnings. A key research finding was that in order to help reduce the prevalence of smoking among adolescents and youth, the socio-economic and cultural reasons for tobacco smoking need to be addressed instead of merely focusing on the physical side-effects. The researcher wanted to investigate the issue on the basis that statistics indicated that Egypt has the highest rate of tobacco consumption in the Arab world, and that most smokers are in their adolescent and late adolescent years.

Findings of the research revealed that various factors usually motivate adolescents and youth to smoke cigarettes: peer pressure and the need to be accepted by peers within adolescent and youth communities; the false beliefs and misconceptions among adolescents and youth about the positive effects of smoking cigarettes on concentration and mood alteration; the misconception that smoking nicotine can help release tension and enhance the ability to

(Continued)

(Continued)

solve problems; the desire to be treated as a grown-up, especially among males who associate smoking cigarettes with the development of their sense of manhood and independence; a sense of normalisation among adolescents and youth due to the prevalence of smoking; and the desire to imitate parents who smoke.

Findings also elucidated that various factors limit the effectiveness of pictorial warnings placed on cigarette packets in Egypt: the idea that photos only reveal the negative health consequences associated with long-term tobacco use among adults; the fact that youngsters do not directly get exposed to the photos placed on cigarette packets due to a lack of financial resources; fear of parental punishment when parents discover that they buy cigarettes, smoking fewer than 20 cigarettes per day and depending on being able to procure cigarettes from friends, which all limit their direct exposure to such photos; the photos being considered offensive and scary from their perspective; the normalisation of photos which technically become 'worn out' after long-term usage; and their suspicions around the photos themselves, which, from their perspective, are not real photos of actual cases of diseases adults suffer from due to the long-term use of cigarettes.

There is no doubt that warnings with pictures on are more effective than text-only warnings, especially in countries like Egypt which have a very high illiteracy rate. They may increase message access to people with low levels of literacy and can help smokers visualise tobacco-related diseases. However, the messages need to be rotated regularly to avoid overexposure. Smoking prevention programmes aimed at Egyptian adolescents should be accompanied by smoking cessation programmes for the family and adult community members. Two main research limitations are noted in the present research. First, the entire sample selected was composed of male cigarette users. Further studies are required to emphasise male–female differences and gender variability in regard to smoking behaviour. Second, the sample selected was composed of young males in their late adolescence. Despite the fact that cigarette warning signs are also viewed by adults, the present research addresses the problem among a certain age group of users. There is still a need to investigate the way adults perceive pictorial warning signs.

When investigating the efficacy of pictorial messages on cigarette packets, the research assumed that targeting adolescents and youth requires a thorough and detailed investigation of cultural variables and other socio-economic factors that may help pictorial messages to target youth effectively. Other researchers who investigated the issue using neuromarketing ended up with different conclusions. One of the surprising findings of the neuromarketing study described by Martin Lindstrom (2008) in *Buyology*, for example, was that not only are the government-mandated warnings on tobacco packets ineffective, they actually promote smoking behaviour by activating the brain's nucleus accumbens, an area associated with cravings. Lindstrom monitored brain activity in smokers using an fMRI while the smokers were exposed to, among other things, smoking warning labels from cigarette packets. The magnetic resonance images showed that this attempt of the international anti-smoking brigade to decrease the impulse to smoke, actually increased cravings for tobacco; anti-smoking advertisements had stimulated the behaviour the campaign sought to prevent. Lindstrom's findings resulted in several arguments, for example that smoking warning labels don't actually discourage smoking in individuals who already smoke heavily. This really makes sense to a certain degree. A heavy smoker has conditioned his brain to the point that it needs nicotine to maintain a happy equilibrium. Lindstrom's results reveal that the implied association between the warning labels and the tobacco and, accordingly, the nicotine that will maintain the brain's equilibrium, stimulates a neurological response through a craving that is much more powerful than the cognitive interpretation of the explicit messages of sickness and death. Such a direct association between the signal of the label and the unconscious response of the craving correlates with Pavlov's classic conditioning theory. Therefore, the warnings practically target non-smokers or youngsters and adolescents who do not already smoke for various other reasons, and not necessarily just pictorial ones.

References

Hussein, N. (2013) Pictorial warnings on cigarette packets: Effectiveness and deterrence among Egyptian youth. *African Journal of Drug & Alcohol Studies*, 12(2), 93–105.

Lindstrom, M. (2008) *Biology: Truth and Lies about Why We Buy*. New York: Doubleday.

Questions for discussion

1. Despite the methodological differences between them, the two studies carried out by Hussein and Lindstrom reached similar conclusions. What does this imply?
2. Do you think that non-smokers actually get affected by pictorial messages, or that there are other reasons that force them not to smoke? Explain.

SUMMARY OF KEY IDEAS

Marketing aims to give decision makers a better understanding of their environment in order to make the right choices. It tries to find a space to enable the creation of value for both the customer and the company. Neuromarketing integrates conscious and subconscious motivations, which can lead to a decision (Georges et al., 2013) and which are also apparent in customers as well as business decision makers. Therefore, neuromarketing must be able to convince customers, so that they buy, and decision makers, so that they agree to fund the resources necessary to please, persuade and interest customers. The literature on neuromarketing reveals different positions on the place of neuromarketing within the scientific spectrum. Viewed mostly as a border science or a management tool (Fisher et al., 2010), neuromarketing may also be approached as a valid research field, being more than the mere application of neuroimaging techniques in marketing products and services or brands (Calvert and Thensen, 2004; Davidson, 2004; Lee et al., 2007; Bogue, 2010). Hubert and Kenning (2008) view neuromarketing as a useful tool to conduct businesses. They emphasise that neuromarketing should be renamed 'consumer neuroscience'. On the other hand, many scholars believe that neuromarketing is a relatively new and controversial interdisciplinary research field, a component of marketing, by means of which one can properly interpret the psychological and neuropsychological knowledge necessary to understand customer behaviour.

According to others, neuromarketing is the process that enables the knowledge and understanding of the mechanisms used by the human brain to process information. Kotler (Kotler et al., 2009; Kotler and Keller, 2012) believes that neuromarketing is a means to describe the activity of the brain under the impact of marketing stimuli, which, by means of specific tools, correlates with the psychological reaction following subjects' exposure to certain advertisements. Thus, neuromarketing helps entrepreneurs develop basic ideas when making decisions about targeting both market and clients and establishing communication with business partners. Labelling neuromarketing as a 'science' per se entails designing and developing a behavioural model capable of highlighting the marketing stimuli that generate a particular type of behaviour. Fugate (2007) believes this would qualify as a feasible endeavour on condition that it comes from marketing practitioners rather than from theorists. One attempt to develop a behavioural model was made by Michael Butler (2008), who believes that four different visions should be combined and interconnected within the model – reporting the results of basic research conducted by academicians, reporting the results of applied research conducted by neuromarketing companies, media reporting of research findings from neuromarketing, and power processes, that is, decisions made on the basis of neuromarketing research.

Classical behaviour research methods and techniques emphasise the visible stimuli which trigger a particular consumption and/or buying behaviour. However, due to neuromarketing investigations, researchers are now getting closer to the invisible side of neural connections (Pop et al., 2014), which leads to a deepening and significant development of marketing research. It is not an attempt to give up on classical market research methods and techniques but an expansion of the latitude of scientific understanding. Neuromarketing has been around for roughly a decade, and only seems to be growing in popularity. Despite its sceptics and pessimists, major corporations have used this technology when designing their products, packaging and advertising campaigns. Marketing research methods constantly develop and, over the last decade, technology has offered solutions to progress this domain. Traditional marketing research methods fail at some point in certain cases, and since emotions are involved in the way consumers process marketing messages, an understanding of cognitive reactions to advertisements has always been an encounter in methodology.

As stated earlier, the application of neuromarketing techniques holds a promising future for marketing research, nevertheless this new practice is facing numerous limitations, including budget, complexity and sometimes the size of the equipment, such as with fMRI scanners (Bogue, 2010). Although neuroscientists believe that by investigating customers' brain inclinations, they can gather marketing preferences, various indicators may intervene when applied globally. Marketing preferences differ cross-culturally, which indicates that neuromarketing still has a long way to go. In light of the paucity of cross-cultural marketing research, neuromarketing would still be an attempt to solve cross-cultural brain mysteries. On the other hand, consumer behaviour is highly influenced by various factors, including economic factors, functional factors (like logic and needs), the marketing mix, personal factors (like age, gender, occupation, lifestyle), socio-economic factors, psychological factors, and other social and cultural factors. Those factors affect the way consumers are usually motivated and oriented. Poverty in different parts of the world, for example, may in itself become a major hindering element that limits the scope and global application of neuromarketing. This is not to underestimate the potential future role of neuromarketing, but it also sheds light on the importance of assessing global trends of consumption.

Chapter Discussion Questions

1. What is neuromarketing?
2. What are the various techniques used in neuromarketing?
3. Clarify the differences between conventional/traditional marketing research and neuromarketing.
4. What are the technical problems associated with the application of neuromarketing techniques? Can they be applied globally?
5. What are the ethical considerations related to neuromarketing?
6. What are the major areas of criticisms of neuromarketing?
7. Based on your understanding of neuromarketing, does it really satisfy global consumer needs? Explain your reasoning.

REFERENCES

Ariely, D. and Berns, G. (2010) Neuromarketing: The hope and hype of neuroimaging in business. *Nature Reviews Neuroscience*, 11(4), 284–92.

Bogue, R. (2010) Brain–computer interfaces: Control by thought. *Industrial Robot: An International Journal*, 37(2), 126–32.

Burgos-Campero, A. and Vargas-Hernandez, J. (2013) Analytical approach to neuromarketing as a business strategy. *Procedia: Social and Behavioral Sciences*, 99, 517–25.

Butler, M. (2008) Neuromarketing and the perception of knowledge. *Journal of Consumer Behaviour*, 7, 415–19.

Calvert, G. and Thensen, T. (2004) Multisensory integration: Methodological approaches and emerging principles in the human brain. *Journal of Psychology Paris*, 98(1–3), 191–205.

Davidson, R. (2004) What does the prefrontal cortex 'do' in affect? Perspectives on frontal EEG asymmetry research. *Biological Psychology*, 67(1–2), 219–33.

Dimoka, A., Banker, R., Benbasat, I., Davis, F., Dennis, A., Gefen, D., ... and Weber, B. (2012) On the use of neurophysiological tools in IS research: Developing a research agenda for Neuro IS. *MIS Quarterly*, 36, 1–24.

Dooley, R. (n.d.) How to Set the Right Price Every Time. Available at: www.neuroscience marketing.com/blog/articles/round-pricing.htm (accessed 11 April 2019).

Dooley, R. (2012) *Brain Influence: 100 Ways to Persuade and Convince Consumers with Neuromarketing*. Chichester: Wiley.

Fisher, C., Chin, L. and Klitzman, R. (2010) Defining neuromarketing: Practices and professional challenges. *Harvard Review of Psychiatry*, 18(4), 230–7.

Fugate, D. (2007) Neuromarketing: A layman's look at neuroscience and its potential application to marketing practice. *Journal of Consumer Marketing*, 24(7), 385–94.

Garcia, J. and Saad, G. (2008) Evolutionary neuromarketing: Darwinizing the neuroimaging paradigm for consumer behavior. *Journal of Consumer Behaviour*, 7, 397–414.

Gatterer, P. (2012) *Neuromarketing and Business Ethics: A Recap of Neuroscientific Methods in Marketing and Rehash of the Theoretical Background for an Ethical Approach*. Saarbrücken: AV AkademikerVerlag.

Georges, P., Bayle-Tourtoulou, A. and Badoc, M. (2013) *Neuromarketing in Action: How to Talk and Sell to the Brain*. London: Kogan Page.

Hubert, M. (2010) Does neuroeconomics give new impetus to economic and consumer research? *Journal of Economic Psychology*, 31(5), 812–17.

Hubert, M. and Kenning, P. (2008) A current overview of consumer neuroscience. *Journal of Consumer Behaviour*, 7(4–5), 272–92.

Javor, A., Koller, M., Lee, N., Chamberlain, L. and Ransmayr, G. (2013) Neuromarketing and consumer neuroscience: Contributions to neurology. *Neurology*, 13, 1–12.

Kenning, P., Plassmann, H. and Ahlert, D. (2007) Applications of functional magnetic resonance imaging for market research. *Qualitative Market Research: An International Journal*, 10(2), 135–52.

Kotler, P. and Keller, K. (2012) *Marketing Management*, 14th global edn. Harlow: Pearson.

Kotler, P., Keller, K., Brady, M., Goodman, M. and Hansem, T. (2009) *Marketing Management*. London: Prentice Hall.

Lee, N., Broderick, A. and Chamberlain, L. (2007) What is 'neuromarketing'? A discussion and agenda for future research. *International Journal of Psychophysiology*, 63, 199–204.

McClure, S., Li, J., Tomlin, D., Cypert, K., Montague, L. and Montague, R. (2004) Neural correlates of behavioral preference for culturally familiar drinks. *Neuron*, 44(2), 379–87.

Madan, C. (2010) Neuromarketing: The next step in market research? *Eureka*, 1(1), 34–42.

Maxwell, S. (2008) Fair price: Research outside marketing. *Journal of Product and Brand Management*, 17(7), 497–503.

Mucha, T. (2005) This is your brain on advertising. *Business 2.0*, 35.

Murphy, E., Illes, J. and Reiner, P. (2008) Neuroethics of neuromarketing. *Journal of Consumer Behaviour*, 7, 293–302.

Nemorin, S. and Gandy, O. (2017) Exploring neuromarketing and its reliance on remote sensing: Social and ethical concerns. *International Journal of Communication*, 11, 4824–44.

O'Connor, C., Rees, G. and Joffe, H. M. (2012) Neuroscience in the public sphere. *Neuron*, 2(74), 220–6.

Pop, N., Dabija, D. and Iorga, A. (2014) Ethical responsibility of neuromarketing companies in harnessing the market research: A global exploratory approach. *Amfiteatru Economic*, XVI(35), 26–40.

Pradeep, A. (2010) *The Buying Brain: Secrets for Selling to the Subconscious Mind*. Hoboken, NJ: Wiley & Sons.

Riedl, R., Hubert, M. and Kenning, P. (2010) Are there neural gender differences in online trust? An fMRI study on the perceived trustworthiness of eBay offers. *MIS Quarterly*, 34(2), 397–428.

Roebuck, K. (2011) *Neuromarketing: High-Impact Strategies – What You Need to Know: Definitions, Adoptions, Impact, Benefits, Maturity, Vendors*. Newstead: Emero Publishing.

Shaw, E. and Tamilia, R. (2001) Robert Bartels and the history of marketing thought. *Journal of Macromarketing*, 21(2), 156–63.

Simon, H. and Dolan, R. (1998) Price customization. *Marketing Management*, 7(3): 11–17.

Solomon, M. and Rabolt, N. (2004) *Consumer Behavior in Fashion*. Upper Saddle River, NJ: Prentice Hall.

Solove, D. (2008) *Understanding Privacy*. Cambridge, MA: Harvard University Press.

Wilson, R., Gaines, J. and Hill, R. (2008) Neuromarketing and consumer free will. *Journal of Consumer Affairs*, 42(3), 389–410.

Zurawicki, L. (2010) *Neuromarketing: Exploring the Brain of the Consumer*, 10th edition. Berlin: Springer.

PART II
Exploring Meanings in Contemporary Consumption

5

THE CONTEMPORARY CONSUMER

Ayantunji Gbadamosi and Adya Sharma

Learning Outcomes

At the end of this chapter, you should be able to understand and discuss:

- Emerging trends in the consumer decision-making process
- Postmodernism and the contemporary consumer
- Consumer culture theory and the contemporary consumer
- Consumer-complicit behaviour
- The changing environment and the change in consumer behaviour patterns
- The difficusion of innovation and the contemporary consumer

INTRODUCTION

Generally, consumption is ubiquitous. Whether you are based in China, studied in the USA, or a fan of a UK football team, you, like everyone else, are a consumer of one product or another. Irrespective of age, gender, lifestyle, income, or any other characteristic, we are all consumers! Meanwhile, the changes in the various elements of the marketing environment, such as socio-cultural and technological, indicate that our consumption patterns and how we go about actualising the satisfaction of our needs are also dynamic. So, the changes we see in the marketing landscape indicate the emergence of a contemporary consumer. As the notion of organisation purchase behaviour (B2B) has been addressed previously this chapter is about those consumers who buy goods and services for ultimate consumption or, better stated, for self-gratification. This could be for personal use, as gifts for others or in any other form that fits the scenario of buying for use, and not business or organisation purposes. Essentially, this chapter addresses the evolving issues around what we buy, how we buy those things and why our decisions are so patterned. The chapter will cover the emerging trends in the consumer decision-making process, postmodernism and the contemporary consumer. We shall also be discussing consumer culture theory and consumer-complicit behaviour in relation to the contemporary consumer. Specific changes in the environment in relation to the consumer and how the new consumer acts in relation to the diffusion of innovation and globalisation are some of the key parts of this chapter. Now, let us begin with the changes associated with the consumer decision-making process.

CONSUMER DECISION-MAKING PROCESS: EMERGING ISSUES

It is now very well established in fundamental discussions of marketing and consumer behaviour that consumers pass through various stages before the purchase of products or services to satisfy their needs. Be it a set of furniture, an automobile, a package holiday, candy or any other product, the ultimate goal of making these purchases is to satisfy needs. While the idea of the consumer decision-making process, as depicted in Figure 5.1, is now quite familiar in the conventional consumer behaviour textbook, our attention in this section of the book turns to a discussion of how each of these stages evolves and demonstrates the consumption system of the contemporary consumer.

More often than not, the process around which fragrance to choose for an occassion, what to eat for dinner, which airline to use to travel to a chosen destination, and many other consumption decisions, begins with a realisation of the need for such a product or service. This is the stage where the descrepancy between the actual state and the desired state comes to the fore – *the need recognition stage*. There are many examples of this in our daily lives that could be considered. We often notice the rumbling of the stomach as a sign of hunger, the breakdown of an old car as a sign that a replacement is needed, and discomfort with a current hairstyle signalling a need to use the services of a stylist – these are some of the day-to-day examples of need recognition as the starting point of a consumer decision-making process. But the critical question for us to consider here is what is new about this. The needs of consumers are increasing in number and diversity, hence they are increasingly

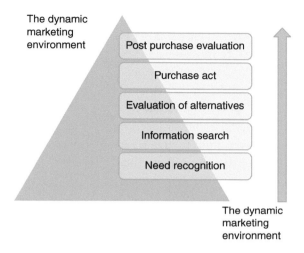

Figure 5.1   Consumer decision-making process

complicated (Gbadamosi, 2015a). For example, the rise in internet usage and consumers' digital skills indicates that their needs have taken on a different dimension. According to the 2015 Mckinsey report, consumers in China spend about 78 minutes a day on social commerce activites (Liu et al., 2016). Meanwhile, global revenue from social commerce is expected to reach USD 80 billion a year by the year 2020 (Farivar et al., 2017; HnyB Insights, 2012). All these are pointers to the fact that consumers' needs for products and services are changing and this will continue to be the case in the foreseeable future.

INFORMATION SEARCH

Increasing use of the internet, as mentioned above, in terms of changing patterns in consumer need is perhaps more significant at the stage of the information search. Essentially, at this stage, the consumer searches for information from various sources that might help them discover what will satisfy the need. The sources of this information could be categorised in a number of ways, such as commercial and non-commercial, personal and non-personal. However, we shall be using the classification of internal and external to explain these sources in order to cover key issues in other classifications. Internal sources of information relate to the individual's experience of using the product or brand and in terms of knowing whether this could be brought to bear on the current decision-making scenario or any direct personal encounter with the market offering. Imagine that you had visited a restaurant for a meal in the past and had a very satisfactory experience – this will make it more likely that the same restaurant will come to mind when the need arises for another meal out. On the other hand, external sources of information are those outside yourself, including marketing communication messages such as advertising, information from sales representatives and word-of-mouth communications from friends and family membes, colleagues and others. In this day and age, the potential sources of such information for the contemporary consumer continue to increase. Smart phones, smart TV and social media sites are among the huge number of opportunities beckoning the consumer to give them information. In fact, while the use of these tools is common among young consumers, increasing use among adults in recent times is evident in all walks of life.

EVALUATION OF ALTERNATIVES

Clearly, consumers are confronted with a myriad of options when it comes to products, especially where several sources of information have been explored at the stage of the search for information. Holiday destinations now compete for consumers' attention, while consumers have a choice of whether to buy their electronic products from bricks-and-mortar outlets through which they can gauge the features of a product before buying it online, which could be relatively cheaper and less hassle than going to a store. Another consideration for the consumer is whether to buy a counterfeit version of the product or insist on getting the authentic item. These are some of the plethora of examples of how consumers are innundated with choices at the stage of evaluating alternatives. The consumer is expected to use some criteria for screening the options down to a shortlist that will eventually lead them to a choice that will satisfy their need. The consumer might use several criteria to achieve this objective such as price, quality, ease of purchase, suitability for a specific use, or comfort. Of course, the type of screening criteria used will be related to the nature of the product involved. Accordingly, you are likely to have considered fuel consumption, fuel type, reliability, brand, the number of seats, and so on, in the purchase of your car. This is understandably different from criteria such as taste, speed of service, and location that will most likely be used for the choice of a restaurant. The outcome of screening will lead to the next stage, which is about making your purchase decision.

THE BUYING STAGE

The buying stage is characterised by the real act of decision. The consumer buys the one considered to offer the utmost satisfaction. The choice of who does the actual purchase varies in relation to the nature of the product, the circumstances surrounding the purchase, societal circumstances, and many other factors. This brings us to the relevance of family buying roles, as depicted in Figure 5.2.

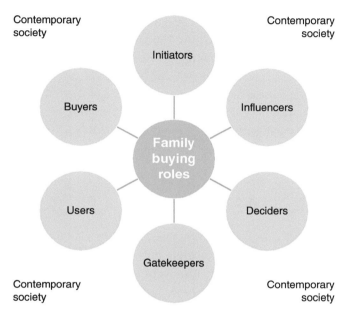

Figure 5.2 Family buying roles

Source: Adapted from Gbadamosi (2018)

The fundamental issue associated with family buying roles is that members of a particular family may play different roles in the purchase of their needed products. While some act as initiators of the idea to buy a particular product or service, others provide support for the initial idea which contributes to strengthening the case for buying it – they are the influencers. Some members of the family make the decision, while others engage in the actual purchase of the product. As shown in Figure 5.2, some are the users of the product. Usually, gatekeepers are associated with organisational buying roles as people who control the flow of information from and to the decision-making unit within an organisation. Similarly, some members of a family tend to control the flow of information to and from other family members. This could be in the form of receiving telephone calls from a salesperson who is following up on a discussion regarding a sale of furniture, receiving email messages relating to family purchases, and so on. Now, what is contemporary at this stage? It is important to note that the individuals playing these roles in families tend to vary, especially due to recent changes in socio-cultural dynamics. While it is likely that the man of the house is seen as having the main say on purchases as he is typically the breadwinner, societal changes mean that the financial standing of women is in some cases greater than that of the men in their households, giving them the final decision on purchases. Interestingly, there is evidence that in some cases, especially for routinely consumed items, children are also involved in decisions, for items such as toys and confectionery (Gbadamosi, 2012, 2015b). Similarly, couples may alternate their purchase roles in relation to normal day-to-day living, depending on who has the most time, or when gifting items on Valentine's Day, anniversaries and birthdays. Apart from this, the growing trend of same sex marriage these days indicates that some of the old assumptions about the dynamics of houseold consumption and buying roles may no longer be generally applicable. So, these roles are not specifically fixed for individual members of a family and adapt to changes in society.

POST-PURCHASE EVALUATION

Whether you have bought a packet of crisps, a new house or paid for the services of a lawyer, the transaction is not deemed totally complete until the post-purchase evaluation stage has been actualised. This is the stage at which we compare the experience of using the product with the expectation we had prior to purchase. Logically, this can result in a number of outcomes which include satisfaction, partial satisfaction or dissatisfaction. This is an important stage in that the outcome might have great implications for whether the consumer is likely to use the product again in the future. At one point or another, we will receive an email or text message from those companies that have served us in the past asking for ratings of their services. Although paper-based evaluation is still relevant and applicable, the use of electronic means to gather this data from consumers is becoming rampant. The use of this shows how businesses are making frantic efforts to be on a par with the contemporary consumer in following the digital revolution.

POSTMODERNISM IN MARKETING

One of the ways of appreciating the dynamics of the contemporary consumer is to look at their roles in the marketplace. This in turn is a very useful approach to understand postmodernism in marketing. The term has been explained as removing the divide that exists between product and consumption, such that the consumer is not only involved in consumption of the goods and services but also in the production of them (Szmigin and Piacentini, 2018).

So, this is closely linked to the value co-creation role of the consumer. To widen our understanding of the term, we turn our attention to the viewpoint of Cova (1996: 16) who states that postmodernism is the 'juxtaposition of the contradictory emotions and cognitions regarding perspectives, commitments, ideas and things in general, and consumption in particular, to wit: heterogeneity with uniformity, passive consumption with active customisation, individualism with tribalism, fragmentation with globalization and so on'. So, this shows the new consumer as an individual that brings their creativity to bear on the marketplace in an unprecedented manner. Table 5.1 shows the characteristics of postmodernism as adapted from the previous work of Brown (1995) and a more recent publication of Parsons et al. (2018).

Table 5.1   Characteristics of postmodernism

Characteristics	Key highlights
Fragmentation	Disjointed consumption pattern
	Customisation
De-differentiation	A blurring of the commonly known pattern
Hyperreality	Actualising the previously known 'dream worlds'
Chronology	A look towards and adoption of the past product/consumption pattern rather than the future
	Nostalgic consumption
Pastiche	Juxtaposition of styles
Anti-foundationalism	A tendency to oppose the conventional pattern of things
Pluralism	Diversity and relativism

Source: Adapted from Brown (1995) and Parsons et al. (2018)

Overall, the postmodern consumer is interested in diverse elements of market offerings, and hedonic gratification more than maximising profit (Badot, 2014). For this consumer, the focus is on customisation, yet still giving credence to diversity and relativism. As is the case with the consumer's taste for goods and services in recent times, a multiplicity of styles thrives in postmodernism.

CONSUMER CULTURE THEORY AND THE CONTEMPORARY CONSUMER

The explanation for consumption and consumer behaviour issues has taken several forms over the years. One of these is the emergence of consumer culture theory (CCT) which was proposed in 2005 by Arnould and Thompson in their seminal paper entitled 'Consumer Culture Theory: Twenty years of research'. In this publication, the authors pinpoint that CCT is a family of theoretical perspectives that focus on addressing the dynamic relationships that exist between consumer actions, the marketplace and cultural meanings. This knowledge is very useful for our understanding of the contemporary consumer as it captures what the consumer buys, how they buy it and why they buy it in contemporary society. As explained by Szmigin and Piacentini (2018), the emergence of CCT is born out of the shift in how consumer behaviour is being investigated as the greater use of qualitative methods and holistic explanation of factors affecting consumption are being emphasised. We can see this clearly in the claim of Arnould and Thompson (2005) in that it is very common to see criticisms around labelling mainstream consumer research as ivory tower, but CCT revolves around cultural meanings, sociohistoric influences and the social dynamics that pattern our consumption and the associated experiences and identities in our everyday life. We can gain a more detailed explanation of this from the view expressed by Catulli et al. (2017) in which they show that CCT is founded in anthropological research, hence it focuses on the role of consumption in relation to how individuals construct their identities, and also recognises the significance of symbolic value. Given this understanding, we can now see that CCT cannot be explained away as an economic perspective on consumption (Joy and Li, 2012). This explanation is also in agreement with the claim of Fitchett et al. (2014) in their paper written on 'Myth and Ideology in Consumer Culture Theory', where the theory is positioned as a significant and coherent alternative to the dominance of microeconomic theory and cognitive psychology-inspired approaches. The basic themes addressed in CCT and examples of studies conducted under each of the themes are explained in Figure 5.3.

In their recent publication on the topic to address the question 'What is Consumer Culture Theory (CCT)?', Arnould and Thompson (2018: 4) indicate that:

> Rather than viewing culture as a fairly homogeneous system of collectively shared meanings, ways of life and unifying values shared by a member of a society ... CCT explores the heterogenenous distribution of meanings and the multiplicity of overlapping cultural groupings that exist within the broader socio-historical frame of globalization and marketing capitalism.

As we can see from the various examples of studies conducted, the way culure is conceptualised in these contexts is different from the conventional understanding of this phenomenon. For example, Hill's (1991) study of homelessness and special possessions transcends the conventional understanding of a cultural divide between a particular society and another. Similarly, the study of Muñiz and O'Guinn (2000) on brand communities does not only break the usual code on culture shared by a particular society but it actually shows consumers as producers of culture. Hence, a critical look at the dynamics of the marketplace of today and the contemporary consumer will show the increasing relevance of CCT.

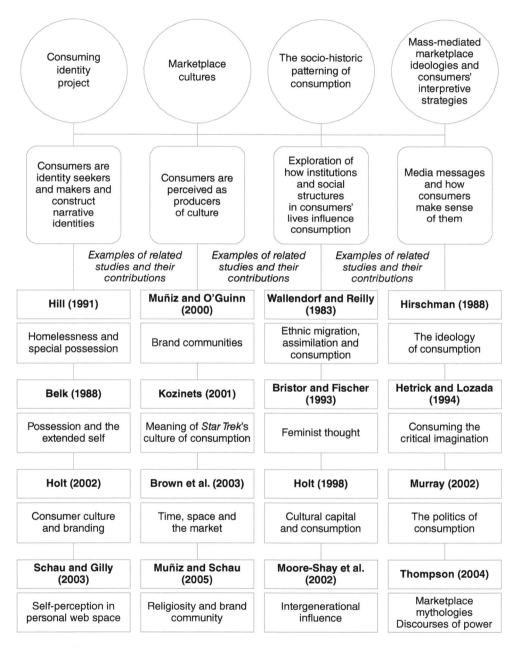

Figure 5.3   The main themes in consumer culture theory

CONSUMER-COMPLICIT BEHAVIOUR: CONSUMPTION OF COUNTERFEIT PRODUCTS

A number of factors make consumer behaviour a very intriguing topic. The diversity in consumption practices which cover the types of products purchased and consumers' response to other marketing mix elements provide an interesting explanation that cannot be ignored (Gbadamosi, 2019). Have you ever wondered why you might prefer to sacrifice something else in order to get your hands on an authentic product? It is also useful to consider why some consumers would knowingly opt to buy items considered counterfeit. An in-depth look at the marketplace will reveal a prevalence of transactions involving counterfeit products in many sectors. Laptops, clothing, beauty products, handbags and some food items are among the very many products whose counterfeit versions can now be found everywhere. Some of these items are conspicuous and open for us to see and admire, while others are not so clearly visible. There have been interesting developments in recent times on these issues and looking at this will provide an opportunity to understand the contemporary consumer further. To give us an early cue on this phenomenon, we shall look at a definition of the term. With reference to a body of literature including Grossman and Shapiro (1988) and Kapferer (1995), Bian and Moutinho (2011) provide a simple definition of counterfeit products as those offerings which bear a trademark that is identical to, or indistinguishable from, a trademark that is registered to another party and which therefore infringes the rights of the holder of the trademark. Evidence shows that various organisations and brands consider consumer-complicit behaviour to be an issue of critical importance, especially as it is closely linked to their proceeds and profitability. The estimated figure provided by Stumpf et al. (2011) indicates that the losses associated with the prevalence of counterfeit sales are approximately over a trillion dollars at the global level. The available evidence shows that not only has the availability of these products increased over the past few years, but the same could be said about the demand for them, with an increase of about 12% each year (Chaudhry et al., 2009a, b; Stumpf et al., 2011). The International Chamber of Commerce (2004) shows that luxury brands lose about $12 billion every year to illicit transactions of luxury brand counterfeit products (LBCP) (Bian et al., 2015). Meanwhile, a whopping $770–960 billion was estimated as the total made in sales of international traded counterfeit products for 2015 alone (BASCAP, 2011). In a more recent publication, in synthesising some ideas into a case study, Szmigin and Piacentini (2018), with reference to Wiedmann et al. (2016), suggest that consumers who buy counterfeit brands are individuals who crave an association with prestige in some way and consider counterfeit luxury brands as an opportunity to signal such status to other people at a far lower price. Figure 5.4, which is based on Chaudhry et al. (2009a, b), provides information on the key elements that distinguish counterfeit products from authentic ones in the marketplace of some countries.

Figure 5.4   Cues for distinguishing between authentic and counterfeit products

Looking at them critically, it makes sense that virtually all key elements in the marketing mix might serve as cues for identifying authentic products in a marketplace where counterfeits are also provided.

Categorisation of consumer-complicit behaviour

While our experience of contemporary society shows the prevalence of consumption of counterfeit products, it is important to know the reason why consumers engage in this. For this, we have two categories of context for the purchase of counterfeit products. As explained by Staake et al. (2009), these are:

- deceptive counterfeiting
- non-deceptive counterfeiting.

Based on this explanation, some consumers are not aware that the items they have bought are not the authentic items they intended to buy. This is deceptive counterfeiting. In this case, both consumer and brand owner are victims of those who engage in the illicit transaction as the product is sneakily sold to the unsuspecting customer while the original and legal owner of the brand does not receive the profit that should have accrued from the sale. On the other hand, in non-deceptive counterfeiting, the consumer who buys the product is fully aware that they have not been sold the legal owner's authentic brand. So, the latter category is related to the consumer's counterfeit proneness (CFP), which is the general tendency of consumers to prefer, like, buy and use a counterfeit market offering (Sharma and Chan, 2016). Given the nature of such transactions, the authorities in most countries frown on them and consider the acts as criminal but the available evidence shows that, in spite of this, about one-third of consumers would still deliberately buy these products (Bian and Moutinho, 2011; Phau et al., 2001). One explanation given for this is that consumers who buy counterfeit willingly may do so for different purposes, such as buying it for use at home while buying the legitimate branded product for use in public (Bian and Moutinho, 2011). Meanwhile, some of the common specific reasons why consumers may engage in complicit behaviour were highlighted by Stumpf et al. (2011), as follows:

- The product is desirable.
- The product is easy to obtain.
- The consumer involved in the purchase is on a low income.
- The consumer views the counterfeit product as acceptable.

Other authors have added to this list. One of the prominent reasons for such a purchase is identified as the need for *social power*. Research suggests that consumers who lack social power will be attracted to status-related goods to increase their power (Bian et al., 2015). So, they resort to acquiring a status product in order to deal with their perceived powerlessness, in that they use such status products to indicate social standing which helps in compensating for social standing which helps in compensating for a low psychological state (Bian et al., 2015). In an explanation provided by Chaudhry and Stumpf (2011), the purchase is related to:

- a hedonic shopping experience
- lack of ethical concern.

This list is extended by Fernandes (2013) whose further reasons are:

- lack of ethical judgement
- self-ambiguity
- value consciousness
- being susceptible to the opinions of others (subjective norm).

The consumer's ethical judgement is their evaluation of what is right and wrong. So, a consumer who does not see anything wrong in the purchase of counterfeit products or brands would be more inclined to make such a purchase on a regular basis. The notion of self-ambiguity explains the lack of clarity about an individual's self-concept which often results in low self-esteem. Meanwhile, the point here is that the consumer whose self-esteem is low would most likely engage in certain consumption acts to foster acceptance among others, which could be in the form of the use of counterfeit products or brands. The value consciousness of consumers is about their willingness to obtain an item for a lower price at lower quality (Lichenstein et al., 1993). So, research shows that consumers who are value conscious would most likely have a favourable attitude towards the purchase of counterfeit market offerings (Ang et al., 2001). Similarly, the culture of consumption in some cases follows a bandwagon effect such as is noticeable among child consumers. Gbadamosi (2012) reports that one of the strategies used by children to influence their parents is the use of 'reference to others' – here, they request a product or service from their parents, justifiying it 'because their friends or neighbours have it'. In the same vein, consumers may buy counterfeit products if they notice that other people have bought similar products. This direction of reasoning is anchored in the notion of the subjective norm, which is a core element in the Theory of Planned Behaviour (Ajzen, 1991). It is about the social pressure on an individual concerning a course of action, which in this case is the purchase of counterfeit goods. So, if the normative pressure from significant others to buy a counterfeit product is great, the higher the likelihood the individual will do it (Fernandes, 2013).

Ethical Focus 5.1

Illegality in consumption of counterfeit products

Be it fragrance, electrical goods or fashion items, consumers buy to enjoy the products or services they have paid for and, in a similar manner, businesses are entitled to their profits when they have operated their business within the remit of the law. However, the activities of dealers of counterfeit goods and brands have been tampering with this balance for some time. It has been reported that 3 million consumers buy counterfeit products annually (Bell, 2016). So, the top brands that own and sponsor the original versions of these offerings are at the receiving end of such transactions. As indicated by the BBC (Bell, 2016), every time a consumer buys a counterfeit item, they help contribute to an unethical labour market,

(Continued)

(Continued)

subsidise the organised crime associated with the act, and steals from the revenue of the company involved. The City of London Police indicate on their website (2017) that apart from funding organised crime, hampering genuine business and the economy, there are safety issues involved in such purchases, in that counterfeit products are often not subjected to rigorous quality and safety checks. This could make the buyer vulnerable to danger of various kinds. As indicated by the police on the website, it is a criminal offence as it involves gaining financially from a trademark without the consent of the owner. This is one of the many factors that make consumer behaviour a complex phenomenon.

References

Bell, B. (2016) What's wrong with buying fake luxury goods? BBC, 15 July. Available at: www.bbc.co.uk/news/uk-england-36782724

City of London Police (2017) Advice and Support|Fraud and Economic Crime|PIPCU|Counterfeit Goods. Available at: www.cityoflondon.police.uk/advice-and-support/fraud-and-economic-crime/pipcu/pages/counterfeit-goods.aspx

Questions

1. Despite current efforts at curbing the menace of counterfeit trade, consumers still engage in non-deceptive counterfeit purchase. Why do you think this is the case and what would you recommend for a total eradication of this practice?
2. Following the notion of value co-creation in marketing, to what extent do you think business and consumers can work together towards solving the problem of counterfeit sales and consumption?

GLOBALISATION AND LOCALISATION

Two words which have influenced the global scenario are globalisation and localisation. Globalisation was welcomed as an economic opportunity for growth (Immelt, 2016). However 'globalisation' was not always perceived as positive. In the beginning, it was defined as a process shaped by and for big business for the systematic reduction of protective barriers to the flow of goods and money by international trade (Hines, 2003). Localisation was promoted as a means to strengthen local culture and to mitigate the movement towards a monolithic undifferentiated global culture (Lucas, 2003). Many factors have been instrumental in shaping the contemporary consumer. Globalisation has increased the mobility not only of people, goods and services but also of information and knowledge. On the other hand, localisation is the rebirth and revival of local culture. It is the intertwining of that which has resulted in a consumer who wants the latest and best, with a desire to have it in the form of their culture.

The view of globalisation has witnessed a change over the years. The scepticism and the negativity have been replaced by positive definitions. It has been argued that the post-modern consumer experience is about participation in shared conversations, and globalisation is that continuous process that helps connect people, ideas and culture (Firat et al, 2013). Globalisation has been defined as the diffusion of different forms and styles from all around the world, breaking through the national boundaries of sovereign states (Grubor and Marić, 2015). The continuous and adventurous journey of globalisation and localisation has shaped a new consumer who wants to return to the roots of their culture but, at the same time, desires global products and services in a manner that fits their culture. Thus, you may eat a McDonalds burger in the USA and India, but the McAloo tikki burger is uniquely Indian.

Ever-changing technology

Every aspect of life, both personal and professional, has been impacted by technology. The pace of change of technology has been unprecedented in the last two decades. Distances have shrunk and information is available on a real-time basis to all. As of February 2017, mobile devices accounted for 49.74 per cent of web page views worldwide, with mobile first markets such as Asia and Africa leading the pack (source: Statista – www.statista.com/topics/779/mobile-internet). In a country like India, 30 years ago having a mobile was considered a luxury and yet the number of users in 2018 is expected to be 775.5 million (source: Statista).

In the business world, the retailer is not only concerned with the payment of online shoppers, but also seeks ways to improve their experience (Claveria, 2018). Technology has provided ways to deliver advertisements specifically targeted at individuals based on their online behaviour (Reczek et al., 2016). Mobile phones have become an important companion for consumers who use them to buy, sell, shop and share their retail experiences with friends, acquaintances, prospects and Facebook strangers everyday. Apps are made to do real-time experience tracking (Macdonald et al., 2012). It is predicted that automation will particularly dominate those transactional interactions centred around speed and efficiency (Gavett, 2015). As technological changes revolutionise the world, it is predicted that marketing will cease to be based on stimulus–response and will instead evolve into a continual process of co-creation (Macdonald et al., 2012). Companies are aided in connecting with customer emotions through big data analytics (Magids et al., 2015). The playing field is becoming more even as cloud computing allows small companies access to those resources which had previously been very expensive for them. All of this has its own challenges too. People now tune out advertisements and messages if they are not interactive and engaging (Claveria, 2018). Technology has made relationships more virtual than physical. Technology may help us reach out to a larger audience but research has also shown that social connections are important for our mental and physical health and a happy individual is one who gets to communicate with others (Gavett, 2015). People are using technology not just to connect on a materialistic level but also to make spiritual bonds (Sharma, 2017). Technology has also blurred the space between home and work. Workplace intrudes into home space very often and in some cases this has distorted human perceptions (Luckett, 2011). Companies are facing their own challenges because the rapid development of new products has been accompanied by a related acceleration in product obsolescence. The learning curve of the consumer is small. On the one hand, the consumer is confused by having too many options and, on the other hand, companies face pressure to innovate at the speed of light. The consumption behaviour of society as a whole has changed. Greater access to education and information has made the consumer more familiar with new means of satisfying basic needs (Haydam et al., 2015). Immediate gratification is becoming more important than asset creation. The power of spending is a representation of social relations, personal and group identity, image and perceptions (Grubor and Marić, 2015).

Digital Focus 5.1

Impact on the consumer

Let us understand the impact of technology on the consumer by way of some interesting examples:

- Until recently, buying clothes meant going to a store, trying them on to check the fit and look, and then purchasing them. 'Fitle' (https://fitle.com/?lang=en) has tried to reinvent the online experience of clothes shopping by allowing the customer to try clothes online. How does this happen?
    - 'Fitle' can access partner brands' databases in real time and generate accurate 3D versions of clothes based on certain specifications.

○   The customer must upload four pictures of themselves and provide details, and then a customised 3D image is generated.
○   The customer can then try clothes online using this image.

● Maths has always been a scary subject for many students. Heymath (https://heymath.com/in), a firm in Chennai, India, has used technology to help students in different parts of the world overcome this fear. The solution comprises of:

○   using the internet as the delivery medium
○   collaborating with centres of excellence in mathematics
○   developing and servicing the product out of India.

Thus, 'Heymath' is an online platform for learning school-level mathematics. Based in India, it reaches students in Singapore, the USA, Africa and beyond.

Questions

1.   What are the advantages of and challenges in using the digital platform for education?
2.   Are relationships going to be virtual in the future?

Very clearly, two major developments in the last two decades can be summed up in two lines:

● technology revolution
● interdependence among nations.

These two things are closely related, resulting in the world being a global village with no secrets. Thus, companies cannot maintain different standards in different countries. Information has empowered the customer who is now aware of their rights. Simultaneously, too many options have also created confusion for them. They are connected to many others but the genuineness of these connections is open to debate. Perhaps in order to overcome these confusions and concerns, the consumer has started playing different roles in the business arena. The empowerment of the customer is now visible in their new avatar.

THE NEW AVATARS OF THE CONSUMER
Consumer as researcher

It has always been important for marketers to understand the decision-making process of consumers. This decision-making process has become more complex, with consumers seeking pricing and product information online well before arriving at a decision (Croome et al., 2010).

In a study done in Japan, it was found that 88% of consumers gather information online after gaining interest in a product offline (Kinomoto, 2015). Online information gains particular significance when a purchase requires a big commitment (Horrigan, 2008). Blogs also play an important role in helping the researcher-consumer gather information before an actual purchase is made. Today, the consumer is not just relying on one source of information but uses several information sources simultaneously (Bronner and de Hoog, 2013). The internet has made every consumer a researcher. It also provides a platform which allows consumers to share their opinions with each other (Gallant and Arcand, 2017). Customers are also using online information to do research on health-related issues, being particularly interested in disovering the available treatment options (Goetzinger et al., 2007). The contemporary consumer brings to every service encounter the collective learning and advice of an extended health network of other patients and doctors (Loane and D'Alessandro, 2014). Consumers' purchase routes are increasingly becoming complicated. Consumers mix and match both online and offline points regularly on their purchase journeys. Multiple types of pathways are emerging. The power of information has broken the barriers of age and gender. Children are active participants in family decision making, thanks to their access to information (Sharma, 2018). The information gathered from different sources means the ammunition is with the consumer now. Discussions with salespeople are informed discussions based on blogs and websites. At the same time, this overload of information is also creating confusion and tension. The authenticity of information is causing problems for the researcher. The consumer is empowered yet handicapped.

Consumer as activist

History is witness to the fact that a certain section of society has always tried to protect the rights of the consumer. After the publication of a causal link between smoking and lung cancer in the 1950s, the consumer movement reached out to educate consumers (Thomson et al., 2015). Due to increased exposure and access to information about global concerns, this activism is now more visible (Shaw et al., 2006). Maybe this is quite timely as it is felt that increasing unethical behaviour in the form of deceptive advertising, etc., may lead to a serious abuse of customer rights (Alsmadi and Khizindar, 2015). Access to information from across the world has made the consumer knowledgeable and aware of his rights. We have a new consumer who is empowered and has donned the role of activist. Advancements in technology have contributed to an increase in the level of information, which in turn has influenced the increase in consumer awareness, reducing social acceptance of enterprises whose activities pose a threat to the environment. Action at the correct time ensures that consumers do not lose faith in the system.

Ethical Focus 5.2

Examples of the consumer as an activist

a. One of the largest student boycotts in history was initiated in 2009 in response to the closure of campus clothing giant Fruit of the Loom's Honduran factory after its workers formed a union. As a result of the campaign, 96 US colleges and 10 British universities terminated their contract with Fruit of the Loom. This cost the firm USD 50 million. The company reopened its factory in 2010, re-employed all its workers, restored all union rights and awarded workers USD 2.5 million in compensation.

b. Singer/songwriter Dave Carroll found a new way of protesting against United Airlines, which broke his guitar due to mishandling in 2008. He wrote and sang the song 'United Breaks Guitars' and posted it on YouTube. The video went viral. Within days, United Airlines' stock price had gone down and the image of United was badly hit. (See Pat Wechsler's 2017 article on boycotts at http://businessresearcher.sagepub.com/sbr-1863-102636-2779297/20170501/the-boycott.)

Consumer as influencer

Another important role that the contemporary consumer plays is that of influencer. There was a time when the company was the main source of information. Now the company is the last source of information. When consumers need opinions and views, they seek out fellow consumers. Consumer-to-consumer interaction has gained prominence.

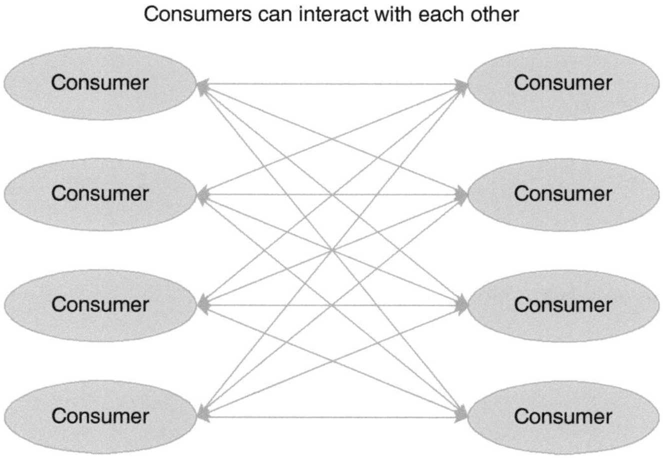

Figure 5.5   Consumer as an influencer

Digital Focus 5.2

Some interesting examples of consumer influence

a. Sperry, which is known for its boat shoes, understood the power of consumers as influencers. In 2016, the company began working with 100 micro-influencers (consumers who were posting popular images of Sperry products on social media) on Instagram to reach out to customers.

b. Sprint (a mobile service provider) featured people with a massive social media presence to start its campaign #Liveunlimited. The company did not insist that influencers play a defined role; rather, it looked for influencers who fit the goal of the campaign.

Point of discussion: Consumer influence

How does one control negative influence?

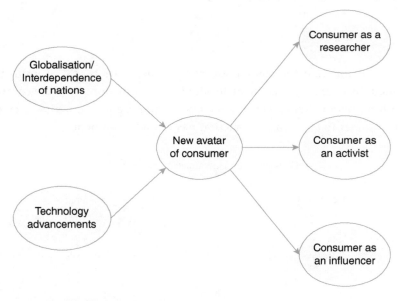

Figure 5.6   The new avatars of the consumer

The interdependence of nations and technology has opened up a new world for the consumer, one with multiple sources of information and knowledge. This new tool of a plethora of knowledge has given the consumer power which they can use both positively and negatively.

Thus, they use this power to gather information about a product/brand or service well before the actual encounter with it. They use this power to fight for their own and other members' rights. They also use this power to share their experiences with others. The customer occupies the central role of business now.

HOW DOES ALL THIS IMPACT INNOVATION AND ITS DIFFUSION?

The theory of diffusion of innovation was introduced by Everett Rogers in 1962. It seeks to explain how innovations spread. According to the theory, the four main elements that influence the spread of innovation are:

- the innovation
- communication channels
- social system
- time.

Let us briefly try to understand these terms:

a.   Innovation comes in various degrees. A continuous innovation includes slight improvement over time. A dynamically continuous innovation involves some change in technology though the product is more or less used in the same way. A discontinuous innovation involves a product that changes the way things are done. An example will make this clearer. When television was first introduced, it was a discontinuous innovation because it completely changed people's view of entertainment. It was something truly new for mankind. When TV changed from black and white to colour, it was a dynamically continuous innovation as it involved change in technology but the function/use remained the same. The various types of colour television over the years (LCD, LED, 3D) are a continuous innovation as these are slight improvements over time.

b.   Communication channel refers to various mediums used to carry messages from one individual to another. It is through the channel of communication that innovations spread across peoples. Thus, in a country like India the print media may still be as important as online media. Use of the correct communication channel helps in reaching the target audience.

c.   Social system refers to all kinds of components which construct society like religion, institutions and groups of people. Thus, in some cultures Friday is considered a very auspicious day and in some cultures buying metal on a Saturday is not considered to be a good thing. This in turn affects the marketing strategy to help reach the audience.

d.   Time refers to the length of time the product takes from being introduced to being adopted. It is the time people take to get used to new ideas.

Adoption of a new idea or product does not happen simultaneously in a social system. There are five adopter categories (see below and Figure 5.7):

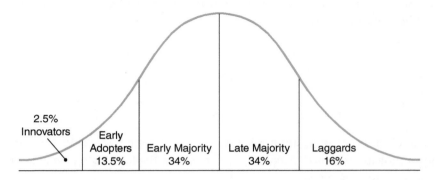

Figure 5.7   Adopter categories

1. Innovators: want to be the first to try the product; they are adventurous and risk-takers.
2. Early adopters: localised opinion leaders who enjoy leadership roles.
3. Early majority: need to see evidence that the innovation is working before they adopt it.
4. Late majority: are sceptical of change and only adopt an innovation after it has been tried by the majority.
5. Laggards: are bound by traditions and are very conservative.

Further, the five main factors that influence the adoption of innovation are:

1. Relative advantage: this measures how much an innovation has improved over a competing option or the previous generation of a product.
2. Compatibility: this refers to how compatible the product is with consumers' lifestyles.
3. Complexity: complexity or simplicity refers to how difficult it is for adopters to learn to use an innovation.
4. Triability: this describes how easily potential adopters might explore your innovation.
5. Observability: the extent to which the results or benefits of using an innovation are visible to potential adopters.

Let us look at some examples to understand this in a more comprehensive manner:

a. Bank cards were adopted quite quickly. People could see the convenience associated with credit and debit cards. They were not difficult to use and they clearly gave a relative advantage over cash.
b. Use of birth control measures has not been successful in many countries where it is not compatible with people's religious views.

c. Mobile phones have been quickly adopted by people everywhere. The reasons for this are given in Figure 5.8.

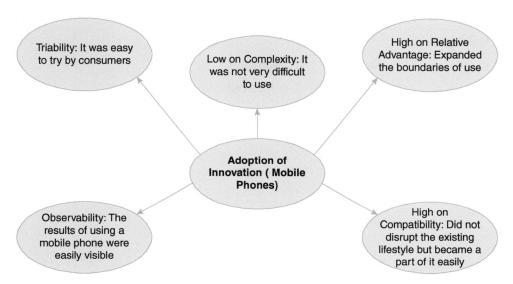

Figure 5.8   Why the mobile phone was adopted easily by consumers

DIFFUSION OF INNOVATION AND THE CONTEMPORARY CONSUMER

The diffusion of innovation theory has been used successfully in many fields. The theory has its own challenges but has witnessed maximum acceptance. The changing dynamics on the global scale have also evoked questions on how the contemporary customer is accepting innovation. Some factors that prove a barrier in diffusion of innovation are a weak education system, unstable political power, a fragile legal system, limited financial resources, poor infrastructure and cultural distances (Zanello et al., 2016). Maybe with the new roles of the consumer, the diffusion of innovation process will also demand an acceptance of parallel processes that are context dependent, mutually complementary and interrelated (Makkonen and Johnston, 2014). Innovation is the lifeblood of today's world and the theory of diffusion is still relevant. At the same time, the theory needs a fresh look and maybe a wider canvas. Use of technical advancements, better communication, the sharing of information and knowledge and efficient processes may emerge as key determinants for the contemporary process of diffusion of innovation.

Digital Focus 5.3

Some interesting statistics

It took the telephone 75 years to reach 50 million users.

It took Facebook 3.5 years to reach 50 million users.

It took the Angry Birds app 35 days to reach 50 million users.

Point for discussion

Why is the rate of adoption speeding up?

Source: https://visual.ly/community/infographic/technology/reaching-50-million-users

Practioners' Perspectives 5.1

The changing landscape of consumer behaviour

'Spiritual texts are my chosen field for writing. My work involves writing, editing and trans-lation. The biggest change as I look back over the last decade and a half is perhaps the digitalisation of information for readers. Digital innovations like Kindle and e-books have radi-cally increased the reach of the written word. Books have gone from being bulky hardbacks to merely a few convenient bytes on one's phone. They've also become far more accessible now, even in remote areas, as opposed to being restricted to a few libraries or shops just a decade ago. In fact, books available only in hardcover/paperback may soon have a limited readership as compared to their digital counterparts.

I also find that my reader base, for an otherwise 'limited interest' subject like spirituality, has actually increased! A changing economy (greater affordability), people's circumstances (more time to discover new reading subjects), increased access to more than just a few texts in the name of spirituality, and a consistently widening base of the literate population may be just some of the reasons. While the actual practice of spiritual living might be going down in today's fast-paced world, spirituality, not to be confused with religion, has anyway never been a 'hot-selling' subject in this ever-materialistic world, and the written word 'per se' is here to stay and thankfully so!' (Megha Sharma, freelance writer, development editor, translator of *Sopan: Steps to Spirituality* by Sadhu Sadanand and other books)

'The way our tax laws are worded, in several cases they are amenable to multiple inter-pretations. Our clients, however, struggle to understand how a clear cut 'yes' or 'no' answer is not possible for several tax issues. Also today, they are generally averse to taking any litigate or aggressive tax positions. They realise that tax litigation is a long drawn-out and costly affair, and prefer to focus their energies on their core business. They also realise that while tax planning is an integral part of business decisions, it cannot be the sole driver in the decision-making process. Due to increased media coverage, clients today are much more aware of the tax concessions and benefits available and the comparable positions in other countries.' (Richa Sawhney, international and direct tax advisor, Richa Sawhney and Associates, India)

'Let me begin by first defining my consumer. It's a corporate entity across multiple industries seeking technology products and services to run its business and also retain its competitive edge in the market. A decade ago when technology was still not very widespread and had a novelty value attached to it, the corporate, while understanding the benefits technology can provide, were still relatively ignorant of what to do, how to implement and maintain it, etc. Skills related to the technology field were concentrated with the technology companies. This in some sense made it a supplier's market, where the customer would engage a technology firm right from strategy formulation up to the implementation and maintenance stage. Now that all the firms broadly have their technology backbone in place and the skills related to technology also in-house, the market has changed to that of a buyer's market. The customer today seeks ready-to-deploy expertise, often has a choice of products or vendors to choose from, and pretty much has their requirements well formulated'. (Pooja Sharma, senior consultant, Tata Consultancy Services)

'In banking, the consumer is no longer interested in walking into a bank branch to fulfill their banking needs. With the advent of tablets and smartphones, customers expect to be served at their fingertips. For loans, they expect documentation to be available through Docu-sign and other secure portals which make the transaction simple, seamless and easy. The other big change is that customers expect you to know them and their financial situation since you have access to all their records. Therefore, the onus is on you to put together an offer that best meets their needs. They want guidance, but they also want you to give them options without making the decision for them. Many organisations, such as ours, have taken this job seriously and are working with technology partners to meet customers' needs. To be suc-cessful in this industry, this is no longer a 'nice to have' but an absolute necessity to survive.' (Reva Rao, senior director, Terafina, USA)

Questions for discussion

1. What evidence can you tease out from the perspectives of these practitioners that indi-cate the changing landscape of consumer behaviour?

(Continued)

(Continued)

2. Assume two of you have been invited as speakers to discuss the topic: *Digital technology: The good, the bad, and the ugly.* The first speaker has spoken at length and emphasised how social media has been used by people for criminal acts and how the involvement of some youth in several criminal acts is linked to the advent of technology. Present your case to show that there is a positive side to the use of technology with reference to the perspectives of the practitioners featured in the above mini case studies.

Case Study 5.1

Confused.com: Expanding possibilities for the contemporary consumer

The options available to consumers on insurance products are increasing by the day. While the ultimate aim of the business will be to relieve the policy holder of the stress of bearing their various risks, ironically the stress associated with meeting several insurance organisations one-after-the other to check and compare their prices and conditions of service could be equally daunting. Drivers would normally need to approach high-street brokers or insurers directly, or through their websites, and in several cases had to spend several hours filling in forms to get a quote for their insurance needs in order to be able to compare the options available. This was the business opportunity spotted by Confused.com in 2002 when it launched its business and became the first to offer the UK car insurance consumer a price comparison website. Generally, as the landscape of marketing acitivities has changed, consumers are becoming more demanding, more educated and familiar with use of the internet. By 2005, Confused.com had expanded its business portfolio to include house, travel, motorbike and pet insurance; now, you can use it to compare utilities like gas and electricity or car purchases, among other products. The company makes it clear to visitors on its website that it does not operate as an insurance broker; rather, its business is to offer the customer a one-stop shop where they may easily compare prices of car insurance, car finance, car purchase and the associated running costs. The idea is that when the consumer recognises the need to buy any of these products, the search for information and evaluation of alternative stages are made easy. According to the company, the process is simple. While the consumer searches for insurance products on Confused.com's website, the company provides the information to a wide range of insurance companies. It basically sends the consumer's information to the site of these insurance partners, which is tantamount to Confused.com completing the form on behalf of the customer. This results in quotes from these various brands, including any special offers they can give the customer based on the given information. Apart from the on-screen listing of the various offers from the different insurance companies, Confused.com also sends an email detailing the quotes to website users to make it easier for them to choose.

In acknowledging that consumers may choose to buy a new car for functional and/or symbolic reasons, as per many other products, and use it to create and maintain an identity, Confused.com provides up-to-date information to consumers on what they should be looking out for in a car in order to be able to get the most from their purchase. This information includes features around style, comfort, fuel efficiency and brand, among others. It also highlights common scams to look out for during the purchase process. As can be inferred from the information available on Confused.com's website, consumers of all age categories can benefit from this: be they young drivers, who have just passed their driving test and are looking to experience the pleasure of driving for themselves, or those who are well experienced but interested in changing their cars to models that might help them meet their lifestyle goals. A part of this commitment is the Confused.com London Motor Show which features talks, demonstrations and family entertainment organised by the company.

The services of this comparison site have been popular among various stakeholders including consumers. This explains the many awards and accolades that have been given to the company over the years. It was declared the Winner of the Best System Integration in the Marketing Specialist category in 2013 under the Sitecore site of the year award; and Best In-house Team under the European Search Award 2014 and 2015, which is an international award recognising the best in pay-per-click (PPC), SEO, digital and content marketing in Europe. The Confused.com team has also been honoured by the Pride Awards (2017) and by the PRCA National Awards (2017) which specifically celebrate the best in the PR and communication industry in the UK. Although Confused.com has won many other awards, which are publicised on its website, and based on a report in the Business Cloud entitled 'Leap In Profits at Price Comparison Giant' its profit in the UK arm of the business alone increased by 40% to £14.3 million for 2018 compared to £10.1m for 2017, the core focus of the company is specifically on making customers happy. This is considered crucial as it is aware of the competition from other sites such as Comparethemarket and Gocompare which were introduced in 2006. So, Confused.com monitors customers' feedback, gathers their reviews, and proudly displays them on the website for others to see how well the company has been rated as excellent.

Another noteworthy contemporary practice of Confused.com is its up-to-date use of social media. It acknowledges that consumers are no longer satisfied with the information they receive from traditional media such as TV and radio. The consumers of today now engage in social media for a number of reasons. They are researchers, activists and influencers. Some are members of brand communities, while others work closely with one another in a group to communicate, expose, boycott or confront the unethical business practices of organisations. They are driven by hyperreality and tend towards user-generated content on a daily basis.

(Continued)

(Continued)

This explains why Confused.com ensures that it has a strong presence on Facebook, Twitter, YouTube and LinkedIn. The approach works, as many consumers are now connected with the company through these media! Clearly, things are ever-evolving and interconnected as the site does not only define the contemporary consumer but also shapes and fine-tunes their consumption patterns.

Questions for discussion

1. To what extent have the activities of Confused.com demonstrated changes in the marketing landscape in relation to the contemporary consumer? How relevant is your answer on this to the consumer decision-making process?
2. The case study suggests that the contemporary consumer may use a car to create an identity. Other than consuming identity projects, briefly explain the remaining key themes of consumer culture theory (CCT).
3. Assume that Confused.com is interested in extending its product portfolio to aid consumers in the search for clothing items. Given the characteristics of postmodernism and the contemporary consumer, would this be a realistic business model for the company? Provide a justification for your standpoint.
4. As shown in the case study, Confused.com also provides price comparisons on mobile phones, among other products. Do you think dealing with this company might help consumers avoid falling victim to deceptive counterfeiting transactions?
5. Confused.com interacts with consumers through various social network platforms which now serve as tools for the empowerment of these contemporary consumers. Explain how consumers might use these platforms as activists and influencers in relation to any two of the products marketed by Confused.com.

SUMMARY OF KEY IDEAS

- There are changes at every stage of the consumer decision-making process in relation to shifts in the marketing environment, such as changes in technology and the dynamics of socio-cultural factors.
- The characteristics of postmodernism indicate that current consumer behaviour is challenging conventional understanding. Similarly, consumer culture theory (CCT) shows contemporary consumers in a new cultural light that is different from the homogeneous system of collectively shared meanings of members of a particular society.
- Consumer behaviour around the consumption of counterfeit products is becoming rampant in this day and age, and the prevalence of it relates not only to deceptive counterfeiting but also to non-deceptive counterfeiting.

- Globalisation and localisation have driven consumption in recent times to unprecedented forms. Hence, consumers are now interested in having a taste of both extremes.
- The new avatar of the customer indicates that contemporary consumers now play the roles of researcher, activist and influencer, and this dynamic is also linked to the diffusion of innovation as moderated by the role of technological advancement and globalisation.

Chapter Discussion Questions

1. In groups of three or four, each member should recall a purchase. This could be a physical product such as a car, an item of clothing, food, a TV set, or a service such as hairdressing, a music event or transportation. Highlight specific points that you think are contemporary about the product/service and the process involved in acquiring it. See if you can compare this for different products on the list.
2. Think of five luxury brands that are sold in your country. In which circumstances do you think consumers might engage in non-deceptive purchase of counterfeit versions of these products? How do you think this consumption behaviour could be discouraged?
3. Give specific examples of postmodernisn in marketing that you have noticed in the global marketing environment. These could be related to your country of origin or elsewhere. Give specific reasons as to why you consider these to be a good fit for this task.
4. Discuss the term 'The new avatars of the consumer'. Cite specific examples that relate to you as a contemporary consumer. Discuss and share these with a member of your group to compare your responses.
5. To what extent would you say the technological revolution has influenced/affected the diffusion of innovation?

REFERENCES

Ajzen, I. (1991) The theory of planned behavior. *Organizational Behavior and Human Decision Processes*, 50(2), 179–211.

Alsmadi, S. and Khizindar, T. (2015) Consumers' perceptions of consumer rights in Jordan. *International Journal of Commerce and Management*, 25(4), 512–30.

Ang, H.S., Cheng, P.S., Lim, E.A., & Tambyah, S.K. (2001) Spot the difference: consumer responses towards counterfeits. *Journal of Consumer Marketing*, 18(3), 219–35.

Arnould, E. J. and Thompson, C. J. (2005) Consumer culture theory (CCT): Twenty years of research. *Journal of Consumer Research*, 31(4), 868–82.

Arnould, E. J. and Thompson, C. J. (2018) Introduction: What is Consumer Culture Theory? In E. J. Arnould and C. J. Thompson (eds), *Consumer Culture Theory*. London: Sage, pp. 1–16.

Badot, O. (2014) Mediterranean marketing and postmodern marketing: An oxymoron? *Journal of Consumer Behaviour*, 13(3), 224–9.

BASCAP (2011) Estimating the global economic and social impacts of counterfeiting and piracy 2011. Report by Business Action to Stop Counterfeiting and Piracy, Frontier Economics. Available at: https://iccwbo.org/publication/estimating-global-economic-social-impacts-counterfeiting-piracy-2011 (accessed 13 April 2019).

Belk, R. (1988) Possessions and the extended self. *Journal of Consumer Research*, 15(Sept.), 139–68.

Bian, X., Haque, S. and Smith, A. (2015) Social power, product conspicuousness, and the demand for luxury brand counterfeit products. *British Journal of Social Psychology*, 54(1), 37–54.

Bian, X. and Moutinho, L. (2011) The role of brand image, product involvement, and knowledge in explaining consumer purchase behaviour of counterfeits: Direct and indirect effects. *European Journal of Marketing*, 45(1/2), 191–216.

Bristor, J. M. and Fischer, E. (1993) Feminist thought: Implications for consumer research. *Journal of Consumer Research*, 19(Mar.), 518–36.

Bronner, F. and De Hoog, R. (2013) Economizing on vacations: The role of information searching. *International Journal of Culture, Tourism and Hospitality Research*, 7(1), 28–41.

Brown, S. (1995) Postmodern marketing research: No representation without taxation. *Journal of the Marketing Research Society*, 37(3), 287–310.

Brown, S., Kozinets, R. and Sherry Jr, J. F. (2003) Teaching old brands new tricks: Retro branding and the revival of brand meaning. *Journal of Marketing*, 67(July), 19–33.

Catulli, M., Cook, M. and Potter, S. (2017) Consuming use orientated product service systems: A consumer culture theory perspective. *Journal of Cleaner Production*, 141, 1186–93.

Chaudhry, P. E. and Stumpf, S. A. (2011) Consumer complicity with counterfeit products. *Journal of Consumer Marketing*, 28(2), 139–51.

Chaudhry, P. E., Peters, J. R. and Zimmerman, A. (2009a) Evidence of managerial response to the level of consumer complicity, pirate activity, and host country enforcement of counterfeit goods: An exploratory study. *Multinational Business Review*, 17(4), 21–44.

Chaudhry, P.E., Zimmerman, A., Peters, J.R. and Cordell, V.V. (2009b) 'Preserving intellectual property rights: Managerial insight into the escalating counterfeit market quandary', *Business Horizons*, 52(1), 57–66.

Claveria, K. (2018) 4 Examples of how Technology is Changing Consumer Behavior. Vision Critical. Updated 2019. Available at: www.Visioncritical.Com/4-Examples-How-Technology-Changing-Consumer-Behavior-1 (accessed 29 April 2018).

Cova, B. (1996). The postmodern explained to managers: Implications for marketing. *Business Horizons*, 39(6), 15–24.

Croome, R., Lawley, M. and Sharma, B. (2010) Antecedents of purchase in the online buying process. *Journal of Internet Business*, 8, 1–40.

Farivar, S., Farivar, S., Turel, O., Turel, O., Yuan, Y. and Yuan, Y. (2017) A trust-risk perspective on social commerce use: An examination of the biasing role of habit. *Internet Research*, 27(3), 586–607.

Fernandes, C. (2013) Analysis of counterfeit fashion purchase behaviour in UAE. *Journal of Fashion Marketing and Management: An International Journal*, 17(1), 85–97.

Firat, A., Kutucuoglu, K. Y., Isil Arikan Saltik and Ozgur Tuncel (2013) Consumption, consumer culture and consumer society. *Journal of Community Positive Practices*, Catalactica NGO, issue 1, 182–203.

Fitchett, J. A., Patsiaouras, G. and Davies, A. (2014) Myth and ideology in consumer culture theory. *Marketing Theory*, 14(4), 495–506.

Gallant, I. and Arcand, M. (2017) Consumer characteristics as drivers of online information searches. *Journal of Research in Interactive Marketing*, 11, 56–74. 10.1108/JRIM-11-2014-0071.

Gavett, G. (2015) How self-service kiosks are changing customer behavior. *Harvard Business Review*, 11 March. Available at: https://hbr.org/2015/03/how-self-service-kiosks-are-changing-customer-behavior (accessed 29 April 2018).

Gbadamosi, A. (2012) Exploring children, family, and consumption behaviour: Empirical evidence from Nigeria. *Thunderbird International Business Review*, 54(4), 591–605.

Gbadamosi, A. (2015a) Brand personification and symbolic consumption among ethnic teenage consumers: An empirical study. *Journal of Brand Management*, 22(9), 737–59.

Gbadamosi, A. (2015b) Family consumption systems in Africa: A focus on children. In S. Nwankwo and K. Ibeh (eds), *Routledge Companion to Business in Africa*. Oxon: Routledge, pp. 146–59.

Gbadamosi, A. (2019) A Conceptual overview of consumer behaviour in developing nations. In A. Gbadamosi (ed.), *Exploring the Dynamics of Consumerism in Developing Nations*. Hershey, PA: IGI Global, pp. 1–30.

Gbadamosi, A. (2018) The changing landscape of young consumer behaviour. In A. Gbadamosi (ed.), *Young Consumer Behaviour: A Research Companion*. Oxon: Routledge, pp. 3–22.

Goetzinger, L., Park, J., Jung Lee, Y. and Widdows, R. (2007) Value-driven consumer e-health information search behavior. *International Journal of Pharmaceutical and Healthcare Marketing*, 1(2), 128–42.

Grossman, G. M. and Shapiro, C. (1988) Foreign counterfeiting of status goods. *Quarterly Journal of Economics*, 103(1), 79–100.

Grubor, A. and Marić, D. (2015) 'Contemporary consumer in the global environment'. In *CBU International Conference on Innovation, Technology Transfer and Education*. Prague, March.

Haydam, N., Edu, T., Negricea, I. and Ionescu, A. (2015) Consumer behaviour mutations and their impact on retail development: Evidence from South Africa. *Transformations in Business and Economics*, 14(3), 187–209.

Hetrick, W. P. and Lozada, H. R. (1994) Construing the critical imagination: Comments and necessary diversions. *Journal of Consumer Research*, 21 (Dec.), 548–58.

Hill, R. P. (1991) Homeless women, special possessions, and the meaning of home: An ethnographic case study. *Journal of Consumer Research*, 18(3), 298–310.

Hines, C. (2003) Time to replace globalization with localization. *Global Environmental Politics*, 3(3), 1–7.

Hirschman, E. C. (1988) The ideology of consumption: A structural-syntactical analysis of *Dallas* and *Dynasty*. *Journal of Consumer Research*, 15(Dec.), 344–59.

HnyB Insights (2012) 'Social commerce strategy and outlook, available at: www.prlog.org/11872607-hnyb-insights-predicts-global-social-commerce-market-to-touch-80bn-by-2020.html (accessed December 5, 2015).

Holt, D. B. (1998) Does cultural capital structure American consumption? *Journal of Consumer Research*, 25(June), 1–26.

Holt, D. B. (2002) Why do brands cause trouble? A dialectical theory of consumer culture and branding. *Journal of Consumer Research*, 29(June), 70–90.

Horrigan, J. B. (2008) The Internet and Consumer Choice, Pew Research Centre, Internet and Technology (https://www.pewinternet.org/2008/05/18/the-internet-and-consumer-choice)

Immelt, J. (2016) Business: Localization can help America win around the world. *Time*, 26 December, 188(27–28), 32.

Joy, A. and Ping Hung Li, E. (2012) Studying consumption behaviour through multiple lenses: An overview of consumer culture theory. *Journal of Business Anthropology,* 1(1): 141–73.

Kapferer, J. N. (1995). Brand confusion: Empirical study of a legal concept. *Psychology & Marketing*, 12(6), 551–68.

Kinomoto, H. (2015) The power of websites in influencing consumer purchasing behavior. Adobe Digital Dialogue, 18 February. Available at: https://Blogs.Adobe.Com/Digitaldialogue/Customer-Experience/Power-Websites-Influencing-Consumer-Purchasing-Behavior (accessed 29 April 2018).

Kozinets, R. V. (2001) Utopian enterprise: Articulating the meaning of *Star Trek*'s culture of consumption. *Journal of Consumer Research*, 28(June), 67–89.

Lichtenstein, D. R., Netemeyer, R. G. and Burton, S. (1990) Distinguishing coupon proneness from value consciousness: An acquisition-transaction utility theory perspective. *Journal of marketing*, 54(3), 54–67.

Lichtenstein, D.R., Ridgway, N.M. and Netemeyer, R.G. (1993) 'Price perceptions and consumer shopping behavior: a field study', *Journal of marketing research, 30*(2), 234–245.

Liu, H., Chu, H., Huang, Q. and Chen, X. (2016). Enhancing the flow experience of consumers in China through interpersonal interaction in social commerce. *Computers in Human Behavior*, 58, 306–14.

Loane Stewart, S. and D'Alessandro, S. (2014) Empowered and knowledgeable health consumers: The impact of online support groups on the doctor–patient relationship. *Australasian Marketing Journal*, 22(3), 238–45.

Lucas, C. (2003) Localization: An alternative to corporate-led globalization. *International Journal of Consumer Studies*, 27(4), 261–5.

Luckett, M. (2011) Relationships between technological and societal change. *Business Studies Journal*, 3(1), 85–93.

Macdonald, E., Wilson, H. and Konus, U. (2012) Better customer insight: In real time. *Harvard Business Review*, 90(9), 102–8.

Magids, S., Zorfas, A. and Leemon, D. (2015) The new science of customer emotions. *Harvard Business Review*, 93(11), 66–8.

Makkonen, H. and Johnston, W. J. (2014) Innovation adoption and diffusion in business-to-business marketing. *Journal of Business & Industrial Marketing*, 29(4), 324–31.

Moore-Shay, E. S., Wilkie, W. L. and Lutz, R. J. (2002) Passing the torch: Intergenerational influences as a source of brand equity. *Journal of Marketing*, 66(Apr.), 17–37.

Muñiz, A. and Schau, H. (2005) Religiosity in the abandoned Apple Newton brand community. *Journal of Consumer Research*, 31(March), 737–47.

Muñiz, A. and O'Guinn, T. C. (2000) Brand communities. *Journal of Consumer Research*, 27(March), 412–32.

Murray, J. B. (2002) The politics of consumption: A re-inquiry on Thompson and Haytko's (1997) 'Speaking of Fashion'. *Journal of Consumer Research*, 29(Dec.), 427–40.

Parsons, E., Maclaran, P. and Chatzidakis, A. (2018) *Contemporary Issues in Marketing and Consumer Behaviour*. New York: Routledge.

Phau, I., Prendergast, G. and Hing Chuen, L. (2001) Profiling brand-piracy-prone consumers: An exploratory study in Hong Kong's clothing industry. *Journal of Fashion Marketing and Management: An International Journal*, 5(1), 45–55.

Reczek, R., Summers, C. and Smith, R. (2016) Targeted ads don't just make you more likely to buy: They can change how you think about yourself. *Harvard Business Review Digital Articles*, pp. 2–5.

Schau, H. J. and Gilly, M. C. (2003) 'We are what we post?': Self-presentation in personal web space. *Journal of Consumer Research*, 30(Dec.), 385–404.

Sharma, A. (2017) Spirituality and modern day life: A conceptual model. *Purushartha: A Journal of Management, Ethics and Spirituality*, 10(2), 69-81.

Sharma, A. (2018) Learning and consumer socialization in children. In A. Gbadamosi (ed.), *Young Consumer Behaviour: A Research Companion*. London: Routledge, pp. 37–58.

Sharma, P. and Chan, R. Y. (2016) Demystifying deliberate counterfeit purchase behaviour: Towards a unified conceptual framework. *Marketing Intelligence & Planning*, 34(3), 318–35.

Shaw, D., Newholm, T. and Dickinson, R. (2006) Consumption as voting: An exploration of consumer empowerment. *European Journal of Marketing*, 40(9/10), 1049–67.

Staake, T., Thiesse, F. and Fleisch, E. (2009) The emergence of counterfeit trade: A literature review. *European Journal of Marketing*, 43(3/4), 320–49.

Stumpf, S. A., Chaudhry, P. E. and Perretta, L. (2011) Fake: Can business stanch the flow of counterfeit products? *Journal of Business Strategy*, 32(2), 4–12.

Symcox, J. (2019) 'Leap In Profits at Price Comparison Giant', Business Cloud, 7 March 2019, https://www.businesscloud.co.uk/news/leap-in-profits-at-price-comparison-giant (accessed 14 May 2019).

Szmigin, I. and Piacentini, M. (2018) *Consumer Behaviour*. Oxford: Oxford University Press.

Thompson, C. J. (2004) Marketplace mythologies and discourses of power. *Journal of Consumer Research*, 31(June), 162–80.

Thomson, I., Dey, C. and Russell, S. (2015) Activism, arenas and accounts in conflicts over tobacco control. *Accounting, Auditing & Accountability Journal*, 28(5), 809–45.

Wallendorf, M. and Reilly, M.D. (1983) Ethnic migration, assimilation, and consumption. *Journal of Consumer Research*, 10 (Dec.), 292–302.

Wiedmann, K. P., Hennigs, N. and Klarmann, C. (2012) Luxury consumption in the trade-off between genuine and counterfeit goods: What are the consumers' underlying motives and value-based drivers? *Journal of Brand Management*, 19(7), 544–66.

Zanello, G., Fu, X., Mohnen, P. and Ventresca, M. (2016) The creation and diffusion of innovation in developing countries: A systematic literature review. *Journal of Economic Surveys*, 30(5), 884–912.

6
BRANDS, BRANDING AND BRAND CULTURE

Aidan Kelly

Learning Objectives

At the end of this chapter, you should be able to understand and discuss:

- What a brand is to different stakeholders and the difficulties of finding an agreed definition
- The role of consumers in the branding process
- How culture impacts on brand meaning and ideology
- Brand architecture and the concept of corporate branding
- The differences between luxury and non-luxury branding
- The potential role that social media can play in fostering consumer engagement with brands

---

INTRODUCTION

Brands are an inescapable part of our culture, whether it's the mobile phones we use, the clothes we wear, the cars we drive or the food we eat – so much of our everyday human behaviour and interaction is mediated through brands. The practices of branding, which arguably date back to ancient Greece and Rome (Moor, 2007), are applied to so much more than traditional, packaged or durable consumer brands such as Nike®, Apple® or

Heinz® – football clubs, websites, universities, governments, protest movements and celebrities are, for better or worse, managed as brands in the marketplaces in which they operate. We as people (or, dare I say, 'consumers') use brands for so many tasks of our lives; for some, our relationship with the brands we consume is inextricably deep, meaningful and long-lasting, while others have a more ambivalent relationship with brands and marketing more generally.

Whether we view brands positively or negatively, it is true to say that brands are an embedded cultural artefact within the fabric of our societies and are, in themselves, worthy of serious academic study. Indeed, many universities in the UK and beyond dedicate entire academic programmes to the study of brands and branding (Brown, 2016). The academic branding literature is itself burgeoning, multi-disciplinary and fascinating, which presents us with two key perspectives on the topic. The first, which is arguably more established, is the managerial literature which tends to focus on the practicalities of managing brands and the steps and challenges involved in creating a successful brand (Keller et al., 2012). This perspective is rooted in the traditional modernist marketing approach which provides us with valuable tools and techniques for creating and managing brands in the marketplace, and is well represented on brand management courses at undergraduate and postgraduate levels in business schools globally. The newer, more emerging perspective is to examine the culture associated with brands and branding, in terms of consumer relationships with brands, their role as cultural symbols and ideological agents, the communities that form around them and the ways in which branding is used in domains not traditionally associated with business (Schroeder and Salzer-Mörling, 2006). Both perspectives offer important insights and ideas in terms of branding, and ecumenical texts on the subject are now usefully combining both managerial and cultural viewpoints on brands in ways that are both fruitful and academically coherent for students and practitioners alike (Beverland, 2018).

The purpose of this chapter is to provide an admittedly selective overview of some key themes of the branding literature for students who may be encountering this subject for the first time. We begin with some basic definitions of what a brand is and outline some of the difficulties and controversies around fixing a single definition to a concept with multiple meanings to different stakeholders. We then outline the relationships that consumers have with brands (both individually and collectively), and the role that culture plays in the creation and development of brand meaning. We consider the role that brands can play for corporate institutions and the importance of branding within organisations to create employee commitment; we also evaluate the luxury context for brands and the unique challenges of managing luxury brands. Finally, we contemplate the role of social media in the context of branding, particularly in terms of what it means for consumer-brand engagement and how it is likely to change brand management practices in the future.

WHAT IS A BRAND?

The term 'brand' is a notoriously difficult concept to define and is not one that academics have universal agreement on in terms of meaning, particularly in a business context. The word 'brand' derives from the old Germanic term 'brinn-an' which means to burn and was associated with burning as a mark of identification, as when a brand signified a burn mark impressed upon cattle and horses to identify ownership (Stern, 2006). The term 'brand' is considered to mean 'burning' or 'fire' from an etymological perspective.

One of the earliest papers in the marketing literature to distinguish between 'products' and 'brands' was published in 1955 by Gardner and Levy, who provided the following oft-quoted definition:

> a brand name is more than a label employed to differentiate among the manufacturers of a product. It is a complex symbol that represents a variety of ideas and attributes. It tells the consumers many things, not only by the way it sounds (and its literal meaning if it has one) but, more important, via the body of associations it has built up and acquired as a public object over a period of time. (Gardner and Levy, 1955: 35)

Later, in 1960, the American Marketing Association provided what is regarded as a standard definition of a brand from a marketing perspective:

> A name, term, sign, symbol or design, or a combination of them, intended to identify the goods or services of one seller or group of sellers and to differentiate them from those of competitors. (AMA, 1960, cited in de Chernatony and Dall'Olmo Riley, 1998: 419).

One very important aspect of defining a brand within the marketing literature has been to define it from the perspective of the consumer, especially in terms of their cognitive associations with the brand. As Brown (1992) notes, 'a brand name is nothing more or less than the sum of all the mental connections people have around it' (cited in De Chernatony and Dall-Olmo Riley, 1998: 419–20). In an insight that was incredibly profound in the branding literature, Levy (1959: 118) reminded us that 'People buy things not only for what they can do, but also what they mean', while Fanning (2006: 10) posits that 'People make decisions with their hearts as well as their heads', so the cognitive and emotional associations around brands for consumers has been a crucial part of defining what brands are. Similarly, an organisational perspective has featured very prominently in definitions of brands, such as that of De Chernatony et al. (2011: 31) who define a brand as 'a cluster of functional and emotional values that enables organisations to make a promise about a unique and welcomed experience'. In highlighting the restriction of defining a brand solely from either a company or consumer perspective, Mulbacher et al. (2006) define a brand as a 'complex social phenomenon' which encompasses brand manifestations, brand meaning and a brand interest group that construct the meaning of the brand within ongoing public discourse. Defining what brands are and to whom has been referred to as a 'holy grail' by some experts (De Chernatony, 2009), and as a polysemic term with multiple meanings it can often mean different things to different stakeholder groups, even within the confines of the marketing academy, let alone if we consider interested groups outside of this.

There are a number of stakeholders with an interest in brands. For consumers, brands are a key way of identifying the goods and services of a provider and act as a promise of quality and reliability (Keller et al., 2012). As we shall see in the next section, consumer relationships with brands can often be deeply important and they create strong bonds with the brands they buy which are often intertwined with one's sense of self and identity. Brands also have an important role for companies as they enable them to differentiate their offering from those of competitors and provide some legal protection for the company name (Beverland, 2018). Brands in and of themselves are of enormous economic value for firms – in a concept known as brand equity, companies now place brands (typically an intangible asset) on their balance sheet and brand valuation firms such as Interbrand® and Brand Finance® regularly engage in financial audits to measure the value of brands either nationally or globally. Similarly, for company employees, brands create an 'espirit de corps' around the organisation and its core meanings and values for the members. Brands also have an immense cultural value too and have played an important role in aesthetics and culture generally. Many artists have worked on brand and advertising campaigns (for brands such as Apple® or Absolut Vodka®), and branded content is often the subject of the artistic gaze since at least the time of Andy Warhol and his famous painting of the Campbell's® soup cans. So, brands matter, economically, socially and culturally to multiple stakeholder groups who have an interest in them, and as a result the meaning of the term 'brand' from a marketing perspective is rather multifarious and disparate (Stern, 2006). Even from a purely educational perspective, the ways in which business schools tend to teach and analyse brands and branding differ enormously from those of media or cultural studies departments, who have an interest in the same phenomena but through a completely different disciplinary and ideological lens. However, it is the diversity and interdisciplinary nature of the branding field that make it such an interesting and vibrant area of study, which is where our interest now turns.

BRANDS AND THE CONSUMER

Consumers have a crucial role to play within the branding process and brands are often seen to exist solely within the mind of the consumer (Ries and Trout, 1986). Cognitive psychology has tended to have a dominant influence on consumer behaviour and marketing theory, and similarly for branding cognitive theories have tended to prevail in terms of conceptualising the role of brands for consumers. Keller's (1993: 2) milestone contribution to the consumer brand psychology literature conceptualised 'customer-based brand equity', which he defined as 'the differential effect of brand knowledge on consumer response to the marketing of a brand'. Keller regards brand knowledge as the primordial factor in the consumer evaluation of brands, which was driven by brand awareness and the types of associations that consumers would make with the brand image. Within this paradigm, branding is something which happens inside people's minds and the purpose of brand research is to examine the cognitive schema through which consumers process brand information and develop brand knowledge.

While the cognitive psychology paradigm was certainly useful in considering how consumers evaluated brands, it gave the consumer a rather passive role in the branding process. In the 1990s and 2000s, a more active consumer was envisaged, where 'value will ... be jointly created by both the firm and the customer ... [with] consumer–company interaction as the locus of value-creation' (Prahalad and Ramaswamy, 2004: 7–10). Consumers were no longer seen as end users in the process of marketing and branding, but as partners in the co-creation of value with companies and thus were willing participants in the process. This idea has found expression in the recent 'service-dominant logic' (SDL) theory of Vargo and Lusch (2004), where value is created 'in use' by consumers rather than in the exchange process, and the consumer is regarded as a co-producer of value for goods and services (which are regarded interchangeably from an SDL standpoint). Empirical research by Fournier (1998) discovered that consumers increasingly saw brands as 'relationship partners' in their lives and developed strong emotional bonds with their brands which were akin to the interpersonal, animistic relationships they had with other human beings. Indeed, consumers often evaluate brands in human terms and attribute personality characteristics to anthropomorphise their favoured brands (Aaker, 1997). Anthropomorphism refers to how people attribute human characteristics to objects, and much practitioner marketing research is concerned with exploring the personalities consumers ascribe to particular brands. This literature portrays a rich and deep relationship with brands for consumers and certainly highlights a two-way co-creative interaction between the firm and the consumer within the branding process.

The materials of the market are often very meaningful for consumers and have an important role to play in the creation of personal identity. Belk (1988) highlighted how possessions form part of the consumer's 'extended self' and these objects contribute toward making up the identity of the individual. Brands have been found to play a similarly important role for the consumer and act as symbolic resources for personal identity construction (Elliott and Wattanasuwan, 1998). They enable us to both distinguish ourselves in society and fit in with various peer groups, and are thus important signifiers of meaning within consumer culture. Consumers buy brands for functional as well as symbolic benefits, however the symbolic value is a powerful vehicle for marketing and is something that has important semiotic resonance for them. Indeed, studies have shown that parents from low-income families will often do without survival necessities such as food or clothes in order to ensure their children can wear branded trainers in school and avoid being bullied by fellow students (Elliott and Leonard, 2004). It is fair to surmise that not all consumers are enamoured with the allure of brands and some actively avoid mass-marketed products entirely (Holt, 2002), however for many consumers brands are important markers of one's identity and help to create a sense of affiliation and belonging within a society.

One relatively recent development in the branding literature has been to consider collective consumer–brand relationships (O'Guinn and Muniz, 2009). These are relationships that are created between consumers based on their mutual affiliation or loyalty to a brand, or what has been termed a 'brand community', defined by Muniz and O'Guinn (2001: 412) as 'a specialised, non-geographically bound community, based on a structured set of social relationships among admirers of a brand'. These are groups of consumers and other stakeholders who have a shared interest in the brand and how it performs in the marketplace. Brand communities share three common characteristics, which are that members share a 'consciousness of kind' or strong connection to each other, they have 'rituals and traditions' associated with the brand (such as brand-orientated events like the Harley Davidson® 'Harley Owner Group' (HOG) rallies) and members share a deep 'sense of moral responsibility' and personal duty toward the brand (Muniz and O'Guinn, 2001). These groups tend to regard the brand as a 'shared cultural property' between the company and themselves (Cova and Pace, 2006: 1089) and play an active role in the development of the brand. The devotion of the consumer community to the brand can take on religious overtones (Belk and Tumbat, 2005), and in some cases the consumer community can take over the marketing of the brand from the parent company in what Muniz and Schau (2007) have referred to as 'vigilante marketing'.

Brand communities are also regarded as key agents in the creation of value. According to Merz et al. (2009: 330), 'brand value is co-created between the firm and its stakeholders … it is process-orientated and views stakeholders as endogenous to the brand value-creation process'. While a recent development in the branding literature, brand communities are seen to create value for companies through their social networking, community engagement, brand use and managing of impressions of the brand for other users (Schau et al., 2009). Community members often get so involved in the brand development that they work with the company to develop new products and volunteer their time and ideas, often for free, for brands such as Alfa Romeo (Skålén et al., 2015), although some have suggested that this could amount to an exploitation of the labour of unpaid consumer volunteers (Cova et al., 2015).

What we have witnessed within the consumer brand management literature has been a rise of the social collective and the impact of their knowledge, expertise and vision on the process of branding. But to what extent should companies try to manage this process and not cede control to consumer brand communities? Fournier and Lee (2009) have argued that brand communities defy managerial control and must be nurtured for the mutual benefit they can generate. Similarly, Cova and Pace (2006) have demonstrated the gains that companies can make if they work with their brand communities and do not try to impose draconian controls on their social interaction or organic creativity. It has been suggested that the key role for companies in the new era of consumer communities is one of facilitation in order to create various forums for value creation between the firm and its various stakeholders (Goulding et al., 2013). The challenge for forward-thinking organisations is to manage the process of multi-stakeholder value creation to an appropriate degree and involve communities in their brand development to achieve the best results for all interested parties. This is a skill set which is relatively new to brand management, although it will be increasingly vital in the age of the consumer–brand collective.

Practitioner's Perspective 6.1

Brands and anthropomorphism

When did you last ask an animal, vegetable, mineral or piece of plastic for its opinion on the state of the world?

Welcome to 21st century brand communications where everything – whether inanimate or an alternate species – is cultivating an online personality and is hungry to engage with an audience.

Survey social media and you'll find yoghurts with opinions about climate change, diarrhoea remedies with views on diversity, bookshops with a sharp line in dry wit, and cathedrals debating which of them is the best in Britain.

The principle of assigning human attributes to non-human objects is nothing new, of course. The stories we've told through history – from ancient myths to modern movies – have often assigned human quirks and qualities to other species, inanimate objects, and all manner of flora and fauna.

So too brands in the 20th century: from drum-beating battery bunnies demonstrating their endurance, to the jolly escapades of Ronald McDonald. But these models of brand identity were limited to their human attributes. They spoke. They acted. They embodied a limited set of values predetermined by the marketing minds behind the campaign.

This anthropomorphic tendency has accelerated in the early years of the 21st century. Brands now attempt to listen, converse with and discuss a broader range of social, cultural and even political issues than the limited parameters of their 20th century iterations. Back

(Continued)

(Continued)

then it was more closely aligned to brands' raison d'etre: buy more, buy now, love us enough to buy again!

Digital media – and particularly social channels – have given brands eyes and ears to see and hear praise and blame, and a voice to answer questions as well as broadcast messages. And with that broader range of senses comes a deeper expectation from consumers of a brand consciousness and conscience.

Marketers talk about the importance of 'authenticity' on digital and social channels – to sound more human than corporate. Inevitably, this leads them into uncomfortable territory. Human voices cover a spectrum of emotions from conviction on contentious issues, to ambivalence on complex questions, and everything in between.

Marketers are having to consider responses to what they don't want to talk about and what's far beyond the relevant field for their product or service.

And how do you scale authentic conversations when you're dealing with audiences in the thousands at least? One emerging answer is chatbots: more technology programmed to sound authentic.

The future looks ever more complex. For every brand that surprises, delights and entertains its audience with an authentic voice, there are others that will mis-speak, cause offence and risk alienating an audience.

The enduring worry for all marketers in the decades ahead is that the messages they really want people to see and hear – buy more, buy now, love us enough to buy again – get lost in a jumble of human-esque chatter.

So, what's the answer? I'm off to ask a yoghurt pot ...

(Paul Hill, award-winning content marketer, writer and journalist)

Questions

1. What is anthropomorphism and why do people apply this process to brands?
2. Why is storytelling so crucial to brand management and brand authenticity?
3. What impact is digital and social media technology likely to have on branding in the future?

BRANDS AND THE CULTURAL WORLD

Culture and business are often regarded as completely separate domains of the world we live in. Cultural products, such as music, art and fashion, are sometimes considered as having little relevance to mass-marketed consumer brands. Yet culture is an inherent part of marketing and branding and, without it, brands would have little meaning for consumers. McCracken's (1986) pioneering work explored how marketing meanings were essentially borrowed or imbued from culture, or 'culturally constituted', drawing meaning from culture to the consumer good and ultimately to the identity of the consumer (see Figure 6.1). Brands incorporate meaning from the cultural world and reconstitute it in the form of marketing communications and advertising (Goldman and Papson, 1998), and art, music, literature, film and celebrities, among others, are often drawn upon to create meaning for brands.

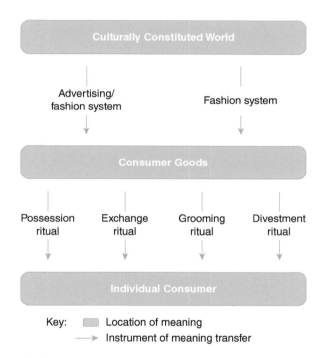

Figure 6.1   Movement of meaning model

Source: McCracken, G. (1986) Culture and consumption: A theoretical account of the structure and movement of the cultural meaning of consumer goods, *Journal of Consumer Research*, 13(1), 71-84, by permission of Oxford University Press.

The ideas of Douglas Holt are particularly compelling in this regard. Holt (2004) demonstrates how certain brands become iconic, by creating myths and stories that are borrowed from potent ideological currents within culture and society. Brands are essentially stories in themselves (Twitchell, 2004a), and Holt demonstrates that iconic brands are essentially a feat of impressive cultural engineering that create identity myths, borrowing their power from cultural products such as movies and music, or exploiting social ideologies or tensions that exist to create brands that are resonant and strong. Pepsi's® recent incorporation of the 'Black Lives Matter' movement in their advertising campaign was an interesting example of how social movements can be co-opted and social tensions mined by brands for commercial purposes. Holt and Cameron (2010) document how Nike® created an iconic brand by tapping into the wider social anxieties faced by Americans in the 1980s and 1990s and identified ideological opportunities to create a compelling story about the brand and enable American consumers to overcome the challenges they faced at the time through the brand. While much of the prevailing orthodoxy on branding suggests that brands become iconic through continuous innovation (or the 'better mousetraps strategy', to use Holt and Cameron's analogy), they argue that it is brands that champion superior ideologies in the marketplace (such as 'Just do it' for Nike®) that will ultimately become icons. This can be true for iconic brands such as Apple®, which sometimes produce products that can be seen as technically inferior to the competition yet still outsell their rivals many times over (Brown, 2016). Brand ideologies can be persuasive, personal, culturally rich and passed down through generations of consumers, as a study of the American Girl® brand has illustrated (Diamond et al., 2009), and other examples have shown that cultural branding is essential to the creation of iconic corporate brands, such as the Post Office® in the UK (Heller, 2016).

As well as considering the consumer response to brands, managers should also consider their cultural relevance and meaning in the ideological marketplace, so much so that McCracken (2009) has suggested that their jobs could be retitled as 'chief culture officers'. Marketing and advertising practitioners who identify cultural trends and create symbolic associations for brands are typically called 'cultural intermediaries' (Smith Maguire and Matthews, 2014), and these individuals have a key role to play in the process of symbolic meaning production and branding. As branding is a managerial as well as a cultural process, it is essential that students of branding are taught the subject from a dual perspective, however the evidence suggests that business schools in particular are sometimes less than enthusiastic about analysing marketing from a cultural perspective (Holt, 2004). This represents a missed opportunity for business students, who will benefit from understanding the cultural as well as managerial processes at play in branding.

Brands themselves often have a very prominent role within our culture, and sometimes to their own detriment they can be a lightning rod for consumer criticism. Books which are critical of brand and marketing culture such as *No Logo* (Klein, 2000) and *Fast Food Nation* (Schlosser, 2002) have often heightened consumer awareness of the darker side of brand culture. Brands themselves have been singled out for parody and attack online, Thompson et al. (2006: 50) have documented the phenomenon of the 'doppelganger' brand, which they define as 'a family of disparaging images and stories about a brand that are circulated in popular culture by a loosely organised network of consumers, anti-brand activists, bloggers and opinion leaders in the news and entertainment media'. These critical brand discourses, which may arguably be hyper-accelerated in the era of social media, can highlight brands whose ideologies may be fading, or when consumers are dissatisfied with the strategic direction or level of service provided by a brand.

The practice of branding is also something that is used well beyond the confines of the business world. Schroeder (2005, 2006) has documented how artists, who are sometimes regarded as separate to or elevated above the commercial world, manage their careers and work as brands and are highly commercially minded in their approach to their work. Books are often marketed with a high level of proficiency and create a lot of hype around the brand, which can be seen with the success of the Harry Potter® books and accompanying films, plays and merchandise (Brown, 2005). Films rely heavily on marketing and are managed as brands, and O'Reilly and Kerrigan (2013) have explored how films incorporate cultural branding techniques to maintain popularity and build a legacy around a film franchise. Celebrities create a culture of their own and are often managed as brands that create followings that many consumer brands can only dream of (Hewer and Hamilton, 2012). Branding can often be used to market historical events that are significant, such as the sinking of the RMS Titanic; Brown et al. (2013) have highlighted the potent myths and stories that are associated with the ship and the merchandise, museums and cultural texts that have followed from the tragedy. Social institutions such as monarchies and religions often employ branding principles to market to their audiences and generate meaning for the brand (Otnes and Maclaran, 2015; Twitchell, 2004b). What much of this research demonstrates is that culture and branding have a symbiotic and intertwined relationship (Tharp and Scott, 1990), in that culture undoubtedly influences brands, but brands and branding have a prominent role to play within culture, also. The expansions of branding research into areas such as art, music, film, literature and celebrity culture are important for business students, as they highlight how branding theory is relevant in different domains and also what business can learn from the creativity of other, related industries (Brown, 2003).

BRAND ARCHITECTURE, CORPORATE BRANDING AND THE EMPLOYER BRAND

The calibration of brands within organisations and the ways in which they are presented to external stakeholders is also an area of vibrant interest within the branding literature. From this perspective, the concept of 'brand architecture' has been introduced, which considers how managers build brands from symbolic and physical infrastructure in a similar way to how an architect would construct a building. Aaker and Joachimstkaler (2000) outline the 'brand relationship spectrum', which highlights the different structure of brand formations within an organisation. Some companies such as Unilever® are what's known as a 'house of brands', as in they operate a number of distinct consumer brands under their stewardship; examples of the brands managed by Unilever include Ben & Jerry's®, Bovril®, Hellman's Mayonnaise®, Lipton® and Marmite®. All these brands operate independently and have separate identities but fall under the Unilever portfolio of managed brands; they all carry the Unilever brand on their packaging but it doesn't feature as prominently as the individual brand name. A 'branded house', on the other hand, has a master brand as the dominant brand name across multiple product offerings or categories, such as Virgin®, and all of the brands marketed by the firm carry the Virgin brand as the primary brand, such as Virgin Media®, Virgin Atlantic® and Virgin Trains®. Companies can have sub-brands that are connected to a master brand in some way, such as Apple TV® or Apple iPhone®, which have to be managed independently from the parent brand. Also, organisations can have brands that they explicitly endorse and are associated with, like Levis Dockers® pants or Polo Jeans® by Ralph Lauren. The key challenge for the brand architect is to consider the portfolio of brands that a company offers and decide how best to organise this, particularly in the vastly competitive world of consumer goods marketing. Uggla (2006) has illustrated the 'brand association base' that brands can use in developing their architecture, which incorporates institutional, partner and corporate brand associations. This research demonstrates that managing brands in the marketplace requires knowledge of semiotic meaning systems within culture and an appreciation of how these can be utilised within a brand's architectural management process.

The process of corporate branding and of how organisations manage their brand identities in the marketplace internally and externally is crucial to their perception. According to Hatch and Schultz (2003), corporate branding is a process that builds relationships with a range of the company's key stakeholders and incorporates the organisational culture, strategic vision and corporate image (see Figure 6.2). The authors' analysis of the British Airways® brand demonstrates that corporate branding is a highly strategic process that requires the integrated effort of the multiple organisational functions and the support of top management. Corporate branding involves organisations aligning their brand identity with their corporate strategy and developing a coherent and coordinated approach which is understood by organisational actors and implemented in a way that engages multiple stakeholders (Balmer et al., 2009; Schultz and Kitchen, 2004). The purpose of managing the corporate brand is to transmit the key values and ideologies of the brand and to develop a strong identity and positioning for the brand. This involves the nurturing of key stakeholder relationships and the management of corporate communications to create a unique corporate identity for the organisation (Balmer, 2017). The development of brand identity can sometimes be conceptualised as a process that is unidirectional and does not involve stakeholder input (Heding et al., 2016), however recent perspectives acknowledge the role of multiple actors in the creation of the corporate brand. Hatch and Schultz (2010) introduce the concept of the 'enterprise brand' that is an amalgam of multiple stakeholder interests, therefore companies should consider brand identity not merely as internally developed and managed but as also socially constructed, co-created and negotiated between the organisation and its various stakeholders. This requires a broader perspective on the management of the brand and frameworks that consider the strategic role of internal and external discursive forces in the creation of the brand (Schultz and Hatch, 2003). To strategically manage corporate brands, senior managers must be good custodians of the brand and give that brand credibility through their actions by managing its covenant (or promise) in the market (Balmer, 2012).

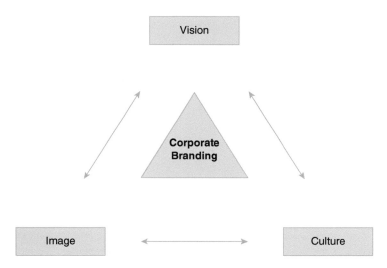

Figure 6.2   Corporate branding

Source: Hatch, M.J. and Schultz, M. (2003) Bringing the corporation into branding. *European Journal of Marketing*, 37(7/8), 1041–64.

While marketing has placed a strong emphasis on consumers as stakeholders in the brand, the role of employees of the company must also not be underestimated in the creation of the corporate brand. Employees are sometimes regarded as 'living the brand' (Maxwell and Knox, 2009) and build a strong sense of identification and belonging with the company. Technology and social media companies such as Google®, Apple® and Facebook® are known for having corporate cultures where employees have a strong affinity with the company, and the organisations themselves have very idiosyncratic workplaces with bean bags for relaxing, comfortable desks and chairs, games rooms and workplaces which are called 'campuses' to create employee identification and foster employee creativity and personal development. Factors such as organisational success, employment conditions, the external image of the organisation and its products and services are seen to positively contribute toward the employer brand

and its attractiveness to employees (Maxwell and Knox, 2009). Similarly, the work content and work culture of a company are regarded as key factors for employees choosing to work for particular brands (Rampl, 2014). The employees of a firm are extremely important as they are the key agents to drive innovation within the company and are also often the external face of the organisation in their interactions with consumers. Companies with incoherent brand identities or poor corporate cultures are unlikely to create an employer brand that their employees will identify with or be productive for, so employees are a crucial stakeholder group that the brand must consider in their strategy. The management of the brand architecture and the corporate brand are vital within this process and the forward-thinking organisation must consider multiple stakeholders, how to incorporate their concerns and market with them (rather than to them) in the era of the co-created brand (Payne et al., 2008). Brand managers and their associated teams have a very large task in managing the architecture and corporate brand and creating a coherent and profitable brand identity for the organisation.

Ethical Focus 6.1

'Dieselgate': The Volkswagen® emissions scandal

Volkswagen is an iconic German car brand with a rich history and millions of consumers worldwide, however the company was rocked in 2015 by the 'Dieselgate' scandal which had a significant impact on its corporate reputation and brand image. The company admitted to rigging 11 million emissions tests for nitrogen oxide on diesel vehicles sold around the world. Volkswagen's then chairman Martin Winterkorn resigned days after the story broke and it is estimated it has cost the company in excess of $30 billion in terms of fines and buying back vehicles from angry customers who felt betrayed by its actions. The company's brand image and international reputation were damaged significantly by the scandal with a 24% fall in its share price after the news broke, and there was a backlash in Germany from consumers who felt the behaviour of the company damaged the global standing of the German nation. Martin Winterkorn was indicted on criminal charges arising from the scandal in the USA in May 2018. While many in the industry were critical of the company's handling of and initial response to the crisis (which has led to three changes of chairman since 2015), the share price and profits have since recovered to pre-crisis levels and consumer confidence in the brand is slowly returning. 'Dieselgate' was nonetheless a landmark event for Volkswagen and one that could have been catastrophic for a brand reputation which had been carefully crafted over many decades. Its passing has heralded a change in organisational culture within the Volkswagen company and demonstrates the importance of ethical corporate governance and management accountability for a corporate brand.

Sources

Anonymous (2015) Fuel on the fire. *The Economist*, 7 November. Available at: www.economist.com/business/2015/11/07/fuel-on-the-fire (accessed 4 April 2019).

Anonymous (2016) A long road to recovery. *The Economist*, 10 November. Available at: www.economist.com/business/2016/11/10/a-long-road-to-recovery (accessed 4 April 2019).

Anonymous (2018) The departure of the VW boss heralds a big shake-up. *The Economist*, 12 April. Available at: www.economist.com/business/2018/04/12/the-departure-of-the-vw-boss-heralds-a-big-shake-up (accessed 4 April 2019).

Ewing, J. (2018) BMW offices raided by authorities in emissions-cheating investigation. *New York Times*, 20 March. Available at: www.nytimes.com/2018/03/20/business/energy-environment/bmw-diesel-emissions.html (accessed 23 May 2018).

Questions for discussion

1. Why was 'Dieselgate' such a large global media story?
2. How has the Volkswagen brand been able to recover so quickly from the 'Dieselgate' scandal?
3. What should Volkswagen do to ensure a scandal like this never happens again?

BRANDS AND LUXURY: THE NICHE CONTEXT

Luxury brands represent a completely different challenge within the context of brand management. While mainstream marketing theories tend to be based on fast moving consumer goods contexts (Brown, 2005), luxury brands tend to require a very different approach. As Kapferer and Bastien (2013: 65) note, 'not only are traditional marketing techniques not suited to luxury, they can in fact be positively harmful to it'. Because luxury brands serve a very unique and niche customer clientele, the marketing approach used by luxury brands needs to be specialist and focused. Luxury brands always have an associated high price (Kapferer and Laurent, 2016), as well as exclusivity, prestige and social status. Luxury brands are based on a strong history and tradition and many luxury brands tend to be European in origin, with companies that have a long heritage in the businesses in which they operate, examples including Ferrari®, Burberry®, Chanel®, Prada® and Hermes®. This is not to suggest that only brands that are European in origin can be considered luxury, but as a continent with a rich history and tradition (something which is essential for a luxury brand), it is fair to surmise that many of the world's most recognisable luxury brands tend to be from Europe (Kapferer and Bastien, 2013). According to Berthon et al. (2009), luxury brands have three specific value dimensions: the experiential value (which concerns what the brand means to the consumer), the symbolic value (what the brand means to others) and the functional value (what physical attributes the brand possesses). Luxury brands adopt a bespoke marketing approach in terms of the product (with a strong emphasis on craft and tradition), communications (aesthetic and stylish), retail (an upmarket and decadent retail space) and segmentation (focusing on consumers who are wealthy individuals). What constitutes a 'luxury' brand can sometimes be a contested space – brands which are prestigious but marketed to a mass audience are known as 'masstige' brands (a portmanteau of 'mass' and 'prestige'), with examples including Coach®, Polo Ralph Lauren® and Calvin Klein®, which offer consumers a more accessible form of luxury (Truong et al., 2009). It is brands that are highly priced and positioned for wealthy individuals for which the term 'luxury' tends to be reserved.

As luxury brands are known for their heritage and tradition, telling the story of that tradition becomes crucial in marketing communications. The 'identity myths' created for the brands draw on their past and create a compelling narrative for the brand (Holt, 2003). Luxury brands are fortunate in that most have a long history to select from and can create a superior sense of cultural authenticity (Beverland, 2009). Luxury brand advertisements are often quite aesthetic in nature and embed signifiers of prestige and high class into their textual structure. Some brands make use of devices such as white space to signify prestige and luxury in their marketing messages (Olsen et al., 2012). Brands have to channel luxury brand ideologies in their advertisements and there are certain cultural codes that are used for this purpose, particularly in terms of aesthetics and style (Holt and Cameron, 2010). Brand storytelling is crucial to build consumer and community interest in the brand (Brown et al., 2003), and for luxury brands the telling of heritage stories via their marketing is essential.

For consumers, luxury brands have an important function. Veblen (1899) first introduced the idea of 'conspicuous consumption' to highlight the ostentatious and wasteful consumption of the upper classes and the role goods play in signifying social status. Consumption and class have been found to be correlated with cultural capital (or cultural knowledge) which is key to understanding what products to buy and what they imply about the consumer (Holt, 1998). Consumers often use luxury brands to signal class, although some evidence suggests that some speak softly and use quiet signals in their consumption (Han et al., 2010). Recent research by Dion and Borraz (2017: 68) has argued that 'the brand is not only a status marker ... it also makes consumers enact a position in the social hierarchy', and brands function to provide social differentiation and distinction for the consumer. Luxury brands are essentially co-created with their audiences and the consumer has a very clear expectation of the value a luxury brand should deliver in terms of intrinsic and extrinsic benefits (Tynan et al., 2010). The experiential aspects of luxury brands in terms of consumer interaction and engagement become very important as they enable consumers to develop touchpoints with the brand (Atwal and Williams, 2009).

Luxury brand retailing is an essential aspect of creating the luxury brand (Chevalier and Mazzalovo, 2012), despite the well-documented decline in high street retailing, particularly in the UK. For some luxury brands, digital marketing and social media can be considered 'down-market' and too democratised for a true luxury brand (Kapferer and Bastien, 2013); as a result, authentic brand experiences in retail spaces become ever more important. Retail brand experiences are profoundly rich and interesting and highlight the epic and spectacular nature of consumption within a shopping centre environment (Brown et al., 2018; Peneloza, 1998). For luxury brands, setting the correct tone in terms of retail experience is a vitally important component of the marketing approach they take. Luxury brands tend to adopt highly aesthetic shop interiors that are beautiful and elegant and have an aura of reverence for the brand, its owners and its heritage (Dion and Arnould, 2011; Joy et al., 2014). The store becomes a key tool for marketing communications and a co-creative space where consumers can experientially engage with the luxury brand and its representatives. Some writers have suggested that luxury brand stores should be exclusionary and go so far as to suggest that retail managers should 'manage exclusion by playing on the social anxiety that people at the bottom of the social hierarchy experience in upper-class locations' (Dion and Borraz, 2017: 81). While the tactic itself may appear discriminatory to some, from a market segmentation standpoint it does make sense for luxury brands to appeal to the most appropriate type of consumer in order for the brand to retain exclusivity. An example of how this can be important was evidenced when lower socio-economic class consumers in the UK, sometimes colloquially referred to as 'chavs', adopted the Burberry® check as a signifier of their social status and created the wrong image for the brand. However, the brand, through its design and innovation, has since managed to distance itself from this image. Meaning matters, particularly for luxury brands, and the management of brand associations, experiences and consumers is extremely important in retaining the magic of a luxury brand in the marketplace.

BRANDS AND SOCIAL MEDIA

Social media has had a profound impact on the ways in which we live, work, communicate and engage with one another. Platforms such as Facebook have over 2 billion users worldwide and President Donald Trump has used Twitter® very effectively (if not to everyone's individual taste) to mould and shape US foreign, economic and domestic policy. Social media provides a platform for consumers of a brand to gather and meet electronically as well as for creating 'user-generated content', which is content that is developed by consumers which can be used by the brand for commercial purposes. Brand communities meet virtually as well as physically, and Brodie et al. (2013) have highlighted how consumer engagement is created online through processes of sharing, co-developing, socialising, advocating and learning. Social media can create a different context in which brand engagement can take place, and it represents a new form of co-creative dialogue between organisations and their customers. Arvidsson and Caliandro (2016: 727) have introduced the concept of a 'brand public', which they define as 'an organised media space kept together by a continuity of practices of mediation'. These differ from brand communities as they are sustained by mediation and the brand is not the focal point, participation is structured in terms of the consumer desire to share experiences or viewpoints, and there is no coherent collective identity articulated around a focal brand. The 'brand public' concept is an interesting one, as social media has provided the forum in which brand interactions can take place and the conversation can be very broad and disparate, not only taking place between loyalists in a brand community, so in the social media age brand publics may be a useful way of thinking about collective consumer-brand engagements in the digital world.

Social media is an important tool for business and for consumers, but it is a relatively young medium (Facebook® was only founded in 2004) and, as such, marketers are still very much understanding how it works and how it can be effectively used for branding. From a consumer perspective, websites and social media channels can be used for the purposes of self-presentation and highlighting personal connections with particular brands (Schau and Gilly, 2003). Blogging is a key consumer practice, where people write about products, services and experiences and share them online for the benefit of other users on a weblog (hence the name 'blogging'). UK bloggers such as Zoella® have created enormous brands for themselves using social media and have amassed millions of followers in discussing the products and services they use, experience or endorse. Blogging is a key way of generating electronic word-of-mouth among consumer communities and co-creating brand meanings online (Kozinets et al., 2010). Bloggers themselves often provide authenticity for products through their use and endorsement of them online (Gannon and Prothero, 2016), which is a new form of product digital demonstration for consumers. Platforms such as Facebook®, Twitter® and Instagram® are absolutely vital in facilitating these sorts of conversations between consumers and generating a buzz around particular brands. Pentina et al. (2018) have outlined how consumer online engagement behaviours can create value for luxury brands and it has been suggested that social media communications can influence brand equity and ultimately consumer purchase intentions (Schivinski and Dabrowski, 2016).

Digital Focus 6.1

General Data Protection Regulation (GDPR), Facebook and permission marketing

Since 25 May 2018, companies have had to comply with General Data Protection Regulation (GDPR) which was passed and implemented by the European Union. The purpose of this is for firms to manage customer data more securely and comply with strict data protection regulations – companies must now appoint 'data protection officers' and customers must give explicit consent for their information to be used. GDPR regulations also apply to companies outside of the EU that engage with EU customers, and the introduction of the legislation comes in the wake of the Facebook® and Cambridge Analytica® scandal where the data of 50 million people was harvested and used for purposes that they had not explicitly consented to. The use of online social media data can be extremely influential not only for marketing purposes but also in areas such as politics where targeted advertising messages can be sent to undecided voters. Seen to be crucial to the 2016 US presidential election of Donald Trump was a political marketing campaign which was devised by Cambridge Analytica and based largely on Facebook customer data. Since the activities of Facebook and Cambridge have come to light, individual citizens have become much more aware of how their data can be used by companies, and online data from Google has suggested that searches for privacy were at a 12-year high in 2018. GDPR was created to ensure companies manage consumer data securely and ethically, and essentially provides a legal framework for the concept of 'permission marketing' introduced by Seth Godin (1999), where marketers must have explicit permission from customers to market to them and manage their data responsibly. Companies that do not comply with GDPR face the prospect of large fines, and this is likely to revolutionise how brands engage with customers and use their data in the digital realm in future.

Sources

Anonymous (2018a) The Facebook scandal could change politics as well as the internet. *The Economist*, 22 March.

Anonymous (2018b) Britain moves to rein in data analytics. *The Economist*, 28 March.

Anonymous (2018c) Europe's tough new data protection law. *The Economist*, 5 April.

Anonymous (2018d) Why is Mark Zuckerberg testifying in congress? *The Economist*, 9 April.

Anonymous (2018e) As GDPR nears, Google searches for privacy are at a 12-year high. *The Economist*, 21 May.

(Continued)

(Continued)

Anonymous (2018f) Europe's tough new data-protection law. *The Economist*, 5 April.

Godin, S. (1999) *Permission Marketing: Turning Strangers into Friends, and Friends into Customers.* London: Free Press.

Questions for discussion

1. Why do you think GDPR regulations were introduced?
2. Facebook was involved in a scandal which uncovered how the data of millions of users was utilised by third parties without explicit consent being provided. What impact do you feel this incident had on the Facebook brand?
3. What impact do you feel GDPR will have on brands that have customers within the European Union?

There can however be an unquestioning assumption that social media is good for brands and can be used effectively for marketing purposes. Fournier and Avery (2011: 193) have cautioned that although social media has been enormously successful in empowering consumer communities, brands are essentially 'uninvited crashers of the web 2.0 party' and are not creating the sort of consumer-brand engagement on social media many are led to believe exists. In a series of highly engaging and entertaining videos on YouTube®, Ritson (2015) has argued that social media is 'social' in that it is created for people, not brands, and is largely a space where brands are not welcomed. To evidence his argument, he highlights how many top consumer brands have pitifully small numbers of consumers who actively follow and engage with their brands online, and he suggests that social media is a much more minor tool of integrated brand communications than many marketers may have been led to believe. Holt (2016: 50) suggests that traditional cultural branding and storytelling are vital using social media and advises brands to harness the power of online 'crowd cultures' to co-create meaning for the brand. It is true that social media has been revolutionary and has changed the way society interacts and communicates, however textbooks in the area of social media marketing have only recently been developed (Dahl, 2018; Tuten and Solomon, 2015), and it remains an area where research knowledge and the ways to foster consumer insight and input are very much in their infancy. Social media and digital technology are the future of branding in terms of development and co-creation with communities in the digital era, and the challenge for brand managers is knowing how to harness and utilise this technology effectively for the benefit of all organisational stakeholders.

CONCLUSION

This chapter has presented a selective review of some key themes of branding research and outlined the development of this research into two key concerns – traditional brand management research and brand culture research. There are some important take-outs that we must consider from this review of the scholarship in the area. First, it is clear that consumers are no longer end users of products (if they ever were), and are conceptualised as active, co-creative agents within the process of branding. Collective communities around brands have become increasingly important, and companies are employing community managers for the explicit purpose of managing engagement with these consumer groups, although the extent to which managers have the requisite skills for this role and even whether consumer communities are capable of being effectively managed are debatable points. Second, brands are very much cultural creations that draw from culture for much of their meaning and the role of traditional storytelling for branding is still crucial – this is an area that business schools should devote much more of their time to developing among students. Third, firms must consider how brands are managed at a corporate level and the ways in which brand architecture is organised and developed both internally and externally. Fourth, luxury brands present a completely new challenge for brand managers as many traditional theories of marketing are not appropriate for managing specialist brands, and new frameworks of knowledge and understanding for managing brands in niche, entertainment or cultural industries will be vital to equip the brand managers of the future in these areas. Finally, social media and digital technology are tools that can be used for building brand engagement, but it's important to put them into context – they represent one tool of many that brands can use for developing an interactive engagement with consumers and communities, and should be viewed in terms of their role within an integrated branding strategy.

Brands are part of our social milieu and their role and impact are fascinating to observe; they are arguably some of the most prominent symbols of a capitalist society and can generate ambivalent feelings among different social groups. This chapter has highlighted how brands have enormous cultural value and are as important as the music, films and literature which they often draw upon for inspiration – they are 'citizen artists' (Holt, 2002) that contribute to our culture in their own right. Our level of interaction and engagement with them is both rich and multi-layered and managing brands in the marketplace is an extremely challenging task for any organisation. It is hoped that this chapter has provided the reader with a useful overview of the landmark scholarship in the field and highlighted how brand management theory is likely to develop in the future.

Case Study 6.1

Supreme® – Selling scarcity

Supreme is a skateboarding shop and brand that was started in New York in 1994 by founder James Jebbia. The brand was initially a specialist company for the skateboarding community, selling skating equipment, clothing and accessories. The store has a number of locations now, including New York, Los Angeles, London, Tokyo and Osaka; in fact, the largest number of Supreme stores is in Japan. The company had its roots within skateboarding culture and was seen as a very authentic and creative brand with a subversive, irreverent attitude to business. The company was regarded as being somewhat 'cocky', with the logo of the company inspired heavily by the work of Barbara Kruger (indeed, some have suggested it is plagiarised), and it even appropriated the branding of Louis Vuitton® at one stage for which it received a 'cease and desist' order from the company. Since its early days as a brand for the skater market, the company has grown enormously in popularity and has recently been valued at $1 billion, with 50% of the company's equity purchased by the Carlyle Group in 2017. So, what is at the heart of Supreme's popularity and how has it managed to capture the imagination of so many, primarily younger, customers?

Supreme clothes are exclusive, very hard to obtain and are released in limited edition batches. The Supreme brand is part of the fashion trend of 'streetwear', which is fashionable urban clothing, and the brand has developed a cult status among its followers. Every Thursday morning, the company has a 'Supreme drop', where new, limited-edition items are released to the public via its website and stores. Customers will queue for days for a chance to buy the latest Supreme items of clothing and the website experiences up to 1700% more traffic on 'drop' days compared to its regular trading days. The clothes typically sell out in seconds online and some consumers of the brand will hire people to queue outside the Supreme store in anticipation of the next Thursday 'drop'. This is part of what is known as the 'hype-beast' scene where customers will seek out hyped streetwear that is released in a particular week. Supreme-branded clothing has a high value in secondary markets such as eBay®, where items fetch many multiples of their original sale price, for example a North Face® nupse jacket which originally retailed at $368 was later resold on eBay® for $4,500. The company releases many limited-edition prints, such as T-shirts bearing the images of Morrissey (which he objected to), Mike Tyson and Michael Jackson, as well as more unusual items such as a Supreme-branded brick and crowbar.

As the brand has grown in popularity, so has its reach in terms of collaboration and celebrity approval. The company has collaborated with a number of major consumer brands including Nike®, Levis®, North Face® and Stone Island® and has also released artwork from Jeff Koons, Damien Hirst and David Lynch, among many others. The brand has even collaborated with its former arch-nemesis, Louis Vuitton®, to create a co-branded range of fashionable luxury clothes. Supreme is also beloved in the celebrity world, and famous people such as Victoria Beckham, Justin Bieber, Kate Moss and Lady Gaga have all been photographed wearing the clothes.

What is particularly interesting about the Supreme brand is its unorthodox approach to marketing. It does not rely on traditional advertising to create an interest in the brand and nothing is done according to tried-and-tested marketing principles. Marketing theory advises businesses to make the customer central to the business, to ensure that products are available and that customers are satisfied, and to communicate value to them via marketing communications. However, Supreme-branded products are positively difficult to obtain, and the company does not tend to rely on marketing research or communications tools to develop interest in its brand. As James Jebbia himself has commented, 'We kind of have a formula, we've got it made. Our formula is there's no formula'. They are a good example of what Stephen Brown (2001) has referred to as TEASE marketing, using elements of tricksterism, entertainment, amplification, secrecy and exclusivity to create hype around the brand. While this approach will not work for every brand and is rather specific to the product category, it has been extremely successful for the Supreme brand and appeals to the consumer tribes that adopt numerous streetwear brands into their cultural repertoires.

While the brand has sold some of its equity, collaborates with major brands and continues to expand globally, for the moment at least its authenticity shows little sign of waning. The founder retains the original punk ethos of the company and its original skateboard followers do not appear to have deserted the brand. Supreme 'drop days' each Thursday are as busy as ever and the allure of the brand continues to grow internationally. A key challenge for the brand in the future is the extent to which it can grow globally and gain a new following yet retain the brand essence which initially brought it to prominence within the skateboarding community.

Sources

Brown, S. (2001) Torment your customers (they'll love it). *Harvard Business Review*, 99(9), 82–8.

Clifton, J. (2016) Why are so many people so obsessed with Supreme? *Vice*, 19 June. Available at: www.vice.com/en_uk/article/5gq393/supreme-and-the-psychology-of-brand-devotion (accessed 23 May 2018).

Cochrane, L. (2017) How streetwear restyled the world – from hip-hop to Supreme and Palace. *The Guardian*, 29 March. Available at: www.theguardian.com/fashion/2017/mar/29/how-streetwear-styled-the-world-from-hip-hop-to-supreme-and-palace (accessed 23 May 2018).

Corbijn, A. (2017) Charting the rise of Supreme, from cult skate shop to fashion superpower. *Vogue*, 10 August. Available at: www.vogue.com/article/history-of-supreme-skate-clothing-brand (accessed 23 May 2018).

(Continued)

(Continued)

Den Broeke, T. V. (2018) What fashionable people actually think of Supreme. *GQ Magazine*, 27 April. Available at: www.gq-magazine.co.uk/article/what-fashion-people-think-of-supreme (accessed 23 May 2018).

Marriott, H. (2017) Two for one: Louis Vuitton presents collaboration with skater label Supreme. *The Guardian*, 19 January. Available at: www.theguardian.com/fashion/2017/jan/19/louis-vuitton-presents-collaboration-with-skater-label-supreme (accessed 23 May 2018).

Trotman, A. (2018) The power of brand: Supreme. *Designdough*, 26 April. Available at: https://designdough.co.uk/the-power-of-brand-supreme (accessed 23 May 2018).

Wolf, C. (2017) Supreme is now a billion-dollar streetwear brand. *GQ Magazine*, 9 October. Available at: www.gq.com/story/supreme-billion-dollar-valuation (accessed 23 May 2018).

Questions for discussion

1. Why is the Supreme brand so popular among consumers of streetwear fashion?
2. The brand famously does not rely on traditional marketing communications. How has its message been transmitted to the public?
3. What is the purpose of 'Supreme drop' days and should the company continue to hold these?
4. How would you advise Supreme on retaining its brand authenticity while simultaneously growing in popularity globally?

SUMMARY OF KEY IDEAS

- Branding scholarship can be defined in terms of two research streams – brand management and brand culture perspectives.
- Consumers are co-creators of value in the branding process and have deep relationships with brands; they also develop relationships with others as part of communities through their mutual admiration of particular brands.
- Brands are inherently cultural creations, which draw influence from culture yet contribute to culture in a bidirectional transfer of meaning.
- Companies must consider how to manage their brand architecture and create employee identification around the core values of the brand.
- Luxury brands represent a niche context and must be managed according to markedly different principles to fast-moving consumer goods.
- Social media is a tool that has changed society and communications but its use for brand building and consumer engagement is still very much in its infancy.

Chapter Discussion Questions

1. What are the differences between the 'brand management' and 'brand culture' approaches to branding and what value does each approach add?
2. What role do consumers play in the branding process and how should organisations harness the power of brand communities?
3. Why is culture important for branding and how might business students study culture for the benefit of learning about brands?
4. Why is corporate branding important and how can organisations organise internally to create effective corporate branding strategies?
5. How are luxury brands different from non-luxury brands and how should they be marketed?

REFERENCES

Aaker, D. A. and Joachimsthaler, E. (2000) The brand relationship spectrum: The key to the brand architecture challenge. *California Management Review*, 42(4), 8–23.

Aaker, J. L. (1997) Dimensions of brand personality. *Journal of Marketing Research*, 34(3), 347–56.

Arvidsson, A. and Caliandro, A. (2016) Brand public. *Journal of Consumer Research*, 42(5), 727–48.

Atwal, G. and Williams, A. (2009) Luxury brand marketing – The experience is everything! *Brand Management*, 16(5/6), 338–46.

Balmer, J. M. T. (2012) Corporate brand management imperatives: Custodianship, credibility and calibration. *California Management Review*, 54(3), 6–33.

Balmer, J. M. T. (2017) The corporate identity, total corporate communications, stakeholders' attributed identities, identifications and behaviours continuum. *European Journal of Marketing*, 51(9/10), 1472–1502.

Balmer, J. M. T., Stuart, H. and Greyser, S. A. (2009) Aligning identity and strategy: Corporate branding at British Airways in the late 20th century. *California Management Review*, 51(3), 6–23.

Belk, R. W. (1988) Possessions and the extended self. *Journal of Consumer Research*, 15(2), 139–68.

Belk, R. W. and Tumbat, G. (2005) The cult of Macintosh. *Consumption, Markets & Culture*, 8(5), 205–17.

Berthon, P., Pitt, L. Parent, M. and Berthon, J. P. (2009) Aesthetics and ephemerality: Observing and preserving the luxury brand. *California Management Review*, 52(1), 45–66.

Beverland, M. (2009) *Building Brand Authenticity: 7 Habits of Iconic Brands*. Basingstoke: Palgrave Macmillan.

Beverland, M. (2018) *Brand Management: Co-creating Meaningful Brands*. London: Sage.

Brodie, R. J., Llic, A., Juric, B. and Hollebeek, L. (2013) Consumer engagement in a virtual brand community: An exploratory analysis. *Journal of Business Research* 66(1), 105–14.

Brown, G. (1992) *People, brands and advertising*. Warwick, UK, Millward Brown International.

Brown, S. (2003) *Free Gift Inside*. Chichester: Capstone.

Brown, S. (2005) *Wizard! Harry Potter's Brand Magic*. London: Cyan Books.

Brown, S. (2016) *Brands and Branding*. London: Sage.

Brown, S., McDonagh, P. and Shultz II, C. J. (2013) Titanic: Consuming the myths of an ambiguous brand. *Journal of Consumer Research*, 40(4), 595–614.

Brown, S., Sherry, J. F. J. and Kozinets, R. V. (2003) Teaching old brands new tricks: Retro branding and the revival of brand meaning. *Journal of Marketing*, 67(3), 19–33.

Brown, S., Stevens, L. and Maclaran, P. (2018) Epic aspects of retail encounters: The Iliad of Hollister. *Journal of Retailing*, 94(1), 58–72.

Chevalier, M. and Mazzalovo, G. (2012) *Luxury Brand Management*, 2nd edn. Singapore: John Wiley & Sons.

Cova, B. and Pace, S. (2006) Brand community of convenience products: New forms of customer empowerment – the case of 'My Nutella The Community'. *European Journal of Marketing*, 40(9/10), 1087–105.

Cova, B., Pace, S. and Skålén, P. (2015) Brand volunteering: Value co-creation with unpaid customers. *Marketing Theory*, 15(4), 465–85.

Dahl, S. (2018) *Social Media Marketing: Theories and Applications*, 2nd edn. London: Sage.

De Chernatony, L. (2009) Towards the holy grail of defining 'brand'. *Marketing Theory*, 9(1), 101–5.

De Chernatony, L. and Dall'Olmo Riley, F. (1998) Defining a 'brand': Beyond the literature with experts' interpretations. *Journal of Marketing Management*, 14(4–5), 417–43.

De Chernatony, L., McDonald, M. and Wallace, E. (2011) *Creating Powerful Brands*, 4th edn. Oxford: Elsevier.

Diamond, N., Sherry Jr., J. F., Muniz, A. M., McGrath, M. A., Kozinets, R. V. and Borghini, S. (2009) American Girl and the brand gestalt: Closing the loop on sociocultural branding research. *Journal of Marketing*, 73(3), 118–34.

Dion, D. and Arnould, E. (2011) Retail luxury strategy: Assembling charisma through art and magic. *Journal of Retailing*, 87(4), 502–20.

Dion, D. and Borraz, S. (2017) Managing status: How luxury brands shape class subjectivities in the service encounter. *Journal of Marketing*, 81(5), 67–85.

Elliott, R. and Leonard, C. (2004) Peer pressure and poverty: Exploring fashion brands and consumption symbolism among children of the 'British poor'. *Journal of Consumer Behaviour*, 3(4), 347–59.

Elliott, R. and Wattanasuwan, K. (1998) Brands as symbolic resources for the construction of identity. *International Journal of Advertising*, 17(2), 131–44.

Fanning, J. (2006) *The Importance of Being Branded*. Dublin: The Liffey Press.

Fournier, S. (1998) Consumers and their brands: Developing relationship theory in consumer research. *Journal of Consumer Research*, 24(4), 343–73.

Fournier, S. and Avery, J. (2011) The uninvited brand. *Business Horizons*, 54(3), 193–207.

Fournier, S. and Lee, L. (2009) Getting brand communities right. *Harvard Business Review*, 87(4), 105–11.

Gannon, V. and Prothero, A. (2016) Beauty blogger selfies as authenticating practices. *European Journal of Marketing*, 50(9/10), 1858–78.

Gardner, B. B. and Levy, S. (1955) The product and the brand. *Harvard Business Review*, 33(2), 33–9.

Goldman, R. and Papson, S. (1998) *Nike Culture: The Sign of the Swoosh*. London: Sage.

Goulding, C., Shankar, A. and Canniford, R. (2013) Learning to be tribal: Facilitating the formation of consumer tribes. *European Journal of Marketing*, 47(5/6), 813–32.

Han, Y.J., Nunes, J.C. and Drèze X. (2010) Signalling status with luxury goods: The role of brand prominence. *Journal of Marketing*, 74(4), 15–30.

Hatch, M. J. and Schultz, M. (2003) Bringing the corporation into branding. *European Journal of Marketing*, 37(7/8), 1041–64.

Hatch, M. J. and Schultz, M. (2010) Toward a theory of brand co-creation with implications for brand governance. *Journal of Brand Management*, 17(8), 590–604.

Heding, T., Knudtzen, C. F. and Bjerre, M. (2016) *Brand Management: Research, Theory and Practice*, 2nd edn. London: Routledge.

Heller, M. (2016) 'Outposts of Britain': The general post office and the birth of a corporate iconic brand, 1930–1939. *European Journal of Marketing*, 50(3/4), 358–76.

Hewer, P. and Hamilton, K. (2012) Exhibitions and the role of fashion in the sustenance of the Kylie brand mythology: Unpacking the spatial logic of celebrity culture. *Marketing Theory*, 12(4), 411–25.

Holt, D. B. (1998) Does cultural capital structure American consumption? *Journal of Consumer Research*, 25(1), 1–25.

Holt, D. B. (2002) Why do brands cause trouble? A dialectical theory of consumer culture and branding. *Journal of Consumer Research*, 29(1), 70–90.

Holt, D. B. (2003) What becomes an icon most? *Harvard Business Review*, 81(3), 43–9.

Holt, D. B. (2004) *How Brands become Icons: The Principles of Cultural Branding*. Boston, MA: Harvard Business School Publishing Corporation.

Holt, D. B. (2016) Branding in the social media age. *Harvard Business Review*, 94(3), 40–50.

Holt, D. B. and Cameron, D. (2010) *Cultural Strategy: Using Innovative Ideologies to Build Breakthrough Brands*. Oxford: Oxford University Press.

Joy, A., Wang, J. J., Chan, T.-S., Sherry, J. F. J. and Cui, G. (2014) M(art) worlds: Consumer perceptions of how luxury brand stores become art institutions. *Journal of Retailing*, 90(3), 347–64.

Kapferer, J. N. and Bastien, V. (2013) *The Luxury Strategy: Break the Rules of Marketing to Build Luxury Brands*, 2nd edn. London: Kogan Page.

Kapferer, J. N. and Laurent, G. (2016) Where do consumers think luxury begins? A study of perceived minimum price for 21 luxury goods in 7 countries. *Journal of Business Research*, 69(1), 332–40.

Keller, K. L. (1993) Conceptualizing, measuring and managing customer-based brand equity. *Journal of Marketing*, 57(1), 1–22.

Keller, K. L., Aperia, T. and Georgson, M. (2012) *Strategic Brand Management: A European Perspective*, 2nd edn. Harlow: Prentice Hall.

Klein, N. (2000) *No Logo*. London: Flamingo.

Kozinets, R. V., de Valck, K., Wojnicki, A. C. and Wilner, S. J. S. (2010) Networked narratives: Word-of-mouth marketing in online communities. *Journal of Marketing*, 74(2), 71–89.

Levy, S. (1959) Symbols for sale. *Harvard Business Review*, 37(4), 117–24.

McCracken, G. (1986) Culture and consumption: A theoretical account of the structure and movement of the cultural meaning of consumer goods. *Journal of Consumer Research*, 13(1), 71–84.

McCracken, G. (2009) *Chief Culture Officer*. New York: Basic Books.

Maxwell, R. and Knox, S. (2009) Motivating employees to 'live the brand': A comparative case study of employer brand attractiveness within the firm. *Journal of Marketing Management*, 25(9–10), 893–907.

Merz, M. A., Yi, H. and Vargo, S. L. (2009) The evolving brand logic: A service-dominant logic perspective. *Journal of the Academy of Marketing Science*, 37(3), 328–44.

Moor, L. (2007) *The Rise of Brands*. London: Berg Publishers.

Mulbacher, H., Hemetsberger, A., Thelen, E., Vallaster, C., Massimo, R., Fuller, J., Pirker, C., Schorn, R. and Kittinger, C. (2006) Brands as Complex Social Phenomena. Available at: http://clemens.pirker.free.fr/publications/brand_social_phenomenon.pdf (accessed 9 May 2018).

Muniz, A. M. and O'Guinn, T. C. (2001) Brand community. *Journal of Consumer Research*, 27(4), 412–32.

Muniz, A. M. and Schau, H. J. (2007) Vigilante marketing and consumer-created communications. *Journal of Advertising*, 36(3), 35–50.

O'Guinn, T. C. and Muniz, A. M. (2009) Collective brand relationships. In D. J. MacInnis and C. W. Park (eds), *Handbook of Brand Relationships* (pp. 173–94). London: Routledge.

O'Reilly, D. and Kerrigan, F. (2013) A view to a brand: Introducing the film brandscape. *European Journal of Marketing*, 47(5/6), 769–88.

Olsen, D. G., Pracejus, J. W. and O'Guinn, T. C. (2012) Print advertising: White space. *Journal of Business Research*, 65(6), 855–60.

Otnes, C. C. and Maclaran, P. (2015) *Royal Fever: The British Monarchy in Consumer Culture.* Oakland, CA: University of California Press.

Payne, A. F., Storbacka, K. and Frow, P. (2008) Managing the co-creation of value. *Journal of the Academy of Marketing Science*, 36(1), 83–96.

Peneloza, L. (1998) Just doing it: A visual ethnographic study of spectacular consumption behaviour at Nike Town. *Consumption, Markets & Culture*, 2(4), 337–465.

Pentina, I., Guilloux, V. and Micu, A. C. (2018) Exploring social media engagement behaviours in the context of luxury brands. *Journal of Advertising*, 47(1), 55–69.

Prahalad, C. K. and Ramaswamy, V. (2004) Co-creation experiences: The next practice in value creation. *Journal of Interactive Marketing*, 18(3), 5–14.

Rampl, L. V. (2014) How to become an employer brand of choice: Transforming employer brand associations into employer first-choice brands. *Journal of Marketing Management*, 30(13–14), 1486–1502.

Ries, A. and Trout, J. (1986) *Positioning: The Battle for Your Mind.* New York: McGraw-Hill.

Ritson, M. (2015) Why Social Media is Mostly a Waste of Time for Marketers. Available at: www.youtube.com/watch?v=MBvCnsxtNsI (accessed 23 May 2018).

Schau, H. J. and Gilly, M. C. (2003) We are what we post? Self-presentation in personal web space. *Journal of Consumer Research*, 30(3), 385–404.

Schau, H. J., Muniz, A. M. and Arnould, E. J. (2009) How brand community practices create value. *Journal of Marketing*, 73(5), 30–51.

Schivinski, B. and Dabrowski, D. (2016) The effect of social media communication on consumer perception of brands. *Journal of Marketing Communications*, 22(2), 189–214.

Schlosser, E. (2002) *Fast Food Nation.* New York: HarperCollins.

Schroeder, J. E. (2005) The artist and the brand. *European Journal of Marketing*, 39(11/12), 1291–1305.

Schroeder, J. E. (2006) Aesthetics awry: The painter of light and the commodification of artistic values. *Consumption, Markets and Culture*, 9(2), 87–99.

Schroeder, J. E. and Salzer-Mörling, M. (2006) *Brand Culture.* New York: Routledge.

Schultz, D. E. and Kitchen, P. J. (2004) Managing the changes in corporate branding and communication: Closing and re-opening the corporate umbrella. *Corporate Reputation Review*, 6(4), 347–66.

Schultz, M. and Hatch, M. (2003) The cycles of corporate branding: The case of the LEGO company. *California Management Review*, 46(1), 6–26.

Skålén, P., Pace, S. and Cova, B. (2015) Firm-brand community value co-creation as alignment of practices. *European Journal of Marketing*, 19(3/4), 0309–0566.

Smith Maguire, J. and Matthews, J. (2014) *The Cultural Intermediaries Reader*. London: Sage.

Stern, B. B. (2006) What does brand mean? Historical-analysis method and construct definition. *Journal of the Academy of Marketing Science*, 34(2), 216–23.

Tharp, M. and Scott, L. M. (1990) The role of marketing processes in creating cultural meaning. *Journal of Macromarketing*, 10(2), 47–60.

Thompson, C. J., Rindfleisch, A. and Arsel, Z. (2006) Emotional branding and the strategic value of the doppelganger brand image. *Journal of Marketing*, 70(1), 50–64.

Truong, Y., McColl, R. and Kitchen, P. J. (2009) New luxury brand positioning and the emergence of Masstige brands. *Brand Management*, 16(5/6), 375–82.

Tuten, T. L. and Solomon, M. R. (2015) *Social Media Marketing*. London: Sage.

Twitchell, J. B. (2004a) An English teacher looks at branding. *Journal of Consumer Research*, 31(2), 484–9.

Twitchell, J. B. (2004b) *Branded Nation*. New York: Simon & Schuster.

Tynan, C., McKenchnie, S. and Chhuon, C. (2010) Co-creating value for luxury brands. *Journal of Business Research*, 63(11), 1156–63.

Uggla, H. (2006) The corporate brand association base: A conceptual model for the creation of inclusive brand architecture. *European Journal of Marketing*, 40(7–8), 785–802.

Vargo, S. L. and Lusch, R. F. (2004) Evolving to a new dominant logic for marketing. *Journal of Marketing*, 68(1), 1–17.

Veblen, T. (1899) *The Theory of the Leisure Class*. New York: Macmillan.

7
MARKETING ETHICS, GREEN AND SUSTAINABLE MARKETING

Ayantunji Gbadamosi

Learning Objectives

At the end of this chapter, you should be able to understand and discuss:

- Philosophical perspectives on marketing ethics
- Major ethical issues in marketing
- Marketing and society: What is sustainable marketing?
- Green marketing strategy and green marketing orientation
- The segmentation of sustainable behaviour
- Consumer behaviour and green marketing
- The meaning of greenwashing and factors that influence it
- Consumerism and consumer protection

INTRODUCTION

Fundamentally, the notion of ethics is about what is right and what is wrong. So, in the marketing context, this is about the morality of marketing and its associated activities. This chapter examines the foundational philosophical underpinning of marketing ethics – the teleological and deontological perspectives. The chapter also highlights and discusses the numerous and growing criticisms levied against marketing. These range from issues around the types of products offered to the market, the mode of pricing and distributing them, to various ways of communicating their value to the target audience. In more specific ways, the chapter unpacks issues around sustainable marketing practices, linking the discourses of business ethics, social responsibility and the environment. For a clearer understanding of the term, a clear discussion of the distinction between sustainable and conventional marketing perspectives is presented as well as discussing notable developments around the notion of sustainable marketing. How are consumers different in their perception and attitude to sustainability and how can the evolving changes in sustainable marketing be effectively managed? This is a key question that will drive the discussion in this chapter.

PHILOSOPHICAL PERSPECTIVES ON MARKETING ETHICS

The issue of morality has been with humanity from time immemorial. According to Caruana (2007), the first significant attempt to address the question of morality was through the ancient discipline of philosophy, but people relied on specific religious institutions that were guiding their particular communities to proscribe directions around issues of morality before this. As pinpointed by this author, 'sometime after the "birth" of philosophy a period of "enlightenment" thinking was ushered in that, in contrast to religious interpretations of the time, conceived Humans and not Deities as the original force of morality' (Caruana, 2007: 213). So, choices of what actions to take around commercial activities have not been in a vacuum all this time.

For our discussion of the philosophical perspective on marketing ethics, we will turn our attention to a widely cited and discussed 'general theory of marketing ethics' proposed by Hunt and Vitell (1986, 1993). This standpoint indicates that ethical issues in how marketing activities are conducted can be positioned under two philosophical stances known as the deontological and teleological perspectives. The deontological process indicates that what is right or wrong can be determined by referring to some independent moral code or set of values that have been predetermined. Since this is rather normative and not determined by the outcome, one cannot assume that the end justifies the means (Nantel and Weeks, 1996). In its strict sense, for deontologists, the only thing that determines a behaviour's ethicality lies in its consistency or inconsistency with such deontological norms as those proscribing lying, cheating, deceiving or stealing and those prescribing honesty, justice, fairness and fidelity (Hunt and Vasquez-Parraga, 1993: 79). On the other hand, the teleological perspective is mainly underpinned by the consequences of the behaviour in the decision situation. In the explanation of Hunt and Vasquez-Parraga (1993: 79), in this teleological philosophical root of ethics, the evaluation of what is right or wrong involves a combination of key issues, which are:

- the forecasting of each behaviour's consequences for various stakeholder groups
- estimating the probabilities of those consequences
- evaluating the desirability or undesirability of the consequences
- assessing the importance of each stakeholder group.

Although the teleological perspective's claim is that 'the end justifies the means', it is still important to differentiate between the beneficiaries of the consequences. If the decision is taken in such a way that it most favours the individual, then it is known as ethical egoism, but if the decision is taken such that the outcome brings the greatest benefit to the greatest number of people, then it is known as utilitarianism (Parsons et al., 2018). It is reasonable to ask which of these guide marketing ethical decisions. Previous studies that have been conducted around this issue in the past, including Akaah (1997) and Hunt and Vasquez-Parraga (1993), indicate that marketing professionals are guided by both perspectives in their decision-making activities. However, these studies show that the influence of deontological processes is primary while teleological considerations are secondary. Meanwhile, it is interesting to know that some factors influence how managers adopt these processes. In the study by Hunt and Vitell (1986), four key factors are presented as being those things that influence a person's process of deontological and teleological evaluation. These are namely:

- the personal experiences and traits of that individual
- the organisational norms and ethical climate
- the cultural norms and ethical climate
- the industry norms and ethical climate.

As an example of this insight into the influences on people's ethical process, we turn our attention to the study of Lu et al. (1994) which centres on the effects of cultural dimensions on ethical decision making in marketing. The findings of this study show that Taiwanese agents, who are notably from the collectivist, high-power, uncertainty-avoidant, Confucian culture, place greater value on the company and fellow employees than do their counterparts in the USA, which is known to be a cultural context with low power distance, being individualistic and masculine. You may be wondering why you have a different experience with hotel staff at different holiday destinations or why the ethical stance of your local supermarket is different from that of your bank. This is a function of many factors which might be personal, organisational, cultural or related to the particular sector of the marketing environment in which the business operates.

MAJOR ETHICAL ISSUES IN MARKETING

The claim of businesses that they create and deliver value has been under scrutiny by critics who question the extent to which that promise is being fulfilled. This is not unconnected to the nature of marketing as a part of the organisation which is a system in that it acts as the glue that brings organisational functions such as production/operation, finance and human resources together within society. It mediates between the organisation and society. For example, marketing brings information about customers' needs from society to the organisation and helps manage how place, possession and time utilities are delivered to consumers. So, the issue of how ethical marketing is vis-à-vis its roles in the organisational system has been a subject of debate on many grounds. It is important to stress that the scope of this topic is considerably wide-cutting across all elements of the marketing mix, various sub-topics of marketing, and areas of connection between marketing and society. We will now examine some of the commonly discussed points in this section.

Unethical pricing

It is often claimed that some of the approaches of many marketers with respect to pricing of their offerings are unethical. In some specific cases, they are confronted with criticism of deceptive pricing, such as presenting items to be on 'special offer' while a critical reflection on the proposed deal will reveal that buyers are not particularly better off. For example, presenting a bar of chocolate which is normally sold at 50p in a special offer of 'buy two for £1' is deceptive in that those buying the products are paying the same amount they would normally pay when there is no offer. Also, in this typical example, the same product may also have the price information presented as 'the price was 65p but now 50p'. While these scenarios do not necessarily indicate charging more than the usual price, they do however indicate a flagrant deception of consumers by the erring organisations in order to purposefully deceive customers into buying, or buying more of, the item in question. Interestingly, while many unsuspecting consumers are caught up in this unsavoury act, some are not unaware of this notoriety. Hence, such cases are sometimes reported to watchdogs and regulatory bodies, which might ensure that action is taken. An example of this is the Advertising Standards Authority (ASA) in the UK, which is an independent regulator of advertising in all media in relation to the guiding codes set by its sister organisation (the Committee of Advertising Practice). Breaches of the code may result in sanctions of various forms being handed out to the organisation.

Moreover, critics of marketing have argued that the prices of some products or services presented by some companies are not proportional to the value offered. This is attributed to inefficiency on the part of these marketers as most of the costs associated with these products could be improved on, but they are just not doing enough in this direction since they know that the burden can be passed on to consumers while still maximising their profits. However, this point could be debunked by marketers – given the intensity of today's competition, charging more exorbitantly than competing firms will only give the latter the opportunity to secure a greater share of the market. It could also be argued that workers will receive their wages whether or not the product moves off the shelf, and that businesspeople are entitled to a return for the risks they have taken, justifying the notion that profit maximisation is a legitimate aspiration (Lanthos, 1987). Nevertheless, ultimately, the issue of ethics in terms of how firms charge for their goods and services should not be taken lightly; firms should ensure that consumers are treated fairly.

Product management

Advocates of consumers have raised some criticisms about the product management of business organisations. These take different forms and include offering shoddy/unsafe products, and planned obsolescence. First, critics have argued that some products offered by marketers are not made well enough to suit the level of quality they project to customers in their claims. The argument is, in these cases, that manufacturers are not effectively ensuring that products deliver form utility to the consumer. Consequently, there are strong links here with questions on the safety of such products. Relevant examples are seen in the automobile industry with some historic cases of vehicle recall from companies like Toyota and Ford. A recent example is the Volkswagen emissions scandal in which the company was dishonest about results in its diesel emission tests in the USA, relating to about 11 million cars worldwide (BBC, 2015). Similarly, the faulty batteries in mobile phones causing problems for buyers, the detection of unsafe products on the shelves of supermarkets and many other similar incidents are sources of worry for some consumers. However, some companies have paid dearly for their neglect and lack of respect for consumer safety in one form or another. Kotler and Armstrong (2018) highlight some of the reasons for problems associated with product safety: increased product complexity, manufacturer indifference and poor quality control. But these are no plausible excuses for marketers, as consumers often expect safety to be incorporated into product design and development. Another closely related issue of ethics in product management is planned obsolescence, which involves deliberately designing a product in such a way that makes it become obsolete easily and quickly, in order to encourage premature repurchase or replacement. Mobile phones, cameras and most other consumer electronics are examples in this respect. There have been claims around the notion that manufacturers of these products deliberately delay the introduction of more attractive and effective models so that when eventually released, they tactically render the existing model 'out of vogue'.

Unethical marketing communication

Marketing communication has been widely acknowledged as one of the essential parts of marketing. While, broadly speaking, marketing is about co-creating with and delivering value to target stakeholders, of whom customers constitute a significant part, marketing communication as an element in the mix helps businesses to communicate this value to the target audience of customers, channel members and a host of other stakeholders. Various tools for achieving this are conventionally advertising, sales promotion, personal selling, public relations and direct marketing (Fill and Turnbull, 2016). So, firms may reach their target audience through media such as TV, radio, newspapers, magazines, trade shows and other traditional modes. However, significant developments in the world of technology have extended the list to include many more new media. The use of mobile technology for communications and social media activities is among the many examples that indicate that the system of contemporary marketing is opening up more communication opportunities for businesses. Meanwhile, the extent to which businesses are ethical in using these tools to communicate with their target audience has been a subject of criticism and debate. It has been argued that, more often than not, the information provided by marketers does not accurately depict the truth about their market offerings. For example, it is claimed that marketers, through the use of advertising, subtly exaggerate the functionality of the product or service being offered, thereby misleading the consumer on the capability of the product. Besides, while advertising has appeared to be regulated in most societies, there are still some ethical concerns about how it is being used. Nantel and Weeks (1996) cite some examples, such as the use of classical conditioning, in which some products with little inherent value are paired with prestigious actors and reputable athletes.

Furthermore, advertising to children is another commonly used example of the issues around ethics in marketing. Essentially, critics argue that advertisers target children, who are not as capable as adults at resisting 'temptation', thereby leading them to engage in the purchase of unnecessary items through the use of pester power. The significance of this issue has led many societies to develop various legal frameworks to bring such actions under control, but the strength of this action varies from one society to another. For example, Vadehra (2004), Cassim (2005) and Gbadamosi (2010) who wrote about advertising to children in India, South Africa and Nigeria, respectively, concluded that further significant efforts are required in these contexts towards reaching a global standard on ethical advertising to children.

From another perspective, the issue of bad faith in visual representation in marketing is core to marketing communications and marketing ethics. In their practices, some businesses may be seen to be biased in how their marketing messages link their market offerings and brands to unique images. Some of the images used are demeaning or stereotypical. Some of the marketing messages that have sparked outraged revolve around gender, race, ethnicity and children. For example, in 1989, Madonna's Pepsi advert, with her singing *Like a Prayer* and showing the image of burning crosses and her kissing a black saint, had to be pulled within 48 hours in reponse to criticism from some stakeholders, notably American religious groups who complained that it portrayed Jesus Christ as being a black man being kissed by Madonna (BBC, 2009). Also, in 2017 Dove presented an advert on its Facebook page showing a black woman removing her top to reveal a white woman underneath – the ad was heavily criticised as racist, and Dove, which is owned by Unilever, had to remove the ad and apologise (Slawson, 2017). These and other examples are part of the reason why Borgerson and Schroeder (2002: 588) suggest that marketing must not contribute to typified images and representational bad faith if it is to be considered as part of the solution rather than part of the problem.

Marketing research

As we have seen several times in this book, the basic tenet of marketing revolves around the notion of value, including satisfying the customer by meeting their needs and wants. In order to fulfil this goal, usually, customer-focused organisations engage in marketing research which often involves the collection and processing of data around an identified problem to aid effective decision making. But the lengths marketers will go to in obtaining the required data is another facet that has ethical implications. For instance, various organisations make calls to customers whose phone numbers have been selected randomly from the available directories to canvass sales of a product or service under the guise of research. Typical examples include asking people whether they have been involved in an accident and would like to make a claim and asking whether the household has insurance cover for one thing or another. This is often considered as impinging on the customer's right to privacy. In some cases, involving the collection of data for specific research objectives, how the exercise is handled prompts many ethical questions. Various authors have written about the widely known ethical issues associated with marketing research. Figure 7.1 synthesises some of these perspectives (Robson, 2002; Malhotra et al., 2012; Ryen, 2016). To be ethical, marketers are expected to avoid these while conducting their marketing research.

On a positive note, there are many national marketing and marketing research associations that have developed a code of marketing research ethics. An example of these bodies is the

European Society for Opinion and Marketing Research (ESOMAR) or the World Association of Opinion and Marketing Research Professionals. The activities of these regulatory bodies are very helpful in terms of providing clear-cut codes that guide marketing research activities. For example, the link between ESOMAR and the International Chamber of Commerce (ICC) has been notably useful in this regard.

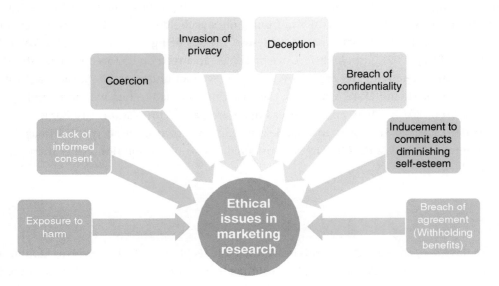

Figure 7.1   Ethical issues in marketing research

Source: Adapted from Diener and Crandall (1978); Robson (2002); Malhotra et al. (2012); Ryen (2016)

Specifically, the ICC/ESOMAR (2016: 7) highlights three elements that fundamentally underpin market, opinion and social research over the years, which could be paraphrased as follows:

- transparency in data collection, the purpose for which the data is collected, and with whom the information will be shared and in what form this will be done
- the protection of personal data from unauthorised people and not disclosing it without the prior consent of the participants
- the need to behave ethically and avoid anything that could cause harm to the data subjects or cause damage to the reputation of market, opinion and social research.

Accordingly, these elements have been broken down into different sections in order to detail the expected conduct on different issues associated with marketing research, such as duty of care and the need to obtain consent from parents or responsible adults concerning data collection from children, young people and other vulnerable individuals. Other related issues include how to act in regard to primary data collection, using secondary data, transparency, publishing the findings, and legal responsibility.

Ethical Focus 7.1

Consumers, ethics and the pharmaceutical traders

The health sector has been consistently acknowledged as an essential part of society. It is crucial to maintaining and developing people's well-being, utilising the services of many professionals such as doctors, nurses, medical laboratory scientists and pharmacists. Meanwhile, there are many ethical issues that revolve around their practices. For example, pharmaceutical companies are expected to operate within a specific code of practice so that consumers and other stakeholders are well covered. One of the bodies playing key roles in this arrangement is the Prescription Medicines Code of Practice Authority (PMCPA), which is a self-regulatory body responsible for administering the Association of the British Pharmaceutical Industry's (ABPI) code of practice for the pharmaceutical industry. This body handles a number of activities, including operating the complaints procedure around materials, pharmaceutical companies and the code; and scrutinising samples of advertising and meetings to be sure they are consistent with the code. To achieve the best in its role, the PMCPA fits very closely with other bodies such as the Medicines and Healthcare products Regulatory Agency (MHRA), which plays a statutory role and administers UK law on behalf of the health ministers. There are different bodies with a similar focus in various other contexts and countries of the world, such as the US Food and Drug Administration (FDA) and the Federal Food, Drug, and Cosmetic Act (FDA) in the USA, Innovative Medicines Canada in Canada, and Pharmacy Board of Australia in Australia. Similarly, there are codes and criteria set down by the European Federation of Pharmaceutical Industries and Associations (EFPIA) and the World Health Organization (WHO). Nevertheless, there are still some occasional breaches of these codes in one form or another at the expense of consumers.

Sources

Prescription Medicines Code of Practice Authority (PMCPA) (n.d.) International and European Codes. Available at: www.pmcpa.org.uk/aboutus/Pages/International-and-European-codes.aspx (accessed 26 November 2018).

Prescription Medicines Code of Practice Authority (PMCPA) (n.d.) Who We Are. Available at: www.pmcpa.org.uk/aboutus/Pages/default.aspx (accessed 26 November 2018).

(Continued)

(Continued)

Questions

1. Research newspaper articles or online materials, or reflect on your experience around a particular breach of an ethical code by a pharmaceutical company. Make notes on the circumstances of the case. Which specific code of practice was violated? What was the conclusion of the case? Was the company sanctioned? Do you agree with the settlement or would you have taken an alternative course of action to resolve the case? Present justifications for your viewpoint.
2. Apart from the pharmaceutical industry, select a profession from any sector of the economy, explore their ethical code of practice and discuss four of these guidelines vis-à-vis the industry and a typical consumer group.

Exploiting disadvantaged consumers

Disadvantaged consumers are those who must live on very little income from whatever source. Hence, this group includes people on a low wage, the elderly, people with a disability, single parents, students, the unemployed and the homeless (Fyfe, 1994). It has been acknowledged many times that marketers devote little attention to such consumers (Anderson, 2002; Edelson, 2005; Hamilton and Catterall, 2005) and rather show a strong affinity for their affluent counterparts. Apparently, one of the reasons for this neglect is the notion that this group of consumers is unprofitable and risky, and marketers' profit motive will be jeopardised if they accord this group of consumers an equal focus. Furthermore, store location may make the disadvantaged consumer even worse off. It is claimed that the disadvantaged suffer a double jeopardy – having less money to spend and being more likely to receive poor value for money or poor quality service (Fyfe, 1994). This is because such consumers have fewer options in terms of retail activities, and are unable to buy in large quantities which have a lower unit rate. No doubt, these criticisms place a considerable ethical burden on marketers as critics believe that the disadvantaged need protection and deserve as much attention as is devoted to those better off.

High-pressure selling

Marketers have been strongly criticised for creating artificial needs which ultimately result in high-pressure selling. Critics claim that salespeople use ingratiatory tactics and place undue pressure on consumers, luring them into buying products they do not need or think of buying at the particular time. This is common in the marketing of insurance services, for example. In these situations, salespeople, who are often most interested in maximising their sales commission, continuously put undue pressure on prospects to buy their offerings. Also, the continuous use of promotional tools to lure consumers to buy items which might eventually go to waste is prone to criticism as far as marketing ethics is concerned. For example, while many individuals in a single-person household might be drawn to buy items on 'extra product' offers such as 'buy-one-get-one-free', in response to the reduction in the unit price, their consumption capacity is limited. Consequently, the unused items may go to waste and constitute additional environmental pollutants. Another side to this argument is the need for the marketer to compensate customers for their loyalty to the brand through some of these offers, such as getting extra for previous purchases. Hence, there is a need to explore the holistic ethical issues around sales activities, to be sure that customers and other stakeholders derive the desired value from these transactions. Some charitable organisations are now working on creating food banks to avoid such associated waste by redistributing within society to areas where such items are most needed.

International marketing

As soon as an organisation decides to enter the international market, its approach to conducting business often takes on a new dimension. Consequently, the company's ethical orientation is expected to broaden to accommodate the cultural implications of its approach in the host country. For instance, an act that is considered ethical in the UK might be viewed otherwise in Asia. This is why Svensson and Wood (2003) stress that the two principal parameters that influence the dynamic of ethics in the marketplace are time and culture. An example of a marketing act with moral questions for international marketing can be seen in the case of the sale of tobacco products that have been banned in some countries being taken to other countries (especially developing countries) where the regulations on such products are not as stringent as in the former. Madichie and Opute (2019) report on the activities of six tobacco companies targeting children in some African countries. According to them, with reference to a BBC-sponsored documentary undertaken by a British entrepreneur, Duncan Bannatyne, these big tobacco giants are exploiting the weak regulatory system in Sub-Saharan Africa (SSA) to encourage kids to smoke (BBC, 2008; Madichie and Opute, 2019). The BBC (2017) also reports further, on an article in the medical journal *The Lancet*, that tobacco companies aggressively make incursions into new markets, especially in developing countries. These are issues of ethical importance in international marketing.

Practitioner's Perspective 7.1

Nudge marketing

'Nudge marketing has become central to the idea of gaining influence (if not winning a direct sale), but its use has come under fire because it challenges the very idea of free will.

Imagine a hospital wanting to increase the amount of people who donate their organs, for the benefit of other patients and medical research. They design a consent form to frame the choice as 'tick this box if you want to opt out of donating your organs'. The hospital would then likely increase the number of organ donors because most people do the minimum, especially when it comes to forms, and go with the 'no effort or thought required' option.

Is the hospital breaking a law, an ethical code or a moral code?

What if a retailer places a highly priced handbag in its shop window, knowing that on seeing the price tag customers will be more likely to pay more for a lower-priced item once inside the store? Shoppers' ability to judge value – and their willingness to part with more money than they would have – has been anchored by the first price tag they saw.

Is that breaking a law, an ethical code or a moral code?

The dilemma is that both patient and shopper may not be aware they're being nudged toward an outcome that benefits the hospital, other patients or the shop's profit margin. In which case, are the choices they make truly theirs, or are they being manipulated against their free will?

So, when is it right and when is it wrong to nudge people?

The answer is critical, and rests directly with each and every marketer who might choose to nudge people, because a defining characteristic of being human is our willingness to be moral and follow an ethical code. Without that, what are we?'

Lee Carnihan, marketing manager, Curveball Media'

Questions

1. Which other specific examples of nudge marketing, as described by Lee Carnihan, have you experienced before or noticed? Provide details around the organisation, its offerings and the reasons why you think the cases you have cited fit this scenario.
2. To what extent would you agree that this approach manipulates people against their free will?

SUSTAINABLE MARKETING

The terms sustainable marketing, green marketing, organic marketing, eco-marketing and other emerging variants are becoming more frequently used. Essentially, the notion of green marketing borrows ideas from the core tenets of contemporary marketing which is about creating, delivering and co-creating value in the marketplace in such a way that all stakeholders – customers, shareholders, society, employees and others – benefit in various ways. Fundamentally, the core focus of green marketing is about achieving marketing objectives in an environmentally friendly way. Hence, the strategic choices of an organisation involved in green marketing in terms of its marketing mix elements and how to operationalise them, should be environmentally friendly. Products to be sold, prices at which they are to be sold, how these offerings are distributed and the way in which their value is communicated should consistently emphasise environmental friendliness. Historically, we can trace the first definition of green marketing back to 1976 and the words of Hennon and Kinnear (1976), in which they define the term as all those marketing activities that have contributed to environmental problems and that may serve to offer a remedy to them. This is an interesting contribution but as the topic has attracted the ever greater attention of stakeholders over the years, further definitions have been provided that are relatively more detailed and contemporary. To guide us in the journey of this segment of this chapter, we will take a look at another definition provided by Kotler and Armstrong (2018), in which they state that while societal marketing concepts revolve around the future of consumers' welfare and strategic marketing is focused on the future of the business, the sustainable marketing concept is about achieving these two ends together by embracing socially responsible action that satisfies the immediate and future needs of both customers and the organisation.

Evidence all around us displays the destructive waste of natural resources by people and organisations. Growing consumption of the environment comes in a myriad of ways. The unnecessary use of electricity and excessive use of natural resources are examples of actions that indicate a lack of care for the environment. This is consistent with the notion of the dominant social paradigm (DSP) which refers to the collection of values, norms, beliefs and habits that constitute the most commonly held perspective within a culture, which has governed the way people act in the developed world since the Industrial Revolution (Pirages and Ehrlich, 1974). So, a discussion of green marketing is not consistent with the world view of DSP which is mainly about continued economic growth and the accumulation of capital (Emery, 2012). Smart (2010) captures this message in his chapter 'An unsustainable all-consuming world' in his book *Consumer Society*. Essentially, the argument is that there are limits to the global consumption growth that can be accommodated. Citing the Global Footprint Network (2008), this publication directs attention to the claim that the world uses the equivalent of 1.3 planets to make the resources we consume available and to absorb our waste. So, by implication, the Earth regenerates what we consume in a year in one year and four months. Hence, there is a shortfall!

Various news media continually echo the view that a 'do nothing' approach to the environment will soon be catastrophic. So, to a great extent, these efforts have brought the issue of environmental sustainability to the table of international politics and increase awareness among societal members. This in turn has served as a key motivation for innovation among companies to develop green products (Dangelico and Vocalelli, 2017). The simple logic behind this drive for innovation is that when consumers demand green products, the onus is on firms to come up with creative solutions. Interestingly, there is stiff competition among firms which implies that businesses that are able to create value for consumers effectively stand a better chance of surviving the turbulent marketing environment. So, it can be a source of competitive advantage.

GREEN MARKETING STRATEGY

In its conventional form, strategy is about the means to achieving set objectives. As in conventional marketing, there are strategic plans amenable to sustainable marketing. This involves acting on segmentation, targeting and positioning, and the marketing mix (Moravcikova et al., 2017). Fundamentally, market segmentation involves dividing the total heterogeneous market for a product or service into smaller units based on specific applicable factors, in such a way that each unit will consist of members with approximately homogeneous characteristics.

Nonetheless, some differences exist in how these are operationalised in sustainable marketing due to the nature of the market offering involved, as there is a claim that psychographics' criteria of segmentation are more effective than demographic alternatives for segmentation in relation to green products (Straughan and Roberts, 1999), and in their study involving classifying consumers based on their pro-environmental behaviour, Modi and Patel (2013) suggest that behavioural variables are more effective than demographics and psychographics. As the topic of green marketing becomes more interesting and attracts greater scholarship efforts, we tend to have various classifications of consumer groups. However, for the purpose of this textbook we will concentrate on one of these classifications (Ottman and Reilly, 1998), as reported by Banytė et al. (2010). Based on this view, we may observe the following consumer groups:

1. *Loyal green consumers:* individuals who are core loyal to the purchase of eco-friendly products in that they are willing to pay up to 40% more for them than cheaper competing products, as they believe that there is a need to have environmental awareness and contribute significantly to conserving the environment.
2. *Less devoted green consumers:* as the name says, these people are also devoted to environmental issues, such that they might pay in the range of 10–22% more to acquire green products over others that are less eco-friendly, but may not change their lifestyle to fit due to a busy schedule.
3. *Consumers developing towards green:* these individuals only embrace green consumption occasionally and subject to situations, and are only able to go as far as paying 4% more for eco-friendly products than their non-eco-friendly counterparts.
4. *Conservative consumers unwilling to change:* the stance of this group of consumers is that environmental issues should be a course of action to be spearheaded and handled by the government, and they are only able to buy eco-friendly products if their prices are the same as those of their non-eco-friendly alternatives.

5. *Consumers completely unwilling to change:* this consumer segment does not consider environ-
    mental issues to be serious and is not making any effort towards environmental protection.

In a conventional marketing sense, market targeting involves exploring the attractiveness of
each of the segments in relation to the purpose of the business and selecting which among
them to focus on for marketing activities. This also applies to green marketing to an extent
but a bit of a noteworthy twist applies in this context. In view of the nature of the market
offering involved, it has been suggested that rather than merely concentrating on targeting
green consumers, efforts should be made to broaden the targeted consumer base by adding
green characteristics to various features of a product (Rex and Baumann, 2007). A similar position has been emphasised by Peattie (2001) who indicates that the green marketing strategy
of a firm should be able to aid the business to enlarge its segments as well as have an understanding of the needs of customers.

Conventionally, positioning is about putting the product in a distinctive place in the mind
of the prospective buyer. Since there are competing market offerings available to consumers,
this gives the position in the mind of the target market in relation to key attributes. In their
study entitled 'Green branding effects on attitude', Hartmann et al. (2005) indicate that firms
can use functional or emotional attributes to distinguish a green market offering from others. The functional positioning strategy involves stressing the environmental benefits of the
product's reduction in air pollution, while the emotional attributes include factors like esteem
where the product/brand is seen as a status symbol. As this study indicates, marketing strategy
that is based exclusively on functional positioning might be insufficient to trigger an action
from the customer. Similarly, using only emotional attributes to position the brand may be
weak too. Hence, a combination of the two will have a stronger attitudinal effect to get potential buyers to act in favour of the offering (Hartmann et al., 2005).

Apart from these two positioning strategies, it is also useful and relevant to indicate that
distinguishing a green market offering from others in the mind of the consumer might be
linked to the firm's stance on environmental friendliness. So, it is important for the firm
presenting the product to be seen as eco-friendly in its ways of managing things to encourage
consumers to favour its brand over others that are non-eco-friendly (Prakash, 2002; Dangelico
and Vocalelli, 2017).

The marketing mix has been a fundamental part of marketing thought and practice
for a long time. It is the combination of elements used by firms to strategically meet the
needs and wants of the target market. As shown in Figure 7.2, they are product, price, place
and promotion and can be effectively applied to the marketing of green products towards
achieving consumer satisfaction and environmental objectives. For example, some of the
key strategies around a product for achieving this include a reduction in packaging and
ensuring that the product can be recycled or reused, fully or partially. Overall, it should

Figure 7.2   Marketing mix for green products

Source: Adapted from Mishra and Sharma (2014); Polonsky and Rosenberger III (2001)

be considered beneficial to both the environment and the consumer buying it. In terms of price, essentially the key focus should be on value. In some cases, eco-friendly products can be more expensive than their conventional product counterparts but the pricing and marketing communication strategies should be effectively managed such that they give the consumer reasons to buy. Hence, the perceived value of the product to the consumer is key in terms of weighing the benefits (functional and emotional) against the cost that the consumer is paying for the item.

As shown in Figure 7.2, a number of marketing communication elements may be applied to emphasise the environmental friendliness of the product and the benefits to the consumer. But developments in digital technology have introduced significant opportunities in various ways through social media such as YouTube, Facebook, Twitter and Instagram to reach a wide audience in terms of what the product has to offer the consumer and the environment. In addition to this, a key part of the system is the activities of channel members to ensure that green products are available to consumers. Around this is the need to consider an efficient transportation system and digital distribution such that they will reduce the cost and ultimately the price to encourage consumption.

A group of researchers (Azad et al., 2013) conducted a study to discover what influences green marketing. Their findings indicate four important factors which are:

- green labelling
- compatibility
- value
- green advertising.

Green labelling is about the ease of identifying green products. So, it should be relatively clear and easy, in relation to the information and design provided on the label, to distinguish a green product from its non-green counterpart. Compatibility covers various issues, including the capacity of a firm to build an emotional relationship with its customers, green packaging, trust in green products and the importance of recycling. Value is about the attractiveness of green product offerings and the presence of a justification to pay more for them. Green advertising is about communicating the value of green products. For instance, consumers need to know why buying green is a better choice than the alternatives.

GREEN MARKETING ORIENTATIONS

Green marketing orientations are the ways an organisation goes about achieving its sustainability objectives. In a review of the existing literature, Papadas et al. (2017) identify three orientations of green marketing which could be sketched out for ease of understanding, as shown in Figure 7.3.

Figure 7.3   Three orientations of green marketing

Source: Papadas et al. (2017)

The strategic green marketing orientation involves approaching environmental strategy on a long-term basis, having top management formulating policies and taking action to facilitate implementation. This reflects a very strong commitment from the organisation. A tactical green marketing orientation, on the other hand, is short term in nature. As indicated by Papadas et al. (2017), the key focus in the tactical orientation is on ensuring a transformation of the marketing mix elements into their greener alternatives. As the name suggests, the internal green marketing orientation focuses on achieving environmental friendliness within the firm through actions such as employee training. As expected, the green marketing strategy of an organisation will have to be a holistic and synergistic approach as the three green marketing orientations are interrelated (Papadas et al., 2017). For example, staff members in research and development will have to work with the marketing department and other parts of the company to ensure adequate training and development programmes are in place that will help the organisation to achieve its corporate green objectives.

GREENWASHING

Following an environmental sustainability course of action might sometimes involve sacrifices from both the consumer's and marketer's standpoint. So, for an organisation to be seen to be embracing sustainability, there are some notable actions required. While there is much more ground to cover concerning the notion of environmental sustainability and consumption, it has become much more pronounced and popular among consumers in recent times than was the case several decades ago. So, businesses are becoming conscious of the need to satisfy the growing demand for eco-products. However, some businesses that would like to benefit from these growing needs are not really addressing environmental issues as expected but would like to take the credit for doing so. This is the main crux of greenwashing. Ross and Deck (2011) give an interesting explanation of the term as the clever interplay of 'white-washing' and 'brainwashing'. These terms are about opportunistic behaviour in not giving the exact, complete picture of a scenario. So, we can sum it together as involving poor environmental performance and yet positive communication about environmental performance (Delmas and Burbano, 2011). As cited in Dangelico and Vocalelli (2017), some of the ways in which organisations engage in greenwashing, as presented by Ross and Deck (2011), include:

- misleading with words
- misleading with visuals/graphics
- exaggeration
- vagueness of claims
- avoidance of helpful information.

Various efforts are being made by different stakeholders such as NGOs and statutory organisations to curb these and other forms of deceptive practices around environmental friendliness claims. In some cases, individuals and pressure groups report erring organisations to various authorities so that they can be called to order. The advice for consumers who wish to avoid being greenwashed is to be educated on which organisations are truly green, be vigilant about the eco-products being presented, and explore the Ecolabel Index to check suspicious ecolabels (Greenpeace; Scientific American, n.d.).

It is also relevant for us to know the factors that drive greenwashing. The work of Delmas and Burbano (2011) presents an elaborate picture of the drivers of greenwashing categorised into: market external drivers, non-market external drivers, organisational drivers, and individual psychological drivers. These four main factors also have sub-factors, as indicated below:

- market external drivers: consumer demand, investor demand, competitive pressure
- non-market external drivers: a lax and uncertain regulatory environment, activists, NGOs, media monitoring
- organisational drivers: firm characteristics, incentive structure and culture, effectiveness of intra-firm communication, organisational inertia
- individual psychological drivers: optimistic bias, narrow decision framing, hyperbolic intertemporal discounting.

Overall, we can see that a myriad of factors contribute to the greenwashing activities of organisations and having this knowledge will aid various stakeholders in curbing the menace. For example, improvements in legislation may strengthen the activities of NGOs, activists and the media whose role in addressing greenwashing could be far-reaching, and having an overarching perspective on how to manage other drivers may increase the incentives for firms to engage in environmentally friendly marketing behaviour.

SUSTAINABLE MARKETING AND CONSUMER BEHAVIOUR

Consumer behaviour is notably intriguing and complex. The question of what people buy and how they do so remains fundamental to any logical discussion of marketing including sustainable marketing. This is especially so as the motives for consumption are many and transcend the functional benefits of such market offerings (Sirgy and Johar, 1999; Gbadamosi, 2015). The available evidence indicates that sustainable marketing has significant long-term advantages for all. However, the issue of how widely shared is this view among consumers remains a blurry terrain. So, it will be useful to consider the dynamics of consumption in relation to sustainability. Let us begin this by examining the information presented in Table 7.1, which shows the categories of consumption and how they relate to sustainability.

Table 7.1   Consumption categorisation and sustainability

Category of consumption	Features
Rational consumption	This is based on the logical decision-making process and assumes that consumers will buy products based on their sustainable credentials. Nonetheless, the limitation of this assumption lies in the fact that rational decision making is most likely to be in favour of personal and short-term interest rather than long-term sustainability in favour of society.
Habitual consumption	This consumption type is based on habit rather than on elaborate information processing. It is about choosing a type or brand repeatedly without any associated sustainable loyalty. Hence, heuristic cues such as the use of the prefix 'eco', or green colouring in the message, label or packaging might help firms that are interested in positioning for routine purchases.
Sociological consumption	This is about making the consumption of green products an issue associated with interpersonal relationships such as relating with friends and colleagues.
Hedonistic consumption	This is based on the underpinning perspective that consumption brings pleasure. This tends to be contradictory to environmental sustainability, but pleasure may come from the act of searching for environmentally benign products.
Self-identity consumption	Consumers tend to use consumption for creating, maintaining and reaffirming identities. This appears neutral and not particularly strongly linked to sustainable consumption, in that identity construction is more closely linked to conventional products. However, it can be linked to sustainable self-identities and lifestyles.
Symbolic and communication-based consumption	This acknowledges that besides the functional roles of products, they have their symbolic roles in that consumption might be used to communicate one's status, taste and identity, and social relationships. Shared experiences of sustainable lifestyles in various social groups might enhance sustainable consumption in this scenario.

Source: Adapted from Emery (2012) and Schaefer and Crane (2005)

ATTITUDE–BEHAVIOUR GAP IN SUSTAINABLE CONSUMPTION

Attitude may be defined as an individual's relatively consistent evaluation of and feelings and tendencies towards a particular phenomenon (Kotler and Armstrong, 2018). Consumers have an attitude towards myriad things including sustainability. The links between our attitude towards something and behaviour in relation to it have been the subject of deep academic study for a long time. Among prominent work on this is the Theory of Reasoned Action (Fishbein and Ajzen, 1975) which indicates that people's attitude leads to intention which also results in behaviour, while the improvement on this theory is Theory of Planned Behaviour (Ajzen, 1985), which indicates the relevance of perceived behavioural control. But there are instances where people have a very positive attitude to something that does not result in the corresponding behaviour – this is the attitude–behaviour gap, and it has been noted in relation to sustainable consumption. An example is the study of Juvan and Dolnicar (2014) within a tourism context, who found that some people seem passionate about environmental protection at home but do not exhibit the same behaviour when they are on vacation. More often than not, we hear people who purport to love the environment, partake in discussion that revolves around improving the ecosystem, but when confronted with a choice between eco-friendly and alternative options, they then favour the latter, especially when it is cheaper than the eco offering. So, what might be responsible for this sort of reaction to environmental issues? Emery (2012) provides a rather broad perspective on various types of unfavourable attitudes to sustainability, which have been adapted into Figure 7.4 for clarity of purpose.

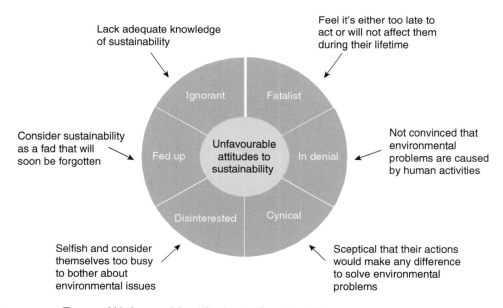

Figure 7.4 Types of Unfavourable attitudes to Sustainability

Source: Adapted from Emery, B. (2012: p.80)

As we can see from Figure 7.4, there are different reasons for people's negative disposition towards sustainable consumption. Perhaps a way of addressing the issues would be to look critically at each of these and develop actions towards changing them in favour of sustainability. For example, providing detailed information through various means about sustainability and its merits might help educate those who are ignorant about it, and showing convincing evidence of the likely damage to the environment if no action is taken might be helpful in converting those who are 'in denial' and 'fed up'.

A number of factors influence the transformation of a green intention into sustainable consumption behaviour. Based on a review of the relevant literature, Signori and Forno (2016) list some of these factors as:

- the individual consumer
- the socio-economic context in which the practices are shaped
- the product
- the company
- the environment in which decisions are made.

It is logical to hold that the holistic interaction of these factors will be greatly helpful in achieving this goal of moving people from the threshold of action to the point of action. For example, willingness on the part of the consumer, supported by the availability of the product from a company that is environmentally friendly itself, and having encouragement from friends, family members or other associates who are already eco-friendly consumers, would most likely be more successful than an environmental context where these factors are not present.

Signori and Forno's (2016) study on closing the attitude–behaviour gap specifically found a strong link to the solidarity purchase group in achieving this objective. This group consists of people who buy food and other daily items that they distribute among themselves. The group, known as 'solidarity based', later spreads from consumers to small producers who supply the products.

Digital Focus 7.1

Paperless correspondence in a digital world: Every little helps

The increasing scale of global consumption is one of the points highlighted as being responsible for the depletion of natural resources. Accordingly, everyone will have to be involved in one way or another to bring a solution to this problem that concerns us all. The Secretary General of the United Nations, António Geterres, in his speech on climate change in September 2018 at the UN headquarters, gave a passionate call for all parties concerned to join forces to keep our planet's warming below 2 degrees for global prosperity. He argued that we, as stakeholders, have the tools to deal with the existential threat of global warming. Consistent with this viewpoint, organisations such as banks, mortgage firms, utility companies and universities now make an effort to encourage their customers to switch to paperless correspondence for telephone bills, mortgage statements and so on. Most of these establishments have various unique apps amenable for use on a mobile device, through which many transactions such as money transfer, checking of balances, making applications and exchanging crucial details, can be done via the system. Evidently, this implies that the less paper and ink used by these bodies to communicate with their customers, the fewer trees and other natural resources will be used, thereby preserving the natural environment. While paperless transactions only address a fraction of the world's environmental issues, small actions like this may be a great gift of the digital economy to society. Nonetheless, while this step, taken by various organisations, has been matched by great enthusiasm from many customers, others have yet to take this small step towards a better world, even when they are positively vocal about the value of it.

Questions

1. Apart from paperless correspondence, identify other measures being adopted in other sectors of the economy and how they are contributing to environmental stability. Discuss how these measures might be improved upon.
2. Why do you think some consumers are not as enthusiastic as others about sustainable consumption? Discuss ways of changing this stance to one of environmental sustainability.

CONSUMERISM AND CONSUMER PROTECTION

The discussion of consumerism and consumer protection is not new per se but has evolved over the years. Nevertheless, there are noteworthy new developments around the issue. Before going deeper into the discussion, it will be very useful for us to examine a definition of the term. In his 1972 article 'What consumerism means to marketers', Philip Kotler defines the term as 'a social movement that seeks to raise the rights and powers of the one that buys in relation to the one that sells' (Kotler, 1972: 49). In simple terms, the core focus in consumerism and consumer protection is on ensuring that consumers' rights are protected in relation to their consumption activities.

The available evidence indicates that we can trace the origin of this phenomenon to the USA around the early 20th century. Its development is linked to mass protests in reaction to the unsavoury business practices of organisations (Bostan et al., 2010). The phenomenon gradually developed in European countries and eventually in several other countries, such that issues around consumer protection are being given fuller attention in one form or another.

Meanwhile, there are guidelines on consumer protection provided by the United Nations, as presented in Table 7.2, with specific objectives which are stated as being to:

- assist countries in achieving or maintaining adequate protection for their population as consumers
- facilitate production and distribution patterns responsive to the needs and desires of consumers
- encourage high levels of ethical conduct for those engaged in the production and distribution of goods and services to consumers
- assist countries in curbing abusive business practices by all enterprises at both national and international levels which adversely affect consumers
- facilitate the development of independent consumer groups
- further international co-operation in the field of consumer protection
- encourage the development of market conditions which provide consumers with greater choice at lower prices
- promote sustainable consumption.

Table 7.2   Consumer protection guidelines

Guideline	United Nations Guideline for Consumer Protection (UNGCP)
Access	Access by consumers to essential goods and services
Inclusivity	Protection of vulnerable and disadvantaged consumers
Safety	Protection of consumers from hazards to their health and safety
Protection of interests	Promotion and protection of the economic interests of consumers
Information	Access by consumers to adequate information to enable them to make informed choices according to individual wishes and needs
Education	Consumer education, including education on the environmental, social and economic consequences of consumer choice
Redress	Availability of effective consumer dispute resolution and redress
Representation	Freedom to form consumer and other relevant groups or organisations and the opportunity of such organisations to present their views in decision-making processes affecting them
Sustainability	Promotion of sustainable consumption patterns
E-commerce	A level of protection for consumers using electronic commerce that is no less than that afforded in other forms of commerce
Privacy	Protection of consumer privacy and the global free flow of information

Source: Consumer International (2016); United Nations (2016)

As evident from the information depicted in Table 7.2, consumerism and consumer protection are matters close to the heart of society and the international community in many ways. The European Union as a region has some guidelines geared towards the same overarching objectives of the broad consumer protection agenda. Table 7.3 shows some of the key issues highlighted on the EU website that are meant to drive commercial interactions in that context.

Table 7.3   Key issues in EU consumer rights

EU consumer rights	Some examples (Extracts from detailed guidelines)
Shopping: Your rights Contract information Pricing and payments Value added tax (VAT) Guarantees and returns	Traders are expected to provide consumers with clear, correct and understandable information about the transaction. They should provide information such as: ☐ email address of the trader ☐ any delivery restrictions in certain countries ☐ the right to cancel your order within 14 days ☐ available after-sales services ☐ dispute resolution mechanisms Consumers must give consent to any additional payment requested by the trader. A trader must repair, replace, reduce the price or refund consumers if products bought turn out to be faulty or at variance from what was advertised.
Internet & telecoms Roaming in the EU Accessing online content abroad Telecommunication services Internet access Data protection and online privacy	Consumers do not have to pay any additional roaming charges while travelling outside their country in any other EU country. Apart from being given a written contract by the telecom provider, the consumer has the right to end the contract if the provider changes the terms of the contract. Consumers must be able to access electronic communication services of good quality at an affordable price. Irrespective of how the data was collected, organisations and EU consumers are guaranteed the protection of their personal data whenever it is collected.
Financial products and services Bank accounts in the EU Payment transfers and cheques Mortgage loans Insurance products Consumer credits and loans Investment products	Banks cannot refuse an EU consumer's application for a basic payment account just because he or she does not live in the country where the bank is established. Consumers can switch their bank account to another bank account in the same EU country. Customers' money in an EU bank account is protected if the bank holding the account fails, up to a limit of EUR 100,000 or the equivalent in local currency. Under EU rules, the lender or credit intermediary has to give consumers at least seven days to assess the offer.

(Continued)

Table 7.3   (Continued)

EU consumer rights	Some examples (Extracts from detailed guidelines)
Unfair treatment Unfair commercial practices Unfair pricing Unfair contract terms	Consumers are protected against two main categories of unfair commercial practices: misleading practices and aggressive practices.
	Sellers must indicate product prices clearly enough for consumers to easily compare similar products and make informed choices. Standard contract terms used by traders have to be fair and drafted in plain and understandable language. Any ambiguities will be interpreted in the consumer's favour.
Energy supply Access to and use of energy services Contract and energy consumption Complaint and dispute resolution	Consumers have the right to have their homes connected to the local electricity network and to be supplied with electricity.
	Vulnerable consumers cannot be disconnected from the electricity network, and may be entitled to benefits to ensure they get the necessary electricity supply.
	Consumers can decide to change their gas or electricity supplier and will not be charged for the change. The network operator in the area must make the change within three weeks.
	Consumers can file a complaint of any noted breach of agreement with the supplier involved. If the way the issue is managed is not satisfactory, the consumer can complain to an independent body for out-of-court dispute settlement such as the energy ombudsman.
Consumer dispute resolution Informal dispute resolution for consumers Out-of-court procedures for consumers Formal legal action for consumers	Consumers should first approach their trader's customer service department – contact details are normally on the trader's website.
	If consumer and trader cannot settle the contractual dispute directly, the trader must inform the consumer about further steps, such as filing a formal complaint and initiating alternative dispute resolution procedures.
	When there is a dispute, consumers can also contact their national regulatory authorities.

Source: (Adapted from European Union Consumers at https://europa.eu/youreurope/citizens/consumers/index_en.htm)
© European Union, 1995-2019

Many examples of inadequacies abound in the business environment, showing how consumers' rights are being infringed upon. Cambridge Analytica, Facebook and Volkswagen are just three examples of businesses that have had to react to allegations of improper conduct in relation to consumers' rights in recent times. Other examples vary across different sectors of the economy such as manufacturing, financial services, retailing, the agricultural/ food sector and the automobile industry. In fact, each element of the marketing mix has been unscrupulously used by marketers to exploit consumers. The rights of child consumers as well as other vulnerable consumers such as older people and those in developing countires, are not always adequately protected. It is important to note that while these activities are still noticeable among marketers, the voices of consumer advocates are now louder than they ever were (Gbadamosi, 2018). Advancements in technology have empowered consumers in the use of consumer-generated content, consumer activists are now more vocal and facilitated to bring the excesses of business into the open, and government regulations are being better established, even in developing countries. Ultimately, the desired state is to ensure that development of the economy, business profitability and consumer satisfaction are well balanced for a better and fairer society (Gbadamosi et al., 2018). Although more can still be done, the significant changes seen so far demonstrate that the contemporary consumer is in a better position than ever in terms of his or her rights.

Case Study 7.1

Apple: Actualising an excellent green agenda

The remarkable news of Apple's recent financial record is a noteworthy development for the business world in 2018. Uncertainty and turbulence in the marketing environment have pushed many businesses off the radar but here we have Apple reporting $53.3 billion revenue for the third quarter ending 30 June 2018. To the excitement of the CEO, Tim Cook, this is the best June quarter record ever known by the organisation. Obviously, this is great news for the company's shareholders as a cash dividend of $0.73 per share has already been declared by the board of directors. However, this is not the only positive news about Apple to be celebrated. The company's ethical record around sustainability is widely acknowledged to be impressive. Apple is not only customer-driven or profit-centred, its focus is also on the long-term good of the environment and society, which is noteworthy. The company has three key priorities as a way of making a huge impact in society: (1) it is strongly determined to reduce its impact on climate change by using renewable energy sources and driving energy efficiency in its products and facilities; (2) it is focused on conserving precious resources to ensure that all can thrive; and (3) it aims to pioneer the use of safer materials in its products and processes.

To date, Apple has already achieved 100% renewable energy in its operated data centre across 24 countries including the UK, Australia, the USA and China; and in 2016, 96% of the electricity used in its global centres was sourced from renewable energy, indicating a reduction in its carbon emissions by approximately 585,000. So, Apple's goal to power all of its facilities worldwide with 100% renewable energy is within reach. Since value creation and delivery in the marketing system goes beyond the internal structures or function of an organisation, Apple works very closely with its suppliers towards ensuring the welfare of society. By the year 2020, the organisation and its suppliers will generate more than 4 gigawatts of new clean power worldwide. The organisation also strictly prohibits human trafficking and

(Continued)

(Continued)

the use of involuntary labour in any part of its processes. So, it works very closely with its suppliers to ensure this policy is adhered to and has an auditing system in place to ensure compliance. Overall, Apple's key focus is to treat everybody working for the organisation or within its supply chain with dignity and respect. Furthermore, it collaborates with multiple teams, such as specialist recyclers and local governments, to ensure that waste created by its supply chains is recycled, reused, composted and converted into energy where necessary. In its 2017 Environmental Responsibility Report, covering the fiscal year 2016, it indicates that it is building the greenest corporate headquarters on the planet. The Apple Park in Cupertino is being positioned to align with the LEED platinum-certified rating. The company is proud to state that this facility is powered by 100% renewable energy, while its 38-acre campus in Austin, Texas, which was opened in 2016, is expected to be certified to Gold level in the same US Green Building Council's LEED rating system.

In terms of product portfolio, Apple is widely acknowledged as being highly innovative. Its market offerings include different items within its main product categories of Mac, iPad, iPhone, Apple Watch and Music. The company is fully aware that customers' expectations in this day and age go beyond the functionality of the products they are buying. For instance, the purchase of an iPhone by a customer is not driven solely by the ability of the phone to allow the owner to receive calls and messages. In fact, it now even transcends the apps that might be used on it. Apple also firmly believes that a device that is durable is greener. The logic behind this perspective is that fewer resources would be needed from the earth to produce new ones if old products can be used for longer. To make products safe for people and the planet, Apple sets strict standards in relation to the materials it uses for producing its devices, which often go far beyond the legal requirement. For example, any product materials that come in contact with the skin such as Apple Watch are carefully and specifically tested, as some people have an allergic reaction to nickel, which is commonly used in many alloys such as stainless steel. Hence, Apple does sweat testing to gauge how quickly nickel moves from metal to sweat. It is therefore not surprising that the firm has been recognised in various ways for its sustainability record and green credentials. As examples, it has been acknowledged as the number one organisation worldwide across all sectors for developing a conflict-free mineral supply chain in the Democratic Republic of Congo; and the Institute of Public and Environmental Affairs, a Chinese NGO, has given Apple the top score on the Corporate Information Transparency Index for the fourth consecutive year.

Source

Apple (2017) Environmental Responsibility Report, Covering Fiscal Year 2016. Available at: www.apple.com/environment/pdf/Apple_Environmental_Responsibility_Report_2017.pdf (accessed 20 December 2018).

Questions for discussion

1. Using Apple as an example; discuss the relationship between an organisation's sustainability record and their business performance (success).
2. Which of the three green marketing orientations is being practised by Apple? Give reasons for your standpoint.
3. Identify specific information from the case study relating to the green marketing mix and specify which element it applies to.
4. What advice would you give to Apple to avoid having its brand tainted in relation to sustainable marketing practices?

SUMMARY OF KEY IDEAS

- The issue of morality has been with man from time immemorial and was mainly addressed by religious codes until the introduction of philosophy. Meanwhile, the main marketing philosophical standpoints on ethics are the deontological and teleological perspectives.

- The deontological perspective holds that the issue of what is right or wrong can be determined by making reference to some independent moral codes or set of values that have been predetermined, whereas the teleological perspective is about the consequences of the behaviour in question, and simply follows the maxim 'the end justifies the means'.

- Some of the commonly discussed ethical issues in marketing revolve around unethical pricing, product management, unethical marketing communications, marketing research, exploiting the disadvantaged consumer, high-pressure selling and international marketing.

- The issue of sustainable marketing is becoming more popular in marketing circles than it was several years ago. Essentially, it is about creating, delivering and co-creating value with all stakeholders in an environmentally friendly way. In the quest to satisfy the growing consumer base for green products, sustainable marketing is now being seen as a source of competitive advantage as it prompts firms to be creative.

- Firms are expected to have a sound green marketing strategy to be able to fulfil their objectives, especially those in terms of satisfying their stakeholders. Hence, the notion of segmentation, targeting and positioning is crucial. However, instead of following the tenet of sustainable marketing effectively, some organisations engage in greenwashing which is about communicating green credentials that they do not have. Similarly, there is a gap between attitude and behaviour among consumers in that some show an interest in the idea of achieving a sustainable environment but do not match it with actions.

- Consumerism and consumer protection revolve around protecting the rights and powers of consumers in relation to those of business organisations. While significant achievements have been made here, some examples of irregularities among businesses indicate that there are further grounds to cover to ensure that consumers' rights are fully protected.

Chapter Discussion Questions

1. Discuss the fundamental differences between teleological and deontological ethical perspectives. Cite specific examples to support your claim.

2. In a group, reflect on your experiences or what you have read in the newspapers or heard in various other news media regarding the unethical marketing practices of some marketers in relation to what has been discussed in this chapter. Discuss what you consider to be the impact of this in relation to specific cases you have identified, among consumers and other stakeholders in society.

3. Assume you have been hired by a multinational company that specialises in sales of toys and children's clothing, to examine the impact of digital technology on children's taste in toys in the curent era. What are the ethical issues that will guide your conduct of this study?

4. Assuming you have been invited to give a talk on 'Greenwashing: The menace of this 21st century', what will be the key highlights of your talk?

5. It has been noted several times that not all consumers who profess to love and care for the environment actually turn this passion into an act of purchase. What are the reasons for this and what would you recommend as action for bridging this attitude–behaviour gap?

REFERENCES

Akaah, I. P. (1997) Influence of deontological and teleological factors on research ethics evaluations. *Journal of Business Research*, 39(2), 71–80.

Anderson, T. (2002) Exploding myths about marketing to Ds and Es. *Brand Strategy*, August, p. 37.

Azad, N., Nobahari, S., Bagheri, H., Esmaeeli, M. and Rikhtegar, M. (2013) An exploration study on factors influencing green marketing. *Management Science Letters*, 3(5), 1369–74.

Banytė, J., Brazionienė, L. and Gadeikienė, A. (2010) Investigation of green consumer profile: A case of Lithuanian market of eco-friendly food products. *Economics & Management*, 15, 374–83.

BBC (2008) Bannatyne takes on big tobacco. *BBC*, 27 June. Available at: http://news.bbc.co.uk/1/hi/programmes/this_world/7477468.stm (accessed 5 April 2018).

BBC (2009) Madonna banned advert. *BBC*, 5 March. Available at: http://news.bbc.co.uk/1/hi/7922129.stm (accessed 24 November 2018).

BBC (2015) Volkswagen: The scandal explained. *BBC*, 10 December. Available at: www.bbc.co.uk/news/business-34324772 (accessed 30 November 2018).

BBC (2017) Smoking causes one in 10 deaths worldwide, study shows. *BBC*, 6 April. Available at: www.bbc.co.uk/news/health-39510728 (accessed 5 April 2018).

Borgerson, J. L. and Schroeder, J. E. (2002) Ethical issues of global marketing: Avoiding bad faith in visual representation. *European Journal of Marketing*, 36(5/6), 570–94.

Bostan, I., Burciu, A. and Grosu, V. (2010) The consumerism and consumer protection policies in the European Community. *Theoretical & Applied Economics*, 17(4).

Caruana, R. (2007) Morality and consumption: Towards a multidisciplinary perspective. *Journal of Marketing Management*, 23(3–4), 207–25.

Cassim, S. (2005) Advertising to children in South Africa. *Young Consumers*, Quarter 2, 51–5.

Consumer International (2016) Consumer Protection: Why it Matters – A Practical Guide to United National Guidelines for Consumer Protection. Available at: www.consumersinternational.org/media/2049/un-consumer-protection-guidelines-english.pdf (accessed 26 December 2018).

Dangelico, R. M. and Vocalelli, D. (2017) 'Green marketing': An analysis of definitions, strategy steps, and tools through a systematic review of the literature. *Journal of Cleaner Production*, 165, 1263–79.

Delmas, M. A. and Burbano, V. C. (2011) The drivers of greenwashing. *California Management Review*, 54(1), 64–87.

Diener, E. and Crandall, R. (1978) *Ethics in Social and Behaviour Research*. Chicago: University of Chicago Press.

Edelson, S. (2005) Missing $100B market: Low-income consumers overlooked by retailers. *WWD: Women's Wear Daily*, 90(79).

Emery, B. (2012) *Sustainable Marketing*. Harlow: Pearson Education.

European Union (n.d.) Consumers. Available at: https://europa.eu/youreurope/citizens/consumers/index_en.htm (accessed 27 December 2018).

Fill, C. and Turnbull, S. (2016) *Marketing Communications: Discovery, Creation and Conversations*, 7th edn. Harlow: Pearson.

Fishbein, M. and Ajzen, I. (1975) *Belief, attitude, intention, and behavior: An introduction to theory and research*, Reading, MA: Addision Wesley.

Fishbein, M. and Ajzen, I. (1977) *Belief, Attitude, Intention, and Behavior: An Introduction to Theory and Research*. Reading, MA: Addision Wesley.

Fyfe, G. (1994) Life on a low income. In G. Fyfe (ed.), *Poor and Paying for It: The Price of Living on a Low Income*. Glasgow: Scottish Consumer Council/HMSO, pp. 1–15.

Gbadamosi, A. (2010) Regulating child-related advertising in Nigeria. *Young Consumers*, 11(3), 204–14.

Gbadamosi, A. (2015) Brand personification and symbolic consumption among ethnic teenage consumers: An empirical study. *Journal of Brand Management*, 22(9), 737–59.

Gbadamosi, A. (2018) The changing landscape of young consumer behaviour. In A. Gbadamosi (ed.), *Young Consumer Behaviour: A Research Companion*. Oxon: Routledge, pp. 3–22.

Gbadamosi, A., Fletcher, K., Emmanuel Stephen, C. and Olutola, I. C. (2018) Consumerism and consumer protection: A focus on young consumers. In A. Gbadamosi (ed.), *Young Consumer Behaviour: A Research Companion*. Oxon: Routledge, pp. 391–413.

Global Footprint Network (2008) 'A Time for Change: Global Footprint Network Annual Report', www.footprintnetwork.org/content/images/uploads/Global_Footprint_Network_2008_Annual_Report.pdf (accessed 14 May 2019).

Hamilton, K. and Catterall, M. (2005) Towards a better understanding of the low-income consumer. *Advances in Consumer Research*, 32, 627–32.

Hartmann, P., Apaolaza Ibáñez, V. and Forcada Sainz, F. J. (2005) Green branding effects on attitude: Functional versus emotional positioning strategies. *Marketing Intelligence & Planning*, 23(1), 9–29.

Hennon, K. E. and Kinnear, T. C. (1976) *Ecological Marketing*. Chicago, IL: American Marketing Association.

Hunt, S. D. and Vasquez-Parraga, A. Z. (1993) Organizational consequences, marketing ethics, and salesforce supervision. *Journal of Marketing Research*, 30(1), 78–90.

Hunt, S. D. and Vitell, S. (1986) A general theory of marketing ethics. *Journal of Macromarketing*, 6(1), 5–16.

Hunt, S. D. and Vitell, S. (1993) The general theory of marketing ethics: a retrospective and Revision. In N. Craig Smith and John A. Quelch (eds), *Ethics in Marketing*. Chicago, IL: Irwin. pp. 775–84.

ICC/ESOMAR (2016) International Code on Market, Opinion and Social Research and Data Analytics. Available at: www.esomar.org/uploads/public/knowledge-and-standards/codes-and-guidelines/ICCESOMAR_Code_English_.pdf (accessed 18 December 2018).

Juvan, E. and Dolnicar, S. (2014) The attitude–behaviour gap in sustainable tourism. *Annals of Tourism Research*, 48, 76–95.

Kotler, P. (1972) What consumerism means to marketers. *Harvard Business Review*, 50, 48–57.

Kotler, P. and Armstrong, G. (2018) *Principles of Marketing*, 17th edn. Harlow: Pearson.

Lanthos, G. P. (1987) An ethical base for marketing decision making. *Journal of Business and Industrial Marketing*, 2(2), 11–16.

Lu, L. C., Rose, G. M. and Blodgett, J. G. (1999) The effects of cultural dimensions on ethical decision making in marketing: An exploratory study. *Journal of Business Ethics*, 18(1), 91–105.

Madichie, N. O. and Opute, A. P. (2019) Regulatory challenges in Sub-Saharan Africa and marketing malpractices of 'Big' Tobacco. In A. Gbadamosi (ed.), *Dynamics of Consumerism in Developing Nations*. Hersey, PA: IGI Global.

Malhotra, N. K., Birks, D. F. and Wills, P. (2012) *Marketing Research: An Applied Approach*, 4th edn. Harlow: Pearson.

Mishra, P. and Sharma, P. (2014) Green marketing: Challenges and opportunities for business. *BVIMR Management Edge*, 7(1), 78–86.

Modi, A. G. and Patel, J. D. (2013) Classifying consumers based upon their pro-environmental behaviour: An empirical investigation. *Asian Academy of Management Journal*, 18(2), 85–104.

Moravcikova, D., Krizanova, A., Kliestikova, J. and Rypakova, M. (2017) Green marketing as the source of the competitive advantage of the business. *Sustainability*, 9(12), 2218.

Nantel, J. and Weeks, W. A. (1996) Marketing ethics: Is there more to it than the utilitarian approach? *European Journal of Marketing*, 30(5), 9–19.

Ottman, J. A. and Reilly, W. R. (1998) *Green Marketing: Opportunity for Innovation*, 2nd edn. Upper Saddle River, NJ: Prentice Hall.

Papadas, K. K., Avlonitis, G. J. and Carrigan, M. (2017) Green marketing orientation: Conceptualization, scale development and validation. *Journal of Business Research*, 80, 236–46.

Parsons, E., Maclaran, P. and Chatzidakis, A. (2018) *Contemporary Issues in Marketing and Consumer Behaviour*, 2nd edn. Oxon: Routledge.

Peattie, K. (2001) Golden goose or wild goose? The hunt for the green consumer. *Business Strategy and the Environment*, 10(4), 187–99.

Pirages, D. C. and Ehrlich, P. R. (1974) *Ark II: Social Response to Environmental Imperatives*. San Francisco, CA: Freeman.

Polonsky, M. J. and Rosenberger III, P. J. (2001) Reevaluating green marketing: A strategic approach. *Business Horizons*, 44(5), 21–30.

Prakash, A. (2002) Green marketing, public policy and managerial strategies. *Business Strategy and the Environment*, 11(5), 285–97.

Rex, E. and Baumann, H. (2007) Beyond ecolabels: What green marketing can learn from conventional marketing. *Journal of Cleaner Production*, 15(6), 567–76.

Robson, C. (2002) *Real World Research: A Resource for Social Scientists and Practitioner-Researchers* (Vol. *2*). Malden, MA: Blackwell.

Ross, D. and Deck Jr, D. W. (2011) Student guide to greenwashing. *B>Quest*, pp. 1–20. Available at: www.westga.edu/~bquest/2011/greenwashing11.pdf (accessed 5 April 2019).

Ryen, A. (2016) Research ethics and qualitative research. In D. Silverman (ed.), *Qualitative Research*. London: Sage, pp. 31–46.

Schaefer, A. and Crane, A. (2005) Addressing sustainability and consumption. *Journal of Macromarketing*, 25(1), 76–92.

Scientific American (n.d.) How Can Consumers Find Out If a Corporation Is 'Greenwashing' Environmentally Unsavory Practices? Available at: www.scientificamerican.com/article/greenwashing (accessed 29 November 2018).

Signori, S. and Forno, F. (2016) Closing the attitude–behaviour gap: The case of Solidarity Purchase Groups. *Agriculture and Agricultural Science Procedia*, 8, 475–81.

Sirgy, M. J. and Johar, J. S. (1999) Toward an integrated model of self-congruity and functional congruity. *European Advances in Consumer Research*, 4, 252–6.

Slawson, N. (2017) Dove apologises for ad showing black woman turning into white one. *The Guardian*, 8 October. Available at: www.theguardian.com/world/2017/oct/08/dove-apologises-for-ad-showing-black-woman-turning-into-white-one (accessed 24 November 2018).

Smart, B. (2010) *Consumer Society: Critical Issues and Environmental Consequences*. London: Sage.

Straughan, R. D. and Roberts, J. A. (1999) Environmental segmentation alternatives: A look at green consumer behavior in the new millennium. *Journal of Consumer Marketing*, 16(6), 558–75.

Svensson, G. and Wood, G. (2003) `The dynamics of business ethics: a function of time and culture – cases and models', *Management Decision*, (41)4, 350–361.

United Nations (2016) Resolution Adopted by the General Assembly on 22 December 2015, UN General Assembly, 4 February 2016. Available at: https://unctad.org/meetings/en/SessionalDocuments/ares70d186_en.pdf (accessed 26 December 2018).

Vadehra, S. (2004) Advertising to children in India. *Young Consumers*, Quarter 4, 75–8.

PART III
Technology, Business and Contemporary Marketing

8
DIGITAL AND SOCIAL MEDIA MARKETING

Vishwas Maheshwari, Paul Dobson and Angela Lawrence

Learning Objectives

At the end of this chapter, you should be able to understand and discuss:

- The importance of digital marketing for optimising business growth
- Various channels of digital and social media marketing
- The use of social media channels as part of inbound and outbound marketing strategies
- The role of digital and social media tools to undertake effective and targeted inbound and outbound marketing practice

---

AN OVERVIEW OF DIGITAL AND SOCIAL MEDIA MARKETING

The rise of digital technology over the past decade has changed the outlook for businesses in the way they promote their brand, products and services and in how they engage with their existing and prospective customers. The use of digital technology in marketing activities is now a *norm* as businesses gain better customer interaction over a range of social media platforms and websites. Digital marketing has a commonly used terminology that includes a variety of online communication channels such as social media marketing, search engine marketing, email marketing and online advertising including paid and display advertising. Digital marketing is carried out using multiple channels (along with traditional media such as print and direct mail) as it supports better and quick identification of customer journeys (Chaffey and Ellis-Chadwick, 2015).

The innovations in digital technology have benefitted the growth of social media marketing strategies within organisations. Through social media, businesses can interact with customers proactively and may also potentially track customer journeys and relative buying intentions. This, in effect, has led to a race among businesses to reach customers through diverse digital channels including social platforms such as Facebook, Twitter, Instagram, Snapchat, YouTube, Pinterest and LinkedIn. Digital and social media marketing has made the marketplace more active and constantly changing but from a customer perspective it has become more transparent, providing clearer choices and enhanced value for money.

The role of digital technologies and the growth of social media channels go hand in hand and have become an active part of contemporary marketing activities, both for interacting with diverse customer segments and understanding behavioural motives. Social media platforms allow for constant engagement by enabling the sharing and building of content, aiding the development of better customer relationships.

So, customers who were beneficiaries of more tangible marketing have been replaced by a generation of experiential marketing consumers: consumers who want to experience brands, talk to brands and feel part of a brand community, but often from within an online environment. The days of one-way marketing communications have been replaced by two-way marketing conversations, where brands and increasingly vocal customers have regular and ongoing digital interactions.

Furthermore, the impact of digital and social media marketing might be established in terms of inbound and outbound marketing techniques, which is similar to traditional 'push and pull' marketing tactics but with the use of high-powered digital technology that can provide a better market reach (access to a higher number of customers) and market depth (establishment of stronger customer relationships for higher brand loyalty).

Both inbound and outbound marketing are discussed in the following sections of the chapter.

INBOUND MARKETING: BACKGROUND AND TERMINOLOGY

Over the last few years, inbound marketing has grown to become one of the major topics in digital marketing. Inbound marketing strategies generate a higher rate of return and have a positive long-term effect. This strategy contacts qualified prospects offering a more targeted approach with relevant content to generate leads and sales. According to Neil Patel (2018), inbound marketing is more of an approach than it is a list of tactics. Inbound marketing, at its core, is about attracting prospects to your business rather than going out to find those prospects. Traditional marketing relied on email lists, cold calling, billboard advertisements and direct mail, and Rudolph (2016) notes that inbound leads cost 61% less on average than outbound ones. Outbound marketing typically interrupts the prospect, via advertising mainly, which causes friction, whereas inbound marketing is designed to provide the information the prospect is searching for, ideally with useful engaging content and leading them to a path of conversion. However, inbound does require more time and effort to develop and see results, but they last longer. For example, when you stop paying for online ads, these ads stop while the inbound marketing can continue a long time after implementation. You need to develop and implement an inbound strategy including content audits, developing a customer persona and developing targeted content. This content curation can take a while before it starts to see results.

Moreover, inbound marketing is a powerful technique using digital marketing tools such as content, search, social and email marketing to drive the growth of a business (Smart Insights, 2018). One of the key tools for doing this is the website. The organisation's website is potentially one of the first impressions that potential customers may have of the company and is a tool that can support all levels of the customer funnel and encourage actions such as sales or subscription to emails. It can also raise the company's presence on search engines and develop the brand as a trusted expert, through the development of well-built home and landing pages with the design and implementation of a good content curation strategy. The other key tools are to get the website seen via social media channels and search engine optimisation (SEO).

The content strategy covers the creating and distributing of relevant and valuable content to attract, acquire and engage a clearly defined and understood target audience – with the objective of driving profitable customer action (Content Marketing Institute, 2012).

A good example of this is Buzzfeed (n.d.), whose aim is to 'connect deeply with our audience, and give them news and entertainment worth sharing with their friends, family, and the people who matter in their lives'. There is a clear strategy of social media-friendly quizzes, including celebrity news for its target audience.

DEVELOPING AN INBOUND DIGITAL MARKETING STRATEGY

In developing a strategy for the inbound website, there are clear steps to follow. This has been adapted from the methodology developed by HubSpot (2018).

Clearly define the digital marketing strategy aims and objectives from the organisation's goals

First, what are the organisation's goals and KPIs? Typically, businesses will have a forward plan of what they want to achieve and by when. The digital marketing strategy should support this by clearly defining key indicators. For example, how many sales are needed per week and therefore how many hits to its landing pages are required? In the context of this, when establishing an online digital marketing agency, the agency can establish for the website KPIs in the areas of: website traffic, bounce rate, subscription to the newsletter, white paper downloads, traffic to key blogs and increase in traffic from social media. Using both this and tools such as Google Analytics and the campaign URL builder, the customer journey can be tracked from social media to sales.

Buyer personas

Second, who is the target audience? Personas are fictional, generalised characters that represent both current and potential customers. These describe their various goals, needs and any concerns to enable segmentation of the market and help understand the customer better. Developing the buyer persona will aid an understanding of what key search terms they use and how, so that the creation and targeting of content are more efficient and effective. When developing the personas of potential customers, consider: what are their interests and biggest fears? What are their objectives, daily challenges and goals? What do they look for when searching online? Use tools such as Google Keyword to analyse what words they use. With this information an interesting, informative website can be developed that clients want to come back to. The personas should also outline what social media platforms they use and when, as this will support your social media marketing.

Competitor analysis

Third, now that the goals and target audience have been defined, the research needs to see what competition is out there, what they are doing and how they are doing it. Competitor analysis can also be a very effective tool for establishing both our position and some characteristics of the market. Typically, there are four key steps involved in competitor analysis:

1. Identifying your competitors

Developing a list of competitors in your target market and for businesses where the location is important, such as builders, gyms, hairdressers, can be done via Google Search using search terms of similar products and services. Also, search for competitors that may not be in direct competition, for example similar businesses across the country, as these can provide marketing strategy and digital marketing tips.

2. Using online tools to analyse competitor strategies and tactics

There are variety of tools such as Buzzsumo, SEMRUSH, SimilarWeb, Builtwith, Spyfu and Ahref to help with this. Look at: who links to what on their website, what estimates of traffic they are getting, what pages are getting the most hits using what keywords, and which keywords get their highest ranking. This gives a good profile of what is working, such as particular blogs or white papers, but also what gaps there are in the market that could be taken advantage of. For example, are customers searching for particular key facts or areas of support that a blog could be written about?

The Google Keyword tool and other search engine tools can help identify the words that clients and potential clients are using to search for the product or service. Check how your competitors compare against these for potential gaps that your business could exploit.

3. Comparing your competitors

This requires just a simple table outlining each competitor's name, products/services, where they compete, i.e. markets (and locations if applicable), distribution channels, their strengths, their weaknesses, and anything else that makes them stand out for their clients.

4. Identifying what makes your business stand out

Add an extra column to the above table and see how the business compares against those of your competitors. If the competitors have been around for a while, it is likely that there are key areas where they stand out, despite having similar products or services to other competitors. Identify the areas your business could develop and stand out in that both current and potential clients would be interested in.

The more you know about your competitors, the better you are prepared for their marketing actions or counter-attacks.

Content audit

A content audit is a qualitative analysis of the content a company has published online. It clarifies where the content is, where the thematic gaps are and, importantly, how it is performing. This helps define what is working, what is not and what you need to do to improve the inbound and SEO results. If your organisation already has a website, the next step is a content audit. The key benefits of a website audit are improving website performance, enhancing SEO and improving the conversion rate (Churt, 2018). A content audit helps to shape content governance and future strategy while ensuring that the quality of content is continuously of superior quality and relevant to its purpose. When auditing the content, consider customer personas and each stage of the customer journey.

In this context, Sizemore (2017) also suggests some important points to assess:

- Is the content relevant to the goals of the organisation and customer?
- Check whether the content is in line with the areas of interest of the client that the company is aiming to attract to the website, rather than covering a service, product or area of interest with no synergy with the company. If there is content that is not of interest to target clients, this can affect the SEO quality score and people will not spend long on the website. It will also be less productive in generating relevant content.
- Is the content accurate and consistent, or does it require copywriting/editing?
- Is the content up to date, or does it contain facts that are no longer relevant or have been superseded? This can be done via a regular, quarterly or similar, scan of the website, including content, in line with any change in regulations and tactics.
- Is it optimised for search? Are the keywords for this content the right longtail keywords in the right areas with the correct density? Currently, the target keyword density is around 2–7% so that it will not trip the filters and put the keywords at the beginning of the page, for example in the paragraph headers, as these have a higher priority.
- Does it speak in the style of the organisation? Is the style consistent across the content and in line with the company style? Consider how this style relates to the companies' social media style. Also think about the target audience – if the target audience is a younger generation, then formal, complicated words may not be appropriate.
- Do the topics of the content overlap? Is there an overlap of content or can the content flow from one piece to another so that you can link the content like a series of pages? Potentially, the longer you can keep an audience on your site, the better its ranking.
- Which content is receiving the most traffic and how do I replicate this? The company's Google Analytics can demonstrate what keywords are effectively being used for what content; this can then be developed to capture more potential clients, for example developing a top 10, white paper or technical support section.

- Which pages are not receiving traffic and need improving, updating, merging or removing? If pages are removed and someone clicks on a link to this area, there is an error so carefully manage your content and pages, including forwarding to other relevant pages or set up a domain redirection. Instead of deleting the page, it might be worth considering developing the content to be more informative and interesting.

Ideally, the website should be optimised for usability, for example ensuring that all of the main value propositions are easily accessible via the navigation menus. In addition, if it is a commercial site, for example with ecommerce or designed to capture potential clients' contact details, HubSpot (2018) suggests key areas to include in the audit to help inbound marketing and sales. These include first checking the shopping experience, especially the shopping cart process to remove any blockages or confusion. This can be done via Google Analytics to see where customers are stopping or leaving in the buying process, and hence where you are losing potential sales. Watching peers and friends having a go at buying something on the website with no hints or interruptions can also help observe where they have issues. Second, ensure that the landing pages are optimised for calls to action (CTAs) and marketing offers by ensuring these are clear and easy to use. Once potential customers are on your website, it is important that, as a minimum, you capture their contact details, for example by offering a free online booklet (PDF) or discount. These contacts can become an important part of your client base and sales campaigns. This can be achieved by a mobile-friendly pop-up window that offers a free information pack if they add their name and email address. Remember to verify the contact request and stay within GDPR guidelines. Third, ensure that the website is fast and mobile-friendly or optimised. Since 2016, mobile internet usage has overtaken desktop internet usage (Titcomb, 2016), therefore it is vital that your website is mobile-compatible. Google is also prioritising accelerated mobile websites, so this might be worth considering. Fourth, broken links on the website can damage the SEO and reduce customer satisfaction with the service. There are free online systems that can be used, such as SEMRush, to test this. If possible, have the page URLs optimised for keywords and do not have session IDs or dynamic parameters such as '?', as these are not SEO-friendly. Having Flash or JavaScript on the website, such as for navigation, is also not good for SEO. Search engines find these difficult to read and understand so they can damage your SEO ranking. Ideally, use SEO-friendly code, for example simple hyperlinks or hyperlinks from graphics. Finally, check that the site structure is optimised for SEO and clearly marked with sitemaps, robots.txt files and tags for search engines where they should/shouldn't index, for example for pages with a lot of duplication.

The content audit could also consider online tools such as Screaming Frog SEO Spider Tool which crawls a site to show how SEO-friendly it is. Google Analytics can give a comprehensive insight into the data and therefore customer flow of the website. This includes Google Users' flow report which is a graphical representation of the paths clients took through the company website, from the source, through the various pages, and where along their paths they exited your site. This lets you compare volumes of traffic from different sources, examine traffic patterns through your site, and troubleshoot. It also includes the Behaviour Flow report, which visualises the path users travelled from one page to the next. This report can highlight what content keeps users engaged with your site and which content is not effective. An example of this is the original Chabanettes Boutique Hotel & Spa website (see http://aubergedecha banettes.com/en). Customers would enter the home page and look at the photos. Although they might spend a while looking at the photos, they then appeared to drop out rather than book a reservation online. This was an area of concern so the owners talked to potential customers, who said they could not find the online booking system so went to other reservation platforms, for example booker.com and tripadvisor.com, and booked through these. This led to a potential loss of customers and income. To help alleviate this, online reservations were moved to the top of the home page which showed an immediate improvement in customer flow to booking reservations.

Editorial calendar and creating new content

An editorial calendar is a plan of marketing activities, for example blogs, newsletters, white papers, ideally supported by social media, that covers what the company is doing over a period of time. Like a traditional calendar, it gives a graphical view of what is going on when. The personas and content audit should be enough information to develop a topics list and editorial calendar. This can include who is writing what topics/keywords for when, and potentially act as a place to help generate ideas. To make these insights actionable, Moz (n.d.) recommend creating a table for each persona with three dimensions: content missing that the audience needs, content titles that address this issue, and content format. Checking customer personas against the content audit may identify gaps in content for the persona. The editorial calendar is also a useful tool to ensure that any upcoming events or sales are marketed effectively. To this end, HubSpot (2018) has developed a list of ideas that might be of some help, as seen in Figure 8.1.

However, if an organisation does not have a website, it will need to choose a content management system. Ideally, it should choose a website development tool that can support search engine optimisation (SEO), such as Yoast for Wordpress.

A way to help keep customers on your website is to create a series of related content, and then, as the reader completes a topic, they are guided to the next one, and so on. New content might also cover issues and recommendations that you know are going to impact

Figure 8.1   List of content formats

Source: HubSpot (2018)

your customers in your area; potentially you could raise this, point out how this will impact them and provide solutions. An important recent feature that Google has developed is the Featured Snippet. These snippets appear at or near the top of the search page when a user asks a question in Google Search. This featured snippet block includes a summary of the answer, extracted from a web page, plus a link to the page and the page title. If you can provide all these, it helps the website appear at the top of a search (see 'Featured snippets in search' on Google).

Content distribution to gain customers

Your website content will be wasted if no one knows it exists. According to Jayson DeMers (2014), founder of AudienceBloom, the real value of content marketing is in the distribution channels. There are various methods to promote your campaigns such as email, social media

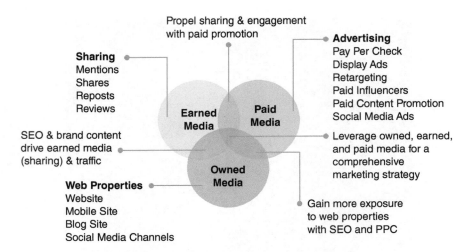

Figure 8.2   Content distribution trifecta – earned, owned and paid media

Source: Fleiss (2017)

and paid campaigns. By developing the personas, the strategy will already encompass the marketing method(s) best to use. According to Fleiss (2017), there are three main types of content distribution channel (see also Figure 8.2):

1. Owned content distribution (owned media): covers the media channels that the company owns and should have direct control over – for example, website, blogs, social media, email newsletters, apps. The company should have direct influence over these channels and can use these in line with their editorial calendar to plan and implement the content. This means that they can support various key stakeholders to build and implement influence, for example creating material for earned content distribution (see next point). The organisation can also develop interesting SEO-targeted longtail keyword-optimised blogs to help insure a lasting and effective series of pages that customers want to keep coming back to read. For example, if you are a firm selling car parts, do not just provide technical information on how to do repairs but also 'how-to' videos, links for ordering car parts and 'Did you know?'-type interactive content; also take customer details so that you have the car make and model.

2. Earned content distribution (earned media): includes the distribution of your content by third parties such as guest blog posts, retweets, shares and PR pieces. This includes your advocates and followers sharing your content with their followers, and having others share or publish your PR. This can be through the organisation developing key advocates and influencers and then giving this group exclusive pre-release information and support for new product launches. These advocates can help build up

interest before a new product release, thereby making a much bigger impression, increasing sales, developing barriers to entry for competitors, and improving and enhancing brand identity.

3. Paid content distribution (paid media): this is where you pay for your content to be distributed, such as through social media advertising and Google AdWords campaigns. The advantage of paid-for advertising is that it can give very quick visibility, such as on Google or FaceBook ads. However, when the company stops paying, this visibility stops as well. To make this effective, it needs careful research and implementation. When implementing this form of digital marketing, you need to be clear what keywords potential customers may use and also what keywords people might search on who are not interested in your product or service but may still see your advert. These adverts are a waste of money and if people visit your site and immediately leave, it will start to give a poor Google result, thereby costing you more to advertise.

Frequently, a digital marketing strategy will include a combination of the above three channels. For immediate effect and content that has proven popular, earned and paid media can be effective, and for longer-term sustainable results, developing the website to be SEO-friendly with a constant monitoring of results to improve inbound marketing.

Search engine optimisation

Search engine optimisation (SEO) is the practice of increasing the quantity and quality of traffic to a website through organic search engine results. Nowadays, consumers are seeking solutions to their problems across multiple platforms, including Facebook, Twitter, LinkedIn, Pinterest and more. However, the majority of searches are still via search engines. Therefore, the website's visibility on this platform is very important. Currently, there are three main types of SEO: on-page SEO, off-page SEO and local SEO.

On-page SEO (also known as on-site SEO) is the practice of optimising key elements on a website in order to rank higher and earn more relevant traffic from search engines. Some of these elements have been described above in the section on the audit. Historically, on-page SEO has been undertaken using keywords and off-page backlinks. With the Google algorithm updates, these have become less important and other factors have started to become more significant, such as the quality of the website content, mobile optimisation and domain power, for instance website age and keyword match domain name. Key areas that impact the SEO ranking are:

- Content quality: content needs to provide real value to viewers, be easy to read and ideally be engaging visually.

- Content length: a study by Neil Patel (2012) demonstrates a correlation between content length and top Google search ranking.
- Mobile first (accelerated/compatible): in November 2016, Google announced its mobile-first indexing. This means that the mobile compatibility of a website now directly affects its search ranking.
- Page speed: the increase in mobile internet and mobile-first indexing by Google has made loading speed a ranking priority.
- Local SEO: search engines are increasingly becoming interested in local businesses so local SEO and schema code is important.
- Brand and social searches: the more traffic you get from branded searches, the more it is recognised by Google's algorithm. Additionally, social searches from Facebook, Pinterest and similar platforms can improve rankings.
- Domain name: the domain name matching the search is still influential but it appears that this has reduced with the latest Google updates.

Off-page SEO (also known as off-site SEO) is the actions taken outside of the company website to impact the search engine rankings. The key element of this type of SEO is the quality and authority of the backlinks to the website. For example, a website with many high-value backlinks will usually rank better than those without other areas being equal. There are three main types of links, defined by how they are developed:

- Natural links are those formed by others linking to a competitor website, for example a newspaper linking to a related and informative blog from an expert in the area. If this link is from a high-profile organisation, for example the BBC, it can have a positive impact on the organisation's SEO ranking. This is an example of why it is worth developing high-quality, interesting content.
- Manually developed links are built through deliberate link-building activities, for example by asking key influencers to share and link to the blogs. Some key influencers have a very strong following, so if they discuss and share a company's content this can raise the profile of the business and the number of hits to the content.
- Self-created links are created by adding backlinks in online directories, press releases, forums and blog comment signatures. Potentially, these may not have a significant impact on the SEO ranking. However, they do help to get the content, and therefore the company knowledge, resulting in increased traffic.

Non-link-related off-page SEO includes social media marketing, guest blogging and influencer marketing. Finally, local SEO is designed to help businesses promote their products and services to local customers at the exact time customers are looking for them. Local SEO uses a variety of tactics, for example getting the website ranked on search engines like Google, business directories such as Yelp, Foursquare, Yell, Google My Business, Bing Places for Business, and also includes localised content on the website, online reviews and other strategies. This has become very important with the increase in customers using their mobile phone for local services, plus it has a high conversion rate. Local mobile search examples are restaurants, plumbers and other domestic repairers.

CONTENT MARKETING

Content marketing is a marketing strategy of creating and distributing informative content such as blogs, videos and photos on a consistent basis to raise the profile of the business or person. The content does not have to be about the business directly, such as an ad, but can be in areas that are of interest to the target audience and therefore help the organisation to receive more traffic or repeated traffic. Although creating content is time-intensive, often businesses change to content marketing because paid-for advertising can be more expensive, ineffective, not scalable, or all three. Content marketing can be shown to help increase sales, is a cost saving compared to paid-for advertising and may help develop better customers who are more loyal (Content Marketing Institute, 2018).

Typically, the content is developed, SEO-optimised, placed on the website, blog or platform and then promoted using social media. Content marketing needs to be part of an overall digital marketing strategy rather than seen as a separate entity, for example incorporated as part of inbound marketing, pay-per-click (PPC), PR and SEO as all of these need good content to be effective. A good example of content marketing is the digital photography school that adds daily hints, tips and advice to its website. To enable this, it has a small team of dedicated and freelance writers who write to a planned schedule of topics.

In addition, it is important to remember that 'content is king'. Emails and PPC will never hit the target without attractive, media-rich, relevant content to appeal to the target audience. Therein lies an overlap between outbound and inbound digital marketing. Social media, considered an inbound digital marketing tool, is also only ever as good as the content that it contains. It is this content, communicated within a one-to-many, inbound digital environment, that can be used to develop appealing, one-to-many, paid-for, outbound digital marketing activities, such as the YouTube clip embedded within the outbound email.

Practitioners' Perspectives 8.1

Interviews on customer focus

'Social media platforms are an extremely effective brand awareness, lead generation and nurturing tool. Businesses of all sizes benefit from using social media as it drives their brand exposure, boosts SEO, represents a global PR tool and helps to monitor industry trends as well as competitors. But using social media aimlessly can have zero or even negative impact on your business.' (Petra Urhofer, marketing consultant, Squirrels & Bears; Urhofer, 2017)

'According to HubSpot, 47% of buyers engage with 3–5 pieces of content before directly engaging with a company. What does this mean? It means that content is key to any digital marketing strategy. By having a clear approach to all aspects of your content creation, your business will be in a much stronger position when it comes to engaging and converting leads to customers.' (Judith O'Leary, managing director, Represent; O'Leary, 2018)

'[B]rands today need to be able to take the unique hobbies, habits, behaviours and interests of consumers into account in order to target them with highly personalised communications, and this requires a major adjustment in marketing approach.' (Thomas Salfischberger, CEO and co-founder, Relay42; Salfischberger, 2018)

'With a rise in social media communications, the goal posts of customer engagement have forever shifted, demanding a more instant and personal approach from brands ... brands need to evolve their CX approach to ensure they can continue to meet the expectations of customers who demand a 24/7 response – those businesses that do this will thrive.' (Simon Fraser, senior director for customer experience strategy, InMoment; Fraser, 2018)

Questions for discussion

1. How are businesses changing their customer focus using digital CX and UX approaches? Discuss with an example(s) which you may have experienced recently or where you have been part of such a development.
2. What do you think are the key ingredients of forming a contemporary brand identity, one that not only appeals to target segments but also creates a seamless personalised relationship with customers?
3. 'Content is king' – discuss this in the context of the application of at least two social media marketing channels that you may have recently experienced. What was the experience, and did it made any difference? Share your perspectives using specific examples of the content identified.

OUTBOUND MARKETING

It does not seem so long ago that the office of a marketer consisted of a row of filing cabinets and a desk with three things on it – a telephone, a computer and a tower of three trays, labelled 'In', 'Out' and 'Pending'. The computer wasn't used for much more than word processing; everything important was stored in hard copy in the filing cabinets. The telephone was in constant use – marketers spoke to their customers, prospects and media contacts regularly. The tower of trays was continuously revolving; post came in, post went out and the pending tray grew as an hour was spent opening mail each morning, shrinking as the day progressed. Nobody had heard of email and the facsimile, or fax machine, was an exciting new form of communication.

The 'Out' tray and the telephone were the marketers' tools for generating business, a method of contacting customers and prospects to discuss new products, prices, promotions and places where products could be purchased. Media contacts worked for magazines and billboard companies. What we now call outbound marketing has derived from these marketing activities, but the difference is that the majority of these communications are now performed within a digital landscape.

Outbound digital communications

Outbound digital marketing, also known as push marketing, is communication that is driven by the digital marketer – the brand initiates contact with the prospect. This is clearly the opposite of inbound, where the prospect independently seeks out the product or brand. Despite being criticised as being out of date, old-hat, untargeted and unsought after, there is without doubt still a place in the digital world for a well-targeted, creative outbound marketing campaign. Indeed, the shrewd digital marketer can make use of a variety of cost-effective tools to implement highly effective, measurable outbound digital campaigns. Gone are the days of mass marketing – targeting and personalisation are considered the norm, resulting in increasingly clever creative concepts that attract audiences amidst the buzz of a crowded marketplace. The ability to be creative is essential in the not-so-new digital environment, where emails are deleted in bulk without being read and advertisements are blocked or ignored.

Making the customer feel that the communication is worth engaging with is the key to a successful outbound marketing campaign. MedTech Europe, Europe's leading medical technology event did this with their integrated marketing campaign.

The campaign resulted in an impressive 369,261 social media impressions with 733 new LinkedIn followers, 16.7% e-blast open rate and 720 attendees to the MedTech Forum event (50% more attendees than the previous year's event), demonstrating the power of a creative, targeted and personalised digital marketing campaign.

Digital Focus 8.1

MedTech Europe

Campaign overview

The MedTech Forum is the largest medical technology industry event in Europe. Welcoming both members and non-members to discuss future trends in the medical device and technology sector.

The Brief

- Attract a new audience to The MedTech Forum 2018 event
- Increase database of prospects for future communication purposes
- Create awareness and visibility of the event online
- Reinforce The MedTech Forum as Europe's leading medical technology event
- Develop new links with key opinion leaders in the medical device and technology sector

The Solution

As the biggest medical technology event outside the USA, award-winning Integrated Communications Agency TMC was commissioned to develop an innovative approach which utilised data platforms to truly maximise reach.

Three target groups were identified, who would benefit most from attending the event. A communication strategy was developed using LinkedIn for acquisition and multiple online channels to illustrate the business benefits of attendance to each of the target audiences.

Dedicated landing pages and email were used throughout the campaign to deliver audience-specific messages, building audience trust and increasing engagement. Social media channels were used to communicate more general messages and to support the LinkedIn activity.

Results

The result was 50% more attendees compared to the 2017 event with a 16.7% e-blast open rate and over 700 new LinkedIn followers.

Questions

1. Why do you think MedTech Europe chose to use LinkedIn and email to connect with its target audiences?
2. What were the possible reasons for email recipients choosing to engage with the campaign?

THE PUSH OR PULL DEBATE

Like many things in life, the decision of whether to use push or pull digital marketing techniques often comes down to timing. We are all too aware of the behaviour of modern, technically savvy consumers who choose to search for what they want from the plethora of pull marketing content available. These confident punters seek out word-of-mouth and reviews to aid their decision making, and may indeed argue that they do not need to have information pushed out to them.

But pull marketing has its disadvantages – creating content, optimising search and responding to the ever-changing algorithms that dictate how easily your content can be found, then waiting for the consumer to find you in the noisy digital world, all take time. The digital environment is fast-paced, and time is a precious commodity for the marketer. Hence, pushing your brand messages out there using outbound digital marketing techniques can lead to being successfully heard above the noise. There are also stages within a brand's or organisation's life cycle when push marketing is always going to be more appropriate. When new products are being launched, push marketing techniques can be essential for building awareness; email, display advertising and PPC are all commonly used to push out the new product message to the uninformed consumer.

When the decision has not yet quite been made, when a consumer has engaged with your brand and come close to committing but has not gone as far as taking the final plunge to buy, a well-timed email or retargeted PPC ad can prompt them to finally say 'Yes, I want this' and make the purchase. Similarly, when the noise of competitors has pulled the consumer away from your content, discount codes, special offers and promotions can be pushed out to tempt them to come back to you to do business.

Outbound email marketing

One thing is for sure: email most definitely is not dead. Contrary to what the apostles of inbound digital marketing would have us believe, email is stronger than ever. The DMA Insight: Marketer Email Tracking Survey (2017) reveals that a staggering 95% of marketers view email as important or very important. However, they agree wholeheartedly that they are not always sending out relevant content, with only 9% stating that their email is relevant to their customers. This begs the question, why would you send out emails that were not relevant and run the risk of annoying or, even worse, losing your customers?

Let us look at a typical example of outbound email usage. Retail outlets increasingly request a customer email address at the point of purchase. The offer of an email receipt pricks our green conscience and we agree. In agreeing to receive the receipt by email, the door is open for the retailer to offer to keep us updated with newsletters, special offers and discount events that they deem relevant or of interest to us. This is the point at which mistakes can be made – loyalty and advocacy can be lost with just one irrelevant or untimely email too many. So, it is not that email is dead, it is simply a case of understanding how to use this powerful outbound digital marketing tool wisely.

> 'If email is to continue to grow and thrive as a channel, then marketers need to heed customer concerns and take care to give them what they want.' (Rachel Aldigieri, MD at the DMA)

Daily deal and discount sites such as VoucherCodes, Groupon, LivingSocial and Secret Escapes are popular with bargain-hunting consumers. The concept of being the first to know about special offers on anything from holidays to hair accessories appeals to the masses, who often proudly boast of their 'wins' on social media. The downside to these popular deal sites can be the over-enthusiastic bombardment of emails to the registered user. Often, the content of many offers, which claim to be targeted to the personal taste of a registrant, appears to bear little resemblance to the bargain of their dreams. Instead, inboxes are cluttered with daily eshots, adding weight to that stark statistic that only 9% of email marketers state that their email is relevant to their customers.

According to statista.com, 269 billion emails were sent daily in 2017 and this figure is expected to increase to over 333 billion by 2022 (Statista, 2018). A visit to internetstatslive.com shows daily emails being sent in a whirr of numbers increasing by millions per second – all this from a standing start of one test email that American pioneer Roy Tomlinson sent to himself, from one computer sat on his desk to another, less than half a century ago in the early 1970s.

Email marketing automation platforms such as Dotmailer, MailChimp and Pure360 make the outbound digital marketer's job so much easier. They offer templates, detailed analysis and reporting, optimisation tips and the opportunity for testing different subject lines to see which has the biggest impact (called A/B testing or split testing), with easy-to-read reporting dashboards containing a plethora of information to guide the user. As with many software packages, these platforms are reported to be underused. The email marketing manager for Smart Insights, Kim Greenop-Gadsby, compares their purchase and functionality under usage to that of a home purchase: 'why would you buy a 5-bedroom house when you have no idea what you would use those rooms for?' This is not to say that marketers should be using their marketing automation platforms to send more emails, but rather that they should be exploring the functionality to send appropriate emails more wisely.

However, such is the confidence in email marketing that, according to a report authored by Dave Chaffey, Robert Jones and Michal Leszczynski, 'Email Marketing and Marketing

Automation Excellence 2018', 50% of marketers do not do any targeting when sending their email campaigns. This is surprising considering increasingly sophisticated email marketing tools can enable targeted, focused and appropriate email to be sent to a receptive customer or prospect who has willingly shared their data with the sender. The platforms and tools available to effectively target, segment and track individual customers and prospects are also increasingly affordable for businesses of all sizes. Some, such as Dotmailer and Emma (https://myemma.com), are single-purpose platforms, while others such as GetResponse, HubSpot and Salesforce are unified CRM platforms capable of co-ordinating both inbound and outbound digital marketing activities to support truly integrated, targeted campaigns (see Figure 8.3).

A section on email marketing would not be complete without reference to the current legislation affecting digital marketers. Headlines telling stories of data breaches and data theft are not uncommon on a weekly basis and the recent GDPR legislation is being described as the gold standard for data protection. Trust is without doubt an issue for email marketers – the DMA Insight, Marketer Email Tracking Survey reports that 'trust is the most important factor in persuading people to sign up for a brand in the first place' (DMA, 2017). Processors and controllers now have obligations under GDPR with regard to both personal data management and their activities. The Information Commissioners Office (ICO) is committed to enforcing legislation under both GDPR and the UK Data Protection Act (DPA).

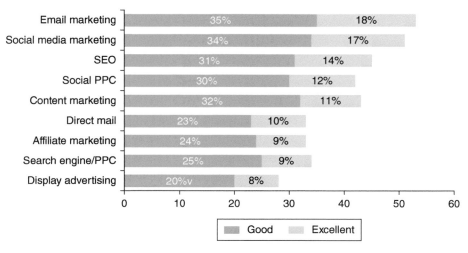

Figure 8.3 Ratings by marketers on the effectiveness of digital media channels

Source: Smart Insights (2018)

Digital giants such as Google faced the wrath of enforcement, but when the legislation was enforced on 25 May 2018, it was reported that the small business was less well prepared for the impact of the new legislation to protect personal data (Information Commissioners Office, 2017). The spring of 2018 saw a flurry of email activity from businesses asking contacts to opt in, but they didn't all get it right, as noted in the tweet from Steve Dinneen, the editor of City AM (Figure 8.4). The fact is, businesses are accountable for the ways in which they use and store personal data … and there is nowhere to hide.

Figure 8.4　Dinneen's tweet on GDPR

Source: Twitter

LOCATION-BASED MARKETING

Location-based technology is hot on the agenda for today's digital advertisers and it seems that George Orwell's Big Brother is indeed watching us. Knowing precisely where our customers and prospects are and what they are doing enables accurate, targeted communications. WiFi and Bluetooth technologies dominate our use of handheld devices, and geofencing enables marketers to transmit targeted messages within a specified area; geofencing is effectively a virtual border, within which mobile devices can be targeted.

There is, however, some negativity around the accuracy of location data used for geofencing. Brand and agency experts speaking to *Advertising Week* at a roundtable event expressed concerns over the perceived estimations of location data (Johnson, 2017). The performances of devices, browsers and users all appear to contribute to inaccuracies, yet, despite concerns, geofencing is a growing outbound digital tool. Data-centred research specialists BIA report that location-based mobile advertising spend is set to reach over $32 billion by 2021.

A typical example of geofencing may be experienced when visiting exhibitions or trade shows. As visitors browse the stands, their mobile device will be detected within the geofence and SMS offers can be pushed out via permission-based digital marketing to attract visitors to stands and engage them with the brand. The limitation of this popular outbound digital tool is that the sender is dependent on the visitor downloading an app, so intelligent planning and possibly event sponsorship may persuade visitors of the benefits of an app which replaces the traditional printed show guide for the digital consumer.

The Museum of Finnish Architecture (MFA) is an international museum in Helsinki and the world's second oldest museum of architecture. The MFA is custodian of an extensive collection of architectural exhibits of international interest.

Examples of Finnish architecture can be seen all around the city of Helsinki, yet the museum itself is limited in space and can only contain photographs, drawings and miniatures of buildings of architectural interest.

To extend the visitor experience and create a unique multi-site experience, location-based marketing techniques were used by app developer Proximi.io – geofencing-enabled users of the MFA app – to continue their visit outside of the museum building and into the city of Helsinki.

A beacon installation within buildings of architectural interest enabled the MFA app to detect nearby buildings, miniatures of which are visible to users of the app.

PAY PER CLICK (PPC) AND BANNER ADS

PPC is the model adopted to use digital advertising to drive traffic to your website. It works on the basis of bidding for keywords – words that you would typically expect the consumer to put into a search engine when looking for products or services that you provide. The most well-known PPC program is Google Adwords, with the model based around advertisers paying a fee each time one of their online ads is clicked. There is a cost per click (CPC) linked to the popularity of the search term and agreed before the campaign begins.

While Google Adwords campaigns can be run in-house, understanding the power and capability of Google's tool, making best use of the wealth of analytics provided and tweaking live campaigns can be a full-time job, hence the growth of PPC agencies, who will do the work for you. Reggie James' blog for Digital Clarity (2018), 'Looking for the best PPC agency can be a challenge', gives sound advice on selection of the right agency, offering questions to ask when seeking a PPC partner, to ensure that you get exactly what you want from your PPC campaigns.

The ability to manage budgets and optimise campaigns is a hugely attractive benefit of PPC – if an ad is not working then changes can be made instantly, to improve its effectiveness. PPC ads can be set up in minutes using keywords, demographics and interests to precisely target the audience that you want to reach, making PPC one of the fastest digital outbound platforms for immediate results. A good PPC campaign comes with a range of metrics to demonstrate its effectiveness, including traffic, click-through rates (CTR), leads, conversions and sales, and PPC is known to deliver high levels of return on investment (ROI).

From a customer viewpoint, digital advertising is getting more and more pervasive, disruptive, intrusive and generally annoying. Pop-ups, banner ads, Facebook ads and online video ads before content loads are perceived to be the most disliked of all, according to HubSpot Research. Ironically, the report 'Why People Block Ads (And What It Means for Marketers and Advertisers)' (An, 2016) itself is hard to read without distraction from a HubSpot pop-up ad encouraging you to subscribe. Consumers respond by installing ad-blocking extensions and it is reported that £27 billion per year will be lost by 2020 as a result. The jury is out over the rights and wrongs of ad blocking but rightly or wrongly, brands still love PPC.

Opinion is further divided on banner ads, which are unpopular with consumers and bear the wrath of the ad-blocking generation. Banner ads sit at the top of web pages and are easily ignored if the content is not attractive. However, dynamic ads which are specific to the interests of the browsing consumer and created in real time according to identified needs and preferences, are far more persuasive. The move towards dynamic ads has led to the development of more successful banner advertising and, along with email, this long-established digital outbound marketing tool is still alive and kicking.

Similarly, affiliate marketing, a form of performance-paid advertising, is still successful when ad blockers are not deployed. For most consumers, a banner ad, whether on an affiliate website or not, is still a banner ad. It will appeal if persuasive and dynamic but is less likely to earn the click-through commission for the affiliate if not appropriately targeted.

CRISIS MANAGEMENT

At times of crisis, the impact of new media is twofold – digital platforms enable swift communication of information to assist the crisis situation, but also facilitate negative rumour dissemination, which can be both inaccurate and harmful. When mistakes are made, organisations and brands need to be quicker than ever to respond with honesty, and apologise where appropriate. To wait or to send out less than candid digital communications is to open a can of worms for the audiences of the unforgiving digital landscape.

The Merlin Group provides an exemplar case of how an organisation responded effectively in the digital environment, at a time of crisis. It was quick to take action following the roller coaster accident at Alton Towers in June 2015, with the CEO Nick Varney fronting the company response in the form of a live heartfelt apology, which was immediately shared and viewed on multiple digital platforms. His measured responses to difficult questions were delivered against a backdrop of graphic videos of the crash emerging across digital channels, along with angry accusations of poor safety procedures. The speed and honesty of his response did much to dampen the finger pointing, and the use of video by Merlin, rather than simply releasing a statement, enabled body language to be read; Nick Varney was clearly devastated for the individuals affected by the incident, and genuinely apologetic on behalf of the Merlin Group.

Compare this to the Grenfell Tower fire in June 2017, when the quick action of community groups communicating via digital platforms to care for the needs of survivors, overtook the response from the Royal Borough of Kensington and Chelsea (RBKC). Criticism of RBKC was quick to appear on social media and a platform for discussion was opened, which RBKC failed to respond to effectively. The broadcasting of the true feelings of the affected community is perceived to have been moved away from mainstream media to the digital environment that was owned by the community itself.

Digital media is highly effective in generating positive marketing messages. The speed and scope of distribution of these messages is far greater than any traditional media and, furthermore, a two-way communication channel is opened. So, at times of crisis, this creates a unique opportunity for organisations or brands to respond to audience opinion and to calm the storm. Astute marketers should prepare for crisis situations and rehearse digital responses, to avoid being overtaken by their digital publics and losing control over a situation, which could result in long-term damage.

Ethical Focus 8.1

Cambridge Analytica/Facebook scandal

The scandal involving Cambridge Analytica, a UK-based company, accused of using Facebook's user data to try and help Donald Trump's presidency campaign, has raised alarms about who (and how and where) is using the personal data of users, especially for political gain.

(Continued)

(Continued)

It is understood that the user data was gathered using Facebook's infrastructure prior to the US presidential elections, and used by quite a few unauthorised entities without the actual user being aware of it. This also involved user unawareness, in the sense that their personal data may have been compromised for political gain, while engaging in personality quizzes and answering profile-related questions. However, Facebook continues to maintain that it had asked for the information to be removed and/or deleted, while Cambridge Analytica claims that it had never used/shared any such data, but also that it deleted it all when requested by Facebook. Either way, the unfolding of this scandal, involving masses of users and their personal data effectively being compromised, has resulted in serious ethical concerns around both the public and private sectors, including the political authorities.

Source: Kleinman (2018)

Questions

1. How can data held online as part of an organisation's digital and social media activity be protected?
2. How do new GDPR regulations in the UK impact ethical concerns for users?

CONTEMPORARY PRACTICES IN DIGITAL MARKETING

Throughout the chapter, we have focused discussion around emerging practices in digital marketing alongside relevant social media applications. Here, we would like to provide brief insight into several contemporary digital marketing practices that are becoming increasingly prevalent as part of marketing planning and strategic implementation by organisations and businesses around the world.

Customer segmentation

Customer segmentation, also known as marketing segmentation, involves examining the overall market for the industry, service or product, and, depending on the characteristics of the customers, dividing this market into segments. The business can then choose key segments that it wants to focus on within its marketing, including digital marketing, which is therefore more targeted and should have an improved return on investment. There are several standard ways of dividing up the markets using customer characteristics. Typically, these segments can be developed from characteristics such as:

- customer channel (or multi-channel) preferences and use: frequently, customers have preferred platforms such as Facebook, Instagram and Snapchat. Potentially, this may include discussion groups such as specialised forums on Yahoo.
- customer profile characteristics: typically, these are characteristics of the population, such as age, gender, geographic distance from the business location, marital status, ethnicity and income. For example, for a beauty therapist this could be a combination of age, geographic location and income.
- customer psychographic characteristics: these can be considered by looking at the customer's lifestyle, including interests, traits, activities and opinions.

This customer buying behaviour can change over time, so it is necessary to undertake primary research as well as analyse marketing data, such as the website Google Analytics, on a regular basis to ensure that the correct segments are being developed and targeted. It is worth noting that even for small businesses it is worth breaking the segments down into their key buying type, for example Prim and Proper beauty treatments (see www.primandproperbeauty. co.uk), where the customer characteristics here might be shown to be: women who are within 10 miles of the salon, have disposable income and are interested in beauty. It can also be further broken down by age and psychographic characteristics, enabling the owner to improve her social media targeting.

It is important to remember that, often, online customer segmentation and the resulting marketing reinforce off-line sales such as the buying of products and services. Therefore, customer off-line characteristics also need to be considered.

MOBILE MARKETING

Mobile marketing is a digital marketing tactic, targeting customers using mobile devices such as smartphones and tablets. This can be via websites, SMS and MMS, social media platforms, email and apps. As many mobile platforms, such as Facebook and Instagram, include marketing tools that allow the targeting of these messages, the marketing can be customised for these targeted audiences, and therefore more effective. Patel (2014) notes that 70% of mobile searches trigger an action.

Mobile marketing can be disruptive, such as SMS, MMS and Facebook chatbots, where the advert potentially interrupts the customer, or non-disruptive such as a customer clicking on a link on a business website that enables the customer's mobile to: call the business, offer travel directions, or offer a customer a call back at a time convenient to them. An example of non-disruptive is a potential customer doing a Google search for 'Chinese restaurants near me'. The search then displays elements the restaurant can have an input in, such as an overview, photos, details about the restaurant, plus options of calling, receiving directions, saving for later and visiting the website. The website could also have disruptive marketing by enabling the customer to subscribe to a Facebook chatbot that sends direct messages outlining the restaurant offers.

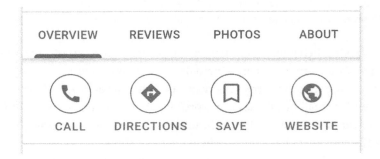

Image 8.1   Phone screenshot

MMS offers a more comprehensive and richer experience than SMS messaging, including graphics, easy shareable options via a social media button and the ability to link to a multi-channel marketing campaign. Therefore, this can be more effective at engaging customers.

As most customers currently use smartphones for social media and online searches, mobile marketing is increasingly important. In addition, there is an increase in mobile marketing tools, especially in social media, such as geolocation tools: geotargeting, geofencing and beacons, where customers can be targeted for adverts depending on where they are. These geolocation tools can be used to send adverts when customers are nearby or, for example, to offer a time-limited discount if they are about to go to a competitor's business location. The knowledge and use of mobile marketing are extremely important for today's businesses to keep in touch with customers and stay competitive.

AFFILIATE MARKETING

The concept of affiliate marketing is very simple – affiliates make money by referring products from their website. Affiliate marketing provides an excellent platform for brands to test new products and services, because payment is by results only. High click-through rates (CTR) can be achieved and sales increased at a fraction of the cost of other forms of digital marketing. Furthermore, affiliate marketing provides detailed metrics giving information such as the type of buyer coming from each affiliate source, which can feed into digital strategy development.

So, for many, affiliate marketing is a key component of a digital strategy. That said, digital marketers must be wary of damage to their brand when considering affiliate marketing. The choice of affiliate and the tactics agreed with them is of paramount importance, as the partnerships represent your brand in one way or other. Heavy discounts, unsolicited emails or pop-up advertisements are all to be avoided if you wish to protect the investment in your brand.

CONTENT AUTOMATION

Changing consumer behaviour has led to the demand for instant response and the fast-paced digital environment has done little to dampen this. In a world where consumers want chatbots to give them the answer now, digital marketers must continually consider the relevance and suitability of their marketing content. Content automation services have fast become an essential part of the digital marketer's toolkit. Thankfully, content automation is both more accessible and less expensive, so these tools are not out of reach for even the most frugal of marketers.

The content that your consumers are exposed to is important at every stage of the buying journey, so content automation is not just one tool, but a range of tools that can be deployed to ensure the provision of relevant and appealing messages every step of the way. Content curation tools exploit algorithms to mine web content and identify what type of content will be most relevant for your customers or prospects; content distribution tools further identify suitable content to be sent to customers or prospects depending on their preferences, as indicated by past online behaviour. Content automation providers such as Marketo, HubSpot and Salesforce can support digital strategies with automated email, mobile, social media, digital advertising and web content, ensuring that your customers see the right content at the right time – exactly when they want it, to make that all-important buying decision.

GETTING IT RIGHT

The secret to successful digital marketing is to employ the right mix of inbound and outbound techniques, to create media-rich content that is relevant to your target audience and to adopt a strategic approach to integrated digital marketing campaign development. With 46% of organisations stating that digital permeates most of their activities (Adobe and Econsultancy, 2017), it has also become increasingly important to integrate both online and offline marketing activities.

The digital and social media marketing impact 'conceptual capture' in Figure 8.5, as a key contribution of this chapter to practice, shows the road map for inbound and outbound marketing channels to achieve optimum and target-driven consumer behaviour that is positive and beneficial for organisations and brands alike.

Figure 8.5   Road map for inbound and outbound marketing channels

It is assumed that both inbound and outbound marketing channels will involve an integrated approach emphasising user-generated creative content that is appealing, and the application of experiential marketing strategies including local-based targeting for better engagement. This should result in the development of informed perceptions within existing and potential consumers that may be positively registered for spontaneous interaction or easily recalled and recognised for future engagement.

Case Study 8.1

The Chabanettes Boutique Hotel & Spa

The Chabanettes Boutique Hotel & Spa (see http://aubergedechabanettes.com/en) is a small, family-run hotel, spa, bar and restaurant. The venue is busy so time is limited and any changes to the hotel's marketing must be cost-effective, with little time spent on developing and maintaining it. The hotel is located far from cities and towns, in pretty countryside with mountain and forest walks all around, including a river flowing near the front of the hotel. It is popular with cyclists and people wanting to get away from the stresses of a busy life. When the family took over the hotel in the Auzelles region of France, after developing the website they registered the hotel's name, address and phone number (NAP), and website, and confirmed that they were the owners. Within a week, the details were available on Google and Google Maps so that if anyone nearby googled details for a hotel, restaurant, bar or spa, the Chabanettes would be highlighted with an option to navigate there, call or book a room via the website. This led to an increase in the number of clients for the hotel, spa, restaurant and bar.

Moreover, on the website, the family regularly adds or updates details of attractions in the local area (see http://aubergedechabanettes.com/en/visit-auvergne-puy-de-dome-livradois-forez). Just by adding this page, the hits to the website increased by over 200% in one month. Although you can get content developed fairly cheaply (for examples, see www.fiverr.com and www.freelancer.com), as businesses start to develop a fan base, visitors may request information or even volunteer to create content for the site. As this is coming from people who are actively interested in the business, this content is usually more relevant and in line with the business profile.

If a business is interested in undertaking online paid-for advertising of content, for example one of its blogs, an effective way of helping to ensure that the advertising achieves good results is to check which content gets the most attention and then undertake paid advertising for that content. This is because it can already be seen to be of interest to readers and therefore help drive traffic and customer engagement. Being selective like this is better than advertising all content, some of which might not be of interest or relevant. The Chabanettes Boutique Hotel & Spa has a quiet period around February when it could develop further content for its website; as it has little time for this activity, the content must be long-lasting, informative and of high quality. Content with a long shelf-life and that is effective at getting customers to repeatedly visit the site is known as evergreen content.

You are tasked with the following:

1. On the website, they are potentially missing out on a number of key market segments/ profiles that might be interested in staying in the location. With a clear rationale as to who

(Continued)

(Continued)

    they are, why have you selected them and what evergreen content would you recommend they develop to help?

2. A large number of customers are families who stay for one night, stopping en route to the south of France or other countries such as Spain. What would you add to the website to encourage these customers to stay longer than one night?

For further advice on starting a content marketing strategy, see the Content Marketing Institute's Getting Started guide at https://contentmarketinginstitute.com/getting-started.

SUMMARY OF KEY IDEAS

- Customers who were beneficiaries of more tangible marketing have been replaced by a generation of experiential marketing consumers, consumers who want to experience brands, talk to brands and feel part of a brand community, but often from within an online environment.
- The content strategy covers creating and distributing relevant and valuable content to attract, acquire and engage a clearly defined and understood target audience – with the objective of driving profitable customer action.
- Earned and paid media can be effective and achieve long-term sustainable results for a company by developing its website to be SEO-friendly with a constant monitoring of results to improve inbound marketing.
- 'Content is king' but emails, SEO, PPC and other digital channels will never hit the target without attractive, media-rich, relevant content to appeal to the target audience.
- Making the customer feel that the communication is worth engaging with is the key to a successful outbound marketing campaign.
- Digital media is highly effective in generating positive marketing messages. The speed and scope of distribution of these messages is far greater than any traditional media and, furthermore, a two-way communication channel is opened. So, at times of crisis, this creates a unique opportunity for organisations or brands to respond to audience opinion and to calm the storm.

Chapter Discussion Questions

1. Identify key aspects of digital and social media marketing that support the optimisation of business growth.
2. Develop an integrated marketing communications plan for a business/organisation/brand of your choice using relevant channels of digital and social media marketing.
3. Why is it important to establish an appropriate understanding of both inbound and outbound marketing strategies?
4. How does investment in organisational digital and social media platforms help achieve an enhanced customer experience?

REFERENCES

Adobe and Econsultancy (2017) Digital Trends Briefing: 2017 Digital Trends. Available at: https://offers.adobe.com/en/uk/marketing/landings/_2017_digital_trends_report.html (accessed 20 February 2018).

An, M. (2016) Why People Block Ads (and What it Means for Marketers and Advertisers). HubSpot Research, 13 July [updated 18 December 2018]. Available at: https://research.hubspot.com/why-people-block-ads-and-what-it-means-for-marketers-and-advertisers (accessed 13 July 2018).

Buzzfeed (n.d.) About Buzzfeed. Available at: www.buzzfeed.com/about?country=en-uk (accessed 20 February 2018).

Chaffey, D. and Ellis-Chadwick, F. (2015) *Digital Marketing: Strategy, Implementation and Practice*, 6th edn. Harlow: Pearson.

Chaffey, D., Jones, R. and Leszczynski, M. (2018) Email Marketing and Marketing Automation Excellence 2018. Available at: https://resources.getresponse.com/en/reports/email-marketing-and-marketing-automation-excellence-2018.pdf (accessed 3 June 2019).

Churt, R. (2018) How to Audit Your Website for Improved SEO and Conversions. HubSpot, 23 April. Available at: https://blog.hubspot.com/blog/tabid/6307/bid/34088/how-to-audit-your-website-for-improved-seo-and-conversions.aspx (accessed 23 April 2018).

Content Marketing Institute (2012) Six Useful Content Marketing Definitions. Available at http://contentmarketinginstitute.com/2012/06/content-marketing-definition (accessed 20 February 2018).

Content Marketing Institute (2018) What Is Content Marketing? Available at: https://contentmarketinginstitute.com/what-is-content-marketing (accessed 18 June 2018).

DeMers, J. (2014) Why No One's Reading Your Marketing Content. Available at: https://hbr.org/2014/11/why-no-ones-reading-your-marketing-content (accessed 24 February 2018).

Direct Marketing Association (DMA) (2017) DMA Insight: Marketer Email Tracking Survey 2017. Available at: https://dma.org.uk/uploads/misc/589c5b9eaaca9-marketer-email-tracking-report-2017_589c5b9eaabde.pdf (accessed 20 February 2018).

Fleiss, W. (2017) Content Distribution: A Basic Primer. Available at: www.outbrain.com/blog/content-distribution (accessed 23 April 2018).

Fraser, S. (2018) Multichannel Communications and the 24/7 Customer. Digital Marketing Magazine, 5 June. Available at http://digitalmarketingmagazine.co.uk/digital-marketing-features/multichannel-communications-and-the-24-7-customer/4900 (accessed 15 July 2018).

HubSpot (2018) Creating an Inbound Strategy. Available at www.hubspot.com/acp/creating-inbound-strategy (accessed 23 April 2018).

Information Commissioners Office (2017) Information Commissioner talks GDPR and Accountability in Latest Speech. Available at: https://ico.org.uk/about-the-ico/news-and-events/news-and-blogs/2017/01/information-commissioner-talks-gdpr-and-accountability-in-latest-speech (accessed 23 April 2018)

James, R. (2018) How to Choose a PPC Agency. Digital Clarity, 15 February. Available at: www.digital-clarity.com/blog/choosing-ppc-agency (accessed 20 May 2018).

Johnson, L. (2017) What Marketers Need to Know About Location-Based Marketing and Where It's Headed. Available at: www.adweek.com/digital/lets-slack-about-location-based-marketing (accessed 20 February 2018).

Kleinman, Z. (2018) Cambridge Analytica: The Story So Far. BBC News, 21 March. Available at: www.bbc.co.uk/news/technology-43465968 (accessed 17 July 2018).

Moz (n.d.) Content Creation. Available at: https://moz.com/beginners-guide-to-content-marketing/content-creation (accessed 22 May 2018).

O'Leary, J. (2018) Why Content is Key to Your Digital Marketing Strategy. Digital Marketing Magazine, 5 July. Available at: http://digitalmarketingmagazine.co.uk/digital-marketing-content/why-content-is-key-to-your-digital-marketing-strategy/4908 (accessed 7 July 2018).

Patel, N. (2012) How Content Length Affects Rankings and Conversions. Available at: www.quicksprout.com/2012/12/20/the-science-behind-long-copy-how-more-content-increases-rankings-and-conversions (accessed 23 April 2018).

Patel, N. (2014) 14 Mobile Marketing Tips that Drive Leads and Sales. Available at: https://neil-patel.com/blog/14-mobile-marketing-tips-to-drive-leads-and-sales (accessed 14 October 2018).

Patel, N. (2018) 6 Inbound Marketing Techniques Every Business Should Use. Available at: https://marketingland.com/6-inbound-marketing-techniques-every-startup-should-use-114306 (accessed 22 May 2018).

Rudolph, S. (2016) Why Inbound Marketing is Your Holy Grail of Marketing: Statistics and Trends. Available at: www.onlinesalesguidetip.com/why-inbound-marketing-is-your-holy-grail-of-marketing-statistics-and-trends-infographic (accessed 26 March 2018).

Salfischberger, T. (2018) Personalising Personalisation. Digital Marketing Magazine, 23 May. Available at: http://digitalmarketingmagazine.co.uk/digital-marketing-features/personalising-personalisation/4890 (accessed 10 June 2018).

Sizemore, E. (2017) *How to Do a Content Audit*. Available at: https://moz.com/blog/content-audit (accessed 21 February 2018).

Smart Insights (2018) Inbound Marketing Strategy. Available at: www.smartinsights.com/digital-marketing-strategy/inbound-marketing-strategy (accessed 22 May 2012).

Statista (2018) Number of Sent and Received Emails per Day Worldwide from 2017 to 2022. Available at: www.statista.com/statistics/456500/daily-number-of-e-mails-worldwide (accessed 23 April 2018).

Titcomb, J. (2016) Mobile Web Usage Overtakes Desktop for First Time. Available at: www.telegraph.co.uk/technology/2016/11/01/mobile-web-usage-overtakes-desktop-for-first-time (accessed 20 April 2018).

Urhofer, P. (2017) Measuring the Impact of Social Media Marketing. Digital Marketing Magazine, 19 July. Available at: http://digitalmarketingmagazine.co.uk/articles/measuring-the-impact-of-social-media-marketing/4492 (accessed 28 June 2018).

9
ENTREPRENEURIAL AND SME MARKETING

Yiwen (Evie) Hong and Sophie Yang

Learning Objectives

At the end of this chapter, you should be able to understand and discuss:

- The concept of SME marketing, examining marketing advantages of SMEs, marketing planning in SMEs and internationalisation of SMEs
- The concept of entrepreneurial marketing in relation to SME marketing
- The differences between entrepreneurial marketing and traditional marketing approaches
- Key dimensions of entrepreneurial marketing
- The emerging research concerns and deficiencies of entrepreneurial marketing

INTRODUCTION

In this chapter, you are going to consider marketing and its relevance to entrepreneurs and SMEs, and how entrepreneurs as well as owners/managers of SMEs adapt and use marketing for their specific requirements during the life of an enterprise. Those areas were covered in this book chapter, as marketing has been seen as one of the greatest problems faced by small and medium-sized enterprises (SMEs). However, marketing is also simultaneously one of the most important activities for the growth and survival of SMEs. Therefore, the purpose of this book chapter is to determine the importance and role of entrepreneurial marketing in relation to SMEs.

Entrepreneurial marketing (EM) acknowledges the interface between entrepreneurship, marketing and innovation. Furthermore, EM also focuses on customer value. An EM approach enhances firms' innovation, proactiveness and risk taking in their marketing strategies, enabling SMEs to better overcome resource constraints.

We will start the chapter first by discussing SME marketing, followed by the concept of entrepreneurial marketing and the dimensions of entrepreneurial marketing.

SME MARKETING
Definition of SMEs

There is no universal definition of small and medium-sized enterprises (SMEs). Definitions and criteria of SMEs vary widely by country and industry sector (Simpson et al., 2011). Often, SMEs are understood in relation to firms' number of employees or turnover. The EU defines SMEs as firms with fewer than 250 employees and whose turnover must not exceed 50 million euros (Hinson, 2011; Wuest and Thoben, 2011). However, within the EU member states, the specific definitions vary. For example, in Germany SMEs are defined as firms with fewer than 250 employees, while in Belgium SMEs are businesses with fewer than 100 employees. Although SMEs are typically officially defined by quantitative criteria, these can also be understood in qualitative terms. Indeed, SMEs can be defined as having the following characteristics (Wach, 2015):

- legal independence of the owners
- simple, flat organisational structure of the firm
- significant role of the owner which places them in the leading position of the firm as entrepreneur/manager and primary decision-maker
- relatively small share of the market.

Marketing of SMEs

Despite the disagreements on the definition of SMEs, the literature tends to agree that SMEs have fewer resources and finances than larger firms. As a result, Simpson et al. (2011) suggest that marketing activities in SMEs often emerge in specific forms, in line with their dynamic internal and external environments, significantly different to marketing practices in larger firms. Due to limited resources, SMEs frequently face significant challenges with the strategic implementation of marketing practices.

Marketing of SMEs is often informal, unstructured, driven by the particular preferences of the entrepreneur (Simpson et al., 2011) as well as reliant on the personal contact networks of the entrepreneur. Due to resource constraints, SMEs maximise marketing opportunities and strategies through networking with partners and other firms. Relationship building with clients, customers and partners is recognised by researchers to be vital to the success of SMEs and their marketing strategies (Simpson et al., 2011).

Practitioner's Perspective 9.1

Interview with a selected SME

Due to resource constraints, SMEs need to adopt innovative techniques to offset the constraints and respond to the problem. By acting innovatively, SMEs can perceive and grasp opportunities in the market and build competitive advantages. Here we show how a Chinese e-commerce shoes company responded to its resource constraints by adopting an innovative business model. Located in Quanzhou, a city famous for shoe manufacturing, the case company sells vintage men's shoes on Taobao, targeting 25–35-year-old customers. The firm has been established for 8 years and has just under 80 employees in total. When operating on Taobao, the firm needs to deal with frequent imitation in this competitive and homogenous online environment.

In the first quotation below, the entrepreneur of the case company discusses how and why the company decided to cooperate with a cladding supplier:

> You know, the online environment proposes new challenges for companies. It is easy to be imitated by competitors. The shoes industry is not a highly technical industry and it is easy for competitors to imitate other companies' shoe design. Therefore, I often explore new business modes to respond to the changes in the online market. Lots of factories produce shoes in this city (Quanzhou, China), while only a few factories produce vintage shoes for companies like us. If we use the factories in other provinces like from Zhejiang or Guangdong, there are delivery costs to pay, which is too high for us. Therefore, we used to work with a factory in Guangzhou, but it's hard for us to control the shoe quality of our partners. Due to finance constraints, we cannot open our own factory currently either. So we decided to develop a comprehensive supply chain system. The normal cycle of producing shoes is 10–15 days, but when we have our own cladding supply chain, we can reduce the production time of shoes to be shorter, allowing us to wait until seeing the latest market data, in order to make a more accurate business decision. We can also use the shoe mould produced in Guangzhou, so other companies cannot copy us. It's hard for our competitors to make similar shoe moulds in Guangzhou. If other companies still want to copy our design, they need to spend some time on it. In the mean time, we can make new shoe styles.

(Continued)

(Continued)

In the next quotation, the same entrepreneur also highlights the reasoning behind the collaboration with an expert photographer:

> Due to the size and location of our company, it is hard for us to retain a specialist in the employment. But you know, for e-commerce fashion brands, we need to control the brand image by presenting high-quality and attractive photos online. We need to make sure the brand image is strong and coherent in our online presence. Therefore, we decided to do it differently by becoming a business partner of a specialist photographer. It benefited our company and allowed us to deliver a coherent brand image online mainly by using professional photographs.

The above interview quotations, with the entrepreneur of a selected SME, provide examples of how an SME dealt with resource constraints and responded to a business problem. By acting innovatively, the entrepreneur grasped opportunities in the market and built competitive advantages.

Questions for discussion:

1. How did the Chinese e-commerce shoes company respond to its resource constraints by adopting an innovative business mode and cooperating with a cladding supplier?
2. Why did the Chinese e-commerce shoes company decide to collaborate with an expert photographer, in order to grasp opportunities in the market and built competitive advantages?

Features of SMEs

The size, resources and structures of SMEs present a number of opportunities and challenges. The informal and less complex organisational structure of SMEs allows them to react more flexibly and quickly to opportunities in the market, in comparison to the lengthy bureaucratic and managerial set-up of larger companies (Wuest and Thoben, 2011). This is one of the ways in which SMEs can gain competitive advantage over larger firms. Additionally, SMEs are more able to make efforts to quickly and effectively meet customer needs and respond to customer concerns (Simpson et al., 2011). Indeed, SMEs tend to develop strong, intimate and personal ties with customers that larger companies are not able to achieve. SMEs can monitor customer feedback, quickly respond to their requests and concerns as well as work closely with customers to co-create value.

However, there are a number of marketing disadvantages associated with SMEs. In particular, SMEs need to deal with human and financial resource constraints, meaning that they tend to lack the staff members to sufficiently develop specialist departments, such as quality control or social media marketing. Often, employees in SMEs work across departments and attempt to adopt multiple roles simultaneously. Financial and human resource constraints are likely to mean that the quality and extent of SMEs' marketing operations are limited and insufficient in nature (Simpson et al., 2011; Wuest and Thoben, 2011). However, despite these numerous constraints, SMEs can develop more innovative and 'nice' marketing strategies given their flexibility and specialist knowledge. This represents a two-sided coin for SMEs' marketing practices.

MARKETING PLANNING IN SMES

Strategic marketing planning is a vital process in order for firms to achieve their marketing objectives. After setting marketing objectives, it is suggested that firms put forward a co-ordinated, strategic and long-term plan to implement these objectives and improve the firm's financial performance (Chaston and Mangles, 2002; Ekwulugo, 2011; Majama and Magang, 2017). The planning process includes three key steps for companies to assess: (1) where they are now; (2) where they want to be; and (3) how to get there. It is the third step in particular which impacts the business growth of firms, as only a formalised and concrete plan can enact the stated marketing objectives.

Majama and Magang (2017: 75) assert that strategic planning can be defined as 'the continuous process of making entrepreneurial decisions systematically and with their greatest knowledge organizing systematically the efforts to carry out these decisions and measuring the results against the expectations through organized feedback'. Chaston and Mangles (2002) suggest that there is significant value for the firm in the process of strategic planning, in enabling greater organisational learning. More specifically, a strategic marketing plan acts as an organisational structure and guide for firms in determining how to market their goods and services (Ekwulugo, 2011).

Strategic marketing planning varies across different organisational forms (Ekwulugo, 2011). Researchers have proposed that SMEs face constraints in carrying out structured, formalised and strategic planning (Chaston and Mangles, 2002). Due to their small size and limited human and financial resources, SMEs are less likely to adopt a strategic and formalised approach to planning for future business performance. While SMEs are aware of the importance of strategic planning, they often lack the capabilities, resources and skilled personnel to conduct it effectively. Thus, in contrast to larger firms, strategic planning in SMEs tends to be informal, flexible and undocumented (Majama and Magang, 2017).

SMEs do well to consider relevant internal and external factors when conducting marketing planning (Chaston and Mangles, 2002). An in-depth understanding of the firm's contexts allows SMEs to better analyse what marketing strategies to produce and how to implement them. Internal factors for the firm to consider when devising marketing plans include its management structure, human and financial resources, financial performance and the skillset of its personnel. On the other hand, external factors to consider should include competitors, market characteristics, development and trends as well as customer needs (Ekwulugo, 2011).

Thus, it is recommended that SMEs develop marketing plans based on an understanding of a firm's internal and external factors. While SMEs cannot influence the external environment, they can attempt to enhance their internal structures, which may generate in-depth, formalised and strategic marketing planning that fits in with the surrounding contexts. Ekwulugo (2011) suggests that SMEs understand and adapt to the fluctuating external environment. Arguably, as SMEs are more flexible than larger firms, they are better equipped to adjust to changes in the external environment.

Analysis of the external environment can be conducted using PEST, for instance, whereby political, economic, social and technological factors are examined. Before developing marketing plans and strategies, SMEs need to adequately understand their current situation and the context in which they operate (Majama and Magang, 2017). An effective and contextualised strategic marketing plan enables SMEs to exploit future opportunities and build a competitive advantage in the market (Ekwulugo, 2011).

There are many theoretical and practical approaches to investigating marketing in SMEs, while there is no unifying theory of marketing in SMEs. It is found that marketing in SMEs is often linked to their entrepreneurial behaviour (Simpson et al., 2011). In addition, marketing in SMEs does not appear to evolve or mature, even when market conditions and business activities change considerably (Brooksbank, 1999). Due to the above, some scholars agree that SME marketing is equivalent to entrepreneurial marketing. Therefore, you will learn about entrepreneurial marketing in the coming sections of this chapter, in order to better understand context-dependent marketing strategies in an ever-changing environment.

Case Study 9.1

Overworking your staff

Due to the limited staff size and high ambitions of SMEs, heavy burdens may be placed on their employees, often without the entrepreneur noticing (Campbell, 2016). Often, this may involve staff members working in multiple departments on multiple tasks or working evenings and weekends. A company culture of overworking may lead to staff members experiencing burnout and negative effects on their lifestyle. Work-related stress can result in a number of health problems for employees, including an increased risk of heart disease, weight gain and digestive problems. Recent studies have found that employees who work 50–55 hours or more per week are more likely than lesser worked staff to experience health issues, lower productivity and increased alcohol consumption. As a result, companies that overwork their employees tend to have greater numbers of employees calling in sick.

Alongside this, employees who are overworked often have little free time for their family or personal life. Instead, they work during the evenings or over the weekends. All of this can result in increased family instability and a stressful lifestyle, which ultimately lead to high employee turnover. Simultaneously, overworked and stressed employees are often less productive and make a greater number of mistakes in the workplace than those who are not.

There are signs for bosses that their employees might be being overworked. For example, a staff member is working longer hours and at weekends. Therefore, they are not taking their designated breaks or are missing family obligations. Employers need to be aware of the pressures that they may be exerting on staff members. In particular, SMEs should take into consideration employees' personality type or ambitions, with those who are overly focused or particularly ambitious more likely to take on a greater workload. SMEs should also consider reducing overwork from an internal marketing perspective. If employees are less overworked and happy, they are more likely to promote the company as a potential employer to others and also to engage with the company's goals, which will ultimately benefit the firm's external marketing strategies and long-term brand building with external customers.

Sources

Campbell, A. (2016) Overworked Employees? 15 Signs You May be Pushing Workers Too Hard. Available at: www.americanexpress.com/us/small-business/openforum/articles/overworked-employees-15-signs-may-pushing-workers-hard (accessed 9 June 2018).

White, D. and White, P. (2017) 5 Signs That You're Overworking Your Employees. Available at: www.entrepreneur.com/article/304970 (accessed 1 June 2018).

Questions for discussion

1. What are the signs of overworking staff members?
2. What are the likely negative consequences of overworking staff members for the firm's long-term external marketing?
3. How can SMEs better manage their staff from the perspective of internal marketing and ensure long-term sustainability of the business?

Internationalisation of SMEs

Internationalisation refers to the process of firms adopting an international outlook and becoming involved in international operations (Ibeh and Analogbei, 2011; Yenera et al., 2014). Firms are motivated to go through an internationalisation process due to both proactive entry conditions (such as increasing international markets, economies of scale, or profits) and reactive entry conditions (such as low profit margins in the domestic market, saturation in the domestic market, or increasing product supply costs) (Yenera et al., 2014).

While internationalisation has traditionally been adopted by large, multinational enterprises, SMEs have increasingly begun to operate internationally and outside of their domestic markets, in line with developments in transport and communication technologies. Although, due to limited capital, SME internationalisation is not very common at the early stages of their development, some firms do begin to internationalise from an early stage, such as 'born globals'. 'Born globals' are firms which are international in focus from start-up, developing new ventures that are global in design and that seek to satisfy a global 'niche' (Tanev, 2012). Given their resource constraints, SMEs' internationalisation tends to emerge as export-based activity from their domestic base, often via the internet (Ibeh and Analogbei, 2011).

However, while research generally suggests a positive impact of internationalisation upon firms' performance, the situation is more complicated for SMEs, who face significant challenges in penetrating international markets and developing internationalisation strategies effectively (Cao et al., 2016). The internationalisation of SMEs tends to achieve an enhanced performance in the long term, while showing an immediate deterioration in short-term performance.

The challenges that SMEs face in internationalisation often relate to their multiple constraints: resource-related, structural or operational. Limited financial and human resources limit the extent and progress of SMEs' internationalisation strategies. Notably, as Ibeh and Analogbei (2011) describe, SMEs often lack personnel who have sufficient knowledge and experience of internationalisation activities. SMEs also tend to face resource-related constraints in accessing adequate infrastructure in foreign markets.

ENTREPRENEURIAL MARKETING

The field of entrepreneurial marketing (hereafter EM) has emerged and grown in importance in recent years, bringing together two previously separate schools of thought – entrepreneurship and marketing. The concept of EM is offered as marketing functions can benefit from the study of entrepreneurship, while entrepreneurship research can also examine firms further through a marketing lens. An EM approach enhances firms' innovation, proactiveness and risk taking in their marketing strategies and enables firms to better overcome resource constraints, useful for both large firms and SMEs.

Since the 1990s, there has been increasing interest in the entrepreneurship and marketing interface. The concept of 'entrepreneurial marketing' has grown as the significant link between marketing and entrepreneurship has been recognised. Indeed, Hills and LaForge (1992) claim that 'marketing behaviour' and 'entrepreneurial behaviour' are similar in nature, given that both concepts (1) interact with environmental and uncertain factors, (2) require evaluation of risk, and (3) provide increased commercial value to firms. Whereas traditional marketing is based on 'managerial marketing' perspectives, EM is focused on entrepreneur-oriented and marketing-oriented perspectives (Hills and Hultman, 2013).

The definition of entrepreneurial marketing proposed by Morris et al. (2002: 5) has been cited by many researchers (e.g. Jones and Rowley, 2011): EM is 'the proactive identification and exploitation of opportunities for acquiring and retaining profitable customers through innovative approaches to risk management, resource leveraging and value creation'.

On the other hand, Hills et al. (2010: 6) identify EM as:

a spirit, an orientation as well as a process of pursuing opportunities and launching and growing ventures that create perceived customer value through relationships, especially by employing innovativeness, creativity, selling, market immersion, networking or flexibility.

As is evident in the above definition, the processes of pursuing opportunities and creating customer value are driven by entrepreneurship characteristics, such as networking and innovation. The entrepreneurial form of marketing highlights the importance of proactively seeking and exploiting opportunities in the marketing process. The proactive opportunity-seeking process was also highlighted when scholars examined international entrepreneurship (Reuber and Fischer, 2011), while the EM perspective focused more on opportunities related to seeking and enhancing customer value. Thus, it can be argued that EM is a subset of entrepreneurship.

On the other hand, Morrish et al. (2010) consider EM as both entrepreneur-centric and customer-centric, where both the entrepreneur and customers are the main actors and are in equivalent positions to conduct marketing activities and strategy. Indeed, Morrish et al. (2010: 304) stated the following:

This paper ... takes the perspective that EM is both wholly traditional AM (Administrative Marketing) and wholly entrepreneurship and not a subset of marketing combined with a subset of entrepreneurial processes; therefore the construct of EM is not simply the nexus between the sets of marketing and entrepreneurial processes that has emerged as the conventional conceptualisation of EM ... but fully includes all aspects of AM and entrepreneurship.

From the perspective of EM, traditional administrative marketing refers to the traditional process of marketing management and strategy (Hills et al., 2008). The above argument considers entrepreneurship as a whole and marketing as a whole, in order to sufficiently understand the nature of EM and its relevant processes. Moreover, EM is more than the summation of aspects of marketing orientation merged with entrepreneurial orientation. Instead, EM is a synergistic, opportunity-driven, innovation-oriented, proactive, risk-accepting set of processes for a marketer to gain competitive advantage (Morrish et al., 2010). Indeed, Kotler (2003) proposes that traditional marketing practices are included within EM practices. Subsequently, EM activity includes all of the core aspects of traditional marketing, such as creating products that meet customers' needs (Morris et al., 2002).

Differences between EM and traditional marketing thought

EM theory can be used to understand firms' marketing approaches and how an entrepreneur's behaviour impacts on marketing approaches. The EM approach is useful for theory development at all stages of a firm's life cycle (Morris et al., 2002). In particular, EM theory may examine the impact of entrepreneurship on the internet-led strategic roles adopted by firms for marketing purposes. EM research shows that firm-level marketing activities are influenced directly by entrepreneurial behaviour. Indeed, Franco et al. (2014) argue that the entrepreneur acts as a central actor in the marketing process rather than through layers of management. An entrepreneurial orientation describes the strategic processes of the firm, as defined by the behaviour of decision-makers (Lumpkin and Dess, 2001).

Indeed, within the entrepreneurial process, the entrepreneur's behaviour and actions are key (Covin and Slevin, 1991; Lumpkin and Dess, 1996). The entrepreneurial process involves three key stages: (1) the discovery phase, (2) involving in a business project, and (3) materialising the idea (Baltar and De Coulon, 2014). Thus, there is a distinction between the discovery phase, which describes the origins of the start-up idea, and the exploitation phase, which refers to materialising the idea and the actions associated with this, such as acquiring resources. Indeed, from an EM perspective, the entrepreneur is an individual who undertakes actions to discover opportunities, innovates products and services as well as meets the need of target customers (Shane and Venkataraman, 2000; Sullivan Mort et al., 2012). The entrepreneur's opportunity creation helps firms to expand existing markets and access new ones.

In EM research, the emphasis is placed on the importance of resource leveraging, in order to gain entry into markets that are 'difficult to penetrate' (Sullivan Mort et al., 2012). Indeed, entrepreneurship research has recognised the key role that the entrepreneur may play in mobilising resources that are external to the firm and in enriching the internal resources of the firm (Barney, 2002).

The entrepreneur drives the firm-level marketing process, facilitating SMEs to gain competitive advantage through proactively seeking opportunities, innovatively developing strategies and engaging with social networks (Hills et al., 2008). A firm's competitive advantage or strategy formulation is influenced by a high level of entrepreneurship characteristics, reflected in the organisational processes and decision-making style of an organisation. Entrepreneurship characteristics affect SMEs through management processes and strategy developments, enabling SMEs to overcome resource constraints to varying extents (Oviatt and McDougall, 2005).

From an EM perspective, entrepreneurs tend to implement marketing strategies that reflect their own characteristics, such as experience and intuition. Entrepreneurs also use their customer knowledge and market probing to develop innovative products (Berends et al., 2014). EM research emphasises the importance of entrepreneurial orientation in seeking and proactively anticipating future customer needs. In contrast, the traditional marketing perspective places greater emphasis on the importance of formal market research when conducting a marketing strategy (Miles and Darroch, 2006). If the firm's marketing strategies are based on formal market research, they are likely to be driven by the needs of the current market. On the other hand, EM strategies are driven by discovering opportunities proactively in order to innovatively exploit opportunities for existing and potential customers (Miles and Darroch, 2006). Table 9.1 compares the key differences between the EM and traditional marketing perspectives discussed above.

Table 9.1   Comparison between EM and traditional marketing

Entrepreneurial marketing	Traditional marketing
Entrepreneur-oriented perspectives	Managerial marketing perspectives
Focus on the characteristics of entrepreneurs to make business decisions	Focus on formal market research to make business decisions
More context-dependent on firms' characteristics	Less context-dependent on firms' characteristics
Seeking and proactively anticipating future customers' needs	Focus on meeting existing customers' needs

Source: Hills et al. (2008); Morris et al. (2002); Sullivan Mort et al. (2012)

Key dimensions of EM

As stated in the definition of EM in the above section, EM embodies seven dimensions which are derived from both entrepreneurship and marketing theory (Morris et al., 2002).

Derived from entrepreneurial orientation, the four dimensions are: (1) proactive orientation, (2) opportunity exploitation, (3) innovation, and (4) risk management. The fifth dimension – resource leveraging – is emphasised in both the marketing and entrepreneurship literature, while the sixth and seventh dimensions – customer intensity and value creation – are reflected in firms' market orientation. The seven dimensions of EM are discussed in detail in the following sub-sections.

Proactive orientation

The conventional role of marketing is to assess industry and market conditions and make suggestions for change through the marketing mix. These conditions can be described as environmental factors, which influence firms' marketing decisions. Entrepreneurial marketing emphasises that firms are not simply reacting to environmental changes. EM does not consider the environmental factors to be a static, non-changeable condition. Therefore, EM suggests that the marketer take the initiative in the market and not be constrained by existing environmental conditions. Proactive-orientated firms tend to be a leader rather than a follower in the market (Schindehutte et al., 2009).

One of the aims of EM is to influence the external environment to some extent and to initiate new developments. The proactive marketer can perceive the opportunity for change and take action to develop new offerings and marketing strategies ahead of the competition. The marketer redefines the environmental changes and makes assumptions regarding when, where and how to grasp the opportunity in these changes. As Lumpkin and Dess (1996) suggest, proactiveness refers to the entrepreneur's ability to take the initiative and to aggressively respond to market opportunities in a competitive and hostile environment.

Opportunity exploitation

The continual opportunity-seeking of the entrepreneur is key to the EM process. Driven by the entrepreneur's proactive tendencies, EM-oriented firms seek and respond to market opportunities. The opportunity exploitation dimension links closely to another dimension of EM, which is proactiveness. The entrepreneur with a proactive posture is expected to take action speedily and move ahead of competitors, after identifying and grasping the market opportunities. By proactively seeking out and exploiting the arising opportunities, EM-oriented firms can achieve competitive advantage in the market (Hills et al., 2008).

Opportunities often arise from the scanning and identification of market needs emerging from external environment changes. Interestingly, the EM perspective emphasises the continuous seeking out of opportunities through the effective exploitation of currently controlled resources. Opportunity exploitation derives from the entrepreneur's knowledge and networks. Furthermore, the discovery of future opportunity requires ongoing learning on the part of the entrepreneur to better understand the evolving environmental changes, such as the impact of technological developments on changes in customer needs. It may be said that opportunity seeking is the predecessor of proactiveness and innovation.

Innovation

The EM literature identifies innovation as a critical element in a firm's development (Hills et al., 2010). EM-oriented firms often take a creative approach to marketing, which may include continually innovating products or strategies (Morris et al., 2002). The firm's ability to develop innovative strategies and products is emphasised as a way of creating added value for customers and maintaining an advantageous position in the market (Morrish et al., 2010).

Sustained innovation refers to maintaining the firm's ability to generate creative ideas from the internal and external environments. These ideas can be transferred to new product development or to updating the marketing process. Other dimensions of EM could combine with the dimension of innovation. For example, innovative products and marketing approaches aid the firm's proactive posture. Further, innovation supports the firm's opportunity for discovery and exploitation.

In summary, innovation is an ongoing process, with the marketer continually updating the marketing mix that enables a firm to build and maintain its position as a market leader.

Risk management

The risk-taking dimension is defined as the willingness of the entrepreneur to commit important resources to opportunities when facing uncertain environmental factors. Risk taking is related to how firms allocate resources to the marketing mix when there is uncertainty as regards the profit outcome, as not all of the risks are calculable and firms cannot avoid risk taking. In the process of EM, the marketer attempts to identify risk factors which exist in both the external and internal environments to see if risk can be reduced.

The marketer can better manage risks through enhancing the flexibility of resource commitment. Also, the marketer can minimise the risk by using innovative ideas or applying advanced technology. For example, e-commerce firms use software to monitor sales trends and plan production, in order to manage the risk of overstock. Firms can also use innovative promotional tactics to attract customers and increase product sales. Ongoing entrepreneurial learning on the environment, network and customers can enhance firms' risk management and enable them to better identify uncertainties when making decisions on resource allocation.

Resource leveraging

Resource leveraging refers to the exploitation of limited resources. As highlighted above, the entrepreneurial marketer's proactive behaviour and opportunity seeking are not limited by the existing resources they currently control. There are different ways to leverage resources (Schindehutte et al., 2009). For instance, the entrepreneur can leverage resources by developing an innovative approach. They should be able to perceive how to innovatively use current resources to maximise their current value. The ability to effectively allocate resources can create a higher combined value, while the ability to motivate employees to become more innovative can generate enhanced performances. Additionally, the entrepreneur may exploit the value of the resources that has not been recognised by using their knowledge, network and experience.

Moreover, the entrepreneur can use existing resources, such as networking, to achieve the firm's marketing aims. For example, a firm may be able to use its brand reputation or network to convince suppliers to agree to delayed payments and to increase the firm's cash flow. Firms can exploit other people's resources by cooperating, borrowing, sharing or outsourcing. The external resources may come from stakeholders, such as suppliers, partners, customers and distributors. The entrepreneur often uses their network to build strategic alliances. For example, an e-commerce shoe brand could cooperate with other clothing brands to expand its customer base when presenting the products online. The model wearing the shoe brand could also wear another brand's clothes to match the shoes, in order to cross-sell both brands. In this way, the two brands are able to share their customer resources.

Customer intensity

EM emphasises customer intensity throughout the firm's marketing decisions, and concepts including customer retention, customer acquisition and customer development are discussed. In particular, the EM perspective places great value on establishing a long-term relationship with customers, in order to build a customer base (Jones and Rowley, 2011).

Sullivan Mort et al. (2012) indicated the importance of customer interaction for building customer intimacy. Interaction is a dynamic process of understanding both customers' evolving behaviour and changes in the external environment. The intimate involvement with customers at the stage of product design enables innovative outcomes on product development as well as increasing customer intimacy. It is therefore suggested that there is a close linkage between customer intimacy and innovative products, whereby they exist in one strategic dimension rather than in two separate dimensions. Accordingly, it is necessary for firms to improve their interaction between the firm and customers to enhance the firm's innovative posture.

The dimension of customer intensity correlates with the creative approach of customer acquisition and customer interaction. Sullivan Mort et al.'s (2012) proposal of intimate involvement in the firm's product development process alludes to the concept of 'co-creation'. 'Co-creation' refers to the collaborative and interactive process between firms and customers in the creation of value, including the development of products and marketing strategies in the firm (Agrawal and Rahman, 2015; Romero and Molina, 2011). Several EM scholars indicate the importance of co-creation in EM practices (Jones and Rowley, 2011).

Indeed, Lee et al. (2012) suggest that customers should be involved in the customer value creation process. Thus, customers themselves can be engaged in the firm's innovative processes. From an EM perspective, it is claimed that interaction between the entrepreneur and her customers will help her gain knowledge of customers' needs and improve marketing practices (Deacon, 2002; Jones et al., 2013).

It is proposed that internet technology can aid the development of innovative strategies which improve interaction with customers and encourage customers to engage in the co-creation process. For example, the entrepreneur can access real-time information from the interaction with customers via online customer forums or online customer reviews. Consequently, the entrepreneur can better understand customers' needs, can proactively identify opportunities from potentially unfulfilled customer needs, and can use an innovative approach to exploit new business opportunities rapidly.

Value creation

The ultimate goals of marketing are to increase customer intention to purchase and to build the firm–customer relationship. The core of EM is proactive and innovative value creation, which ultimately leads to customer purchase and relationship building. Aiming to create value for customers, the entrepreneur must first perceive the potential customer's needs, which may not have been recognised by other competitors, and then to produce values to meet those needs by leveraging resources. Given continual change in the external environment and markets, firms need to keep learning and continually define the potential customer value. The entrepreneur may search and exploit the value by making incremental changes to the marketing mix, such as innovative product design. Value creation links to long-term customer relationship building. For example, a fashion brand may maintain its customer relationships through sharing fashion tips on social media, in order to engage customers and create value that impacts customers' everyday lives.

Case Study 9.2

Rethinking young entrepreneurs' social media strategy

Twenty-first-century young entrepreneurs are increasingly placing social media centrally in their business strategies. Facebook, Twitter, Instagram and YouTube are all popular ways for young entrepreneurs to engage with customers, to communicate and collaborate with partners, to develop their business network and to hire employees. However, there are challenges for a company in making effective use of social media.

Some firms may attempt to manage customer profiles on multiple social media accounts, posting the same updates and content across different media. However, while multiple postings can increase the chances of a company's content being seen, it is necessary to ensure that social media engagement for firms is specifically tailored to the form of social media. It is noticeable that all of the social media channels have points of difference and varied advantages. For instance, YouTube, Twitter and Pinterest are suitable for sharing different kinds of content, in order to maximise the impact of communication.

Young entrepreneurs should clearly and consistently convey the brand image of their firm when engaging with social media, in order to build more long-term connections with customers, clients and partners. It is also suggested that social media strategies should be implemented alongside more traditional forms of communication, for instance telephone conversations and face-to-face meetings.

Questions for discussion

1. How do social media platforms help entrepreneurs to conduct marketing activities and engage a wider range of customers?
2. Can social media help SMEs to overcome the limitation of resource constraints?
3. How might entrepreneurs use social media to maximise the impact of communication?

EM research

In order to better understand the nature of EM marketing, it is necessary to examine how and why SMEs are conducting marketing strategies in practice. Marketing-related decisions often need to be taken in unclear market conditions and in changing external environments. In SMEs, entrepreneurs make the majority of business decisions, including marketing ones. Those business decisions are often made based on the personal characteristics of the entrepreneur, their experience and marketing research (Schindehutte et al., 2009).

Accessing reliable information and market research may inform the entrepreneur's decision making and improve the ability of the entrepreneur to make day-to-day decisions for the firm. While there is no way to avoid uncertain market conditions and to make these stable, entrepreneurs in SMEs can gather rich, in-depth and effective information about the market and the external environment. In doing so, firms can better understand the surrounding environment and adapt to fluctuating market conditions. With a sufficient depth and reliability of knowledge, entrepreneurs are more able to perceive opportunities in the market environment.

SMEs face significant time and resource constraints and are subsequently less equipped than large firms to carry out large-scale, formal market research. This refers to traditional forms of market research that are carried out in larger firms. Those pieces of research typically rely on surveys, are quantitative in nature and are conducted large-scale, often through professional research firms or in formal marketing departments. Thus, there is a formalised research process, in which the existing trends in the market and current preferences of customers are tested in a relatively stable market environment.

On the other hand, SMEs still need to carry out research to enhance their decision-making process. However, given their resource constraints, SMEs might take an alternative approach to research and knowledge gathering that is lower in cost and less complex than it is with larger firms. Instead of simply examining trends in existing customer preferences, EM research focuses on gaining rich insights into customers' emotions and desires. In particular, attention in EM research is placed on 'the customer journey', which includes the customer's needs, desires and expectations and what is behind the customer's decision-making process. EM researchers develop insights based on how and why customers formulate their purchase decisions, rather than simply examining what they are purchasing.

Thus, entrepreneurs base their understanding of the market and the external environment on this rich, qualitative insight, in order to conduct the firm's market research activities. SMEs tend to creatively use customer insights and access this information via their EM research practices, to make sense of the surrounding environment, their competitors and customer needs. The creative use of EM research outcomes often emerges in the form of 'guerrilla marketing', which refers to marketing strategies and campaigns that are innovative, unconventional and operate in contrast to traditional marketing practices.

The way in which entrepreneurs access the information is often innovative, operating outside of the boundaries of formalised marketing research structures. SMEs accumulate knowledge on customer needs and preferences throughout their engagement with them.

For instance, employees can gain insight into customers' behaviour through everyday interaction with them. EM research techniques tend to be low-cost, informal and effective. EM research practices emerge from both qualitative and quantitative forms. Qualitative EM research techniques can include natural observations and in-depth interviews, while quantitative EM research methods incorporate survey research, experimentation and archival studies.

While SMEs conduct simple surveys online (for example, through Survey Monkey), their research into customer behaviour, needs and preferences goes beyond this to extend to day-to-day interactions. This is enabled through technology, whereby employees can, for instance, collect information on customers through social media engagement or the use of specialised software to record customers' journey. From EM research, entrepreneurs in SMEs aim to gain insight into customer behaviour, habits and preferences, and to perceive and grasp opportunities in the market (Schindehutte et al., 2009).

Current EM research concerns and deficiencies

EM research has been conducted in the context of SMEs (Franco et al., 2014; Jones et al., 2013) as well as in both young and large firms (Hills and Hultman, 2013; Jones and Rowley, 2011; Miles and Darroch, 2006; Morris et al., 2002). It has been proposed that SME marketing is equivalent to entrepreneurial marketing, mirroring the entrepreneurial abilities of innovation, competitor analysis, opportunity seeking and leveraging of resources (O'Dwyer et al., 2011). Here, EM-oriented firms may have a superior ability in strategically managing and operating marketing activities in competitive market circumstances. Accordingly, it is necessary to examine the nature of EM in the fast-moving internet e-commerce environment which is dynamic and rapidly changing. The literature has suggested that EM is particularly useful in researching market environments which are rapidly changing (Hills et al., 2008).

There is a dearth of empirical studies examining how entrepreneurship characteristics impact on the firm's marketing activities in an internet-enabled environment. In addition, the importance of EM and the role of the entrepreneur have been highlighted in previous research. However, EM research has not thus far looked at the entrepreneur's role in the EM process, and EM theory has been insufficiently applied to the e-commerce context.

Thus, it is recommended that future researchers conduct EM research in the online context and expand EM research further to include the impact of the individual entrepreneur's entrepreneurship characteristics on firms' marketing processes. In addition, future researchers might examine how SMEs can help make their marketing employees, who have marketing responsibility, become more entrepreneurial. Specifically, while the EM literature has identified some key linkages between entrepreneurship and marketing, future EM research might investigate further the interface between entrepreneurship and marketing in SMEs and how this interface is affected by advanced internet technology development.

Case Study 9.3

TOMS Shoes

The beginning

TOMS Shoes was founded in 2006 by Blake Mycoskie, a Texas entrepreneur. The company sells shoes that are designed around the Argentine alpargata style (a canvas slip-on shoe). After having not previously been involved in shoe design and retail, Mycoskie decided to begin selling alpargata shoes after taking a trip to Buenos Aires. It was here that he also found the inspiration for his unique selling point (USP) of TOMS: its 'one for one' business model. For every pair of shoes that it sells, TOMS donates another pair to an impoverished child, worldwide.

When Mycoskie visited Argentina, he found that many children living in the villages around Buenos Aires did not have shoes and could not attend school because of this. This inspired him to drive his company's mission around the need to give shoes to children in impoverished neighbourhoods. The idea that the company donates a pair of shoes 'tomorrow' after a purchase 'today' inspired its name: 'Tomorrow (or TOMS) shoes'. Having little knowledge of the shoe industry, Mycoskie initially relied on networking to access customers and retail partners. He consulted with his female friends on his idea for TOMS and gave them some trial shoes to test out. They gave him a list of stores that he could approach for selling his products. Following this, Mycoskie took the shoes to a store on the list to sell them. He found that the buyer loved the story as much as the shoes. Here, Mycoskie learnt the benefits of gaining insights from customer feedback, whether a friend or an acquaintance, to expand the business, rather than consulting an 'expert'.

Cause marketing

TOMS stands out in the market because of its unique business set-up and marketing strategy. The strategy of TOMS aligns itself with 'cause marketing': the blending of a product with a social or ethical mission. TOMS has given away 600,000 pairs of shoes in the first four years, or around $33 million worth of shoes. Its success has highlighted that charitable work by businesses can attract the attention of customers and can lead to significant profits. TOMS has

(Continued)

(Continued)

continued to contribute to ethical and social causes through its campaign on podoconiosis, a foot disease.

Customer engagement

Customers are more likely to be loyal and stay with the firm in the long term if they feel tied to the social mission or cause of the company. The one-for-one model generated by TOMS makes use of a varying value combination design. This is where 'social value' is embedded into TOMS' products, thereby transforming customers into benefactors. With customers placing greater value on social issues when making purchases, firms need to increasingly embed cultural capital, ethics and social value into their products. As well as allowing the company to portray a positive image of itself to the world and enhance its reputation, 'cause marketing' also allows customers to feel intimately connected to the firm and feel as if they are playing a role in its social mission, more than a simple transaction. In such a way, the business strategy of TOMS is argued to be more sustainable and can retain customers in the long term.

One of the challenges that TOMS faces is sharing its story in more ways, as the company realises that some of its customers are not aware of its charitable work and unique social mission. Subsequently, it has invested heavily in strategies such as store displays and virtual reality headsets, which show children throughout the world wearing TOMS shoes to spread awareness about its social mission. After one customer becomes aware of TOMS' story, they will begin to share it with others, akin to a 'brand ambassador'. This highlights the importance of 'word-of-mouth' in spreading TOMS' story which is vital to the success of the firm.

Additionally, TOMS also runs an annual co-creation event that challenges customers to go barefoot for one day ('One Day Without Shoes') as a way of promoting the cause of shoeless children. This is a form of customer engagement that allows customers to feel more intimately connected and to become more emotionally invested in its core mission. For instance, two weeks prior to the event, customers are asked to post a photo of their barefoot event. For each photo that is tagged on Instagram, TOMS promises to donate a pair of new shoes to a child in need. This was later extended to incorporate those who had not previously shopped with TOMS. The barefoot event helps to put forward a positive narrative and perception of the brand that ultimately acts to improve TOMS' reputation and brand awareness.

Questions for discussion

1. How did the creator of TOMS Shoes perceive the opportunity to start the brand?
2. How does TOMS engage customers and create customer value in its business strategy?

3. What dimensions of entrepreneurial marketing are reflected in this case study?
4. How did TOMS carry out the co-created barefoot event with customers? What are the benefits of running the event?

Sources

Farrer, S. (2017) Is Social Media a Good Thing for Young Entrepreneurs? Available at: www.virgin.com/entrepreneur/social-media-good-thing-young-entrepreneurs (accessed 1 June 2018).

Haber, J. (2016) How This Company Makes Money While Making a Difference. Available at: www.entrepreneur.com/article/271974 (accessed 1 July 2018).

Lebowitz, S. (2016) On the 10th anniversary of TOMS, its founder talks stepping down, bringing in private equity, and why giving away shoes provides a competitive advantage. Business Insider, 15 June. Available at: http://uk.businessinsider.com/toms-blake-mycoskie-talks-growing-a-business-while-balancing-profit-with-purpose-2016-6?r=US&IR=T (accessed 1 July 2018).

Mycoskie, B. (2011) How I Did It: The TOMS Story. Available at: www.entrepreneur.com/article/220350 (accessed 1 July 2018).

TOMS (2018) Social Enterprise. Available at: www.toms.com/social-enterprise (accessed 1 July 2018).

SUMMARY OF KEY IDEAS

- The size, resources and structures of SMEs present a number of opportunities and challenges. The informal and less complex organisational structure of SMEs allows them to react more flexibly and quickly to opportunities in the market, in comparison to the lengthy bureaucratic and managerial set-up of larger companies. However, the challenges of SMEs often come from human and financial resource constraints.
- While internationalisation has traditionally been adopted by larger enterprises, SMEs have increasingly begun to operate internationally and outside of their domestic markets, in line with developments in transport and communication technologies. This often occurs in the early stages of an SME's development. Given their resource constraints, SMEs' internationalisation tends to emerge as export-based activity from their domestic bases, often via the internet.
- Entrepreneurial marketing focuses on the entrepreneurial orientation in seeking out and anticipating future customer needs. In contrast, the traditional marketing perspective places

greater emphasis on the importance of formal market research when conducting a marketing strategy. As a result, firms that adopt traditional marketing strategies are likely to be driven by the needs of the current market. On the other hand, EM strategies are driven by discovering opportunities proactively, in order to innovatively exploit opportunities for both existing and potential customers.

- EM has seven dimensions, derived from both entrepreneurship and marketing theories. These are: (1) proactive orientation, (2) opportunity exploitation, (3) innovativeness, (4) risk management, (5) resource leveraging, (6) customer intensity, and (7) value creation.
- Attention in EM research is placed on 'the customer's journey', concerning how and why customers formulate their purchase decisions, rather than simply examining what they are purchasing. Thus, entrepreneurs base their understanding of the market and the external environment on this rich, qualitative insight, in order to conduct the firm's market research activities.

Chapter Discussion Questions

1. What are the marketing disadvantages of SMEs and how might internet technology help the internationalisation of SMEs?
2. How do you see the importance and the role of entrepreneurial marketing in relation to SMEs?
3. In your opinion, what are the differences between entrepreneurial marketing and traditional marketing approaches?
4. How can SMEs overcome resource constraints and expand their customer base by applying the dimensions of entrepreneurial marketing in their marketing practices?
5. How can SMEs exploit entrepreneurship characteristics and carry out the most suitable marketing activities in the digital age?

REFERENCES

Agrawal, A. K. and Rahman, Z. (2015) Roles and resource contributions of customers in value co-creation. *International Strategic Management Review*, 3(1–2), 144–60.

Baltar, F. and De Coulon, S. (2014) Dynamics of the entrepreneurial process: The innovative entrepreneur and the strategic decisions. *Review of Business & Finance Studies*, 5(1), 69–81.

Barney, J. B. (2002) *Gaining and Sustaining Competitive Advantage*. Harlow: Pearson.

Berends, H., Jelinek, M., Reymen, I. and Stultiëns, R. (2014) Product innovation processes in small firms: Combining entrepreneurial effectuation and managerial causation. *Journal of Product Innovation Management*, 31(3), 616–35.

Brooksbank, R. (1999) The theory and practice of marketing planning in the smaller business. *Marketing Intelligence & Planning*, 17(2), 78–91.

Cao, Q., Criscuolo, P. and Autio, E. (2016) *SME Internationalisation and Its Impact on Firm Performance: Impact of International Business*. Berlin: Springer, pp. 220–40.

Chaston, I. and Mangles, T. (2002) *Small Business Marketing Management*. Basingstoke: Palgrave.

Covin, J. G. and Slevin, D. P. (1991) A conceptual model of entrepreneurship as firm behavior. *Entrepreneurship Theory and Practice*, 16(1), 7–25.

Deacon, J. (2002), "Contextual marketing-commonalities and personalities-fuzzy experiential excellence", UIC Research Symposium: American Academy of Marketing, San Diego State University, San Diego.

Ekwulugo, F. (2011) Marketing planning in small businesses. In S. Nwankwo and A. Gbadamosi (eds), *Entrepreneurship Marketing: Principles and Practice of SME Marketing*. New York: Routledge, pp. 356–66.

Franco, M., De Fátima Santos, M., Ramalho, I. and Nunes, C. (2014) An exploratory study of entrepreneurial marketing in SMEs: The role of the founder-entrepreneur. *Journal of Small Business and Enterprise Development*, 21(2), 265–83.

Hills, G. E. and Hultman, C. (2013) Entrepreneurial marketing: Conceptual and empirical research opportunities. *Entrepreneurship Research Journal*, 3(4), 437–48.

Hills, G. E. and LaForge, R.W. (1992) Research at the marketing interface to advance entrepreneurship theory. *Entrepreneurship Theory and Practice*, 16(3), 33–59.

Hills, G. E., Hultman, C. M., Kraus, S. and Schulte, R. (2010) History, theory and evidence of entrepreneurial marketing: An overview. *International Journal of Entrepreneurship and Innovation Management*, 11(1), 3–18.

Hills, G. E., Hultman, C. M. and Miles, M. P. (2008) The evolution and development of entrepreneurial marketing. *Journal of Small Business Management*, 46(1), 99–112.

Hinson, R. (2011) Entrepreneurship marketing. In S. Nwankwo and A. Gbadamosi (eds), *Entrepreneurship Marketing: Principles and Practice of SME Marketing*. New York: Routledge, pp. 13–29.

Ibeh, K. and Analogbei, M. (2011) International entrepreneurship and SMEs. In S. Nwankwo and A. Gbadamosi (eds), *Entrepreneurship Marketing: Principles and Practice of SME Marketing*. New York: Routledge, pp. 273–84.

Jones, R. and Rowley, J. (2011) Entrepreneurial marketing in small businesses: A conceptual exploration. *International Small Business Journal*, 29(1), 25–36.

Jones, R., Suoranta, M. and Rowley, J. (2013) Entrepreneurial marketing: A comparative study, *The Service Industries Journal*, 33 (7–8), 705–19.

Kotler, P. (2003) *Marketing Management.* Upper Saddle River, NJ: Prentice Hall.

Lee, S. M., Olson, D. L. and Trimi, S. (2012) Co-innovation: Convergenomics, collaboration, and co-creation for organizational values. *Management Decision*, 50(5), 817–31.

Lumpkin, G. T. and Dess, G. G. (1996) Clarifying the entrepreneurial orientation construct and linking it to performance. *Academy of Management Review*, 21(1), 135–72.

Lumpkin, G. T. and Dess, G. G. (2001) Linking two dimensions of entrepreneurial orientation to firm performance: The moderating role of environment and industry life cycle. *Journal of Business Venturing*, 16(5), 429–51.

Majama, N. S. and Magang, T. (2017) Strategic planning in small and medium enterprises (SMEs): A case study of Botswana SMEs. *Journal of Management and Strategy*, 8(1), 74–103.

Miles, M. P. and Darroch, J. (2006) Large firms, entrepreneurial marketing processes, and the cycle of competitive advantage. *European Journal of Marketing*, 40(5/6), 485–501.

Morris, M. H., Schindehutte, M. and LaForge, R. W. (2002) Entrepreneurial marketing: A construct for integrating emerging entrepreneurship and marketing perspectives. *Journal of Marketing Theory and Practice*, 10(4), 1–19.

Morrish, S. C., Miles, M. P. and Deacon, J. H. (2010) Entrepreneurial marketing: Acknowledging the entrepreneur and customer-centric interrelationship. *Journal of Strategic Marketing*, 18(4), 303–16.

O'Dwyer, M., Gilmore, A. and Carson, D. (2011) Strategic alliances as an element of innovative marketing in SMEs, *Journal of Strategic Marketing*, *19* (1), 91–104.

Oviatt, B. M. and McDougall, P. P. (2005) Defining international entrepreneurship and modeling the speed of internationalization. *Entrepreneurship Theory and Practice*, 29(5), 537–54.

Reuber, A. R. and Fischer, E. (2011) International entrepreneurship in internet-enabled markets. *Journal of Business Venturing*, 26(6), 660–79.

Romero, D. and Molina, A. (2011) Collaborative networked organisations and customer communities: Value co-creation and co-innovation in the networking era. *Production Planning & Control*, 22(5–6), 447–72.

Schindehutte, M., Morris, M. H. and Pitt, L. F. (2009) *Rethinking Marketing: An Entrepreneurial Imperative.* Hoboken, NJ: Pearson Education International.

Shane, S. and Venkataraman, S. (2000) Entrepreneurship as a field of research: A response to Zahra and Dess, Singh, and Erikson. *Academy of Management Review*, 26(1), 13–16.

Simpson, M., Taylor, N. and Padmore, J. (2011) Marketing in SMEs. In S. Nwankwo and T. Gbadamosi (eds), *Entrepreneurship Marketing: Principles and Practice of SME Marketing.* New York: Routledge.

Sullivan Mort, G., Weerawardena, J. and Liesch, P. (2012) Advancing entrepreneurial marketing: Evidence from born global firms. *European Journal of Marketing*, 46(3/4), 542–61.

Tanev, S. (2012) Global from the start: The characteristics of born-global firms in the technology sector. *Technology Innovation Management Review*, 2(3), 5–8.

Wach, K. (2015) Small and medium-sized enterprises in the modern economy. In M. Loera and A. Marianski (eds), *The Challenges of Management in Turbulent Times: Global Issues from Local Perspective*. Sinaloa, Mexico: Universidad de Occidente, pp. 77–101.

Wuest, T. and Thoben, K. (2011) *Information management for manufacturing SMEs*. In *IFIP International Conference on Advances in Production Management Systems 2011*. Berlin: Springer, pp. 488–95.

Yenera, M., Doğruoğlu, B., and Ergun, S. (2014) Challenges of internationalization for SMEs and overcoming these challenges: A case study from Turkey. *Procedia-Social and Behavioral Sciences*, 150, 2–11.

10
BUSINESS-TO-BUSINESS (B2B) MARKETING

Ejindu Iwelu MacDonald Morah

Learning Outcomes

After reading this chapter, you will have learned:

- The meaning and history of business-to-business marketing
- Differences and similarities between B2B and B2C marketing and markets
- The significance of B2B marketing
- How to conduct market segmentation in business markets
- How buying decisions are made in business markets
- How to classify products in business markets
- Marketing programmes in business markets using the 4Ps
- How to forge relationships, networking and key account management in B2B marketing
- The emerging trends in B2B marketing
- An overview of marketing metrics and analytics

INTRODUCTION

The origin of marketing as a field of human endeavour has been the subject of contrasting opinions within the academic community. Although we know that the genealogy of the field of marketing is closely tied to the US industrial landscape, academics including Bartels (1988), Bussiere (2000) and Shaw (1995) have advanced separate and contrasting accounts. While we wouldn't want to add to this debate, we believe it is useful to present some of the early mentions of marketing. First, the *American Encyclopaedic Dictionary*, as far back as 1561, records that the word 'marketing' was used as a noun. But, in 1880, a cookery book titled *Miss Parloa's New Cookbook and Marketing Guide* discussed marketing. Equally, the term marketing was already in use in the *American Economic Review* (AER) in 1897.

While marketing has a long history, B2B marketing is a relatively newer concept. Serious scholarly works on B2B didn't emerge until 1971. A survey of marketing literature suggests that a relatively small amount of scholarly work is devoted to the issues bordering on B2B marketing problems, techniques and practice. This explains why this textbook is relevant to address the traditional, contemporary and emerging issues in marketing.

In this chapter, we will discuss the history of business marketing, its relevance, and illustrate the similarities and differences between B2B and B2C marketing. Market segmentation as a key feature of marketing is explored in the context of business markets. The classification of business products and the characteristics of business markets are explained. This sets the tone for a deeper examination of the various marketing programmes using the marketing mix variables that are available to the business organisation. Relationships and networking are essential to business marketing success, especially given the technology inspiring and changing the business landscape.

Before we begin with a detailed discussion of the entire gamut of B2B marketing, it is necessary to look back at the foundations of this sub-field of marketing.

So, we begin with the history of B2B marketing.

THE ORIGIN AND EVOLUTION OF BUSINESS-TO-BUSINESS MARKETING

In a world that is continually changing, at exponential and at times alarming rates, the need to know the past becomes particularly useful in order to gain a better understanding of the present and be able to predict the future with reasonable certainty. So, let's begin our journey with the history of B2B marketing.

History is the best starting point for every discipline – B2B marketing included. A good understanding of a discipline's past enables both scholars and practitioners to evaluate its current practices, and provides an avenue for sophistication in future research (Culnan, 1986). One of the wise men of modern marketing, George Day (1996), reminds us that history serves several functions, including helping to reveal our origin, celebrate achievements and, importantly, remind us of our indebtedness to our intellectual forbearers.

Marketing academics globally agree that attempts to identify the genesis of industrial marketing are problematic. Although evidence of the origin and practice of business-to-business marketing (B2B) (hereafter referred to as B2B) suggests its recognition immediately after the First World War (that is, the latter half of the 20th century), B2B marketing as a discipline in the realms of marketing didn't begin until 1920. It was originally known as 'industrial marketing' with an emphasis on 'industrial or agricultural products'.

The earliest recorded work on industrial marketing was by Harvard University professor Melvin T. Copeland in 1920 in a classic entitled *Marketing Problems* (a collection of short case studies) and later in another text, *Principles of Merchandising*, published in 1924. Both pieces devoted chapters to industrial and consumer marketing. The first fully fledged textbooks on the subject were J. Frederick's *Industrial Marketing: A Century of Marketing* (1934) and R. F. Elder's *Fundamentals of Industrial Marketing* (1935). Over the years, this field of marketing has metamorphosed into 'business-to-business marketing'.

In the beginning, much of the research and practice of industrial marketing was concentrated in the USA. In the early 1970s, a group of researchers and young academics from France, Sweden, the UK, Italy and Germany were unsatisfied with the theorising and the focus of the larger marketing discourse on consumer goods. The business context confronted in Europe was different from that in the USA. Europe was dominated by business-to-business marketing, especially across national boundaries. This dissatisfaction of European marketing scholars with the dominant marketing paradigm at the time led to the formation of the Industrial Marketing and Purchasing (IMP) Group in Europe. The IMP group drew widely outside of economics – from behavioural theories to sociology and organisational theories.

To educate the world and forge their approach, *Industrial Marketing Management* (IMM) was published in September 1971, as the first journal for the dissemination of industrial marketing knowledge. Through this medium, attempts were made to define and coin the meaning of B2B marketing.

So, what is B2B marketing and why should you bother to study it? What are the contemporary issues in marketing and B2B? In the sections that follow, we will provide answers to the above questions and discuss the wide-ranging issues in this marketing domain.

Let's begin with a definition of B2B marketing.

HOW DO WE DEFINE BUSINESS-TO-BUSINESS MARKETING?

Any business relationship where one business (organisation, institution, government) markets its products (goods and services) to another business for the benefit of both businesses is known as B2B marketing. B2B marketing involves one business (organisation, institution, all levels of government, hospitals, charities) marketing its products (goods and services) to another organisation. B2B marketing encompasses the marketing of business products and develops relationships between organisations for the benefit of all concerned businesses.

Definition of B2B marketing

B2B marketing comprises marketing activities involving two or more organisations in exchange for value. It enables the exchange of value between institutions, organisations, companies and all entities separate and different from the final consumer. For example, for the production and bottling of its carbonated (fizzy) drinks, Coca-Cola may buy sugar from a sugar-producing company and plastic bottles from a plastic bottle manufacturing company. Keep in mind that this sort of marketing relationship is not limited to 'tangible goods' but also, equally, 'services'.

Services emerged and continue to represent a sizeable chunk of B2B marketing business among transacting organisations, thanks to new technologies. This explains why 'industrial services' are an essential element of B2B and are exchanged for value. For example, Nestle, the beverage conglomerate, may seek the services of a marketing research firm to conduct a study on its behalf so it can understand the current and future tastes and preferences of chocolate customers and consumers in the UK. B2B marketing is increasingly seeing the exchange of services as against the original view of the discipline as involving only 'industrial tangible products'.

B2B marketing contributes a huge amount of industrial and commercial transactions across the entire value chain. For example, from sourcing raw materials to industrial services, manufacturers, agents, distributors, wholesalers and even business buyers engage in the exchange process. These actors in the market account for a sizeable share of the entire business activity within a country. In most economies, B2B marketing which creates business markets tends to be larger and, most times, more valuable than B2C markets. So, what are business markets?

BUSINESS MARKETS

Business markets exist whenever organisations buy products from other organisations for the production and distribution of goods and services to other organisations. This includes markets where wholesalers and retailers buy products from a manufacturer for onward sale to the final consumer. The interactions between the producers of raw materials, manufacturers, wholesalers, retailers and other service providers in the manufacturing value chain constitute business markets.

Although B2B and B2C marketing are different in many ways, they share some commonalities. Let us look at the similarities between B2B and B2C marketing.

SIMILARITIES BETWEEN B2B AND B2C BUYING

All organisations that engage in marketing activities, be it B2B or B2C, are focused on providing some form of value to their customers. Within B2B, the customers are mostly other organisations, while B2C customers are the final consumers. Both forms of marketing are substantially similar in their approach by being market-oriented. Regardless of the country or sector within which these firms operate, they share five vital similarities:

1. Both understand that a focus on meeting the needs of customers is essential to their survival.
2. Both know and appreciate the need to collect market-relevant information about their customers, competitors, industry and national economies to achieve their goals.
3. Both ensure that the various functional units within their organisations must be well co-ordinated, to share information about the market and other assets and be effective in delivering customer satisfaction.
4. Both deal with buyers/customers and make purchase decisions.
5. The two buy the same products but for different uses, although there are products that are peculiar to B2B – for example, the purchase of a manufacturing facility, heavy industrial machines and other, related products.

The adoption of market orientation as a business philosophy is fundamental to firm success because it enables firms to understand customers, competitors and the business environment better. This means that accomplishing the above will ensure that, ultimately, firms will survive and thrive in varying business environments.

Now let's look at the more specific and conceptual differences between B2B and B2C marketing.

WHAT ARE THE DIFFERENCES BETWEEN B2B AND B2C MARKETING?

Providing value for customers is at the heart of marketing. Every organisation goes through the basics of identifying and attracting customers and meeting their identified needs and wants in order to satisfy and retain them. This is the focus regardless of the sector and country where they operate. However, there are significant differences in the approach to marketing to businesses vis-à-vis marketing to consumers. The way goods and services are marketed in B2B is often different from that which obtains in B2C markets. Table 10.1 illustrates some of the essential differences between the two forms of marketing.

Table 10.1   Essential differences between business and consumer marketing

Differentiating Factor	Feature	B2B	B2C
Customer/market type	Customer	Organisations, institutions, goverments, non-governmental bodies	Final consumers
	Nature of customers	Heterogeneous	Homogeneous
	Nature of demand	Derived	Direct
	Size of market in terms of monetary value of transactions	Large and growing	Smaller
	Size of market in terms of number of transactions	Narrow	Broad
Environmental factors	Technology	Essential for creating competitive advantage	Used to meet personal needs
	Significance of relationships	Mostly important	Mostly not important
Internal structure and configuration of organisations/ companies	Relationships between units	High interdependence between sections of the firm due to customisation of customer order	Although there is interdependencebetween departments, little or no customisation is required
	Corporate strategy	Marketing strategy is often the same as overall firm corporate strategy	Often seen from the final customer's perspective

The differences between B2B and B2C marketing are based on a number of factors:

- customer/market type
- environmental factors
- internal configuration of companies.

Let's look at each of these factors in detail.

Customer/market type

B2B organisations enter into business relationships with other organisations to meet the needs of the final consumer. This means that B2B companies don't buy raw materials and other products for their private consumption, but rather because they want to use them to produce products that the final consumer will desire. Therefore, the nature of demand in the B2B market is *derived demand*, because the needs of the final consumer inform the type of products companies will produce. However, within B2C marketing, companies transact directly with the final consumer, thus generating a *direct demand*.

While B2B customers are narrow and highly heterogeneous, those of B2C are often homogeneous. A small number of business customers account for a large chunk of their sales, revenue and profitability. It is estimated that B2B transactions double that of B2C. As at 2015, B2B e-commerce transactions in the USA amounted to about $780 billion – which represents 9.3 per cent of all B2B sales (MarketingCharts.com, 2017). In addition, the characteristics (bases) used for segmenting B2B markets differ significantly from B2C markets. B2C adopts demographic and psychographic bases, while B2B uses firm-specific factors (firmographics) including industry classification codes, location, customer size and relevance of products to the buying firm. Also, market segmentation in consumer markets uses simpler methods but B2B uses more advanced and at times complex methods.

Environmental factors

Technology is one of the most visible and well-known game-changers in modern business. While B2C customers are excited about the latest technologies for personal or private use, business demands better technologies. To organisations, sophisticated technologies would help them create better and more sustainable competitive advantage. This explains why firms are continually searching for more advanced and effective ways of employing technology to enhance organisational performance. A mistake in a chosen technology that leads to the production of defective products could amount to losses of unimaginable proportions to the firm.

Internal configuration of companies

High levels of interdependency are the norm in business marketing organisations. Departments, units and divisions within institutions in business marketing work closely to meet customer needs. This explains why no one department in a B2B firm can start and conclude any business process without input from other divisions, departments and units.

The different sections of the entire organisation collaborate to achieve the organisation's over-all corporate goals. For example, if the marketing manager proposes a new product – finance, production, human resources, and so on – other departments would work with marketing to ensure the successful production and launch of the product.

The above differences between B2B and B2C marketing suggest sharp contrasts between them. But how relevant is B2B marketing? And why should you bother to study B2B marketing?

Let's take a closer look at the significance of B2B marketing, why we should bother to study it, and some inherent benefits it brings to our organisations.

THE SIGNIFICANCE OF BUSINESS-TO-BUSINESS MARKETING

According to the US Department of Commerce, the values of B2B and B2C components of the US economy were almost identical in 2007. Here are some of the merits B2B marketing brings to your organisation:

- generates more money for institutions
- means greater business for firms
- contributes greater value–higher quantity per sale
- presents fewer customers to worry about by the firm
- creates huge employment opportunities.

CLASSIFICATION OF BUSINESS PRODUCTS

The classification of B2B products follows a standard approach, which is based on the use of products or materials and the extent to which they are integrated into the final finished product. Some tangible and intangible products that many organisations buy don't directly become part of a finished product but rather act as support for the production process. For instance, a company that manufactures plastic pet bottles would need the services of labourers to load and unload raw materials and clean the manufacturing facility. These services don't become part of the finished product. But the same firm would buy the plastic pellets, which become the critical component of the finished plastic pet bottles. So, how do we classify products in business markets?

B2B products may be classified as:

- *Raw materials*: these form the basic components of all tangible goods. For example, Nestle and Starbucks use coffee beans produced in Africa and South America as the raw material for their finished coffee beverage products. The international price of coffee beans – due to the global forces of demand and supply – often impacts a company's costs and determines its pricing strategies.

- *Installations*: the investments in machines and heavy equipment used for manufacturing – that is, fixed assets. Examples include cutting equipment and moulding machines. They are often expensive and expected to last for a long period. Because this equipment will depreciate due to wear and tear arising from continuous use, organisations make provisions to be able to replace them after a stated number of years. This provision is generally calculated as a yearly percentage charge on the cost of the assets and is known as the *depreciation* charge on the equipment.
- *Accessory equipment*: comprises smaller equipment used for production. For example, hand-held tools including scissors, shovels, etc. are accessory equipment and often inexpensive, and hence treated as expense items and not as investments. For similar reasons, accessory equipment has a short life span, and organisations don't ordinarily calculate depreciation on such items.
- *Business services*: categorised as consulting/business services, maintenance and repairs needed to produce the final product.
- *Maintenance, repair and operating (MRO) supplies*: for the organisation to run smoothly, small and minor items will be required. These include abrasives, stationery, lubricants, etc. Thus, they are used to maintain, repair and serve as operational materials.
- *Manufactured materials and parts*: materials ready to be integrated into the finished product, including processed raw materials like semi-processed rubber also known as Pale Light Crepe (PLC), steel and component parts such as car braking systems, computer hard disks, etc.

The classification of industrial manufacturing organisations into original equipment manufacturers (OEMs) is equally common. OEMs are business organisations that buy component parts from other organisations, integrate them into their finished products and sell the products as their brands. For example, Samsung buys a mobile phone battery, while Toyota buys an automobile breaking system from suppliers, and uses them to produce the final product, which they sell as theirs. While this is a common practice in B2B, it portends several risks and dangers. For instance, in 2016, Samsung Galaxy Note 7 was bursting into flames and was recalled. Similarly, Toyota recalled 437,000 of its third-generation Prius cars in 2010 due to a factory defect. The Toyota Prius had a failed breaking system which caused it to somersault and kill people. These catastrophic consequences arose because the two companies bought their parts from supply organisations; other examples abound.

Although the above classification of B2B products remains popular and widely used, Murphy and Enis (1986) argued that only one classification system is needed and could apply to both B2B and B2C. They proposed a four-fold classification based on the buyer's evaluation of the amount of work involved in acquiring the products, as well as the risks of making a poor decision. Their suggested classification includes:

- *convenience products*: little effort and risks to the buyer are involved
- *preference products*: involves a little more effort than *convenience products* but with higher risks
- *shopping products*: more effort and higher risks than for convenience and preference products
- *specialty products*: these have the highest efforts and risks in their purchase.

SEGMENTING BUSINESS MARKETS

Segmentation, targeting and positioning (STP) are three key marketing practices, often used to design and execute marketing strategies (Dibb and Simkin, 2001). STP applies to both B2B and B2C and across industries – the differences have been discussed in the above section on the differences between B2B and B2C – although the nature and method of its application vary in these two forms of marketing and in some cases across national boundaries. Each element of the STP is essential for effective marketing.

In this section, we will discuss the segmentation of business markets. Let's begin with an understanding of segmentation as a concept in marketing.

Segmentation defined

Segmentation is the division of a mass-heterogeneous market into smaller clusters of buyers with similar needs, known as segments. Customers with similar features (characteristics) are grouped as segments, to ensure that the individual needs of buyers are identified and satisfied. So, to segment a business market, we divide that market into groups of customers with similar requirements and buying behaviours.

Let's look at an example: suppose the customers of a tyre manufacturer are automobile companies. The manufacturer may then segment its market by grouping automobile companies with similar products and in similar climates, and based on their needs. So, they view organisations who need small cars, coaches, earth-moving equipment, trailers, trucks, and so on, as different market segments.

What criteria do we use to segment business markets? In B2B, we use different criteria or variables known as *bases* to segment markets. And these bases can generally be categorised as *identifiers/descriptors* and *response* variables. Identifiers help to identify the organisations. As such *demographic, geographic* and *situational* variables are commonly used to identify and segment organisations, while response variables show how firms respond to the marketing offerings of the seller and include usage rates, and so on (see Table 10.2).

Table 10.2   Bases of segmentation

Identifier/Descriptor variables	Response variables
Firmographics	Service and convenience
Geography	Financial: cost savings
Industry	Usage: usage rate, usage patterns, usage frequency
Company size	Functional: selling firms evaluate the buying firms' main reason for the product, e.g. convenience, value
Order size	Usually medium to High

But why should a B2B firm segment its market? Do you remember the 80/20 rule or Pareto principle? Yes, this rule suggests that 80 per cent of an organisation's revenues and profits are mostly generated from 20 per cent of its customers. This means that we should pay more attention to the 20 per cent of customers needed to provide success.

Well, if the company is to allocate and manage its scarce resources effectively, there is a need to know which customers to serve profitably, and what customer characteristics are common in any segment. This way, similar marketing programmes would be used for each specific segment. This is an approach that ensures firms achieve maximum outcomes from their marketing efforts, by directing a firm's marketing mix elements specifically to meet the needs of the identified and chosen segments of the market. With this, the firm could position itself as one that understands its customers, and that is focused on satisfying customer needs.

Consequently, segmentation enables the B2B firm to customise its offerings to the various segments. But this practice can only be done if the identified market segments possess qualities which are good enough to warrant a firm's investment.

What are the qualities of good market segments?

A segment should possess qualities that would justify the effort and resource commitment of the business marketer. This demands that it should be:

- accessible
- measurable
- profitable
- substantial
- stable.

First, the segment must be customers that the marketer can reach for any form of marketing to take place (*accessible*). Second, knowing the size of the segment (*measurable*) is key before committing organisational resources. Third, the chosen segment must have the potential to generate profits (*profitable*). Fourth, the segment must be large enough (*substantial*) to command the required attention and investment. Finally, the stability of the segment (*stable*) is as vital as every other quality we have discussed.

With these qualities in a chosen segment, the business marketer would be on a journey to helping the firm understand and satisfy its customers, and, by extension, create a competitive advantage by avoiding errors in the process – although many firms make mistakes in segmenting their markets and these are part of the contemporary landscape in marketing.

Errors in market segmentation

Organisations at times commit errors in the way they carry out the tasks of segmentation. Here are four common mistakes business marketers make when segmenting their markets:

- being product-focused instead of customer-focused: that's focusing more on products' features, instead of the needs of customers
- using broad segmentation: they may believe that all customers in the entire market are the same, just because they are in similar locations and of similar sizes
- segmenting too narrowly, thereby missing out on a large chunk of the market and off-course revenue
- making errors in the execution of segmentation.

How then can we avoid or significantly minimise the possibility of committing errors in segmenting our markets? To overcome errors in market segmentation, technical knowledge, marketing analytics and technology are vital:

- *Technical knowledge*: a good knowledge of the industry, market, customers and bases of segmentation would help in avoiding errors in segmenting the market.
- *Marketing analytics*: this employs advanced statistical techniques and powerful data analysis software to segment the market. Cluster analysis (CA) and latent class analysis (LCA) are the two widely used advanced statistical techniques. And the Statistical Package for the Social Sciences (SPSS), SAS and R, is the preferred data analysis software.
- *Technology*: this plays a huge role in our modern business and marketing operations. Current and emerging technologies and proprietary solutions are useful. Just like the geo-cluster approaches, a consumer classification system specially designed for market segmentation and consumer profiling, proprietary technological products are available for the B2B market.

The above three factors have been effective in tackling the issue of errors in market segmentation in contemporary B2B marketing.

You may wonder why we should bother segmenting our markets. Well, we will bother because segmentation done well might prove worthwhile and highly rewarding.

So, let's look at some specific reasons for conducting market segmentation in more depth.

Reasons for segmenting business markets

The process of market segmentation entails taking a closer look at the customer to understand their unique characteristics and needs. Based on this process, customers with similar characteristics are identified for better marketing. This approach yields enormous benefits to the business marketer, including:

- effective and efficient allocation of scarce resources
- superior customer satisfaction
- enhanced revenue generation potential
- identification of new market opportunities
- competitive advantage
- maintenance of market share and position.

Consumer versus business segmentation

The overarching difference between B2B and B2C segmentation lies in the customer type – that is, the 'final consumer' for the B2C marketing firm and 'organisations/institutions' for a B2B marketing firm. Why is this necessary in segmentation? Remember that final consumers are individuals who make buying decisions based on emotions and personal preferences – that is, based on *psychographic variables*, which include individual lifestyles, personality characteristics, habits, states of mind, cravings, likes and dislikes, idiosyncrasies, moods, and so on. On the other hand, human emotions play a limited role in organisational buying decisions, meaning that *psychographics* has no role in the B2B organisational buying decision-making process.

However, both forms of marketing may use some similar bases of segmentation. For instance, geographic, demographic and behavioural variables may be useful to both the B2B and B2C marketing segmentation processes. Care must, however, be taken if you decide to apply some of these bases to both, as poor judgement in their use could lead to unimaginable losses.

Segmentation challenges

The usefulness of market segmentation is well documented in the marketing literature, thus it is not debatable, as detailed above, but some barriers leave business marketers confused as to how to implement segmentation. The barriers that make it difficult for firms to reap the benefits of this marketing practice abound. While marketers understand the concept of segmentation, knowledge on how to implement it remains fuzzy and at best unknown by many business marketers. This lack of clarity, as discussed earlier, has prevented the effective use of this marketing strategy tool.

Here are some of the challenges to segmentation:

- *Infrastructure*: the organisation may lack the relevant infrastructure required to conduct a well-thought-out market segmentation.
- *Process*: some organisations may lack knowledge of the tried and tested process to achieve segmentation. (We will discuss this process further in the following section.)
- *Implementation*: being effective in a marketing effort calls for adequate and careful implementation and market segmentation is no different. Poor implementation would spell a hazard for the firm.

To obviate the effects of segmentation challenges, we should consider how organisations are classified. Every country has its own system which is used for segmentation.

How then are organisations classified? Let's discuss the classification system.

SIC codes

In 1948, the UK introduced a Standard Industrial Classification (SIC) code. At the time, it was formally known as the UK Standard Industrial Classification of Economic Activities. The SIC code is used to classify business establishments and other statistical units based on the type of economic activity they are engaged in. This classification is useful in data collection, analysis and presentation, which provides uniformity among businesses.

The classification was revised in 1958, 1968, 1980, 1992, 1997, 2003 and 2007. Revision is important to align with market dynamics in the current economic and business landscape. Put simply, new businesses in differing industries, which are churning out new products, have emerged over the past few years. (Details of the SIC codes for different industries can be found on the Office of National Statistics' website: www.ons.gov.uk.)

In fact, since 30 June 2016 in the UK, you are required to state the SIC code when forming a company. This code is needed so that your line of business may be ascertained and recognised by the authorities.

So why is the SIC code relevant to business marketing? Because the first two digits in the SIC code represent the industry title, business marketers use this as a guide to achieve four objectives:

- identify businesses in similar industries
- determine industries to serve
- identify potential new markets (that is, ideal customers)
- segment their markets.

Marketers use information on the SIC to identify industries. However, while this approach seems practical, it has been criticised for its shortcomings. This is based on an understanding that although businesses may sit in the same industry, their features and policies might differ significantly. This is why sole use of the SIC code for this purpose may be misleading and counter-productive, and could hamper the process of segmentation.

Let's now look in more detail at the process of segmenting a market.

What is the process of segmentation?

We have looked at the challenges and barriers to implementing segmentation. We also agreed that a lack of clarity and knowledge as to how to segment a business market remains a problem for businesses. Here's a three-step process often employed:

Step 1:   Consider the mass market

Step 2:   Select a market segment

Step 3:   Target the selected segment

The starting point for an effective segmentation task is to identify the mass market of interest. With an understanding of the business needs of customers, we can pinpoint the overall market for our products. We could then use any, or a combination, of the bases of segmentation to create sub-markets by grouping customers with similar SIC codes, needs, characteristics, and so on, in the same segment. While this often proves to be a daunting task in the segmentation process, cluster analysis, a statistical technique, could be employed. Again, this approach is not without its shortcomings, which explains why the use of a combination of bases might prove more effective and efficient. With tailored marketing programmes specifically designed and targeted at the selected segments, marketing performance could be improved. This is effective as organisational resources are used to serve segments with potentially high marketing opportunities. Albert (2003) notes that, within marketing channels, segmentation analysis could be used to design and develop targeted communication strategies, which would help differentiate a firm's value offerings from those of the competition.

So, how do businesses make buying decisions? Let's look at this aspect of B2B closely.

BUSINESS BUYING DECISIONS

Organisational buying usually involves a number of members of staff from various units who take decisions regarding *what to buy, how much to buy, who to buy from, when to buy*, and so on. This group of staff forms a team entrusted with the responsibility of making purchase decisions, and is expected to be rational and less emotional in carrying out its buying functions, although it should be noted that staff are human beings with emotions and often seek to forge relationships with seller organisations. The buying team is often described as the *decision-making unit* (DMU) or buying centre. Due to the size, monetary value and nature of the purchasing activities, the organisational buying process may take several days, weeks, months or even years, depending on the value and size of the products required.

Let's look at the composition of the decision-making unit. According to Webster and Wind (1972), the DMU consists of:

- initiators
- gatekeepers
- buyers
- influencers
- deciders
- users.

Initiators comprise organisational members who often first recognise a problem or identify the need for a product.

Gatekeepers are those individuals who control the flow of information, often filtering it, and access to the buying group. They may influence the buying decision. A gatekeeper might be an administrator who controls access to the DMU, a salesperson's secretary who schedules appointments, or even the finance manager who ensures that purchases are made within budget.

Buyers are those individuals who do the actual purchasing and so source the suppliers. A buyer may or may not be in the firm's purchasing department and his powers vary depending on the situation and from one organisation to another.

Influencers are powerful people who are trusted by the organisation for their expertise and judgements. So, they are respected advisers whose voices are strong and powerful. Influencers may be staff of the firm or external consultants who have been brought in to advise the firm, especially on specific highly technical matters and where the firm lacks such expertise.

The decider or decision maker is the person or committee with the authority to make the buying decision. *Deciders* rely on other members of the DMU for accurate information and advice before making a buying decision. Where strategic issues are involved, the board of directors may assume this role.

Users are the persons or departments within the organisation that will ultimately use the supplied products. The user may be a member of the production, administration or marketing staff. Their evaluation of the product will be sought by members of the DMU, especially the *decider*, and future re-purchase from suppliers will often depend on users' opinions.

Ethical Focus 10.1

The case of Equifax

Marketing organisations depend on an impeccable reputation to thrive. This is far from the practice at Equifax. Equifax is a credit-rating firm and at the epicentre of what customers worry is a growing, discomforting practice with damming consequences. The firm's business model is basically selling customers' personal information to financial institutions and lenders and profiting hugely from it.

In September 2017, Equifax confessed to being at the centre of one of the worst data breaches in recent history. Personal information belonging to 45 million US, 400,000 UK and 100,000 Canadian citizens was compromised. Customers were left open to identity theft and other fraudulent practices.

Consumers and lenders filed lawsuits against the firm, government fines were lacking, but angry consumers attributed the security breach to the firm's disturbing practice. Had customer data been carefully and safely stored, private institutions wouldn't have accessed the data, and data breaches could have been averted. More worrying was the fact that Equifax made this revelation some months after the security breach. Worse still, there was no government punishment as of June 2018. However, by 21st of September 2018 Equifax was fined £500,000 by the Information Commissioner's Office which is the maximum allowed under previous legislation.

Ethical issues

1. Is Equifax's business model ethical?
2. Are Equifax's business customers culpable?
3. Why did the government not impose any financial punishment on the firm?

Source: http://fortune.com

MARKETING PROGRAMMES FOR BUSINESS MARKETING

This section looks at the various elements of the marketing mix: the 4Ps, which are product, price, promotion and place (distribution) in the context of B2B. Remember that the 4Ps refer to tangible products and the 7Ps to services (people, physical evidence and processes are the additional variables, though not discussed in this section). The nature and ways (operationalisation) we use the 4Ps in B2B are different from how we use them in B2C.

Let's look at each element of the 4Ps in more detail.

Managing products in B2B marketing

Every organisation is in operation to offer some form of benefit to its market – that is, the value that the business intends to bring to its customers. This explains why, ideally, we should start the discussion of business-to-business marketing with a clear understanding of what a product means, because all businesses should and ought to have a product from the outset.

But what exactly do we mean by a product? Well, most people see a product as something in a tangible form, which means something that can be felt or seen, but this isn't correct. Admittedly, a definition will bring clarity to the concept of a *product*.

Product defined

A product is anything that offers some form of value to the market. It could be tangible or intangible. For instance, products include ideas, commodities, OEM products, manufactured goods, and services. Surprisingly, ideas remain the least recognised form of product. But, just for a moment, look around you and your business organisation – all you see is the result of somebody's *ideas*. Every product – goods and/or services – begins as an idea in somebody's mind.

Note that:

Product = Tangible + Intangible

Product = Goods + Services

A firm's product portfolio consists of product line and product mix. Here's what they mean:

A *product line* comprises various products produced using the same manufacturing facility, sold together to meet the needs of a specific segment of the market. For example, suppose you are the marketing manager of a mobile phone screen manufacturing company, you may produce phone screens of varying dimensions: 5 inch, 7.5 inch and 10 inch. Each of these screen sizes may be sold together to mobile phone manufacturers like Samsung, Apple, Nokia, etc. The various sizes of screens become a product line.

Product mix consists of all products manufactured by a company. Using the screen manufacturer example, the same firm may also be producing batteries, cameras, phone screens, circuit board, speakers, and so on, used for phone production. All these products form the firm's product mix (see Figure 10.1).

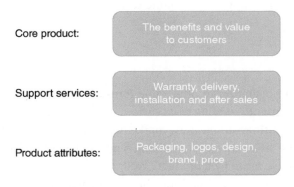

Core product: The benefits and value to customers

Support services: Warranty, delivery, installation and after sales

Product attributes: Packaging, logos, design, brand, price

Figure 10.1   Components of business-to-business products

Therefore, where *product* is mentioned in this section, we are referring to both goods and services. Where necessary and for purposes of specificity and clarity, we will be exact if our discussion relates to either goods or services.

Products are classified according to the standardisation and customisation the organisation chooses.

It should be mentioned, though, that all products have some elements of these two forms. That is, every product has some amount of service and tangible features. Take Dunlop tyres, for example. They consist of the physical tyre that an automobile manufacturer needs to complete the production of a functional automobile. However, Dunlop as an organisation would have to supply or deliver these tyres to business customers that need them. Therefore, the *delivery* is the service element of the tyres. Likewise, if you are on a business trip and book a hotel room, chances are that the hotel will provide breakfast, bathing soap, shampoo, and so on. These tangible products from the hotel are the tangible goods element of the hotel accommodation service.

The intangible elements of a product may include warranties and guarantees, financial services, customer service, and training. Customers use these intangible elements to assess the value of an organisation's market and product offerings. Because any tangible product can be copied, B2B organisations use superior services and firm reputation to create a competitive advantage. For instance, some businesses offer 24-hour support to their clients across the world, which helps clients meet their customers' expectations.

The fundamental characteristic of business products is their functionality, their ability to be used to produce other products the market demands. Business buyers perceive products as bundles of characteristics. As a marketer, it is necessary that you understand which features of the product appeal more to the organisational buyer.

According to Hutt and Speh (2001), product features can be categorised as determinants and non-determinants. The authors suggest that determinants are features that buyers perceive as differentiating and essential, while non-determinants are features that are either differentiating or important but not both.

This means that, as a seller, you must, as a matter of necessity, understand how buyers perceive your product features vis-a-vis your competitors. What you consider as a differentiating product feature may be perceived as a basic and standard requirement by the customer. How then can you tell what the customer wants? The only short cut to knowing how the customer views the features of your product, whether *differentiating* or *important*, is to do two things:

1. Ask the customer.
2. Endeavour to understand the customer's business. What use do they put your product to? What does the customer like?

Knowledge of your customers, as well as their daily, monthly, quarterly, seasonal and possibly annual needs, can give an insight into how they classify your product features.

Why should you bother to know, you may ask? There are two answers to this question:

1. Simply because you want to retain your customers and possibly have them increase their level of business with you.
2. Because you want to enhance the quality of your offering, which means adding new features to satisfy existing customers and attract new ones.

Let's look more closely at business services and what differentiates them from tangible goods.

Service products and differences between tangible and intangible products

So, what are the differences between tangible and intangible products? Intangible products are services. Services by their nature are consumed on production. The value customers attach to any service will depend on the level of involvement in the production process.

B2B services provide much-needed support for manufacturing companies. They usually impact positively on the scale and nature of productivity in manufacturing sectors and, by extension, national economies. In fact, the percentage of the service component of a nation's gross domestic product (GDP) is used as an index for measuring their economic state. That is, the higher the amount or contribution of services to the GDP, the more advanced the economy and vice versa. Based on GDP per capita, in advanced countries, services account for as much as 75% of GDP. While in developing countries, the agricultural and extractive sectors contribute more to GDP.

The points above are essential in B2B marketing since companies are producing for their final customers/consumers.

While tangible and intangible products remain relevant and a critical aspect of B2B marketing, differences in their characteristics suggest different ways of managing these product types. Several marketing scholars, including Lovelock et al. (1999), Grönroos (2000), Kotler (2003) and Palmer (2014), agree with this view.

Let's look further at the features of services.

CHARACTERISTICS OF SERVICES

Services can't be felt, seen, smelt or even touched but can only be experienced. The characteristics of services include intangibility, inseparability, variability, perishability and an inability to be owned:

Intangibility: services are often intangible. The intangibility feature of services creates measurement problems, especially across national boundaries.

Inseparability: it is often difficult to separate the production and consumption of services, as both processes are done simultaneously.

Variability: because humans are involved in the production of many services, very often, the quality of services rendered will vary.

Perishability: any service produced and not consumed is lost.

Inability to be owned: unlike goods, services are intangible and perishable, hence they can't be owned.

Table 10.3 highlights the attributes of services that differentiate them from tangible goods.

How then do we manage business products to ensure success? Fortunately, there are several strategic tools to help manage business products. They include product analysis, product life cycle (PLC), portfolio analysis and others needed to innovate new product offerings.

Table 10.3   Characteristics of services

Characteristics	Effect on customers	Effects on organisation
Intangibility	• Perceived as high risk • Use price to assess quality • Difficulty in comparing competing services • Emphasis is on information sources	• Focus on improving service quality • Hang on simplicity of service, avoiding complexities • Facilitate word-of-mouth advertising • Emphasise tangible elements of the service
Inseparability	• Business and customer co-produce services • Business delivers services in customer's chosen location • Similar services are delivered to customers in same sector	• Improves service delivery system • Better management of business–customer interactions • Conscious attempt to separate service production and consumption
Variability	• Produced and consumed simultaneously • High perceived risks • May not identify brand differences • Identifies weaknesses in the process of production	• Difficulty in control and monitoring to maintain consistency • Difficulty in blueprinting the service process • No chance to correct mistakes before consumption
Perishability	• Careful planning before buying • Evaluation of suppliers • Up-to-date knowledge of market conditions in terms of demand	• Fluctuation in availability of services • Demand patterns fluctuate • Services can't be stored • Congestion in peak periods • Huge losses for non-consumed services • Use of appropriate pricing and promotional tools
Inability to be owned	• No transfer of ownership from seller to buyer • Buys the right to use	• Impact on design of channels of distribution • Use of direct distribution • Intermediaries act as co-producers of services

Source: Adapted from Palmer (2014)

Let's look at each of these tools and how we can apply them in more detail.

PRODUCT ANALYSIS

One of the fundamental principles of marketing is 'know thy product'. The following are some vital questions you should consider, ask or have at the back of your mind to help you *know* your product:

- Who are the users of your products?
- How do customers use your products?
- Where and how do they buy?
- How often do customers buy and use the products? Are the products used once or multiple times?
- What quantity of a product do customers buy?
- Why do they buy the products? Why don't they buy them? The benefits sought must be well understood.
- What price are your competitors offering?
- Are customers loyal to your brand? What about your competitors' brands?

These considerations are necessary because of their substantial impact on market share. Answers to the above questions demand that we conduct both market and marketing research.

Understanding product analysis is useful, but detailed knowledge of the stages a product goes through in its life will guarantee success in terms of profits and volume.

Let's focus on these stages as we discuss the product life cycle.

PRODUCT LIFE CYCLE (PLC) AND PRODUCT MANAGEMENT

To better manage a product, you should have a good knowledge of its life cycle, especially as varying strategies might be required to effectively manage the different stages of the product over its life cycle.

So, what is the product life cycle and how is it used in business marketing?

PLC defined

The product life cycle (PLC) is a concept that describes the stages a product goes through in its life. It is analogous to the biological life-to-death stages in living organisms.

Dean (1950) is credited as the pioneer of the PLC model, even if he didn't use the term 'product life cycle'. Figure 10.2 shows the classical model of the PLC, which details the stages gone through from when the product is first introduced to the market up until it declines.

The principle is that as products go through the stages of their life cycle, different marketing strategies might be needed to guide this transition, which follows an S-shaped curve or path. But note that the nature of the product determines the speed with which it progresses through the phases of the PLC. Technology-based products move faster than agricultural and fast-moving consumer goods. The application of a strategy that is inappropriate for the stage of a product in its life cycle would spell failure.

The following are the five stages of the PLC:

- pre-launch
- introduction
- growth
- maturity
- decline.

The *pre-launch* stage involves thought processes, ideas, time and financial investments, marketing, and market research and other series of activities, all required to conceptualise the product.

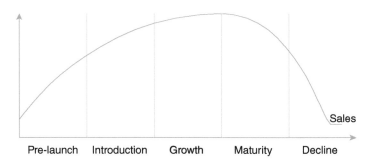

Figure 10.2   Stages in the life cycle of a product

The *introduction* stage is when the product is first presented to the market. Profit is zero or negative due to heavy investment in research, development and other promotional costs. Because the product is new, sales will typically be low, while the costs of other activities in bringing the product to market continue to increase. Creating awareness is the focus and heavy promotion is needed to communicate the product value to buyers.

In the *growth* stage, as the product gains market acceptance, sales and profit will increase. This explains why it is also known as the 'take-off stage'. Existing and new customers will be attracted and demand may rise.

In the *maturity* stage, with competition, demand continues to increase but at a reduced rate. Eventually, the rate of sale growth slows. The competition often adopts discounting and other price-based strategies to win more sales. This is rarely a good strategy, as it focuses on market share. Instead, you should design and develop more valued offerings that customers can recognise to help maintain and possibly enhance your margins.

In the *decline* stage, several factors may lead to a decline in sales or, more likely, in demand for a product, such as technological advancements or a rise in competitive pressures. As competition intensifies and new technologically sound products become available, sales will begin to drop rapidly, as will profit margins.

Finally, based on the above discussion about PLC in B2B, the following should be noted:

- The nature of the product determines its speed in transitioning the stages of the PLC. Agricultural products will transit slower than technology products.
- Average profitability and sales rise and slow as the product goes through the various stages.
- To extend the life of a product, several strategies could be adopted, including product extension, adding new features, finding new uses for the product, creating a foreign market, enhancing service support.

Although the PLC concept looks intuitively appealing, its validity has come under scrutiny.

Let's look at the criticisms of the PLC concept.

Criticisms of the PLC

Marketing academics including Dhalla and Yuspeth (1976) have criticised the PLC theory from several standpoints. The view is that the sequential nature of the concept is the major weakness in its validity. These scholars argue that the theory misleads organisational managers by making them ignore existing products and instead focus on new products. Also, the simplicity and intuitive appeal of the theory challenge its validity and practical use as a planning tool. Finally, others argue that it might be difficult to clearly recognise the stage of a product in its life cycle.

But what role does technology play in the use of PLC?

PLC and technology

The criticisms of the PLC theory remain part of the contemporary issues in marketing, but technology provides support to marketing managers as they adopt the PLC theory. This, to a significant extent, has addressed this contemporary marketing issue. Modern software and statistical techniques are known to be useful in solving the problems highlighted as the criticisms of the PLC theory.

Some specialised forms of product life-cycle management (PLM) solutions are now available for this purpose, some of which are software-based and others web-enabled technologies. Examples include computer-aided-design (CAD), computer-aided manufacturing (CAM), enterprise resource planning (ERP) and product data management (PDM). Two well-known organisations that provide these systems are SAP and IBM. The key to the effective use of PLC theory is to understand the appropriate marketing actions needed at any stage of the life cycle. With a good product(s) on its stable, the next step is for the B2B firm to price all products appropriately.

WHAT ARE THE PRICING STRATEGIES IN BUSINESS MARKETING?

Pricing is one of the most important elements of the marketing mix. It has a direct impact on sales and profitability. Although important, research in the field of B2B pricing has been relatively neglected (Liozu, 2015). This may be due to the general notion that firms are price-takers, or to a lack of understanding regarding its execution – to set appropriate prices for their products. So, what is price?

Price defined

Price is the value customers ascribe to a product. Organisations set the price of products, but it is the customers that decide if the value in a product is equal to the monetary cost attached to it by the seller. Customers often evaluate the utility, satisfaction or value they derive from using a product and match it against what they have been asked to pay to get it. If the value is more than the financial cost, customers gladly pay, but if the opposite is the case, customers look for other, competing products in the market.

But why should B2B marketers care about pricing their products? You should note that mistakes in pricing can be detrimental to an organisation's corporate existence. If done well, sales volume and profitability will soar; if poorly executed, losses and possible liquidation are the results. Business managers are often confused as to whether to increase the price of their products or not, which is mostly due to the 'follow the followers' syndrome.

According to Hinterhuber (2004), a 5 per cent increase in price may increase earnings before interest and taxes (EBIT) by 22 per cent, but a 5 per cent increase in sales and turnover increases EBIT by 12 per cent, and a 5 per cent reduction in the cost of goods sold increases EBIT by 10 per cent. This clearly shows the effect price has on the earnings and profitability of a business.

In pricing, organisations should pay attention to three key elements that determine appropriate pricing. These elements are known as the 3Cs of pricing:

- costs
- customers
- competitors.

Costs: these are all the essential costs incurred in producing a tangible good or delivering a service. They may include the cost of raw materials, logistics, production, wages, salaries, and so on. Careful identification and consideration of these, divided by the total quantity produced, generates the cost per unit. You then add a mark-up or a reasonable profit to set the price for your product. This approach to pricing is known as the *cost-plus pricing* method.

Customers: customers make the final decision of whether or not to purchase a particular product. In pricing a product, the business marketer should consider the demand structure for the product. That is, you should know the responsiveness of demand to changes in price – *demand elasticity*. The elasticity of demand for your product depends on several factors, including the unique value of the product, whether or not it is necessary, the availability of similar products, competitor prices and the available quantity.

If the product has an *elastic demand*, a 1 per cent change in price will lead to more than a 1 per cent change in the quantity demanded. However, if your product has an *inelastic demand*, a 1 per cent change in price will cause less than a 1 per cent change in the quantity demanded.

Why is elasticity of demand relevant to the business marketer? The relevance of the elasticity of demand is that it determines the sales volume and, by extension, the profitability of your firm.

Here are some facts about the elasticity of demand and price:

- If demand is *elastic* and you increase the price, then there will be a significant reduction in demand for your product. So, sales and profit will fall drastically.
- Where demand is *inelastic*, you can increase the price to generate higher revenue, while a reduction in price would mean a cut in revenue.

Competitors: knowing your competitors is a key to effective pricing strategy in business marketing. You should have a good knowledge of your competitors, their products and prices. It's essential that you don't set your prices far and above those of the competition – accept that your value proposition is unique and the benefits significantly different. But ensure this is recognised by customers, as anything short of that will lead to a loss in sales.

So, how would the 3Cs of pricing be used within a business organisation? An understanding of the above 3Cs of pricing is necessary for determining appropriate pricing methods and strategies. Pricing methods involve setting a product price based on the costs incurred in the process of design, development and production. This takes the form of the inside-out approach or cost-based pricing approach. These pricing methods include *marginal cost, mark-up, break-even, peak-load, product line* and *competitive bidding* pricing.

The problem with cost-based pricing is that it ignores the customer's perception of the value vis-à-vis the price the seller sets. It focuses mainly on costs to arrive at a price. The effect is that prices may become higher than the customer can afford or is willing to pay.

Let's look at B2B pricing strategies in more detail.

B2B PRICING STRATEGIES

To be effective, the B2B marketer should first set their pricing objectives to inform pricing decisions and strategies. Why are you pricing your product? What do you intend to achieve? What level of profit do you desire? To what extent do your relationships matter? Do you want to be the dominant force in your market? Responses to these questions will determine the appropriate pricing strategies to use, for example:

- price skimming
- penetration pricing
- follow the leader
- price leadership.

Price skimming: when an organisation invests heavily in research, development and production of a new and innovative product, it is bound to set prices to recoup its investments. Such organisations set high prices when a new product is launched and introduced into the market. Customers are often willing and happy to pay the high price if the perceived value and benefits of the new product are high. It is a strategy mostly used in high-technology and pharmaceutical industries. The price-skimming strategy is effective where there are few competitors with similar products or customers perceive the product to be of high quality, prestigious and high status. The point is that customers must identify, understand and recognise the distinguishing features of the new product and the benefits they may derive from it before buying.

Penetration pricing: in using this strategy, organisations set a low price during the introductory and growth stages of the product's life cycle. This is often done in low-technology markets, with the aim of winning a large share of its markets. The strategy deters competitors from entering the market due to the low price. Penetration pricing is the opposite of price skimming and may be useful in achieving and retaining high sales, significant market share and profitability.

Follow the leader: there are situations where there are few ways of reducing costs or adding value to a product relative to the competition. In such cases, you may opt to follow the market leaders as anything short could mean a loss of sales. Traditionally, this strategy is used for commodities, although it is apparent that commodities can be differentiated in some respect. For instance, an organic commodity will sell for higher than non-organic ones.

Price leadership: when you have better technology and/or other capabilities that enable you to produce at low prices, then you can set low prices for your product offerings. In this way, more customers will buy from you. With this, you become the price leader and command a significant share of the market.

Winning a sizeable share of the market demands that we communicate our product and its benefits to the customer. So, let's now take a look at B2B marketing communications.

MARKETING COMMUNICATIONS IN B2B MARKETING

To attract customers, the business marketer must learn to communicate the unique benefits of the firm's products and to interact and create dialogue with the market. Generally, an organisation seeks to enlighten the market about itself, promote its values and policies and essentially endeavour to create a positive self-image.

So, what is marketing communication?

Figure 10.3   Basic communication model

Marketing communication defined

This involves creating awareness about an organisation and its products. The aim is to reach customers and change the behaviour of a target market in some respect. Marketing communications are a series of activities designed to inform the market about an organisation and its products and persuade customers to buy. Within B2B, the quantity of business transactions is small, but the value is much larger than B2C, which explains why personal contact is extremely vital. Thus, personal selling is used to communicate and demonstrate the unique features and benefits of a product to the market. Although there are similarities between B2B and B2C marketing communications, differences abound (see Table 10.4). Unlike in B2C marketing, mass advertising plays a less meaningful role in B2B marketing communication (Zimmerman and Blythe, 2013).

Table 10.4   Differences between B2B and B2C communication

Variable	B2B	B2C
People/customers	Small number	Large number
Expected transactions	Large in value	Small in value
Strategy	Mostly pull	Mostly push
Medium	Person-to person mostly possible	Non-human media/person-to person mostly not possible
Feedback	More immediate	Complicated but directly not expected
Type of relationship	Long-term with companies	Long-term with market segments

What tools are used for marketing communication?

The B2B marketer employs several tools to communicate to their market effectively. These tools include advertising, trade shows, exhibitions, personal selling, sales promotion and public relations.

The marketing communications objectives of the organisation will determine the tools they use to reach and interact with customers. It is essential to state the marketing communications objectives as clearly (and measurable) as possible. For instance, the objective could be to increase sales of *Brand X* by 15 per cent in three months within Europe or to achieve a 10 per cent increase in new customers in Africa or North America within 12 months. These are clear objectives that can be measured. You should avoid ambiguity as it creates fuzziness in crafting the message, in deciding which communication tools to use, as well as in how they are used.

Why do we use marketing communications to converse with customers? We adopt marketing communication tools in order to:

- differentiate a company and its product offerings
- inform the market about the company and its offerings
- persuade customers to purchase
- educate the market
- reinforce perceptions and images associated with the products and the company, that is, highlighting its unique selling proposition (USP)
- sell products.

Let's look at each of these marketing communication tools in more detail.

Advertising

Advertising is a paid form of non-personal communication using a specific medium. Business advertising is aimed at organisations, which means it needs to appeal to different people. Members of the DMU rarely buy products using advertising alone. Rather, they use adverts as a supporting tool instead of being the primary method of communicating with the market. The following media could be used for advertisement purposes: TV, print (newspapers and magazines), trade or industry journals, online databases, directories, and so on.

Advertising is less effective than other promotional tools in business marketing. Due to the characteristics of business marketing activities, personal selling produces a stronger result in creating product awareness and achieving sales.

In modern times, advertising has become more interactive and faster, and has given the business marketer many technology-inspired options to communicate. Likewise, customers now have the power to respond to an advert immediately. So, we now have a two-way advertising process, which is different from that employed previously, and one which provides more effective communication.

With this, organisations hope to ensure their products are identified and better recognised, and sales leads are generated in a timely and structured manner. But, above all, the business marketer aims to interact with the customer more to learn better about their current and changing needs. Remember that as firms adopt new technologies, their need for products as inputs for production changes. Knowing when and what informs these changes might help put firms in a position to take advantage of the new and emerging opportunities within their markets.

Trade shows and exhibitions

This is an essential marketing communication tool used by many organisations in the B2B sphere. Trade shows are platforms that bring together suppliers and buying organisations in a specific location. They are often sponsored by trade/industry associations, which cater to the needs of a specific industry. At trade shows, suppliers use the opportunity to display and demonstrate their product features, benefits and workings, as well as any new technology. Buyers attend such events to find better products – those that are more cost-effective, advanced in design, of better quality and with a better company support system. At a trade show, suppliers occupy different booths and buyers visit their stands to see new products and possibly structure deals.

To be successful at a trade show, you must plan it out by identifying the customers you seek to meet. If possible, schedule meetings in advance with members of the companies' DMU who may be attending. The idea is for the business marketer to meet and discuss business and close a sale during or immediately after the event. Trade shows are usually held for between two days and two weeks, in order to allow time for companies to showcase their products.

Trade Fairs and Exhibitions UK is sponsored by Trade Partners UK and is the official website for the UK exhibition industry. Examples of B2B UK trade exhibitions can be found at www.exhibitions.co.uk. Examples of B2B trade exhibitions in the UK include:

- International Direct Marketing Fair (IDMF), Earls Court, London
- National Franchise Exhibition, NEC Birmingham
- Retail Interiors, Earls Court, London
- Total Marketing Solution, NEC Birmingham.

Trade missions

Trade missions are government-sponsored events. They are usually organised and promoted by governments who seek to facilitate economic growth in their countries. UK Trade and Investment is the government body which provides financial support for companies to take part in identified and selected industry exhibitions – for example, the Paris Airshow in France; oil and gas shows across the world. Governments use trade missions to encourage foreign companies to invest in their country. They boost economic activity and, by extension, economic development.

Public relations (PR)

Organisations use PR to create and maintain a favourable image of themselves about all stakeholders (internal and external). The PR personnel in the company ensure that a cordial relationship exists between the company and its key public. The focus is to build and maintain harmonious relationships between the company and its stakeholders. Due to the huge size of B2B publicity vis-a-vis B2C, many companies have designated or fully fledged PR departments to manage their affairs both with the public and with PR agencies. Let's distinguish between 'PR' and 'publicity'. PR is what a PR manager does (that is the work), while 'publicity' is what she creates for the company and its products. PR managers adopt different strategies to achieve their objective. One strategy is to strategically plant in the media those company news stories that portray the company in a good light. With this, free media exposure is achieved, and the public will see the company in a positive light. Publicity must be planned and well integrated into the company's communication mix and strategy. The following are some of the tools and techniques needed to gain publicity: lobbying (yes, companies use it!), events, news conferences, sponsorship, press releases, press conferences, interviews, corporate advertising, investor relations and crisis management.

Personal selling

Personal selling plays a considerable role in B2B. Personal selling is a form of promotion that involves the physical and direct interaction between a company's sales representative and a customer. It is adjudged as the most expensive B2B promo tool. The salesperson's role is to engage, inform and persuade the customer to buy. Most technical products demand demonstration for the customer to evaluate its performance and decide if it is consistent with the company's focus. For instance, the buyer would want to see if the product being demonstrated might enhance quality, effectiveness and efficiency. This means that sales representatives must have in-depth product knowledge and should be skilled in human relations. This is essential as they are needed to communicate the unique benefits of the product and demonstrate why the buyer should patronise their company.

Sales and trade promotions

These are short-term incentives often used to encourage and persuade buyers and customers to buy more from a company. They take various forms, for example a reduction in the unit price of the product or an increase in the quantity of a product – such as two for the price of one. Sales promotions are more effective in B2C marketing situations. The business buyer doesn't only look at price, but also overall effectiveness and efficiency. Sales promotions are often used when there are low sales on a product, and the company is looking to increase sales of the product. So, it is used to stimulate higher demand for an underperforming product, to encourage consumers to try a new product or where a firm is trying to clear its existing stock to enable it to bring new stock to the market. Although buyers are incentivised, companies highlight the key product benefits in communicating to the market.

One of the contemporary issues in marketing is that, in recent times, customer behaviour, tastes and preferences have changed significantly due to the dynamics of the digital landscape, calling for the use of contemporary marketing communication tools to reach and engage with customers in our changing digitalised business environment.

What contemporary marketing communications tools are used in B2B marketing?

The Internet of Things (IoT) has changed the way organisations carry out the task of advertising, both regarding the tools used and how it is done. Nowadays, and with the use of digital media, many organisations use the latest technologies in communicating with their markets. Some of these tools are apps, software, social media platforms, and others are web-based tools. For example, it is no longer uncommon to find businesses using the following tools to reach their target business markets:

- Instagram
- Twitter
- Facebook
- email
- pay-per-click and banner and digital display advertising
- internet, extranet and intranet advertising (company website)
- telemarketing and direct response
- search engine marketing (SEM)
- Google AdWords
- apps.

Although most of the above tools are mainly associated with B2C, a growing need to reduce costs and enhance speedy interactions with customers has led businesses to employ social media for B2B marketing communications.

The old approach involved the firm coding and sending out advertising messages to the customer without immediate interaction. The new model, using new technologies including social media, requires that the customer interact with the advert online, in real time. Figure 10.4 illustrates this new communication concept.

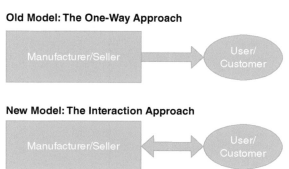

Figure 10.4   Models of marketing communications

The focus of marketing communication is to differentiate the organisation and persuade customers to buy. So, using more interactive approaches to conversing with a market is a more contemporary way to execute marketing communication.

Marketing communication is achieved through the use of the AIDA model.

WHAT IS AIDA?
AIDA hierarchy of effects model

The ability of an organisation to effectively use the communication tools discussed so far will depend on its objectives, which inform its communications strategy. The AIDA model is often used in developing a communications strategy. The model was developed to help organisations understand why it is necessary to use different tools and techniques to achieve different communication objectives. AIDA is an acronym for Attention, Interest, Desire and Action.

Let's discuss the AIDA model further. Understandably, we may all agree that customers will not buy from a company they do not know. So, let's say the problem is that the customer is unaware of our company and products, or that they are just not interested in us, or that they need to be persuaded. Well, in these three instances, our communication task would be to create that awareness, stimulate interest and make the customer buy from us. This means taking the customer through different stages of enlightenment before the eventual buying decision. To achieve this, we would have to adopt different techniques and tools suitable for our purpose.

According to the AIDA model, we need to communicate to customers to create awareness, find a way to stimulate their interest, cause them to desire our products and make them take action, by buying from us. This suggests, as you may imagine, the use of several communication tools depending on the type of products and customers in question.

So, we must carefully and thoughtfully state our communication objectives if we are to achieve success. But, how can we set SMART communication objectives? This calls for us to ensure that the stated objectives are SMART, that is:

Specific

Measurable

Achievable

Realistic

Time-based.

It is essential at this point to mention the concept of DAGMAR. Russell Colley (1961) developed the DAGMAR concept. DAGMAR is an acronym for Defining Advertising Goals for Measured Advertising Response – and it is the basis of the AIDA concept. According to Colley, it is better to evaluate advertising goals using communication goals instead of sales. He proposes that separate behavioural objectives should be set for the different methods used and for the various stages of the AIDA process. The reason is that we need to adopt a back and forward movement within the process – because customers will be at varying stages of the process. This suggests, therefore, that organisations must adjust their communications campaigns to allow for the identified differences.

Producing, pricing and communicating the product to the market are necessary but not sufficient without the use of an appropriate marketing channel to get the products out to market.

So, what does a B2B marketing channel entail?

ORGANISATIONAL MARKETING CHANNELS

Marketing channels consist of organisations who jointly develop and produce products. Each organisation adds value to the product before moving it to the next organisation and finally to the end user. Also known as *distribution channels*, marketing channels are concerned with ensuring that quality products pass from the manufacturer to the end user. Within B2B marketing channels, different organisations assume different responsibilities and play different roles.

Let's now look further at channel memberships and roles.

Channel membership and roles

Here are the various players in the B2B channel of distribution:

- *manufacturers*: the sources of the products and those who bear the highest risks
- *distributors and retailers*: link manufacturers to end users
- *agents*: function like distributors but work mostly for the manufacturers
- *wholesalers*: buy in large quantities from the manufacturer and sell to other channel members
- *dealers*: act as a platform bringing customers to producers

- *value-added resellers*: often break bulk and act as strong market information collectors for producers
- *end users*: the final users of the products and an integral part of the channel, without whom there would be no business.

While some firms manufacture, others act as distributors and retailers, agents, wholesalers, dealers and value-added resellers. All members of the distribution channel, apart from the manufacturer, are known as *intermediaries*. Intermediaries function as a link between manufacturers and end users, although there is a technical difference between distributors and wholesalers. Distributors sell directly to end users, while wholesalers distribute to other intermediaries. Each entity is usually a customer to the previous one in the value chain, and there is a close interrelationship among collaborating firms.

Two elements are involved in the distribution of products. The first is concerned with the management of all activities needed to move the physical or tangible product from the manufacturer to the end user – this is known as *logistics*. The second involves managing the intangible elements related to matters of product ownership and flow, and control of information between all organisations in the value chain that make the product available to the customer. This second element is commonly referred to as *channel management*.

In this section, we focus on how B2B organisations might manage their distribution channels (i.e. channel management). Why is B2B channel management important? As you might imagine, the task of producing and distributing products across a value chain can be a prohibitively expensive and risky process for one entity to manage. This explains why organisations tend to interrelate and cooperate with others to share the workload and reduce the costs and inherent risks to any single firm. Each company uses its expertise to add value, which helps reduce uncertainty. This collaboration enhances end users' perceived value of the product and, by extension, leads to higher competitive advantage. In sum, B2B channel management is important for:

- reducing workload, risks and uncertainties for all collaborating firms
- enhancing the quality and perceived value of the product in the mind of the end user
- creating a competitive advantage, since entities combine using their distinct specialties.

To achieve all this, the firm must do the following:

- enter exchange relationships with other companies who possess complementary strengths
- specialise in improving product value
- collaborate to reduce complexities in the value chain; this is achieved by the use of intermediaries.
- collaborate to increase value and competitive advantage.

Let's now discuss the various distribution channels used in B2B markets.

TYPES OF DISTRIBUTION CHANNELS IN B2B MARKETS

Most producers have to contend with various market decision issues. For instance, should they sell directly to the end user or push the product through the distribution channel, engaging the services of other organisations as intermediaries? Thus, the question of using a *direct channel* or an *indirect channel* is what a firm must decide on. There are pros and cons to these two approaches, although the choice of which to adopt depends on several factors, including the level of risk involved, the quality of the product, the strength of the competition, the existence and quality of intermediaries and the availability of reliable suppliers.

In the following sub-sections, we will look at the features of the two approaches to distribution.

Indirect channels

Whenever the risks and uncertainties with regard to meeting the needs of the end user are beyond an acceptable level, firms will often adopt the indirect channel approach. If the product is new and untested, its risk of failing to impress end users would naturally be high. In such a situation, the manufacturer opts to use the indirect approach, which means bringing other companies on board to share in the costs and risks of taking the product to market. This is the firm's technique and method of reducing risk – which also means that cooperating firms will come with their expertise, financial strength and market knowledge. This may enhance the product's potential market success.

The configuration of the channel depends on the number of intermediaries. Figure 10.5 details the indirect channel, which shows the possibilities within the business channel. These are non-existing in a direct channel, which we will consider next.

Direct channels

In a direct channel, the manufacturer sells directly to the end-user organisation. This approach is preferred by producers who are confident in the ability of the products to generate and keep end-user interest. Also, some producers adopt this approach for fear of adulteration. In such situations, retaining the quality and image of the seller and its product is of paramount importance. For example, poultry and other farms tend to sell their products directly to user organisations.

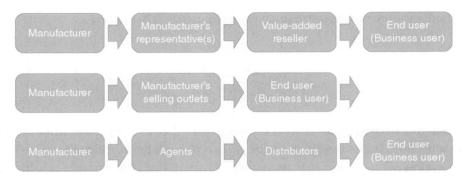

Figure 10.5   Indirect channels in B2B market

Contemporary marketing issues in B2B channel management suggest the role of technology in our current markets. Modern technologies now help to fuel the direct channel business. For example, with e-commerce and similar digital or web-based channels, organisations are able to reach large and far-flung markets. As a consequence, larger quantities, units and volume of products and businesses are sold. Figure 10.6 is a diagrammatic representation of the direct channel.

Figure 10.6   Direct channel in B2B markets

So, how does technology influence B2B channel distribution? Let's take a further look at technology in B2B marketing channels.

TECHNOLOGY AND MARKETING CHANNELS

Technology is pervasive and impacts on every aspect of modern life, B2B inclusive. The growth and latest developments in internet technology have and will continue to dictate how B2B organisations carry on the channel distribution function. For instance, buying organisations are now able to place orders online using the websites of several producers, and these products can be delivered to the organisation directly. Latest reports suggest that corporate customers are now able, more than ever, to shop online, as per B2C. This means that firms are now using their websites to sell products. This process of selling and fulfilling orders online is known as *e-commerce.* It should be noted that this is a direct channel of distribution approach, and it is attractive due to its convenience and speed.

Technology has various impacts on channel marketing. Specifically, technology impacts B2B channel distribution in the following ways:

Increased service outputs: organisations selling online can carry a vast array of products which they display on their websites.

Flow of information in channels of distribution: because of the very nature of technology, information flows are fast and accurate. This enhances product delivery and the overall customer shopping experience. Those firms that understand, appreciate and use this tool for communication purposes often outperform those that don't. Because information flows digitally on websites, companies are able to collect rich data. The analysis of data will generate rich insights into customer behaviour and shopping preferences. This is essential to guide marketing decision making and, by extension, marketing performance.

Physical distribution (PD): this entails that the right product is in the right place at the right time and at the right price. This means that the firm must pay attention to key components that make PD useful. These components of PD include:

- inventory: the products developed to meet the needs of the customer
- order processing: this includes the decisions and processes involved in planning to ensure the right products are delivered to the right customers in good condition and on time
- warehousing: this involves keeping the inventory in the warehouse while awaiting orders or during order processing
- transportation: the movement of the physical products or items and manpower required to meet service needs.

To ensure that PD adds value, the firm must foster strong and relevant relationships with other entities in its value chain. So, what role do relationships play in business marketing?

RELATIONSHIPS AND NETWORKING IN BUSINESS MARKETING: THE EMERGING TRENDS

Relationships play a massive role in B2B marketing, which underpins the *marketing concept*. Although the decision-making units (DMU) of businesses tend to make rational buying decisions, the personalities of individuals who represent a supplier company convey the image and philosophy of that supplier. People often do business with people they appreciate. This is no different from the practice in B2B marketing.

Why are relationships important to the B2B marketer? The sales representative of a supplier must forge strong ties with the members of the DMU of the buying organisation to be able to make sales. Hence, personal selling is a key function in the process of developing and nurturing relationships and building networks. Imagine if you were the buyer and a sales representative calls and you perceive her as unprofessional, unfriendly and technically deficient. Would you do business with such a rep and her company? I am sure your answer would be a resounding no! To establish rapport with the buyer, you must demonstrate an understanding of their needs and clearly show how your product(s) can satisfy these needs more efficiently and effectively.

Here are some specific reasons why it's essential to develop and maintain cordial relationships with customers in B2B marketing:

- gives rise to fewer conflicts
- there is greater understanding, leading to higher collaboration
- leads to synergistic effects and outcomes of relationships
- engenders enhanced performance outcomes: higher revenues, profits, etc.
- achieves organisational effectiveness and success.

For all intents and purposes, developing relationships is an essential part of modern marketing, but several issues arise as buyers and sellers interact and engage in the exchange business. Relationship-based theories and variables provide conceptual yet practical insight into the nature of relationships between organisations. So, what are these contemporary marketing issues related to buyer–seller relationships that determine a firm's B2B marketing performance?

CONTEMPORARY ISSUES IN BUYER– SELLER RELATIONSHIPS

Key issues that arise in buyer–seller relationships include the following:

- *Relationships with suppliers*: this relates to the extent to which suppliers cooperate and coordinate. Closer cooperation will lead to higher levels of relationships and vice versa. Use of technology (digital media, internet, etc.) is helpful here.
- *Level of adaptations required*: this will depend on how well different organisations working together are able to resolve all conflicts arising from their relationships. A better conflict-resolution strategy will lead to better cooperation and, by extension, benefits for all involved. Digital tools will help to speed up adaptation and create better understanding among contracting firms.

- *Relationships must be seen as investments*: the relevant parties must see their developing relationships as a good investment and key to sustainable long-term success. This way, every contracting firm would be expected to make efforts in creating better understanding and cooperation.
- *The role of trust and formality*: because written contracts at times prove to be unenforceable, the need to develop trust between contracting bodies becomes essential. Parties tend to trust those from their own country due to sharing a common culture and other similarities. For instance, a Japanese company would be happier doing business with another Japanese company due to a common understanding of the Japanese business culture – unlike dealing with an American firm. Such organisations value trust far and above formal contracts.
- *Cooperation and conflict*: as firms with differing goals and histories must relate to each other, there is bound to be some misunderstandings as they transact, which may lead to conflict. The ability of the firms to resolve any such conflict and grow stronger ties will lead to more beneficial cooperation.
- *Level of complexity in relationships*: this depends on the closeness of the buyer and seller. Relationships are often complex and are described using several wide-ranging variables. Hence, the more firms interact, the closer they become but the more complex their relationship becomes. This is especially the case when there are several touchpoints or points of contact.
- *The role of power and dependence*: this relates to the extent to which one contracting party may or may not make life difficult for the other. This is usually evident if one party has less negotiating power than the other and must depend on the other. The other firm dictates the terms of the business relationship which may or may not be in the best interests of the weaker party.

To create value that is beneficial to all parties in the exchange process calls for strategic understanding and the use of networking. What is networking and how would you use it to your benefit?

NETWORKING IN B2B MARKETS

As discussed earlier, developing strong relationships is fundamental to the success of the B2B organisation. But firms must network to achieve success. Networking involves the meeting and striking of accords between firms and their representatives. To achieve this, there must be platforms to engender the meeting between personnel in both buyer and seller organisations. But how do B2B entities network to develop and sustain relationships? What is the role of going digital in B2B (i.e. using contemporary technologies in marketing)?

Digital Focus 10.1

Contemporary issues in B2B marketing

All businesses are turning to the use of digital resources, and B2B marketing has not been left out. In recent times, the modern business environment has grown and become more competitive across industries and regions. Communicating to and engaging with customers with a view to establishing and maintaining business relationships, is no longer sufficient. But the speed and ease with which these marketing activities are carried out are now more vital to the B2B firm.

To achieve speed, effectiveness and efficiency, B2B firms now adopt social media. Social media has become a powerful tool, as are e-functions like e-logistics and e-procurement.

In an exploratory study of the use of social media in B2B marketing and branding, Brennan and Croft (2012) observe that social media use is more common among US-based B2B marketing firms. And these firms use social media to position themselves as thought-leaders, grow their markets and engage with different stakeholders.

It appears that there is a need for B2B marketers to employ other digital resources, although the full effects of these resources are not yet known. However, with burgeoning technological breakthroughs, digital media inclusive, it is not certain what the future holds for the B2B marketer.

Questions

1. What digital resources do you consider to be inevitable in our modern times?
2. How well have we used social media, e-logistics and e-procurement tools?
3. What future development in the digital sphere do we foresee?

KEY ACCOUNT MANAGEMENT

Key account management (KAM) entails identifying customers that contribute more to an organisation (in terms of sales revenue and profitability) and then treat them in a way that further enhances future trust and the quality of the relationship. This means that customers that buy more from us are of strategic importance to us and should be given better deals, discounts and other support services. This group of customers is referred to as 'key accounts'.

Several academics including Millman and Wilson (1999), Spencer (1999) and Pardo (1999) have argued about the exact meaning of KAM and used different terminologies to describe the concept of KAM. This obfuscation in the meaning of KAM is one of the contemporary issues in marketing. For instance, some marketing scholars refer to KAM as strategic account management, national account marketing, major account management and key account management. Regardless of the term used, the reasoning is the same in that customers who give us higher-value business should be noted and taken care of. End of story!

Part of the question raised by Boles et al. (1999) is how firms should decide which customers to identify as key accounts. Well, the simple answer to this somewhat difficult question is that we need to borrow knowledge from the quantitative marketing discipline and, specifically, marketing metrics. In the realm of marketing metrics, you might use the concept of 'customer lifetime value' (CLV) to calculate the net present value of all future revenue from every customer of the firm. Customers with higher CLV are contributing more and are more valuable to the firm. This group of customers then become the 'key accounts'. Problem solved!

Part of the role of relationship management is to ensure that customers who are of strategic importance to the firm, based on the volume and value of business they do with the firm, are treated with better care. This is logical! In addition, KAM relationship managers facilitate the further development of valued customers and act as problem-solvers in case of issues arising in customer–firm relations.

So how do we develop a KAM relationship? Here is Millman and Wilson's (1995) six-stage model of key account relationship development:

1. Pre-KAM: here we identify those customers qualified to become key account candidates.
2. Early KM: we continue to search for opportunities for closer collaboration with the identified customers of value.
3. Mid-KAM: this is where we develop more cross-boundary relationships.
4. Partnership KAM: this stage views suppliers as part of our external resources.
5. Synergistic KAM: here we jointly create value with our suppliers.
6. Uncoupling KAM: if it's no longer sustainable, we may then dilute the KAM relationship at this stage.

In addition to KAM, there are current market trends that determine how B2B business relationships are further developed. Let's now look at these current trends in B2B marketing.

EMERGING TRENDS AND TECHNOLOGIES AND THEIR IMPACT ON BUSINESS MARKETING PRACTICE

The 21st century has witnessed advances in technological breakthroughs. A large part of this is fuelled by the advent of the Internet of Things (IoT). The IoT now has and will continue to have a significant impact on the way business is carried out all over the world.

Technology and IoT now dictate how B2B marketing activities are conducted and the resulting outcomes of these activities. We'll next discuss current and future technologies and their effects on B2B.

Let's begin with the current trends in B2B. There are several effects of technological break-throughs on the theory and practice of B2B marketing.

Current trends in B2B marketing

Technology in sales: organisations now use technology to enhance effectiveness, including in their selling activities. Available evidence suggests that firms now use technology to automate their selling functions. The automation helps to achieve lower selling costs, better communication with customers, superior customer relationship management (CRM) and an improved process of gathering market and customer information.

Widmier et al. (2002) note six different sales functions that technology now enhances. Table 10.5 details these sales functions and the various technologies used to execute them.

Table 10.5   Sales functions and technology

Sales function	Technology used
Organising	Electronic call schedule and meeting management
Communication	Emails, internet including social media, mobile phones
Sales presentation	The use of digital media and multimedia platforms
Transaction support	Use of ERPs for order tracking, status and inventory management
Reporting sales	Electronic call reports, expense claims and performance related
Informing customers	Product performance, prospecting and configuration

Social media: although social media is well known and used to promote and sell products within B2C, B2B seems to lag in its use. But in a recent publication, Badnar and Cohen (2018) suggest that B2B is better than B2BC at social media. According to the authors, when social media is done well in B2B, several advantages accrue to the firm, including increased lead volume, a reduction in marketing expenditure and provision of a clear and measurable return on marketing investment. They further provide the five steps to B2B social media lead generation:

- getting the basics right
- maximising content discovery
- creating conversion ubiquity
- test and fail fast
- optimising for effective lead flow.

e-procurement: within B2B, many multinationals have employed and still use e-procurement. The benefits of this approach to sourcing production inputs are phenomenal. For example, IBM and Ford report massive savings in millions of dollars due to the use of e-procurement.

e-logistics: a special type of ERP is used to set up and support e-logistics activities. This way, the firm spends less time and other financial resources on its logistics efforts.

Enterprise resource planning (ERP) software: ERPs are software now used for several marketing functions including B2B. For example, the use of sales and distribution and materials management modules of the SAP ERP helps the firm with better scheduling of sales and selling, materials and channel management, inventory control and much more. This practice produces greater efficiency and effectiveness, which leads to higher cost and time savings and more revenue and, by extension, higher profitability.

Information technology and B2B relationships: technology remains the most critical driver of the current and possibly future dynamics in B2B relationships. For example, we now use social media (Facebook, Twitter, Instagram, WhatsApp, IMO, etc.) to inform our customers about the latest products and sell to them using our e-commerce platforms. We expect this trend to continue and grow in relevance and volume in the coming years. But what future trends should the B2B marketer expect?

Future trends

We expect technology to continue to dominate and dictate B2B business practice. The outcome of this has been, and will remain, huge in the markets. More technologically advanced approaches will emerge, and technology will support existing processes.

Also, marketing accountability will increase. To ensure we are ready for this and use it to our benefit, we must learn how to measure our marketing performance and predict future customer behaviour. To achieve this, two key aspects of marketing must be embraced: marketing metrics and marketing analytics.

Let's look at these two aspects of marketing capable of dictating future dynamics and B2B marketing performance.

Measuring marketing performance (marketing metrics)

Marketing metrics belong to the marketing science domain. It involves the measurement of marketing performance. This means that you and I, as marketing managers, should be able to identify key metrics and use them to continue to measure our marketing performance. Every aspect of the organisation's marketing functions – Product, Price, Promotion, Distribution, People, Processes, Physical Evidence, and Customers – can be measured to ensure optimum productivity.

To this end, commonly used marketing metrics include return on marketing investment (ROMI), customer lifetime value (CLV) and the customer satisfaction index (CSI). Let's take a more in-depth look at these concepts.

Return on marketing investment (ROMI): the metric that enables us to measure how much return our marketing investment brings. Which means we should be able to calculate and establish how much in sales, revenue and profit the money we invest in marketing generates. Suppose you are the marketing manager of a B2B firm and you have been given £1 million as your marketing communication budget for this financial year. At the end of the year, management and the board of directors would want to know how you have 'spent' your marketing budget and what benefits the firm has enjoyed from it. So, to prove your worth as a manager, you should compute how much in sales, revenue and profit your investment in marketing communication has contributed to your firm.

Customer lifetime value (CLV): CLV is the present value of all future cash flow from our customers. This means that every single customer has a monetary value to our firm. The trouble is we may not know if we don't calculate their CLVs. So, to help us manage customers better, we should calculate how much revenue we expect from all customers for a defined number of years, mostly between three and five. Those customers with a higher CLV are contributing more and are more valuable to us. This knowledge will help us to treat these customers differently. For example, for high CLV customers, we might give higher discounts, better customer service and other advantages; and then offer them higher value products (upselling) and other, similar products to the one they have been buying (cross-selling). In this way, we maximise our customer relationships and spend fewer resources on customers with low or negative CLVs.

Customer satisfaction index (CSI): We continually measure customer satisfaction to ensure our customers are getting value from us. This practice gives us an idea of the mood of the markets to inform us of new market developments. For instance, an unhappy customer might tell us what our competitors are doing differently, and we will try to match them. This is useful if we wish to continue to be relevant in our markets and to our customers.

While marketing metrics are useful, they often rely on historical data which would not be great at predicting the future. So, to take our business to a higher level of marketing performance calls for the use of marketing analytics. So, what is marketing analytics?

THE USE OF MARKETING ANALYTICS TO INFORM MARKETING DECISIONS

Analytics is the use of tools, techniques and models in analysing data to inform marketing decision making. It is the analysis, interpretation and communication of data for better marketing decisions. The focus of marketing analytics is to make data-driven marketing decisions – that is, decisions based on the information generated from analysing organisational data. Analytics is fast becoming a tool that gives the firm a powerful competitive advantage.

Better marketing analytics means that the firm has a better understanding of its customers and can predict what, when, how much and how frequently the customer will buy. There are four types of analytics used by organisations: descriptive, diagnostic, predictive and prescriptive. Let's take a closer look at each of these.

Types of analytics

Descriptive analytics uses historical data to gain a better understanding of the firm's business. Descriptive analytics asks the question: 'what happened?'. It uses infographics to show a firm's key metrics, including sales, profit, market share, and so on.

Diagnostic analytics is used to diagnose the happenings within the firm. It asks the question: 'why has this happened?'. It uses statistical and quantitative techniques to identify relationships in data sets. With this, it helps to pinpoint causes of problems and enables the firm to find timely solutions.

Predictive analytics is used to predict future events and customer behaviour. It asks the question: 'what could happen?'. For instance, if we increase promotional spend and customer service, what impact would this have on sales?

With the use of powerful statistical techniques, the marketing manager can predict demand, the effect of price changes and essentially customer behaviour.

Prescriptive analytics asks the question 'what should we do?'. Prescriptive analytics uses powerful statistical techniques, mathematical models and algorithms to suggest the optimal cause(s) of action. With this, it makes a recommendation as to what actions would yield the optimum benefit to the firm.

These are some of the approaches and trends that will shape the B2B marketing dynamics now and in the foreseeable future, as well as the contemporary issues in marketing.

Practitioner's Perspective 10.1

The revolutionary role of big data and data analytics in B2B marketing

We live in digital times! This is the reality as digital technology has assumed a more prominent position in how smart businesses are conducted in modern times. The same digitalisation witnessed in consumer marketing is revolutionising the B2B marketing domain; the difference is in

(Continued)

(Continued)

scale and form. Digital technology has made marketing automation possible; it supports business data capture and how B2B firms now use data analytics in making data-driven marketing decisions. Ted Dunning, a US-based chief applications architect of a big database technology company MapR, states that at the heart of the changes in B2B marketing is the fusion of big data with marketing automation.

B2B marketing enjoys similar automation and data analytics to the technological breakthroughs used in consumer marketing. These technologies are used to capture tons of data (structured and unstructured) from customer interaction. This sort of data is known as 'big data', due to its size and form.

The use of data analytics tools in analysing big data generates insights and helps firms gain a better understanding of their customers and markets. Through data, B2B firms can now predict customer behaviour and make relevant marketing decisions. For instance, firms can predict what quantity of products customers might need, when certain customers are likely to buy and how much they are willing to pay for the product. This knowledge affords the B2B firm the ability to target and automate marketing messages and actions at certain groups of customers and set up the selling process.

Source: Adapted from CMO (2018)

Discussion Questions

1. To what extent do you agree with Dunning's perspective on the role played by big data and automation in B2B marketing?
2. How can B2B marketing managers use analytics to enhance customer relationship management?
3. What benefits could accrue to the B2B firm from the use of data analytics?

Case Study 10.1

Honda out to beat competition: The supplier collaboration and technology imperative

The global automobile industry is changing at an unprecedented pace and technology is fuelling developments in the sector. Many players are visible in the market and with this come stiff competition and shrinking margins. The competition is rife and, it is suggested, to make gains in this environment, firms must not only innovate using technology but, in addition, must adopt approaches that improve business processes and outcomes.

One of the prominent players in this industry, Honda, has a rich history and has been in business for 72 years. The company has a constellation of products including cars, motorcycles, special equipment, engines and marine equipment. In 2005, Honda surprised the world by entering the aircraft production market with the unveiling of its first aircraft, named the Honda HA-420 HondaJet. The company has recorded remarkable successes. For instance, it employs 215,638 people, operates more than 120 facilities in 33 countries, 34 automobile production operations in 18 countries and territories, churns out about 20 million cars and motorcycles per year, and total global units of more than 31 million. It is the world's fourth-largest automobile manufacturer, with a revenue market share of 5.5% as at 2017, behind Toyota (9.2%), Volkswagen (7.2), Ford (6.5%), and global net sales of 15.4 trillion Japanese yen as at 2018.

Its outstanding performance is due mainly to the company's business philosophy – 'Sangen Shugi' – which means the actual place, the actual part, the actual situation, a policy that is pervasive in the company and is attributed to the uniqueness of its purchasing function. Honda is a market-oriented organisation and ensures that the sales, manufacturing, purchasing and design departments' activities are well coordinated to achieve company-wide consistency and harmony. With the customer at the centre of its operations, Honda focuses on cost-cutting, supplier satisfaction, supplier training, supply chain management and advancement of its technology. Its cost modelling is now part of the company's capability which makes it possible for any employee to easily identify the essential cost components of any part.

Honda's philosophy is 'purchase where you produce', which helps the company manage suppliers. This explains why it has been successful in developing and building a network of supplier companies. In North America, supplier companies supply over 80 per cent of the component parts, materials and services used for Honda's automobiles, engines and motorcycles. The company's focus is on ensuring suppliers' activities are fully aligned with the company's philosophy. Relationships with suppliers are highly valued, and staff see suppliers as an extension of Honda.

To further support suppliers and create harmoniously beneficial business relationships, Honda established several morale-boosting programmes including suppliers' development programmes and activities, supplier awards and other forms of supplier incentives. While these programmes are similar to industry practice, the former vice president Dave Nelson adds that Honda's approach is different due to the amount of money, time and effort the company invests in developing and sustaining the network of supplier relationships. In one collaborative effort with a supplier – Tower Automotive – Honda helped the supplier double its production output from 63 to 125 parts per hour, and the useful life of the parts was extended from 50,000 to 250,000 welds.

With its design in process, Honda focuses on supplier involvement to leverage supplier innovation. This process brings several designers from supplier organisations into Honda's

(Continued)

(Continued)

facilities to work with the company's technologists and design engineers – an approach often used at the start of every new project. According to Honda's Charles Baker, 'Our focus on building cooperative relationships requires getting the outside designers' input at the very beginning of a project, while we're still in the planning phase for the vehicle. By involving these suppliers early on, we can pick up their latest technology to make sure we're integrating it into our vehicle'. Based on its desire to compete favourably and lead the competition, the automobile giant developed technology roadmaps, and often shares these with suppliers. The roadmaps also double as a tool for showing suppliers the company's focus and for setting high expectations from suppliers. To this end, suppliers are encouraged to view new product development as a strategic process that requires innovation, technology and focus.

Honda thrives on advancing its technology to guarantee more powerful products and cooperation with its markets. In 2017, the company unveiled its self-balancing motorcycle, developed with the safety of the rider at the very heart of the design and the product. This was achieved due to its increased automation and technology. Based on its extensive in-camera and radar technologies, Honda is about to launch the world's first predictive cruise control system. This smart system is capable of foreseeing and automatically adapting to other vehicles 'cutting in' to the car's lane. It can predict the chances of the cut-in happening up to 5 seconds before it occurs. Honda has been visible in the use of modern technology to communicate with suppliers and customers alike. For example, the firm uses social media in its operations, to establish brand awareness, announce new product launches and influence future brand development and other activities.

Sources

Autonews (2018) How Honda Cuts Cost and Satisfies Suppliers. Available at: www.autonews.com/article/19981109/ANA/811090765/how-honda-cuts-costs-satisfies-suppliers (accessed 15 December 2018).

CMO (2018) How Data Analytics is Transforming B2B Marketing. Available at: www.cmo.com.au/article/563176/how-data-analytics-transforming-b2b-marketing (accessed 15 December 2018).

Fortune (2018) Biggest Corporate Scandals and Misconduct. Available at: http://fortune.com/2017/12/31/biggest-corporate-scandals-misconduct-2017-pr (accessed 15 December 2018).

Honda (2018) History. Available at: https://global.honda/about/profile.html (accessed 15 December 2018).

Mydriftfun (2018) About Honda. Available at: https://mydriftfun.com/20-interesting-facts-honda (accessed 15 December 2018).

Office of National Statistics – www.ons.gov.uk

Questions for discussion

1. What are the main factors that account for Honda's success despite stiff competition in the automobile market?
2. Explain the term 'relationships' as it relates to Honda's operations.
3. Why are supplier relationships vital to Honda?
4. In a recent opinion poll, an interested supplier itching to establish a business relationship with Honda argued that Honda should add suppliers far from its production facilities. To what extent do you agree with this?
5. What should Honda do differently to harness the power of social media in its B2B relationships?

Group tasks

1. In groups of five, discuss what new features you might add to a B2B service product targeted at airline manufacturers.
2. Assuming the position of the buying centre members of a mobile phone manufacturer, what factors would you consider in establishing a B2B relationship with an OEM manufacturer?
3. Identify five B2B products and discuss how you would market them to manufacturers.

SUMMARY OF KEY IDEAS

- B2B is the marketing business relationship between organisations, where one firm does business with one or more organisations.
- B2B marketing comprises marketing activities involving two or more organisations in an exchange of value.
- B2B and B2C marketing share a nomological similarity as both focus on offerings that will meet customer needs.
- B2B marketing is significant to the firm as it generates a high volume and value.
- Business products are classified as raw materials, installations, accessory equipment, business services, maintenance, repairs, operating supplies (MRO) and manufactured materials and parts.

- Business markets can be segmented using different bases – identifiers and response variables.
- Market segmentation is useful as it helps organisations to achieve effectiveness and efficiency, although it might have infrastructure, process and implementation challenges.
- Business buying decisions are based on rational decisions made by the decision-making units (DMU). DMU comprise initiators, gatekeepers, buyers, influencers, deciders and users.
- A product is anything that can be exchanged for value.
- Services are intangible products. They possess the qualities of intangibility, inseparability, variability, perishability and the inability to be owned.
- The product life cycle describes the stages a product goes through in its life. The stages include pre-launch, introduction, growth, maturity and decline.
- New products are the lifeline of every business, B2B inclusive.
- Price is the value customers ascribe to a product. Pricing strategies include price skimming, penetration pricing, follow the leader and price leadership.
- Promotions are used to communicate product features to customers. Promotional tools used in B2B include trade shows, trade missions, public relations, personal selling and sales, and trade promotions.
- Organisational channels of distribution include direct and indirect channels.
- Relationships play a huge role in B2B marketing situations, and it is beneficial to the firm to develop relationships to reduce conflict and improve performance.
- Key accounts are those customers with high value to the firm. Thus, the identification and management of this group of customers with high CLV is known as key account management.
- Technology powers both current and future trends in B2B marketing. Some trends involve the use of technology to improve B2B marketing functions, including e-procurement, e-logistics, social media, etc.
- The use of marketing metrics and analytics will have a significant role in determining the success of B2B. Organisations who adopt these marketing approaches will develop a competitive edge over those that don't.

Chapter Discussion Questions

1. Describe four ways in which technology might be used to enhance B2B marketing functions.
2. Evaluate the place of key account management and consider its benefits.
3. What are the key features of B2B markets and how would they impact on the B2B marketing manager's role?
4. Evaluate the bases used in segmenting business markets.
5. Describe the role of relationships in B2B marketing effectiveness.

REFERENCES

Albert, T. (2003) Need-based segmentation and customized communication strategies in a complex-commodity industry. *Industrial Marketing Management*, 32(4), 281–90.

Badnar, K. and Cohen, J. L. (2018) *The B2B Social Media Book: Becoming a Marketing Superstar by Generating Leads with Blogging, LinkedIn, Twitter, Facebook, E-mail, and More*. Hoboken, NJ: Wiley.

Bartels, R. (1988) *The History of Marketing Thought*, 3rd edn. Columbus, OH: Publishing Horizons.

Boles, J., Johnson, W. and Gardner, A. (1999) The selection and organization of national accounts: A North American perspective. *Journal of Business and Industrial Marketing*, 14(4), 264–75.

Brennan, R. and Croft, R. (2012) The use of social media in B2B marketing and branding: An exploratory study. *Journal of Customer Behaviour*, 11(2), 101–15.

Bussiere, D. (2000) Evidence of a marketing periodic literature within the American Economic Association: 1895–1936. *Journal of Macromarketing*, 20(2), 137–43.

Colley, R.H. (1961) *Defining Advertising Goals for Measured Advertising Results*. New York. Association of National Advertisers.

Copeland, M. T. (1920) *Marketing Problems*. New York: A.W. Shaw Co.

Copeland, M. T. (1924) *Principles of Merchandising*. Chicago: A.W. Shaw Co.

CMO (2018) How Data Analytics is Transforming B2B Marketing. Available at: www.cmo.com. au/article/563176/how-data-analytics-transforming-b2b-marketing (accessed 15 December 2018).

Culnan, M. J. (1986) The intellectual development of management information systems, 1972–1982: A co-citation analysis. *Management Science*, 32(2), 156–72.

Day, G. (1996) Using the past as a guide to the future: Reflections on the history of the journal of marketing. *Journal of Marketing*, 60(1), 14–16.

Dean, J. (1950) Pricing policies for new products, *Harvard Business Review*, 28 (6), 45–53.

Dhalla, N. K. and Yuspeth, S. (1976) Forget the product lifecycle. *Harvard Business Review*, 54, 102–4.

Dibb, S. and Simkin, L. (2001) Market segmentation: Diagnosing and treating the barriers. *Industrial Marketing Management*, 30(8), 609–25.

Elder, R. F. (1935) *Fundamentals of Industrial Marketing*. New York: McGraw-Hill.

Frederick, J. (1934) *Industrial Marketing: A Century of Marketing*. New York: Prentice-Hall.

Grönroos, C. (2000) *Service Management and Marketing*, 2nd edn. Chichester: Wiley.

Hinterhuber, A. (2004) Towards value-based pricing: An integrative framework for decision making. *Industrial Marketing Management*, 33(8), 765–78.

Hutt, M. and Speh, T. (2001) *Business Marketing Management*, 7th edn. Fort Worth, TX: Harcourt.

Kotler, P. (2003) *Marketing Management*. Upper Saddle River, NJ: Prentice Hall.

Liozu, S. (2015) Cambridge marketing handbook: Pricing points. *Journal of Revenue & Pricing Management*, 14(2), 134–5.

Lovelock, C., Vandermerwe, S. and Lewis, B. (1999) *Services Marketing*. Hemel Hempstead: Financial Times/Prentice Hall.

Marketingcharts.com (2017). E-commerce share of total B2B Sales in the US 2015–2021. Available at: www.marketingcharts.com/forrester-e-commerce-share-total-us-b2b-sales-2015-2021-jun2017 (accessed 1 March, 2019).

Millman, T. and Wilson, K. (1995) From key account selling to account management. *Journal of Marketing Practice: Applied Marketing Sciences*, 1(1), 9–21.

Millman, T. and Wilson, K. (1999) Processual issues in key account management: Underpinning the customer-facing organization. *Journal of Business and Industrial Marketing*, 14(4), 328–37.

Murphy, P. E. and Enis, B. M. (1986) Classifying products strategically. *Journal of Marketing*, 50, 24–42.

Palmer, A. (2014) *Principles of Services Marketing*, 7th edn. London: McGraw-Hill.

Pardo, C. (1999) Key account management in the business-to-business field: A French overview. *Journal of Business and Industrial Marketing*, 14(4), 276–90.

Shaw, E. H. (1995) The first dialogue on macromarketing. *Journal of Macromarketing*, 15, 7–20.

Spencer, R. (1999) Key accounts: Effectively managing strategic complexity. *Journal of Business and Industrial Marketing*, 14(4), 291–309.

Statista (2018) *Global Automotive Market Share in 2017, by Brand: UK*. London: Statista.

Webster, F. E. and Wind, Y. (1972) *Organizational Buying Behaviour*. Englewood Cliffs, NJ: Prentice Hall.

Widmier, S. M., Jackson, Jr, D. W. and McCabe, D. B. (2002) Infusing technology into personal selling. *Journal of Personal Selling and Sales Management*, 22(3), 189–99.

Zimmerman, A. and Blythe, J. (2013) *Business to Business Marketing: A Global Perspective*, 2nd edn. Oxon: Routledge.

PART IV
Marketing Non-Conventional Market Offerings

11
SOCIAL AND NON-PROFIT MARKETING

Nayyer Samad

INTRODUCTION

Social marketing is the use of marketing concepts in programmes designed to influence the voluntary behaviour of target audiences in order to improve health and society (Stead et al., 2007). Marketing until the early 1950s was considered an economic activity to maximise return on investment through sales of products and services. Non-profit marketing evolved together with marketing when sociologists argued about whether ideas could be sold like commercial products and services. Wiebe (1951) suggested that the success of a social change campaign improves significantly when commercial marketing techniques are applied to the campaign.

By the late 1960s, the significance of commercial marketing in social campaigns had been recognised by academics. Kotler and Levy (1969) invited marketers to expand their thinking and apply marketing skills to the increasingly diverse range of societal activities. A couple of years later, the term social marketing was introduced by Kotler and Zaltman (1971) to sell ideas, attitudes and behaviours using the same marketing principles used for selling products and services. The new concept met with instant resistance from critics who argued that the replacement of products with ideas in marketing would threaten the fundamental concept of exchange, and also feared that it would be used for propaganda purposes and would discredit marketing in general (MacFadyen et al., 1999; Andreasen, 2006). Nonetheless, the use of social marketing continued, particularly in family planning campaigns in developing countries and for prevention of heart disease in America (Fox and Kotler, 1980). While many of the earlier social marketing campaigns were primarily a social communications exercise, they neverthe-less laid the foundations for subsequent integrated social marketing programmes (MacFadyen et al., 1999).

By the 1980s, social marketing was recognised as a discipline and researchers started exam-ining various social marketing projects and identified their design and application weaknesses (Bloom, 1980). They also advocated the need for more research to inform practitioners about planning and implementation issues (Bloom and Novelli, 1981). By the turn of the century, social marketing was established as an effective method for addressing public health and environmental issues by both academics and practitioners (Hovig, 2001; Kotler et al., 2002; Armand, 2003). Social marketing campaigns for dealing with obesity, tobacco consumption, recycling waste in developed countries, and family planning and disease prevention in devel-oping countries are good examples of successful interventions (Domegan, 2008).

DEFINITION OF SOCIAL MARKETING

There is no single definition of social marketing. Both academics and practitioners have been regularly coming up with new versions. The major challenge in presenting a precise defini-tion is the many criteria involved in the social marketing process. Like commercial marketing, it is not a theory in itself but a framework or structure that draws from psychology, sociology, anthropology and communication theory to understand how to influence people's behaviour (Kotler and Zaltman, 1971). It focuses on target audiences and uses research to improve mar-keting activities. But, unlike commercial marketing, it targets complex, often controversial behaviours with no immediate benefits to the target audience (Smith, 2006).

Some of the popular definitions of social marketing are as follows. Kotler and Zaltman (1971: 5) described social marketing as:

> The application of principles and tools of marketing to achieve socially desirable goals, that is, benefits for society as a whole rather than for profit or organizational goals and includes the design, implementation, and control of programs calculated to influence the acceptability of social ideas and involving considerations of product planning, pricing, communications and marketing research.

Kotler and Zaltman's (1971) definition, although still considered the cornerstone of all subse-quent definitions, was too broad and did not capture the element of behaviour change that later became the central theme of all social marketing interventions. There is no mention of behaviour change in their definition.

Andreasen (1995: 7) provided a more precise definition that included behaviour change and combined both individual and societal goals:

Social marketing is the application of commercial marketing technologies to the analysis, planning, execution, and evaluation of programs designed to influence the voluntary behaviour of target audiences in order to improve their personal welfare and that of their society.

Kotler et al. (2002) presented an improved version of Kotler and Zaltman's (1971) definition that was similar to Andreasen's (1995) in many respects, as follows: 'Social marketing is the use of marketing principles and techniques to influence a target audience to voluntarily accept, modify, or abandon a behaviour for the benefit of individuals, groups, or society as a whole'.

The new definitions by Andreasen (1995) and Kotler et al. (2002) illustrate four key features of social marketing:

1. The behaviour change is voluntary.
2. There is a clear benefit for the target audience.
3. Social marketing utilises the same techniques as commercial marketing, such as consumer research, market segmentation and the strategic application of a marketing mix.
4. The goal is to benefit society and not the organisation. (Stead et al., 2007)

The last point – that organisations must not benefit from social marketing interventions – was the major departure from commercial marketing (MacFadyen et al., 2002). The other differentiating point was the emphasis on behaviour change without any reference to products and services, while in commercial marketing an increase in the demand for products and services is always the main objective and is linked to positive results (Dann, 2006). The similarities and differences between commercial and social marketing are discussed in detail in the next section.

KEY CONCEPTS IN SOCIAL MARKETING

It is not always necessary to apply all social marketing principles to every intervention. Similarly, many interventions claimed to be social marketing are actually not social marketing interventions because they do not meet the criteria of social marketing, particularly the behaviour change component. A review of over 50 interventions suggested that most of the social marketing programmes did not focus on the behaviour change component because interventions were not defined in terms of behaviour change (Stead et al., 2007). In one family planning study, social marketing was described as the distribution of free contraceptives (Price, 2001), while in another social marketing programme for nutrition and physical activity, social advertising and communication were treated as social marketing (Alcalay and Bell, 2000).

Due to the absence of profit-related objectives, it is sometimes confused with other marketing concepts like societal marketing and non-profit marketing (Kotler et al., 2002; MacFadyen et al., 2002). To differentiate social marketing interventions from others, McDermott et al. (2005) developed a framework using six benchmark criteria for identifying legitimate social marketing interventions based on Andreasen's (2002) definition. The McDermott framework, adapted by Stead at al. (2007), is shown in Table 11.1.

Table 11.1   Andreasen's benchmark criteria

Benchmark	Explanation
1. Behaviour change	Intervention seeks to change behaviour and has specific measurable behavioural objectives
2. Consumer research	Intervention is based on an understanding of consumer experiences, values and needs. Formative research is conducted to identify these. Intervention elements are pre-tested with the target group
3. Segmentation and targeting	Different segmentation variables are considered when selecting the intervention target group. Intervention strategy is tailor-made for the selected segment/s
4. Marketing mix	Interventions consider the best strategic applications of the 'marketing mix'. This consists of the 4Ps of marketing: product, price, place and promotion. Other Ps might include policy change or people (e.g. training is provided to intervention delivery agents). Interventions which only use promotion are social advertising, not social marketing
5. Exchange	Intervention considers what will motivate people to engage voluntarily with the intervention and offers them something beneficial in return. The offered benefit may be intangible (e.g. personal satisfaction) or tangible (e.g. rewards for participating in the programme and making behaviour changes)
6. Competition	Competing forces to the behaviour change are analysed. The intervention considers the appeal of competing behaviour (including current behaviour) and uses strategies that seek to minimise this competition

Source: Stead et al. (2007: 129)

SOCIAL MARKETING FRAMEWORK

Social marketing is derived from the commercial marketing notional framework that is based on exchange theory and uses research, segmentation and the marketing mix to influence behaviour. The extent to which commercial marketing concepts have been adopted by social marketing, and their effectiveness in addressing social issues, are critical in understanding the difficulties and challenges faced in the application of commercial marketing concepts to the social marketing context, particularly those related to behaviour change.

Behaviour change

The main goal of social marketing is to improve the personal welfare of the target audience as well as that of society by changing voluntary behaviour (Andreasen, 1995). Social marketing products may include a particular practice or a tangible product but the main aim is to change behaviour (Kotler and Roberto, 1989). For example, the family planning campaign in Pakistan may include the marketing and distribution of contraceptive products and services but the primary aim of the programme is to induce change in the behaviour of the target population. Similarly, in the five-a-day campaign in the UK and other European countries, the main product is not to promote the consumption of fruit and vegetables but to develop the habit of healthy eating. Since behaviour change requires considerable effort and commitment, like giving up smoking or increasing physical activity, with no immediate benefit to the target audience (McDermott et al., 2005), the social marketing strategy must provide the environment that facilitates the desired behaviour, and remove or reduce the competition. Competition in this situation involves those factors that interfere with the willingness or ability to change, like inertia, enjoyment of the current behaviour or the absence of options (MacFayden et al., 1999; MacAskill et al., 2002; Hastings, 2003).

Since the acceptance of behaviour change as the central theme of all social marketing campaigns, the interest of programme managers in behavioural research has intensified. Until the late 1960s, factors influencing behaviour have been a subject of discussion for social psychologists only. Studies examining the relationship between attitudes and behaviour by Wicker (1969) suggested that attitude has no influence on behaviour. However, the relatively new and widely acknowledged *Theory of Reasoned Action* (TRA) by Ajzen and Fishbein (1980) concluded that there is an indirect role for attitude in predicting behaviour. TRA states that individual behaviour is determined by one's intention which is the function of attitude towards behaviour and subjective norms. Critics of TRA like Härtel et al. (1998) and Albarracín et al. (2001) argue that the relationship between attitude and behaviour is reciprocal and behaviour can influence intentions and attitudes, and the degree of association depends on past experience.

Ajzen's (1985, 1991) *Theory of Planned Behaviour* (TPB), considered as an extension of TRA, included an additional variable, *perceived behavioural control*, along with *attitude* and *subjective norms* as determinants of behaviour, as shown in Figure 11.1.

Perceived behavioural control refers to people's perception of the ease or difficulty in performing the desired behaviour, and is more significant than actual behavioural control (Ajzen, 1991). TPB suggests that perceived behavioural control along with intention can be used to predict behavioural achievement. It further suggests that the ability of perceived behavioural control to predict behaviour is restricted when the information on the behaviour is limited or the requirements or resources are changed (Ajzen, 1985).

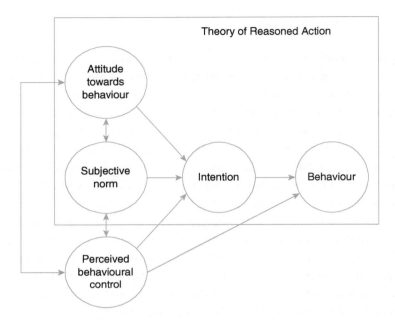

Figure 11.1 The Theory of Planned Behaviour
Source: Ajzen (1991)

While the TRA has been useful in explaining a variety of conditions, it assumes that all behaviours are under voluntary control (Madden et al., 1992; Taghian and D'Souza, 2007), suggesting that intention can only predict behaviour that is under voluntary control and where there is no constraint on action, but in a situation where the action is constrained the intention alone cannot predict behaviour. The TPB, on the other hand, is useful in predicting behaviour not under voluntary control; rather, it explains the potential constraints on the action as perceived by the individuals. The role of perceived behavioural control in the theory of planned behaviour has made a major contribution to the cognition model designed to predict health (desired) behaviour (Armitage and Conner, 2001).

The behaviour change process involves several steps: (1) customer insight, (2) segmentation and targeting, (3) competition, (4) exchange, and (5) the marketing and intervention mix (Morris and Clarkson, 2009). The starting point is an understanding of the existing knowledge, attitude and behaviour of target customers and the nature of competition. This can be compared with what is called customer insight in commercial marketing. The social marketing framework aims to change attitude by improving knowledge of the target audience and by creating an environment to facilitate the adoption of desired behaviour.

Consumer orientation

The main feature of marketing is exchange theory, described as the willingness of individuals or groups to exchange resources for perceived benefits. It is based on the key philosophy of consumer orientation (Lefebvre and Flora, 1988). Consumer orientation is a strategy for achieving and maintaining competitive advantage in any environmental situation (Slater and Narver, 1994). It involves structuring the organisation towards the generation and delivery of sustainably superior value for customers (Narver and Slater, 1990; Deshpandé et al., 1993). The social marketing framework requires a strong commitment to understanding the target group, whose behaviour needs to be changed. While significance of exchange has been highlighted in social marketing (Bagozzi, 1975), there are many practical difficulties in explaining the process due to the considerable efforts required to change behaviour with no immediate benefit to the target audience (McDermott et al., 2005). To overcome these difficulties, Grier and Bryant (2005) suggest that social marketers must find ways to offer benefits that consumers value, and recognise the intangible cost that consumers pay such as experiencing the discomfort associated with changing behaviour. There are other obstacles, according to Lefebvre and Flora (1988), that may interfere with the adoption and maintenance of customer orientation. These include: (1) lack of clear objectives, (2) poor knowledge of customer needs, (3) pressure to achieve other programme objectives above consumer needs, (4) expert-driven strategies, and (5) dilution of messages due to the involvement of several intermediaries. Awareness about these barriers during the planning phase can be helpful in developing strategies to address them.

Formative research

Information on consumer behaviour is the prerequisite to any successful programme seeking behaviour change (Grier and Bryant, 2005). It facilitates the development of effective marketing strategies and their smooth implementation. The research plan is designed to: (a) inform its segmentation strategy, (b) identify attitudinal and behavioural barriers, and (c) assess the programme impact. Formative research involving the pretesting of ideas and material prior to implementation, using techniques like focus groups, intercept interviews and pilot studies, is described as essential for effective programme implementation (Lefebvre and Flora, 1988).

Formative research, according to Thackeray and Neiger (2003), includes audience analysis, channel analysis and market analysis. Audience analysis provides information regarding the needs of the target population and the costs associated with it, while channel analysis seeks to identify the most efficient way to reach the target audience. Marketing analysis involves gathering information relating to the other players in the market and their influence. Formative research can therefore be described as a tool to understand the needs of the target audience and their perceptions of product benefits and costs, as well as social and market influences that deter them from healthy behaviour.

Segmentation

Segmentation has two main objectives: to define homogeneous groups according to one or more criteria such as geographic, demographic and behaviour, and to target segments for the design of marketing mix strategies (Andreasen, 1995; Kotler et al., 2002). While the lack of proper segmentation of the target market into meaningful sub-groups defies the basic marketing philosophy of consumer orientation, many social marketing interventions appear not to segment their market and try to reach everyone using all available channels (Fine, 1990). The non-availability of relevant data necessary for proper segmentation has been cited as the reason for non-usage of segmentation (Bloom and Novelli, 1981).

In social marketing, segmentation is done on the basis of current behaviour and future intentions rather than age, ethnicity or other demographic variables. It then uses tailor-made strategies to address the requirements of individual segments (Forthofer and Bryant, 2000). For example, a social marketing programme for family health (SMPFH) in Pakistan defined target groups in terms of shared demographic, attitudinal and behavioural characteristics. This approach helped in the identification of target groups as well as in the development of audience-focused marketing strategies to achieve the desired behavioural outcomes. The SMPFH used research to identify barriers among the target groups in terms of attitude and behaviour towards the use of family planning products and services, in addition to their income and lifestyle.

Marketing mix

The adoption of the marketing mix, also known as the 4Ps, to influence behaviour is the central theme of social marketing interventions. The marketing mix is often used in marketing parlance to describe the set of marketing tools that an organisation uses for implementing its strategy (Kotler and Armstrong, 2010). Hardly any meaningful discussion on marketing strategy can be done without making an adequate reference to the marketing mix as it constitutes one of the core concepts of marketing theory (Rafiq and Ahmed, 1995). The blending of product, price, promotion and place defines the planning and implementation of an integrated marketing strategy. The relevance and applicability of the 4Ps in social marketing programmes is discussed below:

Product: traditionally, product is considered as something tangible, a physical entity or service that can be exchanged, but in social marketing products may be ideas, social causes or a change in behaviour (Lefebvre and Flora, 1988). Kotler and Lee (2008) identified four distinct groups of issues based on the types of behaviour that social marketing can impact: (a) *health related behaviour*: obesity, tobacco use, fruit and vegetable intake; (b) *injury-related prevention behaviour*: drink and driving, seatbelt, and domestic violence; (c) *environmental behaviour*; waste reduction, air pollution from automobiles and energy conservation; and (d) *community involvement behaviour*: organ donation, voting and literacy. It is therefore difficult to formulate a concept for social marketing product vis-à-vis a consumer product like toilet rolls (Bloom and Novelli, 1981). The other issue is with the target audience who may not perceive the need or want for behaviour change as they do not see any immediate benefit from behaviour modification (Kotler and Roberto, 1989). This is a major challenge for programme managers as they need to offer something of equal or higher value to the target group in exchange for the desired behaviour. According to Wood (2008), in practice, whatever is offered in exchange is considered of little or no value. It is therefore necessary to understand the concerns of the target audience and manage all elements of the marketing mix to make the desired behaviour an attractive option and remove any barriers to change.

Kotler et al. (2002) described social marketing products using the three levels of product: the core, tangible and augmented levels. They referred to the benefit people would gain from performing the desired behaviour as the core product and the behaviour as the actual product. The products and services used to facilitate behaviour change were defined as augmented product. This is in contrast to commercial marketing where the actual product is tangible and the augmented product is intangible (Kotler et al., 2005). The reversal of tangible and intangible products in the social market confuses many programme managers. Wood (2008) states that the social marketing product model is difficult to understand and implement, therefore programme managers tend to push the augmented products instead of the core benefits. This underscores the need for a greater emphasis on behaviour change communication in programmes as compared to actual products and services (Grier and Bryant, 2005).

Price: in commercial marketing, pricing is described as the most important element of the marketing mix as its generates revenue for the organisation and pays for the costs of product, distribution and promotion, but in social marketing price can be monetary as well as non-monetary, like time, effort or change in lifestyle (Kotler and Roberto, 1989). The monetary price plays an important role in positioning products in terms of quality and improving access to social products – for example, a high price suggests better quality, while a low price facilitates access to social products by a poor population. The monetary price is also used to limit the usage of non-healthy products like tobacco and alcohol. However, many social marketing products or services have little or no monetary price (Rothschild, 1979; Bloom and Novelli, 1981); the costs are usually intangible in nature, such as diminished pleasure, embarrassment and the psychological discomfort that accompanies change (Grier and Bryant, 2005). Considering the significance of monetary and non-monetary price, the challenge is to address the psychological barrier/cost and encourage people to continue their healthy behaviour. Studies in social learning also suggest that people are motivated by tangible incentives immediately following the behaviour (Bandura, 1977).

Place: place in social marketing is more than just providing a convenient location for exchange, it also involves measures that make the desired behaviour more appealing to the target population (Kotler et al., 2002). It includes the provision for a place where the desired behaviour is facilitated through the use of tangible products. It also includes intermediaries that can provide products or information or perform other functions to support behaviour change (Grier and Bryant, 2005). Alcalay and Bell (2000) suggest 'social availability' as an important distribution objective in social marketing. It is described as support and acceptance of healthy behaviour by society. This can be achieved through advocacy and mobilising opinion leaders to support healthy behaviour, such as religious leaders' support for contraception. Other methods for encouraging target groups to adopt healthy behaviour include a community outreach programme that builds the individual's ability and intent to practise the desired behaviour. Small community meetings for women and men are a cost-effective mechanism for facilitating discussions about people's concerns regarding family planning and HIV/AIDS prevention programmes in the Indian subcontinent.

Promotion: promotion is referred to as persuasive communications to convey the product benefit, price and availability to the target audience. It involves a clear definition of the target audience, communication objectives and optimum methods including media and frequency to reach the target groups. Promotional activities generally include advertising, sales promotion, public relations, direct marketing and personal selling. However, recently there has been a tremendous increase in a new, interactive form of communication due to the widespread availability of internet and digital technology (Fill, 2002). This effect can be seen in social marketing promotion where products such as behaviours (physical activity), ideas (recycling), tangible items (bicycle helmets), services (mammography screening) and causes (energy conservation) are being promoted through the internet (McKenzie et al., 2009). Since the primary objective in marketing communication is to promote the organisation and the products and services it offers, therefore, in addition to commercial marketing communications tools, social marketing also utilises professional training, community-based activities and skill building to encourage the adoption of desired behaviours (Grier and Bryant, 2005). Due to the high visibility of promotion in the marketing mix, many believe that promotion is the only relevant element in social marketing. Bloom and Novelli (1981) state that, until recently, promotion was restricted to creating awareness, with very little being done to sell the benefits of behaviour change. The problem has been attributed to the nature of the products in social marketing and difficulties in building product ideas around product benefits (Wood, 2008). Nonetheless, researchers (Lefebvre and Flora, 1988; Glenane-Antoniadis et al., 2003; Grier and Bryant, 2005) agree on the need to integrate promotion with product, price and the distribution channel that is directed towards the target population. This is because each element of the marketing mix has a role in communication: *products* represent benefits or values that satisfy the needs of the customer, and in the communication programme branding and packaging are all designed to present an image or positioning beyond physical attributes; *price* from the communication standpoint has to be consistent with the product and the communication strategy. A high-quality product at a low price may create confusion among customers; *place* or distribution is about making the product available to the customer. Any information about the product is of no value if the products are not available where the customer wants them to be.

While the *4Ps* discussed above have been widely mentioned in the literature, it is also noteworthy to point out the arguments in the extant literature which introduce three additional elements – *process, people* and *physical evidence* (Boom and Bitner, 1981). Although these authors argue that the inclusion of these elements is to make the marketing mix amenable to transactions of services, their introduction has received strong support (Goldsmith, 1999; Solomon et al., 2009; Kotler et al., 2012). Hence, this extension of marketing mix elements also has some relevance in social marketing. For example, people are often involved in managing social marketing programmes, and the process of managing them could have significant implications for how successful or not they are in achieving the desired impact. As stated by Zeithaml et al. (2012), customers judge services on the basis of how efficient and effective the service process is. Hence, the relevance of the efficiency and effectiveness of the process adopted by various social marketing organisations cannot be ignored in terms of the perceptions of stakeholders regarding the quality of offerings. Maintaining a physical presence in various forms such as logo, offices and buildings can also go a long way towards 'tangiblising' the programme of social marketing organisations. A review of branding strategies used in the social marketing of the Family Health Project (FHP) in Pakistan suggests three different approaches: the conventional approach which involves development of a new brand for the local market; a second approach which entails promoting a commercial brand and is driven by economic reasons as it is considered to be more cost-effective and sustainable; a third strategy which uses umbrella branding for social marketing programme components, including socially franchised clinics for family health consultations and for generic promotion of contraceptive methods (Samad et al., 2010). Brands and logos have been extensively used for promoting their clinics and other services as well as for creating a generic demand for family health (FH) products and services. Hence, branding has not been restricted to product-based interventions only but effectively used in all social marketing interventions. Furthermore, there is evidence that branding facilitates the design and implementation of effective marketing campaigns and subsequently in building brand equity. Examples of successful brands and/or logos used in social marketing campaigns worldwide are 5 A Day, Click It or Ticket, Think! and Change4Life.

Monitoring and evaluation

Programme monitoring is an integral part of all social marketing interventions. Each intervention is evaluated against the programme objectives and its effectiveness is assessed. The process is designed to provide longitudinal data for programme delivery and utilisation trends (Lefebvre and Flora, 1988). Programme managers use continuous monitoring to gauge the consumer's response to marketing strategies. The messages and material are often revised based on this information (Balch and Sutton, 1997). The monitoring of progress is essential for effective implementation, including adjustments of activities according to the requirements of the target population.

The FH programme conducted population-based surveys to evaluate the impact of the programme on knowledge, attitudes and behaviours among priority groups, including a selection of project indicators to measure ability and intent to change behaviour as well as actual use of FH services. The VERB™, a social marketing campaign to increase physical activity among youth in the USA, used observation and intercept interviews at sponsored events to assess visitor demographics and interactions of the target groups with the activities (Grier and Bryant, 2005).

BARRIERS IN SOCIAL MARKETING

Most social marketing concepts derived from commercial marketing fit well in social marketing practice; there are, however, a few issues involved in understanding social products in terms of behaviour and exchange theory, particularly in the absence of any immediate and tangible benefits (Wood, 2008). The social marketing framework nevertheless offers a broad guideline for planning and designing social marketing interventions for tackling obesity (Rayner, 2007). Just as any intervention using some social marketing principles cannot be classified as a social marketing intervention, not all principles need be applied in every social marketing intervention.

For example, in an obesity context, if target groups must give up their old behaviour (eating habits or lifestyle), they should receive something of equal or higher value. Wood (2008) argues that the target groups in these situations do not believe that they need the products or services that are being offered in exchange. This makes it necessary for programme managers to understand the requirements of service users and to manipulate the marketing mix accordingly to maximise the impact (Armand, 2003; Thackeray and Neiger, 2003). This highlights the need to make the new behaviour an attractive option, as well as reducing cost and competition.

Governments and health organisations are recognising the importance of social marketing strategy in changing behaviour and are adopting the social marketing framework (six interdependent steps: initial planning, formative research, strategy development, programme development, implementation and monitoring) in obesity control programmes. The behavioural control of obesity through the social marketing framework is an essential component of obesity control strategies recommended by Bristol Social Marketing Centre (BSMC) at the University of the West of England, Bristol, and the Department of Health (DH).

BSMC guidelines on social marketing strategy for addressing obesity in a specific region suggest that the adoption of social marketing principles based on behaviour change and exchange theories can produce positive results (Tapp et al., 2008). The guidelines recommend the application of marketing technologies, including research, segmentation and effective use of all elements of the marketing mix, to achieve behaviour change. Recognising the complexity of the issues surrounding obesity, the report also cautions that social marketing alone may not suffice and should be applied in conjunction with other, long-term public health programmes.

The Department for Health (DH) strategy for obesity control, as outlined in the Change4Life marketing strategy (DH, 2009), also adopts a social marketing framework and suggests the use of research, targeting an integrated communications campaign for behaviour change. Both strategies suggest involving government, non-government and commercial organisations and recommend a combination of activities directed at individuals as well as groups.

The identification of relevant target groups in a social marketing campaign is a major point of concern. A social marketing product or social proposition is a behaviour, and, according to Andreasen (2002), behaviour change is the responsibility of the individual, therefore it is only logical to direct the campaign towards individuals. Other researchers (Hastings et al., 2000; Donovan and Henley, 2003) however suggest that an environment must be created to facilitate behaviour change. For this reason, many interventions are based on creating an environment for healthy behaviour by improving the access to affordable alternatives (Meadley et al., 2003). The strategy is influenced by the socio-economic context, particularly in developing countries marked by widespread poverty, a lack of resources and poor infrastructure. Practitioners' attention to socio-economic context has been recognised by academics (Hastings et al., 2000; Donovan and Henley, 2003) and supported by the National Social Marketing Centre (UK), which describes an intervention or planned process targeting behaviour change, directly or indirectly, by providing the environment for positive behaviour, as social marketing (NSMC, 2006). It can therefore be concluded that with the exception of a few disparities in principles, researchers agree that social marketing is an effective method for influencing behaviour change (Meekers and Rahaim, 2005; Domegan, 2008).

FUTURE OF SOCIAL MARKETING

In order to facilitate the application of social marketing theory into practice, certain social marketing concepts like product and exchange theory should be further defined (Wood, 2008). The language of social marketing also needs to be simplified in order to be understood by those delivering it. There are suggestions that regular training and even formal education at the highest level be provided to those involved in programme design and delivery (Grier and Bryant, 2005).

Charity marketing and new forms of philanthropy

Philanthropy is defined by the Oxford Living Dictionary (Oxford Dictionaries, n.d.) *as the desire to promote the welfare of others, expressed especially by the generous donation of money to good causes*. Charities are organisations involved in philanthropy. Also known as *not-for-profit* or voluntary organisations, charities must fulfil certain requirements defined by the relevant authorities in order to be classified as such. For example, in England and Wales the organisation must be for the benefit of the public and should fall within the description of purpose in the Charities Act (Charity Commission, 2013).

An act of charity may include helping a homeless person with food and shelter or donating money to a good cause such as providing clean drinking water in an under-developed country. Philanthropy is a relatively more complex phenomenon, due to the nature of the activities involved, for example establishing community libraries to support education and thereby empower people and reduce poverty (Lucas, 2000). According to Wall (1970) (cited in Lucas, 2000), the difference between charity and philanthropy was described a long time ago by Andrew Carnegie in his essay 'The Gospel of Wealth'. Here Carnegie described philanthropy as the process of transforming the surplus wealth of the few for the benefit of the many, which is much more impactful than the distribution of small amounts individually.

Philanthropy is not a new concept – donations from rich businessmen for social causes have been common since the 17th century in the USA. The donations however were made by the individuals in their personal capacity and not by their companies. The situation changed in the 1960s, when US companies established their own foundations to demonstrate their participation in the welfare of society (Smith, 1994). Since then, more and more companies all over the world have made the social welfare of society, or philanthropy, an integral component of their organisational objectives.

Charities can be described as non-profit-organisations involved in philanthropy. The list of charitable purposes is long and includes relieving poverty, education, health, human rights, and so on. Although the primary purpose of charities is to alleviate social problems from society, securing funding is the prerequisite philanthropic programme. Therefore, one of the main functions performed by charities is arranging funds or fund raising.

Funds are usually provided by: (1) national government and international agencies such as the UK Department for International Development (DFID), the United States Agency for International Development (USAID), the German Development Bank (Kreditanstalt für Wiederaufbau or KfW), the United Nations (UN); (2) private foundations such as the Bill & Melinda Gates Foundation and the Packard Foundation; (3) businesses such as Lloyds Bank, Marks & Spencer, John Lewis, and so on; and (4) individual donors are another source for funding. The individual donor source is gaining attention due to its huge potential. The method used for reaching a target audience includes direct mailing, advertising, face-to-face and online contact. The online system of donation collection is quite common and frequently used by charities. The site used by Population Services International (PSI), a Washington-based NGO involved in social marketing and communication for health worldwide invites donations online through its webpage. It includes eight different options:

- online donation
- donation by mail or phone
- monthly donation
- employer matching
- gift of stocks
- donor advice funds
- management of monthly contribution
- combined federal campaign.

These options provide a choice to either participate individually or as part of a group along with your employer or the federal campaign. It also allows individuals to make a single one-time contribution or participate on a regular basis.

Case Study 11.1

Change4Life

The first national social marketing campaign to address the obesity problem in England was launched in 2009. The campaign, labelled as the Change4Life Strategy or C4L, was developed by the Department of Health (DH), England under the Healthy Weight, Healthy Life strategy, in consultation with academics and the commercial sector using behaviour-change theory and the lessons learned from similar campaigns in other health interventions (DH, 2009). Change4Life initially focused on prevention rather than treating obesity. It targeted young children under 11 with the objective of changing unhealthy lifestyles by providing opportunities to avoid weight gain and influencing them to adopt healthy behaviours.

The campaign was divided into five distinct phases to create preconditions for behaviour change and to support their efforts to achieve behaviour change targets. An important feature of this campaign was the emphasis on prelaunch activities, including a briefing on research findings for those involved in implementation. The C4L campaign heavily relied on social marketing for achieving healthy weight. This was based on the assumption that social marketing is a systematic approach for addressing barriers to behaviour change through the use of several interdependent activities.

C4L assumptions

Social marketing will support the overall Healthy Weight, Healthy Lives strategy by:

- creating a segmentation model that allows resources to be targeted at those individuals who are most in need of help (i.e. whose attitudes and behaviours place their children most at risk of excess weight gain)
- providing insight into why those individuals hold those attitudes and behave as they do
- creating a communications campaign to change those attitudes
- providing 'products' (such as handbooks, questionnaires, wall charts, web content) that people can use to help them change their behaviours
- signposting people to services (such as breastfeeding cafés, accompanied walks, free swimming and cookery classes)
- bringing together a coalition of local, non-governmental and commercial sector organisations that will use their influence to change behaviour.

Source: Adapted from Samad et al. (2016); DH (2009)

C4L outcomes

However, despite a strong theoretical base and systematic implementation, the results of the C4L campaign remain less than satisfactory. The obesity data suggest that there is no sign of any improvement in the final outcome. According to a recent survey by the NHS, 24% of men and 26% of women were found to be obese. Based on current trends, 60% of adult men and 50% of adult women will be affected by obesity by 2050 (McPherson et al., 2007).

A review by Croker et al. (2012) indicates that while there was a significant improvement in the awareness of C4L, the campaign had very little impact on attitude or behaviour. The study was commissioned by the DH for independent evaluation of the Change4Life strategy. The main objective of the study was to evaluate the impact of the communication material (the family information pack) component of C4L on (a) parents' attitudes towards their children's eating and physical activity behaviour, (b) their intentions to change, and (c) the reported diet and activity behaviours of parents and children.

The poor impact of the C4L campaign on attitudes and intentions is not in line with other social marketing campaigns in the USA, Australia and Europe, where some positive results have been observed in all cases (Bauman et al., 2001; Wammes et al., 2005; Huhman et al., 2010). However, the impact on behaviour has been mixed; in certain studies, a positive impact was noted, while in others no change in behaviour was found (Huhman et al., 2005; Craig et al., 2009).

The possible explanations for a poor response can be summarised in five points: (a) a relatively low level of engagement; (b) targeting of multiple and complex behaviours instead of focusing on a specific behaviour; (c) lack of clarity on the target groups – it was not clear whether the target was parents or children; (d) use of untested behavioural models; and (e) no evidence of any social marketing criteria actually being applied. The relevance of these points is well documented (Sweet and Fortier, 2010; Evans et al., 2011; Croker et al., 2012) and they could have been responsible for the low impact of the C4L campaign.

Questions for discussion

1. What are the reasons for a poor response to the C4L campaign?
2. Is social marketing a relevant option for controlling obesity?
3. Can legislation on the marketing of food products help in improving the obesity situation? Explain.

Digital Focus 11.1

PSI and digital technology

The use of digital technology by charities is becoming increasingly relevant in recent times. A clear example is the use of digital technology by PSI, a Washington-based global charity

(Continued)

(Continued)

operating in 50 countries, to generate funds from individual donors across the world. The scope of internet-based communication in social marketing has tremendously increased due to newer applications (Web 2.0) providing more control to users with regard to how the information is generated, organised and shared.

Social media can significantly enhance the effects of efforts made within social marketing communications. It can directly engage consumers in the campaign process by both producing and distributing information through *collaborative writing, content sharing, social networking, social bookmarking* and *syndication* (Thackeray et al., 2008). Social media can also enhance the power of viral marketing by increasing the speed at which consumers share experiences and opinions with progressively larger audiences.

While the widespread use and potential effectiveness of social media applications cannot be denied, strategic issues need to be considered by social marketers before incorporating related applications into campaign plans. The strategic issues to be considered include target audience preferences, the selection of appropriate applications, tracking and evaluation, and related costs. Once these issues are carefully considered, use of social media will expand to allow practitioners more direct access to consumers with less dependency on traditional communication channels. There are a number of ways to incorporate social media into a social marketing campaign plan, and, as technology advances, social media applications will again expand to allow programme managers greater direct access to clients. Programme planners need to be creative in their social marketing efforts and to consider how social media can be incorporated to better market their products to the target population.

Source: Adapted from Thackeray et al. (2008)

Questions for discussion

1. How can digital technology be used to enhance the impact of social marketing?
2. Do you agree that social media applications will expand with time and subsequently replace the traditional communication channels for social marketing? Give reasons.

Case Study 11.2

Greenstar Social Marketing, Pakistan

Greenstar Social Marketing (GSM) was established in 1991 as a social enterprise, to improve the family health of people in Pakistan by increasing choices and access to quality modern family planning methods and products.

Since GSM's inception in 1991, it has been working ceaselessly to increase awareness of, availability of and access to affordable, quality, modern family planning (FP) products.

Today, the GSM Sabzsitara logo is synonymous with reliable family planning information, products and services all across the country. As the largest private sector provider of reproductive health products, GSM is responsible for the provision of approximately 53% of all FP products and services, distributed by the private sector, in Pakistan.

GSM implements a total market approach in which those activities that are serving the poorest in rural areas will continue to be subsidised, while people in urban areas will increasingly pay closer to cost recovery prices for products.

GSM's primary goal is to increase quality family planning services and reduce maternal mortality throughout Pakistan. Our premise is that every pregnant woman is a client for FP services. The reach to these potential clients can be increased, on the one hand, by motivating our network providers for better FP counselling and, on the other hand, by providing access to better antenatal and postnatal services, including FP counselling and method adoption.

Our key objectives include:

1. To improve the quality of health service provision by Greenstar franchise providers, specifically training them in the new initiative of antenatal FP counselling and the adoption of an FP method postpartum.
2. To improve access to and availability of quality reproductive health and maternal and child health services for low socio-economic classes in urban areas and rural areas through Public Private Partnership.
3. To increase access to affordable reproductive health and maternal and child health products, particularly in rural areas.

Message from Dr Rehana Ahmed, Chairperson, Greenstar Social Marketing, Pakistan

The reality is that family planning is one of the most powerful investments in the development of our country. Its benefits cascade across all sectors, leading to a healthier, better educated and prosperous nation.

The mission of Greenstar Social Marketing (GSM) is 'to contribute to the development of Pakistan through family planning'. GSM is a national organisation that has already celebrated 25 years in operation, increasing access to and enhancing the quality of products and services provided for family planning and maternal and child health.

GSM sees the power in collaboration with the different development sectors, because it is only through combining skills that we can build an effective model for the universal

(Continued)

(Continued)

coverage of family planning in Pakistan and achieve the government's promises to the international community.

The GSM Board, management and staff own this mission and pledge to address the ongoing challenges, facing the future with a determination to serve those low-income families whose aspirations are 'not more children but more for their children'.

Source: https://www.greenstar.org. pk/

Questions for discussion

1. What are the benefits and challenges of the 'total market approach'?
2. Do you think Dr Ahmed's perspective on the social marketing of FP in Pakistan can stand the test of time and/or change government policy? Discuss.

Ethical Focus 11.1

Can we rely on the information provided by food marketers?

Obesity is described as excess body fat. It is generally caused by an imbalance between food intake and physical activity. Body Mass Index (BMI) is a simple and reliable method to measure the level of obesity. BMI is a person's weight in kilograms divided by the square of height in metres. According to the NHS, a BMI of 18.5 to 24.9 is a healthy weight, while a BMI of 25 to 29.9 is considered to be overweight, and over 30 is obese.

There are several factors that can lead to obesity, such as genetic, demographic and, in many cases, behavioural (NIH, 2012). Obesity treatment includes behavioural therapy, drugs and, in extreme cases, surgery. Behavioural therapy targets eating and exercise habits, and attempts to provide individuals with the necessary skills, motivation and environment for behaviour modification. Interventions in this regard are guided by two distinct models: the medical model focuses on treatment and is directed toward individual patients, while the public health model concentrates on prevention and focuses on risk factors within the target population (Adler and Stewart, 2009). Most of the interventions use a combination of both models, as individually they are considered incomplete.

In the UK, until recently, the government's focus has been more on highlighting the problems caused by obesity than on providing solutions (Martin, 2008). Even the current government policy is to pass responsibility to the individual, with no change in public health law for control of obesity. The population is expected to make an informed decision in terms of food intake but the problem is can we rely on food marketers to be honest in their advertising? Martin (2008) concludes that a government obesity strategy based on research is a good start but the policy can only be effective if supported by changes in legislation.

Questions for discussion

1. What is the significance of providing a necessary environment for the obesity prevention programme?
2. Do you agree that under the current legislation we cannot rely on the information provided by food marketers? Is there any role for government?

REFERENCES

Adler, N. E. and Stewart, J. (2009) Reducing obesity: Motivating action while not blaming the victim. *Milbank Quarterly*, 87(1), 49–70.

Ajzen, I. (1985) From intention to actions: A theory of planned behavior. In J. Kuhl and J. Beckman (eds), *Action Control: From Cognition to Behaviour* (pp. 11–39). Heidelberg: Springer-Verlag.

Ajzen, I. (1991) The theory of planned behavior. *Organizational Behavior and Human Decision Process*, 50, 179–211.

Ajzen, I. and Fishbein, M. (1980) *Understanding Attitudes and Predicting Social Behaviour.* Englewood Cliffs, NJ: Prentice Hall.

Albarracín, D., Johnson, B. T., Fishbein, M. and Muellerleile, P. A. (2001) Theories of reasoned action and planned behavior as models of condom use: A meta-analysis. *Psychological Bulletin*, 127(1), 142–61.

Alcalay, R. and Bell, R. (2000) *Promoting Nutrition and Physical Activity through Social Marketing: Current Practices and Recommendations.* Center for Advanced Studies in Nutrition and Social Marketing. Davies, CA: University of California.

Andreasen, A. (1995) *Marketing Social Change: Changing Behaviour to Promote Health, Behaviour, and the Social Environment.* San Francisco, CA: Jossey-Bass.

Andreasen, A. (2002) Marketing social marketing in the social change marketplace. *Journal of Public Policy and Marketing*, 21 (1), 3–14.

Andreasen, A. (2006) *Social Marketing in the 21st Century.* Thousand Oaks, CA: Sage.

Armand, F. (2003) *Social Marketing Models for Product-Based Reproductive Health Programs: A Comparative Analysis*. Washington, DC: USAID/Commercial Market Strategies Project.

Armitage, C. and Conner, M. (2001) Efficacy of the theory of planned behaviour: A meta-analytic review. *British Journal of Social Psychology*, 40, 471–99.

Bagozzi, R. (1975) Marketing as exchange. *Journal of Marketing*, 39(4), 32–9.

Balch, G. and Sutton, S. (1997) Keep me posted: A plea for practical evaluation. In M.E. Goldberg, M. Fishbein and S.E. Middlestadt (eds), *Social Marketing: Theoretical and Practical Perspectives* (pp. 61–74). Mahwah, NJ: Lawrence Erlbaum Associates.

Bandura, A. (1977) *Social Learning Theory*. Englewood Cliffs, NJ: Prentice Hall.

Bauman, A.E., Bellew, B., Owen, N. and Vita, P. (2001) 'Impact of an Australian mass media campaign targeting physical activity in 1998', *Am J Prev Med*, 21: 41–47.

Bloom, P. (1980) Evaluating social marketing programs: Problems and prospects. In *The 1980 Educators Conference Proceedings*. Chicago, IL: American Marketing Association.

Bloom, P. and Novelli, W. (1981) Problems and challenges in social marketing. *Journal of Marketing*, 45(2), 79–88.

Boom, B. H. and Bitner, M. J. (1981) Marketing strategies and organisation structures for service firms. In J. Donnelly and J. R. George (eds), *Marketing of Services*. Chicago, IL: American Marketing Association.

Charity Commission (2013) What Makes a Charity CC4? Charity Commission for England & Wales. Available at: www.gov.uk/government/publications/what-makes-a-charity-cc4/what-makes-a-charity-cc4 (accessed 9 July 2019).

Craig, C.L., Bauman, A., Gauvin, L., Robertson, J. and Murumets, K. (2009) 'ParticipACTION: A mass media campaign targeting parents of inactive children; knowledge, saliency, and trialing behaviours', *Int J Behav Nutr Phys Act*, 6: 88.

Croker, H., Lucas, R. and Wardle, J. (2012) Cluster-randomised trial to evaluate the 'Change for Life' mass media/ social marketing campaign in the UK. *BMC Public Health*, 12(1), 404.

Dann, S. (2006) Exploring the cross compatibility of the Andreasen (1995) definition of social marketing and the AMA (2004) definition of commercial marketing. PHILICA.COM. Article number 62.

Department of Health (DH) (2009) Change4Life Marketing Strategy. London: DH Communications Directorate. Available at: https://webarchive.nationalarchives.gov.uk/20130124053508/http://www.dh.gov.uk/prod_consum_dh/groups/dh_digitalassets/@dh/@en/documents/digitalasset/dh_115511.pdf (accessed 16 May 2019).

Deshpandé, R., Farley, J. U. and Webster, F. E. (1993) Corporate culture, customer orientation, and innovativeness in Japanese firms: A quadrat analysis. *Journal of Marketing*, 57(1), 23–37.

Domegan, C. T. (2008) Social marketing: Implications for contemporary marketing practices classification scheme. *Journal of Business and Industrial Marketing*, 23(2), 135–41.

Donovan, R. and Henley, N. (2003) *Social Marketing: Principles and practice*. Melbourne: IP Communications.

Evans, W., Christoffel, K.K., Necheles, J., Becker, A.B. and Snider, J. (2011) 'Outcomes of the 5- 4-3-2-1 Go! Childhood Obesity Community Trial', *Am J Health Behav*, 35: 189–198.

Fill, C. (2002) *Marketing Communications: Contexts, Strategies and Applications*, 3rd edition. Harlow: Financial Times Prentice Hall.

Fine, S. (1990) *Social Marketing: Promoting the Causes of Public and Nonprofit Agencies*. Boston, MA: Allyn & Bacon.

Forthofer, M. and Bryant, C. (2000) Using audience-segmentation techniques to tailor health behavior change strategies. *American Journal of Health Behavior*, 24(1), 36–43.

Fox, K. and Kotler, P. (1980) The marketing of social causes: The first ten years. *Journal of Marketing*, 44, 24–33.

Glenane-Antoniadis, A., Whitwell, G., Bell, S. and Menguc, B. (2003) Extending the vision of social marketing through social capital theory: Marketing in the context of intricate exchange and market failure. *Marketing Theory*, 3(3), 323–43.

Goldsmith, R. E. (1999) The personalized marketplace: Beyond the 4Ps. *Marketing Intelligence & Planning*, 17(4), 178–85.

Grier, S. and Bryant, C. (2005) Social marketing in public health. *Public Health*, 6(3), 19–39.

Härtel, C., McColl-Kennedy, J. R. and McDonald, L. (1998) Incorporating attributional theory and the theory of reasoned action within an affective events theory framework to produce a contingency predictive model of consumer reactions to organizational mishaps. *Advances in Consumer Research*, 25(1), 428–32.

Hastings, G. (2003) Competition in social marketing. *Social Marketing Quarterly*, 9(3), 6–10.

Hastings, G., MacFadyen, L. and Anderson, S. (2000) Whose behaviour is it anyway? The broader potential of social marketing. *Social Marketing Quarterly*, 6(2), 46–58.

Hovig, D. (2001) *The Conflict between Profits and Public Health: A Comparison of Contraceptive Social Marketing Models*. Working Paper No. 43. Washington, DC: PSI Research Division.

Huhman M. E., Potter L. D., Nolin M. J., Piesse, A., Judkins, D. R., Banspach, S. W., and Wong F. L. (2010) The influence of the VERB Campaign on children's physical activity in 2002 to 2006. *Am J Public Health*, 100, 638–45.

Huhman, M., Potter, L.D., Wong, F.L., Banspach, S.W., Duke, J.C., Heitzler, C.D. (2005) Effects of a mass media campaign to increase physical activity among children: Year-1 results of the VERB campaign. *Pediatrics*, 116 (2), e277-e284; DOI: 10.1542/peds.2005-0043

Kotler, P. and Armstrong, G. (2010) *Principles of Marketing*, 13th edn. Upper Saddle River, NJ: Pearson.

Kotler, P., Keller, K., Brady, M., Goodman, M. and Hansen, T. (2012) *Marketing Management*, 2nd edn. Harlow: Pearson.

Kotler, P. and Lee, N. (2008) *Social Marketing: Influencing Behaviors for Good*, 3rd edn. Thousand Oaks, CA: Sage.

Kotler, P. and Levy, S. (1969) Broadening the concept of marketing. *Journal of Marketing*, 33, 10–15.

Kotler, P. and Roberto, E. (1989) *Social Marketing: Strategies for Changing Public Behaviour*. New York: Macmillan.

Kotler, P., Roberto, W. and Lee, N. (2002) *Social Marketing: Improving the Quality of Life*, 2nd edn. Thousand Oaks, CA: Sage.

Kotler, P., Wong, V., Saunders, J. and Armstrong, G. (2005) *Principles of Marketing*, 4th edn. Harlow: Prentice Hall.

Kotler, P. and Zaltman, G. (1971) Social marketing: An approach to planned social change. *Journal of Marketing*, 35(July), 3–12.

Lefebvre, R. and Flora, J. (1988) Social marketing and public health intervention. *Health Education Quarterly*, 15(3), 299–315.

Lucas, A. (2000) Extracts from a paper presented at a workshop on Public–Private Partnerships in Public Health, Massachusetts, USA, 7–8 April. Available at: www.who.int/tdr/publications/documents/public-private-partnerships.pdf (accessed 9 July 2019).

MacAskill, S., Stead, M., MacKintosh, A. and Hastings, G. (2002) 'You cannae just take cigarettes away from somebody and no' gie them something back': Can social marketing help solve the problem of low-income smoking?, *Social Marketing Quarterly*, 8(1), 19–34.

MacFadyen, L., Stead, M. and Hastings, G. (1999) A synopsis of social marketing. *Institute for Social Marketing*. Available at: www.qihub.scot.nhs.uk/media/162221/social_marketing_synopsis.pdf (accessed ?).

MacFadyen, L., Stead, M. and Hastings, G. (2002) 'Social marketing'. In M. J. Baker (ed.), *The Marketing Book*, 5th edn. Chapter 27. Oxford: Butterworth Heinemann.

Madden, T., Ellen, P. and Ajzen, I. (1992) A comparison of the theory of planned behaviour and the theory of reasoned action. *Personality and Social Psychology Bulletin*, 18(1), 3–9.

Martin, R. (2008) The role of law in the control of obesity in England: Looking at the contribution of law to a healthy food culture. *Australia and New Zealand Health Policy*, 5(21).

McDermott, L., Stead, M. and Hastings, G. (2005) What is and what is not social marketing? The challenge of reviewing the evidence. *Journal of Marketing Management*, 5(6), 545–53.

McKenzie, J. F., Neiger, B. L. and Thackeray, R. (2009) *Planning, Implementing, and Evaluating Health Promotion Programs* (5th edn). San Francisco, CA: Benjamin Cummings.

McPherson, K., Marsh, T. and Brown, M. (2007). Modelling Future Trends in Obesity and the Impact on Health. Foresight Tackling Obesities: Future Choices. Available at: https://assets.publishing.service.gov.uk/government/uploads/system/uploads/attachment_data/file/295149/07-1662-obesity-modelling-trends.pdf (accessed 14 May 2019.)

Meadley, J., Pollard, R. and Wheeler, M. (2003) *Review of DFID Approaches to Social Marketing*. London: DFID Health Systems Resource Centre.

Meekers, D. and Rahaim, S. (2005) The importance of socio-economic context for social marketing models for improving reproductive health: Evidence from 555 years of program experience. *BMC Public Health*, 5 (10).

Morris, Z. and Clarkson, P. (2009) Does social marketing provide a framework for changing healthcare practice? *Health Policy*, 91(2), 135–41.

Narver, J. C. and Slater, S. F. (1990) The effect of a market orientation on business profitability. *Journal of Marketing*, 54, 20–135.

NIH (2012) Overweight and Obesity Statistics. Weight-control Information Network. *NIH Publication No. 04-4158.*

NSMC (2006) *Social Marketing Pocket Guide*. National Social Marketing Centre, London: Department of Health and National Consumer Council.

Oxford Dictionaries (n.d.) Oxford Living Dictionary. Available at: https://en.oxforddictionaries.com/definition/philanthropy (accessed 9 July 2019).

Price, N. (2001) The performance of social marketing in reaching the poor and vulnerable in AIDS control programmes. *Health Policy and Planning*, 16(3), 231–9.

Rafiq, M. and Ahmed, P. K. (1995) Using the 7Ps as a generic marketing mix: An exploratory survey of UK and European marketing academics. *Marketing Intelligence and Planning*, 13(9), 4–15.

Rayner, M. (2007) Social marketing: How might this contribute to tackling obesity? *Obesity Review*, 8(1), 195–9.

Rothschild, M. (1979) Marketing communications in non-business situations or why it's so hard to sell brotherhood like soap. *Journal of Marketing*, 43(2), 11–20.

Samad, N., Nwankwo, S. and Gbadamosi, A. (2010) Branding in contraceptive social marketing: The Pakistani experience, *Social Marketing Quarterly*, 16(2), 50–68.

Samad, N., Samad, N. and Aftab, N. (2016) Re-examining obesity prevention strategy: Is social marketing still a relevant option? *The Marketing Review*, 16(3), 322–41.

Slater, S. F. and Narver, J. C. (1994) Does a competitive environment moderate the market orientation performance relationship? *Journal of Marketing*, 58, 46–55.

Smith, C. (1994) The new corporate philanthropy, *Harvard Business Review*, 72(3), 105–16.

Smith, W. A. (2006) Social marketing: an overview of approach and effects. *Injury Prevention*, 12 (1), 38–43.

Solomon, M., Marshal, G., Stuart, E., Barnes, B. and Mitchell, V. (2009) *Marketing: Real People, Real Decisions*. Harlow: Pearson.

Stead, M., Gordon, R., Angus, K. and McDermott, L. (2007) A systematic review of social marketing effectiveness. *Health Education*, 107(2), 126–91.

Sweet, S. and Fortier, M. (2010). Improving physical activity and dietary interventions with single or multiple health behaviour interventions? A synthesis of meta-analyses and reviews. *International Journal of Environmental Research and Public Health*, 7(4), 1720–43.

Taghian, M. and D'Souza, C. (2007) A cross-cultural study of consumer purchase intention and planned behaviour. In M. Thyne, K. Deans and J. Gnoth (eds), *ANZMAC 2007: 3Rs – Reputation, Responsibility, Relevance, 2009–15*. University of Otago, School of Business, Dunedin, New Zealand.

Tapp, A., Eagle, L. and Spotswood, F. (2008) Social marketing-based strategy for obesity interventions. Project report. University of the West of England (UWE). Available at: http://eprints.uwe.ac.uk/79 (accessed 9 July 2019).

Thackeray, R. and Neiger, B. (2003) Use of social marketing to develop culturally innovative diabetes interventions. *Diabetes Spectrum*, 16(1), 15–20.

Thackeray, R., Neiger, B. L., Hanson, C. I. and McKenzie, J. F. (2008) Enhancing promotional strategies within social marketing programs: Use of Web 2.0 social media. *Health Promotion Practice*, 9(4), 338–43.

Wall, J. F. (1970) *Andrew Carnegie*. Pittsburgh, PA: University of Pittsburgh Press.

Wammes, B., Breedveld, B, Looman C. and Brug, J. (2005) 'The impact of a national mass media campaign in The Netherlands on the prevention of weight gain', *Public Health Nutr*, 8:1250–1257.

Wicker, A. W. (1969) Attitudes versus actions: The relationship of verbal and overt behavioral responses to attitude objects. *Journal of Social Issues*, 25, 41–78.

Wiebe, G. D. (1951) Merchandising commodities and citizenship on television. *Public Opinion Quarterly*, 15(4), 679–91.

Wood, L. (2008) Brands and brand equity: Definition and management. *Management Decision*, 38, 662–9.

Zeithaml, V. A., Bitner, M. J. and Gremler, D. D. (2012) *Services Marketing: Integrating Customer Focus Across the Firm*, 6th edn. New York: McGraw-Hill.

12
NATION BRANDING AND PLACE MARKETING

An Amalgamation of Theory and Practice

Rula M. Al Abdulrazak

Learning Objectives

At the end of this chapter, you should be able to understand and discuss:

- The significance of nation branding and place marketing
- The strategic thinking behind nation and place branding
- The most common applications of nation branding and place marketing in relation to customer perceptions and consumer experiences
- The concept and its applications in place branding, public diplomacy and cultural diplomacy

---

INTRODUCTION

As the globalised market has evolved, it has enabled leading multinational corporations to not only challenge regional and local markets and businesses, but also to create a major challenge to states. Mega international and multinational organisations' contribution to the national economy can be significant to the economic stability of a nation, such as in the oil industry. This significant contribution gives these corporations leverage when negotiating contracts and tax relief. The negotiations for the UK's exit from the European Union (Brexit) are leading many major businesses to threaten to move their manufacturing and European headquarters outside the UK, unless the British government gives them assurances of stability and offers them advantages such as customs and tax relief. In August 2018, Panasonic, for example, announced that it was moving its headquarters to Amsterdam to avoid potential tax issues. Multinational organisations in automobile and advanced technology industries can pressure governments to offer them special deals, in comparison with small businesses.

Countries are competing for resources more than ever before, where nations are displaying their hunger for increased wealth. The need for financial capital to build an economy and gain worldwide power to survive has become their main purpose. With marketing knowledge and practices expanding beyond products and services to brand people, policies, ideas and places, a significant interest in marketing skills and knowledge has emerged. A wide range of titles is allocated to skilled marketers to perform delicate jobs in terms of positioning and communication that affects our lives socially, politically and/or financially. Thus, understanding the role of branding in national development is key to comprehending contemporary marketing knowledge and practice, and may open up new career opportunities for marketers.

This chapter introduces you to the phenomenon of nation branding, and to the different schools of thought on the role of nation branding. This is followed by an exploration of the different applications of nation branding and place marketing that reflect different career paths. The chapter takes a critical approach to the concept and applications of nation branding to develop your ability to make marketing decisions which are ethical and to help you consider social consequences in the future.

EVOLUTION OF THE NATION BRAND

Nation brand is derived from the concepts of nation and brand, which are concepts that have emerged in different disciplines. History, politics, sociology and culture have examined the notion of nation (e.g. Anderson, 2006; O'Shaughnessy and O'Shaughnessy, 2000; van Ham, 2001), while marketing developed the concept of brand. Applying the concept of brand was initially limited to products and profit organisations but a call for broadening the marketing discipline took centre stage in 1969. Kotler and Levy (1969) suggested applying marketing concepts and practices to a wider scope of tangible and intangible assets including ideas and nations. Marketing scholars have also been studying extensively the effect of the country-of-origin image on buyer behaviour (Schooler, 1965, 1971). In the mid-1990s, marketing scholars (e.g. Kotler et al., 1997) began studying place marketing more closely. International relations scholars encouraged politicians to become brand managers to manage the nation brand in the early 2000s. One of the champions of the nation-state brand in international relations is van Ham with several publications in this respect (2001, 2002, 2005, 2008a and 2008b). However, these studies remained separate and without clear interdisciplinary links until the emergence of nation-branding studies in the late 1990s through the efforts of practitioners such as Wally Olins and Simon Anholt and academics such as Philip Kotler in the 1990s and Keith Dinnie in the mid-2000s.

To understand nation brand, it is important to define the two concepts of brand and nation. Brand in summary is the projected perception of an object, whereas nation is a group of people who share a cultural identity and a history. They usually, but not necessarily, share a territory, which in most cases is located in a country or more, or spread across a geographic region or more. With this definition in mind, one state or more can govern a nation. Therefore, it is important to differentiate between the nation and the state.

The state is the governing authority of a nation over a specific period of time. In her book *The Need for Roots* (1952 translation into English), Simone Weil embraces the importance of national roots. However, loving one's roots does not necessarily extend to one's support of state politics. The relationship between a nation and its state is complex. Weil's love of France, thus, does not necessarily extend to the empire, and led to her active support of political and social movements. Schaar (1981) and Viroli (2003) argue that nationalism and patriotism share a history, but assess it differently. Nationalism seeks exclusivity as it aims for cultural homogeneity, while patriotism is about social justice in a multicultural society that is non-exclusive (Visvanathan, 2006). As such, patriotism is suggested to be an alternative to nationalism.

There is a difference between a nation brand and a country brand, because political borders and the governing state define a country, which is a self-governing political entity; a nation, however, can spread across more than one country. The Arab League, for example, includes countries from North Africa, the Mediterranean and Asia, all of which speak the Arabic language and thus have a shared history. It is also not the same as place brand because a place can be as small as a street and as wide as a continent, regardless of the inhabitants. In reality, of course, you cannot brand a place without the engagement of the locals who are affected by the consequences of the branding process; however, focusing on the place in place branding can limit the locals' engagement.

When a nation of people has a state or country of their own, it is called a nation-state such as France, Egypt, Germany and Japan. Some states, however, have more than one nation, such as the UK, Canada and Belgium. The USA is referred to as a nation-state regardless of its multicultural society as a result of the perception that its people share an American culture.

THE PROMISE OF NATION BRAND

The nation brand phenomenon has been introduced and promoted widely by branding practitioners such as Wally Olins and Simon Anholt. Olins (1999) addresses nation brand as a corporate brand that has a collective identity. Through the process of branding such an identity, a commercially attractive image that contributes to a country's wealth can be created (Foroudi et al., 2016). Anholt (2003, 2005) extends this idea further in his book *Brand New Justice*, arguing that branding countries can help redistribute the world's wealth, benefitting developing countries' interests. Here, Anholt addresses the criticism of the consumptive, materialistic culture and marketing role in creating a nation's brand. Branding detractors, such as Naomi Klein in her book, *No Logo* (2000/2010), perceive a move towards cultural commodification; that is, when cultural symbols are reduced to commodities and fashion statements, they become meaningless and lack integrity. Anholt (2005: 164) calls upon marketing to 'do its community service' by providing the governments of poorer countries with the marketing skills required to establish a positive and powerful nation brand. As such, a brand can lead to a fairer redistribution of the benefits of globalisation and in turn 'make a real difference to the cultural and economic prospects of more than half of the world' (Anholt, 2005: 165). Branding advocates such as Dinnie (2008) believe that a nation brand encourages cultural diversity and allows smaller and less powerful nations to compete effectively in the global market. A nation with limited resources can be highlighted on the world map for a recognisable positive accomplishment. With a nation-branding strategy based on a sustainable development agenda, Nepal has been able to achieve an impressive rank in environmental stewardship indexes, which is a positive differential advantage (Dipak R. Pant in Dinnie, 2008). Nations may also have a favourable position in specific markets due to shared events or history. For example, Nepal has its place in the UK as the Gurkha soldiers from Nepal and northern India fought some of the bloodiest battles for the British on the frontline, opening the door for the British Army. Thus, the nation is known for its bravery rather than its brutality in Britain.

In contrast with the harsh reality of economic survival and the nature of political crises, a nation functioning as a brand can come across as trivial. The idea of understanding and managing public perceptions for many is a luxury that can only be afforded in times of growth and prosperity. However, the nation-branding argument is that perceptions regularly surpass reality. A financial crisis is highly affected by perceptions, hence financial markets are volatile: 'it's all about the survival of those *perceived to be* the fittest' (Anholt, 2009: 88). Competence in managing perceptions such as a nation's image is as significant as military, political or fiscal competence in earlier times.

Companies' experience in times of crisis, such as a recession, also shows that in a time when the back office cost may be reduced and more efficient use of resources is needed including marketing communication, successful companies increase their brand communication and emphasise their position in the market to keep the business alive and developing. Such companies make sure they are still relevant to their customers as times change; they develop and communicate appropriate and attractive value propositions. They intensify their communications and enhance their focus, turning it into an opportunity to attract new customers who will be happy to switch suppliers, particularly when these suppliers are limiting their communication with customers.

However, the branding of nations has been addressed as part of public diplomacy propaganda. Some even consider cultural diplomacy, political communication, international public relations, democracy building, military information operations and branding, to be public diplomacy that is a type of propaganda (Potter, 2009: 36). Nonetheless, none of the above, especially branding, would be effective if found to be untruthful by consumers and the media since a lack of truth is often found in propaganda. As the CBS broadcaster and director of the US Information Agency Edward R. Murrow said, more than 45 years ago: 'Truth is the best propaganda … To be persuasive we must be believable; to be believable we must be credible; to be credible we must be truthful' (cited in Lugar, 2009: 7).

Anholt (2009) suggests that the success of any propaganda is conditional on two requirements: the nation being a closed society, and it having central control over the sources of information reaching the target market. Globalisation has made it very difficult to achieve these requirements. Thus, a nation-branding attempt that addresses image alone without dealing with its roots, in reality is nothing but a plan to damage the credibility of the nation. When the brand promise cannot be met and reality contradicts the communicated message, people's experience of the country will more likely leave them with a negative perception.

COMPETITIVENESS AND NATION BRANDING

The nation-branding industry is much wider today as many branding and marketing practitioners expand into place and nation branding. Branding is promoted aggressively to the extent that in some cases it appears as if a nation's existence might depend on it, with globalisation positioned as a 'threat' and the probability of 'unbranded' nations missing out on potential gains underscored. Several indexes which rank nations according to their brand, economy, human developments, sustainability or reputation are being widely communicated, inflaming the competitive atmosphere among nations and creating a sense of urgency for states to employ a branding programme within their national development agenda. Simon Anholt today presents himself as a policy adviser rather than a marketer. This shift emphasises that marketing today plays a role in policy making. At the same time, he created the Good Country Index, offering an alternative way for nations to compete.

As a result, the motives behind the engagement of governments in nation-branding programmes are very competitive. The phenomenon of rating nations through a competitive index is not new, however nation-branding practitioners fanned the flames of the process by increasing the number of indexes with a focus on nations, places and cities as brands and putting them under the spotlight through effective marketing communication.

In 2005, Anholt and GfK, a research company, established the Anholt-GfK Nation Brands Index^{SM} (NBI^{SM}) to measure nations' image around the world, and to track their profiles as they rise or fall. Today, there are several nation, country and city brand indexes, such as the Country Brand Index (CBI) by Future Brand, the Nation Brand Ranking (NBR) by Brand Finance, the Country Brand Ranking (CBR) by Bloom Consulting, and the Good Country Index (GCI) by Simon Anholt. This is in addition to city brand indexes and other subject-specific indexes that rank nations, such as the Global Competitiveness Ranking, the Human Sustainable Development Index by Our World, the Perceived Corruption Index by Transparency International and many others. Regardless of how comprehensive and realistic their ranking is, these indexes put unprecedented pressure on governments to compete.

Nation, country and city brand indexes are based on perceptions of panels of tens of thousands of respondents from a number of countries. However, the representation of these panels is questionable. For example, although the Anholt-GfK NBI ranks 50 countries, its respondents are from 20 countries only and they total just over 20,000 respondents. Moreover, not all countries are considered in every ranking and since the majority of these indexes are established in the west and the majority of their panels are located in the west, there may well be biases embedded in the ranking. In 2009, the Middle Eastern countries included in the Anholt-GfK Nation Brand Index were only four: Egypt, Saudi Arabia, the United Arab Emirates and Iran. Later on, Qatar was added and Iran is missing in the 2017 ranking. The African continent has only three countries represented in the 2017 ranking: Nigeria, South Africa and Botswana. Egyptian respondents are considered less experienced in completing online surveys – after a decade of involvement in this survey – and as such, the survey's length has been reduced, resulting in each nation getting approximately 200 ratings from Egypt, 300 fewer than the ratings received from the other panels, knowing that Egypt is the only Middle Eastern panel involved in Anholt-GfK NBI's survey.

Ranking nations is problematic due to the complexity of nation identity and its various traits. Some indexes' approaches are more comprehensive than others. Future Brand's Country Brand Index focuses on the brand as a place to visit by measuring: awareness, familiarity, associations, preference, consideration and decision/visitation. In terms of associations, five associations are considered in two categories: (1) status, which includes value system, quality of life, business potential; and (2) experience, which includes heritage and culture, tourism and made-in. Without familiarity with the nation in question, completing questions related to the above measures would be problematic. Anholt-GfK NBI, on the other hand, focuses on respondents' perceptions of nations' performance in six categories: culture and heritage, people, exports, tourism, investment and immigration, and governance. Thus, the ranking of these indexes suggests an indication of an international image of a nation that does not make much sense, except in comparison with other nations ranked in the same index, based on the same measures and by the same panel. In 2014, for example, Future Brand ranked Japan number one in its CBI, while Brand Finance ranked the USA number one in its NBR, and Germany came first in the Anholt-GfK NBI. CBR by Bloom Consulting and NBR by Brand Finance ranked the USA number one in 2017, while Germany climbed to number one in the Anholt-GfK NBI, pushing the USA down to sixth place.

Considering such conflicting results while drawing a national development policy can be confusing, and following any of these indexes may lead to a misleading strategic focus, as the results cannot represent the global market or a specific country view due to limitations in methodology, measuring criteria, sampling size and selection criteria (Al Abdulrazak, 2018). Such results also make it difficult to indicate the progress and performance of nations following a long-term nation-branding programme(s). For example, nation-branding rankings cannot claim to accurately measure the achievements of the 'Great' campaign of Great Britain.

Practitioner's Perspective 12.1

Interview with Simon Anholt

In London on 5 May 2015, Alain Elkan interviewed Simon Anholt, policy advisor and former nation-branding consultant, after he established the Good Country Index. Anholt helps national, regional and city governments earn better reputations – not by launching advertising or PR campaigns, but by changing the way they behave.

What is the Good Country Party about?

Two things. The first thing is to create a space where everybody in the world who cares about the future of humanity and the future of the planet can gather together ... as a group of people with a common philosophy, and a common worldview ... The second purpose is to try to change the culture of government worldwide. Traditionally governments have a simple mandate. They represent the interests of their own population and their own territory. My view is that today this is leading us to disaster.

Why?

Because it means that all countries are in competition against each other.

(Continued)

(Continued)

Was it not always like that?

Yes, that's the problem. Today we live in the age of globalisation and our problems are not national, they are global.

How can you cancel history? Look how difficult it is to create a political European consensus

Difficult, but not impossible. I don't think you can cancel history, but the future does not have to be the same as the past. You see the government of Matteo Renzi in Italy and Angela Merkel in Germany can't fix the global crisis and ensure stability. The government of Mexico cannot fix narco-trafficking. The European Union can't fix migration or poverty. America can't fix terrorism or climate change. We must collaborate more and compete less.

Yes, but how?

I believe that at least 10% of the world's population and possibly much more would prefer to live in a good country than a competitive country ... I use [in the Good Country Index] 35 indicators, mainly from the United Nations, which measure the contributions, both positive and negative, which each country makes outside its own borders. So these are contributions which include aid, culture, knowledge, peace and security, health and wellbeing and so forth. So, for example, if a country is responsible for killing people outside its own borders it loses points on the index.

But today political campaign debate is mostly about the economy and taxes?

Yes, and this is part of the reason people are voting less and less ... personally I want to vote for a government that considers all of these things, both domestically and internationally.

You also advise governments. Which ones?

53 so far, all over the world, from very rich to very poor and very large to very small. If you want extreme examples, as big as Mexico down to the Faroe Islands, population 50,000; from Austria to Sierra Leone.

What do you advise them?

It all comes under the general heading of engagement, helping countries to collaborate more effectively with other countries and the international community.

What about an old and common disease called war?

I think that war is another consequence of the old style of competitive governance: my nation against your nation. And we must move beyond that.

Questions for discussion

1. Considering the competitiveness that brand and nation indexes are causing, do you think the Good Country Index can reduce the competitiveness among nations? Why or why not?
2. Keeping in mind that some politicians come from a creative background – such as Arnold Schwarzenegger, a former US governor, and the former US president Ronald Reagan, who were both Hollywood actors before starting a career in politics – discuss the phenomenon of marketing practitioners advising governments on international and national policies.

Source: www.alainelkanninterviews.com/simon-anholt

NATION BRANDING: SCHOOLS OF THOUGHT
Nation branding stimulates national development

In 1997, Kotler, Jatusripitak and Maesincee published *The Marketing of Nations: A Strategic Approach to Building National Wealth*. The book begins with an exploration of the challenges of economic development, followed by the means of formulating a strategic national vision, then the development of policies, infrastructures and institutional frameworks, and concludes with the mechanisms that nations and businesses can use to unite their efforts towards prosperity (Kotler et al., 1997). The book provides governments and business leaders with managerial guidance to bridge the gap between state policies and the actual business environment. It encourages nations to assess their strengths and weaknesses, identify their opportunities and implement competitive global policies and strategies designed to achieve long-term prosperity. It suggests strategic marketing as part of national economic development or reform in order to market a nation and communicate its changes.

Within a strategic framework that links macroeconomic state policy with the microeconomic industrial behaviour of firms and consumers, the intention is to provide a comprehensive synthesis of economic, political and cultural factors that influence economic progress in both developed and developing nations, instead of depending on one of these forces to drive national growth. Kotler, Jatusripitak and Maesincee adopt a strategic approach to marketing a nation that addresses the nation's development programmes as well as the communication of the achievements of such programmes. It does not, however, discuss nation-branding techniques and nation brand management, both areas of some complexity in themselves.

More recently, Odia and Isibor (2014) suggested a strategic approach to nation branding through four steps of a process from start-up and organisation to implementation and follow-up, which involves the nation's leading sectors, and led by governments with a focus on brand communication. They examine Nigeria as a potential brand and address the possible synthesis between different sectors under state leadership and control; however, they focus on the process without clearly defining the scope and timescale; they also do not consider the challenges of such a complex process.

In the UAE, which has proved to be relatively successful in developing a positive nation image, there is no strategic marketing plan as part of its development strategy (Al-Abdulrazak, 2016). However, there is a strategic understanding to market its development programmes and all projects involved. This is because marketing is deemed an essential part of every successful project, and, as the UAE tends to attract and hire a skilled workforce to plan and deliver its projects, giving great care to marketing, this is not a surprise. Journalists are on the hunt for a good story, especially if it is different (Anholt, 2007). The UAE offers many impressive stories through its ambitious development and business projects, such as Ski Dubai in the middle of the desert, Masdar the zero-carbon dream city, and Saadiyat Island, a cultural destination that includes Louvre and Guggenheim Abu Dhabi. Countries and nations need to provide such stories because it makes them a place or nation attractive enough to be discovered, or friendly enough to be dealt with.

Nation branding – a culture-based brand

A growing consultancy market has evolved over the last decade and governments are keen to seek advice on communication across nations and place promotions, which may include advice on policies that can impact their image and in turn their power and commercial opportunities (Rasmussen and Merkelsen, 2012). Brands of Swiss chocolate, French perfume and Japanese electronics are meaningful and recognisable. This is due to the sponsor nation acting as a brand that represents an entire product category and cultural history. Such brands are closely associated with the identity of their nation. Dinnie argues that nation brand is 'the unique, multi-dimensional blend of elements that provide the nation with culturally grounded differentiation and relevance for all of its target audiences' (2008: 15). No matter whether a nation brand is an economically or politically oriented brand, it is a cultural brand. People's perception of a nation is believed to be the nation's culture. So, if it is a promise of wealth such as the 'American dream' or the UAE's more recent image, the culture associated with this promise will be one of luxury and privilege for business-oriented communities.

This is also the case where it is a politically oriented image led by conflict in the region and ideological disagreement, such as Syria's image in the UK decades ahead of the Syrian crisis in 2011. British people may well envision Syria as a country of extremists, with an ill-educated population and powerless women. Ultimately, a perceived culture will be branded as the nation culture, whether factually accurate or not. Neither the United States of America nor the United Arab Emirates has a nation-branding programme, but they do have an image within the UK market. A nation image could be limited in awareness, poor in knowledge and strongly influenced by media coverage and stereotypes, which will influence consumer decisions in relation to the country and its people (Al-Abdulrazak, 2016). Such nations, therefore, would be better off in terms of their relations with the British people if they effectively manage how they are perceived in the UK. Nation branding can offer a systematic approach to influencing international nation image.

Here, nation branding is a process that achieves differentiation. As with any brand, a nation brand is a differentiating factor, albeit a complex one with a multi-dimensional blend of elements, all of which are grounded in cultural differentiation and relevance to the target market (other nations). Elements of any culture can be commercial and have their roots in and implications for a nation's economy. Others are political, producing internal and external policies, which in turn influence the nation's culture. Consequently, politics, economy and culture shape a nation brand as they shape the nation identity (see the examples in Tecmen, 2017).

Nation branding – a marketing communications technique

Fan (2006) focuses on nation branding as a marketing tool to communicate a national vision and promote a favourable image. As such, nation branding helps in emphasising the distinctive characteristics of a place to act as a competitive advantage. This is a widely applied concept in marketing places to promote them as a destination for tourism, education, private health care and foreign direct investment.

Considering nation branding as an application of 'marketing communications techniques to promote a nation's image' (Ahn and Wu, 2015), however, can lead to superficial campaigns that concentrate on what is relevant and appealing to the target market, without giving due consideration to how relevant this is to the national people. Fulfilling the promise of the campaign is reliant on effective involvement from locals. It requires having infrastructure in place and the necessary resources, which include a skilled workforce. Nation branding can be costly to national resources and have economic and environmental consequences.

Effective campaigns that attract many visitors, talents and investors will eventually have a significant impact on the social fabric of the nation and its culture. Cultural change can face serious resistance from the nation, particularly if it brings with it negative change such as human and drug trafficking. In the case of Bangkok, sex tourism from the 1980s flourished particularly after an increase in health care tourism, leading to unresolved tensions between vice and virtue in the area (Cohen and Neal, 2012).

Ethical Focus 12.1

Mari El Republic as a tourist destination

Human agency plays a significant role in nation- and place-branding practices and the subsequent expected and unexpected consequences. Typical examples are the tension between sex and health care tourism in Bangkok; the Emiratisation programme in the United Arab Emirates that aims to nationalise most jobs after the country became a magnet for a workforce seeking prosperity; and a London real estate market where first-time buyers are struggling to purchase a home due to high prices, with one of the major contributors to this being high foreign investment in buy-to-let properties.

Every nation-branding programme needs to consider two major ethical questions:

- To what extent is the programme a true representation of the nation identity, resources, capabilities and aspirations, so that it is a sustainable and positive contributor to national development?
- What are the long- and short-term effects of the programme on the nation's social fabric, environment and economic stability?

Mari El Republic is located in what is considered to be the European part of Russia, along the northern bank of the Volga River. It is the home of almost 700, 000 people. It is an ethnic republic, representing native Mari people. The place is full of natural beauty and has a unique heritage but also limited resources; hence, developing it as a tourism destination could prove helpful in improving its economy.

The suggestion is to position Mari El Republic as an attractive destination for rural and ethno-tourism, taking into account the unique character of the Mari settlements in terms of their history, culture and ecology. Understanding, however, the socio-cultural specifics of a tourism destination is key to ensuring the sustainability of the destination, not only in terms of the prosperity of local communities but also as regards their happiness.

In a piece of research regarding the socio-cultural fabric of the region, although over 80% of residents are happy living there due to its beauty and tranquility, 95% of respondents expressed their intention to relocate in search of progress and prosperity (Sheresheva and Polukhina, 2018). The Mari El Republic population has been declining in the last decade as young families choose to move out of the region, seeking opportunities that the region lacks.

Strong believers, up to 90%, dominate the region and some have 'dual faith', combining the Orthodox religion with the traditional Mari pagan faith. These strong believers, particularly at the age of retirement, are reluctant to support tourism for fear of it affecting their privacy in practising their beliefs.

Questions for discussion

1. Sustainable tourism development in this region is in need of an appropriate brand positioning strategy for target audiences. For Mari El Republic, ethno-tourism based on preserving paganism, the traditional religion of the Mari people, can become a solid basis for positioning. Discuss.

2. Local Mari communities are still preserving ancient cultural and religious traditions (paganism) and opposing the idea of ethnographic tourism, as they feel that this is a threat to the national identity and spirit of Mari people. However, there are other nationalities, cultures and religions situated in the region. Suggest a positioning strategy that is true to the nation's identity and may help resolve this conflict, engage the Mari people and offer sustainability.

Source: Based on Sheresheva and Polukhina (2018)

Nation branding – propaganda promoter

Szondi (2008) examines the two concepts of nation branding and public diplomacy as two emerging fields of study, although traditional public diplomacy as a discipline developed a few decades earlier than nation branding. In a lecture Snow delivered in Tokyo (in 2013), the two terms (nation branding and public diplomacy) are used interchangeably as if they are a two-faced coin. In 1963, Edward R. Murrow, a director of the USIA, stated that 'Public diplomacy ... involves interaction not only with governments but primarily with nongovernmental individuals and organisations' (Leonard et al., 2002: 1). Leonard et al. (2005: v) address the necessity for governments to communicate to the public and to extract 'a premium from their national reputation'. Sceptics consider such involvement as a government's 'manipulation' of its nation image (O'Shaughnessy and O'Shaughnessy, 2000).

In comparison, nation branding is a people-to-people process, requiring the coordination of governments and a wide range of individual and institutional stakeholders (Anholt and Hildreth, 2004). Different parts of a nation's identity come to the attention of consumers at different times as a result of political events, media news and entertainment. To manage the impact of disseminated news about a nation or its nation image, Kotler et al. (1999) suggest the implementation of an image-management programme, employing a process of researching, segmenting, targeting, positioning and communicating the place's benefits to a target audience.

The challenge of such a high-involvement approach from government and non-government institutions is the issue of propaganda. It is a major limitation in political marketing as it may allow a group of people to manipulate a society and a nation (Baines et al., 2010). Propaganda was of central importance to Italy's Fascist dictatorship – in his article 'Mobilizing the Nation: Italian Propaganda in the Great War', Thomas Row (2002: 169) examines Fascist propaganda based on an examination of artwork and visual adverts in a historical study, exploring the role of propagandist art during and following the First World War in Italy. Harris and Lock (2010: 297) address such manipulation as 'the black arts of propaganda'. Social pressure groups may also use a mixture of marketing and propaganda or a marketing/propaganda hybrid (O'Shaughnessy, 1999) to change a government policy. Baines et al. (2010) argue that even terrorist organisations utilise political marketing/propaganda techniques to recruit sympathisers or even would-be suicide bombers, mainly through persuasive audio-visual communications.

NATION-BRANDING APPLICATIONS AND PLACE MARKETING
Branding destinations

Destinations are places, and destination branding, in most cases, focuses on places' unique offers and characteristics. Some of these characteristics may be directly related to the inhabitants of the place and those delivering these offers. With a focus on place, it is easy to define place branding. Papadopoulos (2004) defines it as the broad set of marketing efforts that local government and businesses of a country, region or city apply to market the places they represent. The aim of marketing a place may be to encourage all types of inward investment, tourism or international trade, for example UK Trade and Investment efforts to market the UK as a business-friendly place and as a stable international trade partner.

Destination branding, on the other hand, is more specific. It is a sector-based type of branding that aspires to highlight what places stand out for in a specific sector, whether tourism, investment or trade. For example, Brazil is known for its music and vibrant culture but it has an issue with a high crime rate which has affected its information technology (IT) industry. This has led Brazil's IT and technological innovation institutions, such as the Brazilian Association of Information Technology and Communication Companies (Brasscom), to market Brazil as a destination for IT to the global IT market, targeting IT businesses to encourage business-to-business transactions and collaborations.

Being focused on one sector, destination branding requires engagement with a relatively limited number of stakeholders – in comparison with nation branding, destinations' stakeholders are usually expected to be relevant to the sector. For example, a tourism destination involves tourism authorities, tour operators, the hospitality and entertainment industry, and environmental bodies.

The sustainability of destination offerings is a dilemma faced by destination marketers. Branding can offer a competitive edge and highlight a destination's unique selling points, but if its promises are not met through the customer experience, whether tourists, investors or buyers, there will be no sustained business. Destination branding depends not only on the uniqueness of the place, but also more importantly on its substance and the destination's ability to deliver and sustain what the slogan promises (Cai, 2009).

Digital Focus 12.1

Tourism in Belize

With its sandy beaches, Belize is a typical Caribbean destination offer for tourists. However, the Belize Tourism Board and its marketing agency, Olson, decided to change tourists' expectations by highlighting the unique experiences Belize has to offer through a destination marketing campaign, to reposition Belize as the place to be to re-discover yourself. They also made flying to the country easier by working with Southwest airlines and WestJet airlines to open more routes and direct flights to Belize from the USA and Canada.

Belize launched 'Discover How To Be', a campaign that showcased the natural and cultural wonder tourists can expect to experience there. The campaign is built around a series of videos that allow the audience to experience moments of aspiring to live in a world with rich nature, culture and heritage, a place of adventure and natural beauty. The campaign is designed to leverage technology and digital marketing in destination branding and communication to increase the number of tourists visiting Belize.

Belize Tourism Board targeted new segments and niche markets to attract more adventurous tourists from the USA and Canada, and capitalise on the usual tourist segments showing them what else they can experience other than the usual beach holiday. Being a small Caribbean country, Belize needed to connect with well-defined target segments through detailed online profiling, sharing with them the unique experiences the country has to offer.

Videos proved to be one of the most effective online communication tools with more than 1 billion hours spent on watching videos watched daily on YouTube alone (Youtube, 2017;

(Continued)

(Continued)

Bergman, 2017). The Belize video campaign, shown on the official website of the Tourism Board, and shared over a wide range of social networks (see Table 12.1), each targeting a specific segment of users, generated a wide enough audience base to secure an 8.7% average annual growth in Belize tourism between 2012 and 2015. The increase was 321,000 tourists in 2014, a trend that has continued. In 2016, the country's GDP increased by 2.24%, as reported by the Central Bank of Belize, due to the tourism boost.

Table 12.1   Social networks utilised in Belize's destination-branding campaign

Youtube
Facebook
Twitter
Instagram
Pinterest
Snapchat
Vine

Kevin McKeon, chief creative officer at Olson, summarises the campaign message: 'We set rules from the beginning – no honeymooners, no frozen drinks, nobody getting a massage by the pool. We want to go for someone who's a little more ambitious about what they're looking for in a vacation. The takeaway is you're going to meet some fascinating people and come back with a story you didn't expect to have.' 'The locals are so passionate about their country, and that adds to the campaign because you can see their passion', adds Karen Bevans, director of tourism at the Belize Tourism Board. Targeting ambitious holiday seekers who are looking for a different experience and eager to meet the locals and experience their culture continues with videos featuring the likes of a Belizean climbing a tree upside down and cutting down coconuts.

Sources: Birkner (2016), Moreno and Larrieu (2016), and www.belizetourismboard.org

Questions for discussion

1. The case suggests that Belize's campaign 'Discover How To Be' increased the number of tourists to Belize. What impact do you think the campaign had on positioning Belize as a tourism destination?

2. Video content is key to engaging customers with the Belize national identity and culture. The campaign assumed that videos are part of choosing a destination. On reflection, in your own experience do you agree with this assumption? Why or why not?

3.   The campaign attracted more than a hundred thousand followers on social networks. Why have none of these videos gone viral and achieved millions of views? Would viral video be useful in achieving this campaign's goal? Why or why not?

You will find some of these videos at: www.travelbelize.org

State policies and public diplomacy

Anholt (2007) focuses on the synergy between public diplomacy and other activities that represent the nation internationally in terms of international trade, tourism, and so forth. This synergy combines three main components of a nation's life: commerce, culture and politics.

Halsall (2008: 17) considers 'nation branding' as the new justice that allows nations to redistribute the world's wealth more fairly, proffering the need of countries, cities and regions to manage their reputations, the ultimate stage of 'post-colonial capitalism'. Halsall (2008) challenges the cultural discourse of the 'brand state' – as expressed by consultancy Place Brands, which mixes brand management and development policy to redefine the nation purely as a business location. Indeed, 'the tendency to see the nation as a brand', according to Halsall (2008: 26), 'stems largely from ignorance, from the fact that contemporary consumers of the global media actually know very little if anything about other nations and cultures'. This means that '[n]ation branding is not just the benevolent application of marketing tools to improve the images of nations' (Halsall, 2008: 27); rather, it adopts an ideological perspective that assumes a nation should be run like a company. For example, the UAE derives from a post-colonial settlement that adopts the assumed link between economic gains and culture within the capitalist models of the 1990s, which were exported from one culture to another and led to the 'brand state'. As stated by the Prime Minister and Ruler of Dubai (Kroft, 2007), the country is run as a corporation that aims to achieve the vision of its leader.

Running a country as a company suggests an ideological difference in understanding nation branding. The nation-state is reconceptualised as a corporation, where the role of politicians is to manage the brand and manipulate the nation's international image (van Ham, 2001); however, politicians tend to have a short life cycle while a national vision, as it is in a corporate vision, is long term and requires a long-term commitment to the same priorities.

Politicians also tend to look inwards for leverage in their political campaign and prioritise some local interests, whereas the globalised market has forced many companies to adopt an international outlook; the global market exerts a strong and magnetic force. Companies that have taken the decision to avoid internationalisation or global trends have found themselves alienated from the mainstream and have faced multinational corporations who have far greater resources to compete with.

Cultural diplomacy

Shared cultural values, customs and other common dominators help in shaping a nation's identity and in understanding the motivations behind differences in lifestyle, ideology and policy (Hurn, 2016; Cassinger and Eksell, 2017). Independent cultural activities free from state intervention underline the influential power of culture (Bound et al., 2007). Intervention from government authorities, social institutions and opinion leaders as part of a nation-branding programme may undermine this power and its authentic representation of the nation. The existence of a cultural ministry, according to a study of art and nation branding by Ahn and Wu (2015: 168), 'had a negative influence on the effect of the creative sector output on the country's brand value'. A possible approach to limiting the potential use of culture as a means to serve public policy and diplomacy (cultural diplomacy) is for cultural institutions and others in this sector to collaborate in the process of relevant policy making. Although, in the long run, this may blur the distinction between the interests of these parties and lead to less independence.

One of the most effective cultural diplomacy ambassadors, as seen in the experience of the British Council, is higher education. Williams, et al. (2012) appreciate the role that higher education institutional brands such as Kwame Nkrumah University of Science and Technology (KNUST) play in brand Africa and Ghana. They also argue that to change a negative nation image (e.g. corrupt and unsafe), having stakeholders including academics, celebrities and sports stars (Fetscherin and Marmier, 2010; Osei and Gbadamosi, 2011) effectively and positively representing the nation brand individually and in groups can create success stories, as they do for multinational corporations (Omar et al., 2009; Williams et al., 2012). Such institutions and personalities reflect the nation's culture and capabilities, offering an opportunity to build credibility and eventually change a nation's image.

Case Study 12.1

The 'GREAT Britain' campaign

The UK's GREAT Britain campaign was launched in 2012 to capitalise on the publicity and positive image that the London 2012 Olympic Games provided. The campaign's aim is to communicate the distinctive and appealing characteristics of the UK and to capitalise on a favourable market position. The London 2012 Olympics was a great success, offering the UK a unique opportunity to communicate what the UK can be great at, and appealing to today's target audiences: creativity, technology, innovation, entrepreneurship, culture and heritage. The end goals of the campaign are to achieve a direct economic return, positively influence the buying intentions and preferences of the target audience, and increase UK brand value.

It is suggested that the GREAT Britain campaign is the British government's most ambitious international marketing campaign thus far. It was developed to stimulate growth and employment. It highlights the best the UK has to offer to encourage the world and, more precisely, its target audiences to visit, study in, invest in and trade with the UK. This is a highly complex process as to achieve consistency, effectiveness and efficiency in raising brand awareness, being true to the brand identity and emphasising a clear brand position, extensive coordination among over 20 government departments and over 350 private and public partners in 144 markets around the world was needed.

The campaign resulted in collaboration among a wide range of institutions and government bodies. Her Majesty's Treasury, the Foreign and Commonwealth Office, UK Trade and Investment, the Cabinet Office, the British Council, the Department for International Trade, and the Department for Digital, Culture, Media and Sport are just some of these bodies. Coordination among these bodies allows the campaign to convey a unified message that emphasises a clear brand position in the global market and attains the objectives of the campaign.

The designed logo provided the brand with a unified voice that helps in establishing awareness and stimulating interest, particularly with the word 'Great', which offers relevance in meaning and direct association with the country name. It also links the past with the present and future as it is easily relatable to the British Empire heritage, today's creativity and culture, and future innovations. 'Great' is memorable and wide in scope which reflects a wider vision where Great can continue to expand and progress in the long term. To secure the association with Britain, the logo includes the British flag which is recognised worldwide.

In its efforts to publicise the campaign, disseminate and emphasise the value of greatness, the campaign's website offers organisations access to high-quality images of the logo to be used in a wide range of promotional activities. This helps to showcase what is great in Great Britain and what the British are great at, for example, 'Study is GREAT' and 'Music is GREAT'.

Through the GREAT Britain campaign, Visit Britain is drawing on the key triggers for travel to Britain – culture, heritage and countryside – alongside shopping, food, sport, adventure and music in order to: build awareness of Britain's attractiveness as a tourism destination among those who have not yet visited Britain; encourage prior visitors to return; and provide a series of opportunities and incentives to visit Britain in partnership with the private sector.

(Continued)

(Continued)

The Department for International Trade launched an international, interactive digital service online (www.great.gov.uk) to familiarise international buyers and sellers with the British market and offer local businesses practical advice for entering the global market. This service includes a searchable export directory, the 'Find a Supplier' tool for international businesses to identify their perfect trade partner, sector-based information to help international investors navigate the UK market from food to technology with ease and make informed decisions, while an overseas sales service, country guides and export opportunities are also shared online, and investment support service is offered.

Many companies partnered with the Great campaign and showcased for international trade and investment such as Touch Bionics, an innovative and world-leading British provider of prosthetic technologies in the health and life science sector, with revenue exceeding £39 billion and over 107,000 jobs. Another international company showcased in the campaign is a Danish energy company, Dong Energy, the largest wind developer worldwide with the largest portfolio of offshore wind farms in the UK.

The campaign started by targeting two obvious major markets with strong economic growth and collaboration opportunities, building on assumptions rather than robust research to secure return on investment. However, as the campaign progressed, it became evident that target markets were prioritised, securing a higher return on investment, such as the USA, Germany, Brazil and France. The Department for International Trade, for example, created pages for its priority markets: Brazil, India, China, Germany, Japan, Spain and the USA. This is in addition to dedicated translated content in Chinese, German, Japanese, Spanish and Portuguese, highlighting UK investment opportunities.

By 2017, the campaign reported a return of £2.2 billion to the British economy (great.gov.uk) on an investment of £133.5 million up to 2016 (DBA, 2016). This is due to a 16% increase in intentions to visit and invest in the UK, and a 12% increase in intentions to procure British products (DBA, 2016).

For more information read: Yeldar, R. (2015), Great Britain Campaign: creating impact for Britain around the world, *DBA Design Effectiveness Award Entry 2016*; and see www.greatbritaincampaign.com; www.gov.uk/government/news/new-campaign-highlights-trade-and-investment-opportunities-in-global-britain; www.great.gov.uk; and www.visitbritain.org/introducing-great-tourism-campaign

Questions for discussion

1. In relation to the different types of nation-branding practices reviewed in this chapter, would you classify the GREAT Britain campaign as a nation-branding programme? Why or why not?
2. Discuss how effective the GREAT Britain logo is in representing British identity and aspirations.

3. It is not clear how the campaign's return on investment is calculated. Do you believe that the hundreds of millions invested in the campaign are justified?

4. Suggest other effective marketing approaches which are less demanding financially that could promote Britain industries and culture.

5. How long do you think the GREAT Britain campaign will last, and why?

SUMMARY OF KEY IDEAS

- This chapter highlights the important role branding plays in raising nations' profiles to attract favourable interest from the rest of the world, in particular any target markets. Place branding, for example, helps market tourism and foreign investment destinations, and cultural nation branding widens the effect of cultural diplomacy in reaching other nations and building bridges across cultures.

- The chapter demonstrates the underpinning ideologies that affect nation-brand applications and effectiveness, whether by taking a strategic approach where the nation brand is embedded in a nation's long-term development vision and plan, or by creating a short-term campaign to market a specific sector to particular target markets.

- The chapter also explores common applications of nation branding and place marketing that aim to change a nation's international image and target market perceptions of the nation's people and/or state, and to influence the consumption experience of the campaign, national people and places. Relevant examples of such applications are given throughout the chapter to enhance the reader's understanding.

- The chapter critically evaluates the concept of nation branding and its applications, addressing some of the challenges such a complex marketing endeavour faces and the serious social and national implications that may result from cultural and social dynamic changes or resources and environmental challenges.

Chapter Discussion Questions

1. Why do governments seek the services of nation- and place-branding consultants, and what are the benefits of having a nation-branding programme?

2. As a nation-branding consultant, you have been approached by Vladimir Putin's administration to work on a nation-branding programme that informs Russia's public diplomacy to improve the country's international relations. Working with such a powerful and influential country is a dream come true for your consultancy career. Discuss how you would approach such a request and form a decision to accept the job or not, and if you accept it consider what approach you would take to develop such a programme.

3. What are the different applications of nation branding? Explain them with examples.
4. Think of your local area or a village you are familiar with, identify the development needs of the place and its local people, then discuss what you can apply from what you have learned in this chapter to help the local area achieve its ambitions or face its challenges.
5. Critically evaluate nation-branding concepts and practices and consider the future of this phenomenon in the long term.

REFERENCES

Ahn, M. J. and Wu, H. C. (2015) The art of nation branding: National branding value and the role of government and the arts of culture and sector. *Public Organisation Review*, *15*(1), 157–74.

Al-Abdulrazak, R. M. (2016) The Branded Nation: A Comparative Analysis with Reference to Syria and the United Arab Emirates. Thesis, University of London.

Al-Abdulrazak, R. M. (2018) *Is the promise of nation branding sustainable?* In 6th International Conference on Contemporary Marketing Issues (ICCMI), Athens, Greece, 27–29 June.

Anderson, B. (2006) *Imagined Communities: Reflections on the Origin and Spread of Nationalism*. New York: Verso Books.

Anholt, S. (2003) Elastic brands: How far can you stretch the idea of 'brand'? *Brand Strategy*, 28–29 February.

Anholt, S. (2005) *Brand New Justice: How Branding Places and Products can Help the Developing World*. Oxford: Elsevier Butterworth-Heinemann.

Anholt, S. (2007) *Competitive Identity: The New Brand Management of Nations, Cities and Regions* Basingstoke: Palgrave Macmillan.

Anholt, S. (2009) Endnote: Nation 'branding': Propaganda or statecraft? *Public Diplomacy Magazine*, No. 2, Summer, 88–90.

Anholt, S. and Hildreth, J. (2004) *Brand America: The Mother of all Brands*. London: Cyan Communications.

Baines, P. R., O'Shaughnessy, N. J., Moloney, K., Richards, B., Butler, S. and Gill, M. (2010) The dark side of political marketing: Islamist propaganda, reversal theory and British Muslims. *European Journal of Marketing*, *44*(3), 478–95.

Bergman, S. (2017) We spend a billion hours a Day on YouTube, more than Netflix and Facebook video combined, Forbes. Available at: https://www.forbes.com/sites/sirenabergman/2017/02/28/we-spend-a-billion-hours-a-day-on-youtube-more-than-netflix-and-facebook-video-combined/#10ac3b0b5ebd (accessed 11 May 2019).

Birkner, C. (2016) This Tourism Campaign's 'No Beachside Honeymooners' Rule Boosted Belize's GDP, Promoting the Culture and More Direct Flights', Brand Marketing. ADWEEK, 26 August. Available at: www.adweek.com/brand-marketing/tourism-campaigns-no-beachside-honeymooners-rule-boosted-belizes-gdp-173150 (accessed 29 July 2018).

Bound, K., Briggs, R., Holden, J. and Jones, S. (2007) Cultural Diplomacy. *Demos report.* Available at: www.demos.co.uk/files/Cultural_diplomacy_-_web.pdf (accessed 2 May 2019).

Cai, L. A. (2009) Tourism branding in social exchange system. In L. A. Cai, W. C. Gartner and A. M. Munar (eds), *Tourism Branding: Communities in Action.* Bingley, UK: Emerald Group Publishing, pp. 89–104.

Cassinger, C. and Eksell, J. (2017) The magic of place branding: Regional brand identity in transition. *Journal of Place Management and Development*, 10(3), 202–12.

Cohen, E. and Neal, M. (2012) A Middle Eastern Muslim tourist enclave in Bangkok. *Tourism Geographies*, 14(4), 570–98.

Dinnie, K. (2008) *Nation Branding: Concepts, Issues, Practice.* London: Butterworth-Heinemann-Elsevier.

Fan, Y. (2006) Branding the nation: What is being branded? *Journal of Vacation Marketing*, 11(5), 543–61.

Fetscherin, M. and Marmier, P. (2010) Switzerland's nation branding initiative to foster science and technology, higher education and innovation: A case study. *Place Branding and Public Diplomacy*, 6(1), 58–67.

Foroudi, P., Gupta, S., Kitchen, P., Foroudi, M. M. and Nguyen, B. (2016) A framework of place branding, place image, and place reputation: Antecedents and moderators. *Qualitative Market Research*, 19(2), 241–64.

Halsall, R. (2008) From 'business culture' to 'brand state': Conceptions of nation and culture in business literature on cultural differences. *Culture and Organisations*, 14(1), 15–30.

Harris, P. and Lock, A. (2010) 'Mind the gap': The rise of political marketing and a perspective on its future agenda. *European Journal of Marketing*, 44(3–4), 297–307.

Hurn, B. J. (2016) The role of cultural diplomacy in nation branding. *Industrial and Commercial Training*, 48(2), 80–5.

Klein, N. (2000/2010) *No Logo.* London: Fourth Estate/Harper Collins.

Kotler, P. and Levy, S. J. (1969) Broadening the concept of marketing. *Journal of Marketing*, 33(1), 10–15.

Kotler, P., Aspland, C., Rein, I. and Haider, D. H. (1999) *Marketing Places Europe: Attracting Investment, Industry, and Tourism to European Cities, States and Nations.* Upper Saddle River, NJ: Financial Times/Prentice Hall.

Kotler, P., Jatsuripitak, S. and Maesincee, S. (1997) *The Marketing of Nations: A Strategic Approach to Building National Wealth.* New York: The Free Press.

Kroft, S. (2007) Dubai 60 Minutes: A Visit To Dubai Inc. Steve Kroft reports on a success story in the Middle East, *CBS News*, originally broadcast October; updated 30 July 2008, re-broadcast 3 August 2008. Available at: www.cbsnews.com/stories/2007/10/12/60minutes/main3361753.shtml (accessed 20 May 2009).

Leonard, M., Small, A. and Rose, M. (2005) *British Public Diplomacy: In the Age of Schicisms*. London: The Foreign Policy Centre.

Leonard, M., Stead, C. and Smewing, C. (2002) *Public Diplomacy*. London: The Foreign Policy Centre.

Lugar, R. G. (2009) Public diplomacy: The next 100 days. *Public Diplomacy Magazine*, No. 2, summer, 6–7.

Moreno, J. M. and Larrieu, M. (2016) Belize and the importance of video marketing in tourism campaigns. In *Destination Branding: A Compilation of Success Stories*, coordinated by J. L. R. Real, IBRAV and Erasmus+ programme of the European Union.

O'Shaughnessy, J. and O'Shaughnessy, N. J. (2000) Treating the nation as a brand: Some neglected issues. *Journal of Macromarketing*, 20(1), 56–64.

O'Shaughnessy, N. (1999) Political marketing and political propaganda. In B. Newman (ed.), *Handbook of Political Marketing*. Thousand Oaks, CA: Sage.

Odia, E. O. and Isibor, F. O. (2014) Strategic approach to nation branding: A case of the Nigerian brand. *International Journal of Business and Management*, 9(3), 204–16.

Olins, W. (1999) *Trading Identities: Why Countries and Companies are Taking Each Others' Roles*. London: The Foreign Policy Centre.

Omar, M., Williams, R. and Lingelbach, D. (2009) Global brand market entry strategy to manage corporate reputation. *Journal of Product and Brand Management*, 18(3), 177–87.

Osei, C. and Gbadamosi, A. (2011) Re-branding Africa. *Marketing Intelligence and Planning*, 29(3), 281–304.

Papadopoulos, N. (2004) Place branding: Evolution, meaning and implications. *Place Branding*, 1(1), 36–49.

Potter, E. H. (2009) Navigating the middle: A new architecture for Canadian public diplomacy. *Public Diplomacy Magazine*, No. 2, summer, 36–40.

Rasmussen, R. K. and Merkelsen, H. (2012) The new PR of states: How nation branding practices affect the security function of public diplomacy. *Public Relations Review*, 38(5), 810–18.

Row, T. (2002) Mobilizing the nation: Italian propaganda in the great war. *Journal of Decorative and Propaganda Arts*, 24, 141–69.

Schaar, J. H. (1981) The case for patriotism. In J. H. Schaar (ed.), *Legitimacy in the Modern State*. New Brunswick, NJ: Transaction Press.

Schooler, R. D. (1965) Product bias in the Central American common market. *Journal of Marketing Research*, 2(4), 394–7.

Schooler, R. D. (1971) Bias phenomena attendant to the marketing of foreign goods in the US. *Journal of International Business Studies*, 2(1), 71–81.

Sheresheva, M. Y. and Polukhina A. N. (2018) *Marketing issues of sustainable tourism development in Russian regions*. In *6th International Conference on Contemporary Marketing Issues (ICCMI)*, Athens, Greece, 27–29 June.

Smith, C. (2018) 160+ YouTube stats and facts (May 2018): by the number. DMR, Business Statistics, 30 July. Available at: https://expandedramblings.com/index.php/youtube-statistics/, (accessed 30 July 2018).

Snow, N. (2013) Japan: The super nation brand. Public lecture video, Institute of Contemporary Asian Studies (ICAS), Temple University, Japan, 11 November. Available at: www.youtube.com/watch?v=iNC6kQU0C_o (accessed 18 August 2014).

Szondi, G. (2008) Public diplomacy and nation branding: Conceptual similarities and differences, Discussion Papers in Diplomacy. *The Hague: Netherlands Institute of International Relations, 'Clingendael'*. Available at: www.kamudiplomasisi.org/pdf/nationbranding.pdf (accessed 1 May 2019).

Tecmen, A. (2017) Nation branding and right to brand: Brand Turkey. *Research and Policy on Turkey*, 2(1), 76–89.

Van Ham, P. (2001) The rise of the brand state: The postmodern politics of image and reputation. *Foreign Affairs*, 80(5), 2–6.

Van Ham, P. (2002) Branding territory: Inside the wonderful worlds of PR and IR theory, Millennium. *Journal of International Studies*, 31(2), 246–69.

Van Ham, P. (2005) Branding European power: Opinion piece. *Place Branding*, 1(2), 122–6.

Van Ham, P. (2008a) Place branding: The state of the art. *Annals of the American Academy of Political and Social Science*, 616(March), 126–49.

Van Ham, P. (2008b) Place branding within a security paradigm: Concepts and cases. *Place Branding and Public Diplomacy*, 4(3), 240–51.

Viroli, M. (2003) *For Love of Country: An Essay on Patriotism and Nationalism*. New York: Oxford University Press.

Visvanathan, S. (2006) Nation. *Theory, Culture and Society*, 23(2–3), 533–8.

Weil, S. (1952) *The Need for Roots*. London Routledge.

Williams, Jr., R., Osei, C. and Omar, M. (2012) Higher education institutions' branding as a component of country branding in Ghana: Renaming Kwame Nkrumah University of Science & Technology. *Journal of Marketing for Higher Education*, 22(1), 71–81.

YouTube (2017) You know what's cool? A billion, Official Blog, Monday, February 27, available at: https://youtube.googleblog.com/2017/02/you-know-whats-cool-billion-hours.html (accessed 11 May 2019).

13
ARTS MARKETING

Nnamdi O. Madichie

Learning Objectives

At the end of this chapter, you should be able to understand and discuss:

- The ongoing debate between the notion of 'arts marketing' vis-à-vis 'marketing of the arts'
- Various art forms – visual, poetry, literature, music and the performing arts, and any intersections between these
- The varied challenges across diverse art forms and the debates surrounding these
- How to mitigate identified challenges confronting the arts marketing discipline

---

INTRODUCTION

The main preoccupation of this chapter is to explore, highlight and situate 'arts' in the broader business and management framework. The chapter explores and highlights the place of arts in the business and management discipline, taken from the perspective of marketing management. The chapter follows in the tradition of non-business disciplines that have now been appropriated into the business and management curriculum, such as events management, sports marketing and/or management, film marketing and, more recently, the creative industry. Most of these adjacent disciplines have now become titles of numerous business and management journals and texts. For example, in the Emerald portfolio a journal dedicated to the study of the arts, i.e. *Arts Marketing: An International Journal*, which launched in 2010, morphed into a more befitting title, *Arts and the Market,* only five years later in 2015 – thus reflecting a sign of the times. Indeed, the fifth volume featured a Special Issue on 'Design of titles, teasers and trailers'.[1] Interestingly, and related to the need to shed some light on what arts marketing entails, another Special Issue on 'Music, culture and heritage',[2] was published in 2015. What this means is that arts transcend mere drawing and painting, i.e. visual and still arts. Performing arts (theatre, dance, film and music) have become a 'new normal' of cultural products and/or production, embellished with heritage cues – and sometimes discussed under the label of 'creative industries'.

However, even as the arts market grows and gathers wider global recognition, there remain voids to be filled as the discipline transits from the margins to the mainstream. For example, scholars such as Sozuer (2017) observed 300,000 global art dealings, less than 2 per cent (about 5000) of which accounts for about 80 per cent of total sales (see Figure 13.1). This obviously warrants further research enquiry – some of which is touched upon in this chapter. It has also been suggested that there is a need to forge strategic alliances wherever possible, in the view that such partnerships should be between institutions supported by an online presence to secure the bottom line. To achieve this objective, however, there are two key ingredients for success – aspiration and persistence. In addition to these ingredients is, arguably, creativity, as pointed out by Robert Dex (see Images 13.1–13.3):[3]

A disused petrol station is being transformed into a contemporary art gallery as part of the multi-million-pound regeneration of White City in London. Staff from *Elephant Magazine* will curate a series of shows in the building, renamed Elephant West, when it opens in the autumn, including film screenings and dance performances.

For the former two, i.e. aspiration and persistence, art galleries were the main focus of Aytug Sozuer's study on contemporary art taken from the purview of the Turkish city of Istanbul (see Sozuer, 2017), which shows that the annual sales volume in the global art market between 2007 and 2016 was around US$60 billion. Research has also shown that the annual sales volume in the global art market within this period was around US$60 billion on average (McAndrew, 2017; Sozuer, 2017). According to Sozuer (2017), 'almost 85 percent of sales is realised only in three countries – namely the United States, China and the United Kingdom'. These countries form the backdrop of the vignettes/boxes dotted across this chapter.

It is worth highlighting, however, that the art gallery management practices investigated by Resch (2016a, b) demonstrate how small steps can be effective. Indeed, Sozuer (2017) argued that art galleries 'should adopt [a] *state-of-the-art* business making rule'. In other words, there is a need for professionalisation of all functions from marketing and public relations

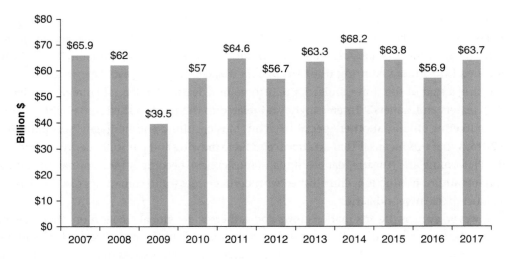

Figure 13.1 Sales in the global art market 2007–17

Source: Arts Economics (2018). Retrieved from: www.artsy.net/article/artsy-editorial-art-market-hit-637-billion-2017-key-takeaways-art-basel-report

Image 13.1 Street art gallery

Source: www.standard.co.uk/go/london/arts/a-disused-petrol-station-has-been-turned-into-a-contemporary-art-gallery-in-west-london-a3839566.html

to legal and general management of the arts. Overall, therefore, this chapter explores and documents various dimensions of the arts and the marketing of the 'cultural' product in its various forms, notably art forms.

In the first section, some discussion of the commonly confused art form (i.e. still art or drawing and painting), and the marketing of this, is undertaken. In the second section, an attempt is made to highlight the place of art within the context of the creative industry (book publishing, film production and animation, music, theatre and even fashion). The third section is dedicated to another art form, which is poetry and/or literature. The emphasis here is on books, fairs and script writing, which paves the way for the next section with its emphasis on the enactment of these scripts. In the fourth section, the focus shifts towards entertainment of the performing arts (notably film and music production and consumption).

The methodological consideration follows in the tradition of Preece and Kerrigan (2015: 1213), which, in itself, 'follows previous studies of the art market, including Plattner's (1998) call for an ethnographic study of artists' careers'. Furthermore, Fillis (2011) specifically recommended the use of biographical and narrative methods (arguably poetics) to examine entrepreneurial marketing and applied this approach to the study of artists in a previous study (see Fillis, 2004). Since the interpretive research process offers an open, flexible and experiential approach, the examination of the dynamic nature of the careers and relationships through which the artistic brand is constructed can be effectively achieved with this approach.

'ARTS MARKETING' AND THE 'MARKETING OF ARTS': CLEARING UP THE CONFUSION

In this section, some discussion of the commonly confused art form (i.e. still art or drawing and painting) and its marketing is undertaken. Four key studies have been used in the development of this section – notably Butler (2000), which explored the marketing of the arts from a demand perspective; and Fillis (2006) who highlights the dichotomy of the arts for its own sake or for business. The remaining two studies call for a rethink of arts marketing in a changing cultural landscape (see Lee, 2005a and b), and the construction of artistic brands (Preece and Kerrigan, 2015). Fillis (2006: 36) explored 'the debate surrounding the art for art's sake versus art for business sake philosophies found within the industry, with particular emphasis on the visual arts'. He points out that 'New art marketing theory needs to be constructed around ... the realisation that the artist and the artwork are the focus of consumption, and not the consumer as modelled in marketing frameworks'. Barrere and Santagata (1999: 35; cf. Fillis, 2006: 36) distinguish art versus market orientation:

> Freedom from the market is sought by carrying out the antieconomic logic of 'art pour l'art' ... praising ... that which is creative against that which is saleable ... The artist is indifferent to ... commercial success ... Market dependence ... induces artists and art collectors to become managers of themselves. They spend their time controlling the system of sales and the process of valorisation of their works of art. (Fillis, 2006: 34)

In discussing the philosophy of 'Art for Art's Sake Marketing', Fillis (2006: 35) argues that 'within the network of forces impacting on the artwork, the gallery owner is seen as having an important part to play, with interpretation and mediation impacting on the process of converting art into product'. He goes on to highlight that 'other contributing factors include the way in which the art product is exhibited and the amount of recognition given by critics in terms of style, quality and suggested interpretation'.

Art critics (and dealers or curators) are gatekeepers, as illustrated in the construction of the artistic brand in Figure 13.2 where the diffusion process is shown to spread from the brand identity to the consuming audience. As part of this process, the artist and

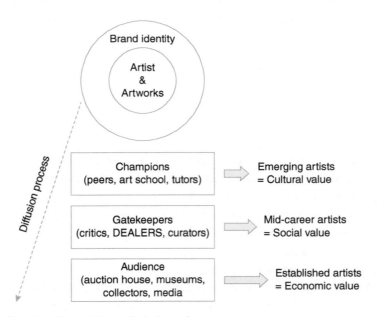

Figure 13.2   Construction of the artistic brand

Source: Preece and Kerrigan (2015: 1225)

his/her artworks filter down through champions such as art tutors or art schools, to these gate-keepers (including art critics, art dealers and curators), before finally reaching the arts audiences.

Preece and Kerrigan (2015: 1226) sum up their ascription to artistic brands in terms of the artist and their artworks, and the diffusion process emanating thereof as follows:

> Artistic brands make the first steps towards demonstrating concrete ways in which a brand can be positioned and perceived as legitimate and the difficulties in this process, particularly in highlighting that a person brand cannot be constructed by one person alone but must be socially co-constructed and negotiated by a variety of individuals, including its consumers.[4]

According to these authors, there is a focus on the interplay between the product, the producer (the artist) and the stakeholders, notably the audience and gatekeepers (see Figure 13.3 on the 'Daisywheel model of artistic brand stakeholders'), and the way these come together to create a mythical narrative of which the artist is the protagonist. Other stakeholders have also been identified to include institutions such as the media and the museum, as well as art dealers and the 3Cs (curators, collectors, critics). As Preece and Kerrigan (2015) point out, this multiple interaction enables the development of a process through which value is created, co-created, experienced and consumed. Artists may appear to make mythologies but their

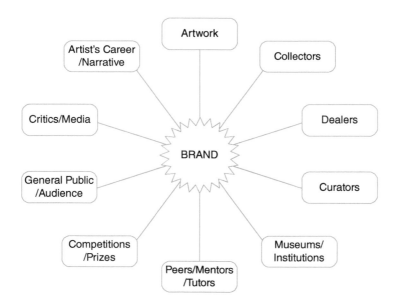

Figure 13.3   Daisywheel model of artistic brand stakeholders

Source: Preece and Kerrigan (2015: 1218)

actions alone are not sufficient to mythologise the artwork; this process occurs through multiple interactions in culturally and historically situated contexts. Indeed, as Mañjon and Crum (2017) point out, 'the model of a successful artist has changed'.

Artists have forged an entrepreneurial quest – paving the way for the term ARTrepreneur,[5] whose attributes, among many others, include working collaboratively with other parties such as arts organisations and artists. These authors highlight the need for educators interested in supporting the entrepreneurial dreams of artists to de-mystify the passion-centred trajectory, stress that commodifying their craft is not creative blasphemy, and explain that the art world is not grounded in meritocracy. Collaboration was also pointed out as being the key to success (Mañjon and Crum, 2017). Such collaborative initiatives, especially with critics and curators, may take many forms including poetry, which is discussed next.

ART FORMS: POETRY AS ART

Although rather fragmented, the interactions between poetry and the arts have been highlighted in the literature from those between poetry and music (Masserman, 1986), styles in poetry, painting and music (Martindale, 1990), to writings through music, poetry and art (see the edited volume by Bernstein and Hatch, 2010). In a study on poetry as music, Masserman (1986) argued that 'poetry and music are thematically and philosophically related in their abilities to be used as therapeutic modalities and satisfy an individual's physical, social, and existential needs'. This link between poetry and music is also extended to the realm of painting and architecture in the work of Martindale (1990) on the predictability of artistic change. In that study, Martindale (1990) sought to establish what determined the evolution of styles in poetry, music and architecture as well as whether there were universal laws of art history to which 'even Shakespeare, Beethoven, and Picasso were subject'.

Furthermore, Bernstein and Hatch (2010), in their article 'Writings through John Cage's music, poetry, and art', investigated the creative work of the great avant-gardist John Cage from an exciting *interdisciplinary* perspective, exploring his activities as a composer, performer, thinker and artist. Although entrepreneurially oriented and equally published in a journal with that label, one study highlights the convergence of poetry and art using aesthetics as a common denominator. According to Smith (2015: 452), 'aesthetics is related to semiotics and is concerned with an appreciation of artifactual objects establishing a link between art, creativity and entrepreneurship'. He goes on to highlight that 'Art possesses representational, expressive qualities and has form and substance'. The ongoing debate ensues as follows (Smith, 2015: 452):

- Langer (1953) suggests that art conveys various emotions, while verbal language conveys thoughts. This notion of entrepreneurship as an art form is of interest because it has long been debated whether entrepreneurship is an art or a science.
- Livesay (1982: 13) claims that entrepreneurship is an art form.
- Aldrich and Zimmer (1986) consider entrepreneurship as both an 'art' and a 'science'.
- Drucker (1985: 10) sees entrepreneurship to be 'neither a science nor an art. It is a practice'.
- Anderson and Jack (1997) view entrepreneurship to be closer to an art form than a science.

Besides the above debates on the artistry embedded in entrepreneurship, there have been a few studies around the topic of poetry (see Brown and Patterson, 2010; Brown, 2015a), the 'theoretics' of poetry (Kerrigan et al., 2011) and case illustrations such as Andy Warhol (Currid, 2007; Kerrigan et al., 2011; Foster, 2014), Pablo Picasso (Muñiz et al., 2014), John Cage (Bernstein and Hatch, 2010; Smith, 2015) J. K. Rowling (Brown and Patterson, 2010) and T. S. Eliot (Brown, 2015a). It is worth stating, however, that not all entrepreneurs are artistic, nor all artists entrepreneurial (see Smith, 2015). Furthermore, although it possesses artistic qualities, the end-point of entrepreneurial achievement is not directed towards creating art. As pointed out by Smith (2015: 452), 'cultural factors such as play, charisma and aesthetics affect identity creation [and the] entrepreneurial narrative possesses an aesthetic quality which inspires others to emulate the success embedded in the story'. It is from such a story or stories that the importance of narration (or curation) may be connected to yet another art form, i.e. poetry. For example, Smith (2015: 452–3) 'uses aesthetics to investigate an important facet of entrepreneurship from a fresh perspective – namely poetry and poetics', and points out that 'the boundary between poetry and literature is blurred'. Case Study 13.1 provides an illustration of engaging audiences with literature on TV with government support.

Case Study 13.1

Creativity in Chinese arts

In recent years, China has created a large number of products based on its cultural traditions, ranging from souvenirs developed by museums to products with modern design. Recently, *China Week: Inherit and Innovate*, a set of exhibitions that is being staged in about 30 cities around the globe, including Seoul, Brussels and Mexico City, is showcasing these products to the world. The exhibitions, which began on 10 May 2018 and run through June 2018, are organised by China Cultural Centres – the country's institutions for cultural diplomacy under

(Continued)

(Continued)

the Ministry of Culture and Tourism – in those cities (Kaihao, 2018a). In another report, an outreach programme highlighted that 'the slow pace and soft focus of a CCTV [i.e. China Central Television] literary show seem to be appealing to viewers'. Former NBA superstar Yao Ming is taking to a new kind of stage. Unconventionally, the man, who is probably one of the best recognised Chinese athletes in the international arena, is showing people another side to his personality with *The Readers*, a TV programme produced by China Central Television. He is reading a Chinese translation of *True Nobility*, a work of prose written by American novelist Ernest Hemingway (Kaihao, 2018b). Last year, the first series of *The Readers* broke the mould and taught Chinese TV audiences that a talk show does not have to simply be about amusement. Now, in its second series, the show returns with its trademark slow pace, warm touch and mesmerising vocal rhythms set in an intimate atmosphere. Dong Qing, producer, director and anchor of the show explains that the aim of the programme is to arouse people's memories of literature and allow them to cast a retrospective eye over their developing attitudes toward life.

Sources

Kaihao, W. (2018a) Exhibitions showcase traditional creativity. *China Daily*, 11 May. Available at: www.chinadaily.com.cn/cndy/2018-05/11/content_36180014.htm (accessed 18 June 2018).

Kaihao, W. (2018b) Subtle touch of 'The Readers' proves a hit. *China Daily*, 10 May. Available at: www.chinadaily.com.cn/a/201805/10/WS5af38b86a3105cdcf651d033.html (accessed 18 June 2018).

Questions for discussion

1. What benefits does the cultural diplomacy of the Chinese government bring to global arts marketing?
2. To what extent would you agree that a talk show does not have to be simply about amusement? Justify your position.

Two studies (Brown, 2007; Brown and Patterson, 2010) demonstrate capturing the power of literature in 'selling stories' and the 'retro-dominant logic of marketing' of the arts through stories. There is also mention of the power of literary criticism (see Brown, 2015 – see page 3 on funnelling Franco, which talks about 'the laws of literature' and 'the coming-of-age novel').

ART FORMS: VISUAL AND FINE ARTS

In an article entitled 'What is Art Marketing, and Why Bother?', Aletta de Wal (2012) points out some ground rules for arts marketing as involving 'a series of conversations designed to build a bridge between you, your art, and your audience' (see practitioner's perspective 13.1 for insight into an artist in residence project at a higher education institution). As one visual artist pointed out:

> when someone looks at my art, they have thoughts and feelings about what they see, how they interpret my visual message and whether or not they like it enough to buy it. I can't get inside people's heads, so I ask them to tell me what they see, feel, and think about what I have created. I watch their facial expressions and listen carefully. As soon as I can, I write their words down in my notebook, for future reference. Their words help me when I need to create marketing messages for future buyers. (de Wal, 2012)

The narrative is quite revealing: 'that's how I approach art marketing, and trust me, it's worth the effort. I do it this way because I've found that artists who market their art correctly end up with three very important things – credibility, visibility, and desirability' (de Wal, 2012).

Starting with *credibility*, the issue of trust and fair pricing are the main pillars. As for *desirability*, both allure and appeal seem to take centre stage. As the author points out:

> you need to make your work more desirable than any other artwork on the market. You need to make 'you' more interesting than other artists ... You may have the best art in the world, but if you're talking to the wrong people, you won't have a business. Conversations with the right people at the right time, in the right place, about the right things can lead to relationships. It's those relationships, carefully nurtured, that lead to sales.

In terms of visibility, De Wal (2012) points out that it 'attracts attention and relationships that lead to referrals, representation and purchases'. In other words:

> You're in charge of building your own visibility in the real world and in cyberspace. Make a point to regularly exhibit your art at appealing events in your studio, galleries, museums and alternative spaces. When you're there, start lots of conversations. You have to get the word out more than once in person, in print and online to be noticed.

Such conversations are evident in the study Cellini and Cuccia (2014: 57) on 'the relationship between the artist and the art dealer'. These authors point out that artist and art dealer are:

two members of a 'marketing channel', as defined by industrial organization and marketing science literature. The result for both parties depends on the individual effort that each of them puts in; uncoordinated effort levels are shown to result in an inefficient outcome.

It must be added, however, that the study had 'specific reference to the visual arts'. According to them (Cellini and Cuccia, 2014), interpreting the relationship between the artist and the art dealer, as being two members of a marketing channel as in the case of a painter and an art gallery manager, is imperative. Furthermore, the authors point out that:

> creation of different artistic goods, such as the creation of editorial or musical products [such as between] a writer and a publisher, or a singer and their event organizer, or a musician and the disco-producer may represent different specific examples of marketing channels in artistic fields [which share] some features with cases of manufacturing and retailing industrial production: with the success of artistic production depending on the artistic effort of the 'creator' (the manufacturer), as well as on the promotional efforts made by the retailer, be it the art dealer, the event organizer, or the publisher, on the other hand. (Cellini and Cuccia, 2014: 57)

Still on the subject of visual arts, Solkin (1993) once explored the discipline through the lens of the public in a book entitled *Painting for Money*. This view is further illuminated in another study, labelled 'Art infusion', where Hagtvedt and Patrick (2008) investigated the 'influence of visual art on the perception and evaluation' of products by consumers. Finally, Arora and Vermeylen (2013) highlight the role of the art connoisseur in a digital context (see digital focus 13.1).

Digital Focus 13.1

Digital issues around the arts

Arora and Vermeylen (2013: 194) sought to address:

> popular notions on participation and expertise concerning social media in the art world through a historical lens by re-examining and positioning art experts from past to present. Particularly, characteristics of intermediaries in the art market are looked at closely and their strategies in knowledge production and establishment of expertise. This historical situatedness enables us to move beyond the hype of new media expectations, generating more appropriate avenues of investigation to better grasp possible changes among actors within the contemporary art world.

In a separate study, He et al. (2018: 127) examine the impact of information type (dynamic verbal versus dynamic visual cues) and augmenting immersive scenes (high versus low virtual presence) on visitors' evaluation of the AR-facilitated museum experience and their subsequent purchase intentions. As augmented reality (AR) has been increasingly adopted by various industries as a marketing tool, tourism practitioners have come to recognise its promising potential in staging experiences. Despite the extensive discussions around AR's managerial implications, academic inquiry into how to adopt AR technology in museum tourism contexts remains rare. Using an experimental approach, the results demonstrate that compared with dynamic visual cues, dynamic verbal cues lead to visitors' higher levels of willingness to pay more and such an effect is more salient when environmental augmentation provides a high level of virtual presence. Such effects can be explained by the psychological mechanism of mental imagery.

Sources

Arora, P. and Vermeylen, F. (2013) The end of the art connoisseur? Experts and knowledge production in the visual arts in the digital age. *Information, Communication & Society*, 16(2), 194–214.

He, Z., Wu, L. and Li, X. R. (2018) When art meets tech: The role of augmented reality in enhancing museum experiences and purchase intentions. *Tourism Management*, 68, 127–39.

Discussion questions

1. To what extent would you agree on the impact of 'augmented reality' on museum visitor experiences?
2. Why would visitors be willing to pay higher prices? Are visual cues more effective than verbal cues?

Practitioner's Perspective 13.1

Artist in Residence Project

Fiddian Warman (Founder of the Society of Digital Artists (SoDA), is at the London School of Business and Management in Fitzrovia, London Bloomsbury where he works as Artist in Residence. Fiddian describes himself as a 'middle-class white male' who takes inclusivity seriously. He is, therefore, keen on issues related to ethnicity, diversity and inclusiveness. He encourages people to share their stories in conversational style and uses roadshows/salons

(Continued)

(Continued)

in and around London Bloomsbury, to bring these stories to life. One of these salons is the Shoeshine Stories initiative – a project where he invites both staff and students to sit down with him as he shines their shoes and chats with them about their experiences at the institution. He then articulates these stories in texts etched into the table tops and other work surfaces of the student hub and Guild Office to showcase the identity construction of the staff and students at the institution.

Source: Author online at: https://www.linkedin.com/feed/update/activity:6432287422456823808/

Questions for discussion

1. What are the pros and cons of the Shoeshine Stories?
2. Could this project be better undertaken? How and why?

Ethical Focus 13.1

From Gotham City to Gotham Town: Unintended place marketing through art

Didcot is a railway town and civil parish in the ceremonial county of Oxfordshire and the historic county of Berkshire – about 15 miles (24 km) south of Oxford, 10 miles (16 km) east of Wantage and 15 miles (24 km) north-west of Reading in the UK. It was only recently, however, that the little railway town made news headlines following an act undertaken by a street artist who used humour to change street names (see Images 13.1 and 13.2). Didcot Mayor Jackie Billington said:

> I saw it online and thought I would go and have a look but I never made it to Middle-earth ... I'm concerned that a tourist could be driving around for hours trying to find Gotham City. Someone has obviously gone to a lot of trouble. You can't tell the difference, they are exactly the same font and look like any other normal street sign.

Most residents welcomed the road sign modifications, describing the move as 'genius' and 'so cool'. Then Mayor Billington struck a more serious note, saying that ultimately taxpayers would end up paying for the fake signs' removal.

Source: Lumley, S. (10 May 2018) WTF's going on as street artist alters a city's signs. UK *Metro* Newspaper. Retrieved from: https://www.metro.news/wtfs-going-on-as-street-artist-alters-a-citys-signs/1050576/

Questions for discussion

1. There have been mixed views as to how ethical the events and signs in Didcot are. Debate these contentions and take a stand.
2. Can you explain the motivation for the artist who has been described as 'someone [who] has obviously gone to a lot of trouble', to replicate signs looking like normal street signs?
3. What does the signage say about 'art for its own sake'?

Table 13.1   Key reading (by year of publication)

Author/ Year	Title	Synopsis
Kim et al. (2018)	Why do non-profit performing arts organizations offer free public access?	This article draws on benefits theory and resource dependence theory to explore the relationships between different types of revenue and the extent to which performing arts nonprofits offer free access.

(Continued)

Table 13.1   (Continued)

Author/ Year	Title	Synopsis
Wiid and Mora-Avila (2018)	Arts marketing framework: The arts organisation as a hub for participation	This paper proposes a framework for the marketing of arts based on participation, cocreation and social networks. The arts marketing framework provides a view of art organisation in relation to its funding partners and audiences. The framework also proposes the use of social media and collaboration to create social value.
Mañjon and Crum (2017)	ARTrepreneurship: Shifting to a business mindset in a creative world	Mañjon and Crum (2017) report that the model of a successful artist has changed, as artists have forged an entrepreneurial quest – paving the way for the term ARTrepreneur. These authors highlight the need for educators interested in supporting the entrepreneurial dreams of artists to demystify the passion-centred trajectory, stress that commodifying their craft is not creative blasphemy, and explain that the art world is not grounded in meritocracy. This requires collaborative efforts.
Preece et al. (2016)	Framing the work: The composition of value in the visual arts	This study examines value creation within the visual arts market and argues for a broader, socio-culturally informed view of value creation. The authors develop an original conceptual framework to model the value co-creation process through which art is legitimised. Using an illustrative case study of artist Damien Hirst, the study illustrates how value is co-constructed in the visual arts market, demonstrating a need to understand social relationships as value is dispersed, situational and in flux.
Preece and Kerrigan (2015)	Multi-stakeholder brand narratives: An analysis of the construction of artistic brands	These authors sum up their ascription to artistic brands in terms of the artist and their artworks, and the diffusion process emanating thereof as follows: 'Artistic brands make the first steps towards demonstrating concrete ways in which a brand can be positioned and perceived as legitimate and the difficulties in this process […] A person brand cannot be constructed by one person alone but must be socially co-constructed and negotiated by a variety of individuals, including its consumers' (p. 1226).
Rodner and Preece (2015)	Tainted museums: 'Selling out' cultural institutions	This study examines the role of museums as repositories of cultural meaning and symbolic capital. As educational and cultural institutions, museums serve to legitimise works of art within the frame of an art historical context. Attention is devoted to how these pressures can affect the production and consumption of art, offering an alternative perspective on the development of museum policies.
Brown (2015a)	Selling poetry by the pound: T. S. Eliot and the Waste Land brand	Although the battle between culture and commerce isn't over, the conflict has entered a new phase. Elite artists like Picasso and Warhol were canny commercial operators who knew their own worth and weren't reluctant to exploit it.

Author/ Year	Title	Synopsis
Pusa and Uusitalo (2014)	Creating brand identity in art museums: A case study	This study argues that the combination of marketing and art has been considered ill matched, almost unthinkable – based partly on the assumption that marketing will automatically degrade the inner value and distinctiveness of art and favour only the most popular and superficial. Traditional cultural curators tend to believe that a reverse association holds true between the popularity and quality of art.
Lehman and Wickham (2014)	Marketing orientation and activities in the arts-marketing context: Introducing a visual artists' marketing trajectory model	This article aims to build an 'arts-marketing orientation' model by exploring the parallel relationship between the product life cycle and the notion of the 'career trajectory' (as it applies to visual artists). Unlike customer orientation (central to traditional marketing theories), this research suggests that in the arts-marketing context, the marketing orientation and activities of visual artists change according to the career trajectory stage in question.
Rodner and Kerrigan (2014)	The art of branding: Lessons from visual artists	This conceptual paper highlights the importance of the field of visual arts marketing in the development of wider branding theory and practice. Drawing on examples from visual artists and the art mechanism that connects them, the paper reveals how artists and art professionals foster various types of capital (social, cultural, symbolic) as a way of developing a brand name, ensuring longevity in the field and gaining financial value on the market.
Muñiz et al. (2014)	Marketing artistic careers: Pablo Picasso as brand manager	This study develops the proposition that successful artists are powerful brands. It explores the branding acumen of Pablo Picasso and highlights how he maneuevred with consummate skill to assure his position in the art world. By mid-career, he had established his brand so successfully that he had the upper hand over the dealers who represented him, and his work was so sought after that he could count on selling whatever proportion of it he chose to allow to leave his studio. In order to achieve this level of success, Picasso had to read the culture in which he operated and manage the efforts of a complex system of different intermediaries and stakeholders that was not unlike an organisation. Based on an analysis of Picasso's career, the authors assert that in their management of these powerful brands, artists generate a complex, multifaceted public identity that is distinct from a product brand but shares important characteristics with corporate brands, luxury brands and cultural/iconic brands.
O'Reilly and Kerrigan (2013)	A view to a brand: Introducing the film brandscape	The study develops the cultural approach to branding through introducing the idea of the granularity of the brandscape: particular brandscapes can be viewed as loosely bounded sites within which meaning is derived from making sense of the various, interrelated brands within this brandscape.

(Continued)

Table 13.1 (Continued)

Author/ Year	Title	Synopsis
		Such meaning is dependent on cultural cues which evolve over time. Managerial decision making can be understood through considering the various cast and crew decisions, genre and positioning. Through understanding the granularity of the brandscape, marketing and branding practitioners can have a greater understanding of consumer sense making which can be used in strategic decision making.
Kerrigan et al. (2011)	'Spinning' Warhol: Celebrity brand theoretics and the logic of the celebrity brand	The paper takes as its subject celebrity and consumption and the cultural logic of the celebrity brand. It introduces the concept of celebritisation as the engine of celebrity culture, discussing ways in which celebrity brands operate as 'map-making' devices which situate consumers within networks of symbolic resources. This paper builds observations from documentary accounts of the life and work of Warhol.
Brown and Patterson (2010)	Selling stories: Harry Potter and the marketing plot	This paper plots the Harry Potter stories onto Booker's seven-element theory of narrative emplotment and considers how consumers interact with the Harry Potter brand phenomenon. Three consumer narratives of engagement are evident – discovery, diachronic and denial – as is the disagreement between battling plots.
Fraser et al. (2004)	Key issues in arts marketing	This chapter provides a recap to the book and, in so doing, explores the notion of arts for business vis-à-vis arts for art's sake, as well as the relationship of artworks with their respective publics. The marketing concept espouses the importance of understanding the needs and wants of the customer. However, in the arts environment, the product is regarded as the brainchild of the producer, who, through a belief in its intrinsic value, seeks ways of bringing it to an appreciative audience (p. 195).
Fillis (2006)	Art for art's sake or art for business sake: An exploration of artistic product orientation	This study explores the debate surrounding the art for art's sake versus art for business sake philosophies found within the industry, with particular emphasis on the visual arts. Market orientation has received a large amount of attention in the marketing literature, but product-centred marketing has largely been ignored. Many studies have found that market orientation is positively linked with improved performance, but others have shown that the relationship is tentative at best. The arts have long been a domain where product and artist-centred marketing have been practised successfully. Drawing on Hirschman's seminal 1983 paper on artistic ideology and aesthetics, this article considers the merits and implications of being prepared to ignore market demand and customer wishes.

Author/ Year	Title	Synopsis
Schroeder (2005)	The artist and the brand	This study discusses the cross-fertilisation of art and branding, focusing on three contribution areas: the interactions between art, brands and culture; the self-reflexivity of brands; and brand criticism. Several prominent, successful artists served as case studies to illuminate the potential for insights into the interconnections between art, branding and consumption by turning to art history and visual studies. Successful artists can be thought of as brand managers, actively engaged in developing, nurturing and promoting themselves as recognisable 'products' in the competitive cultural sphere.
O'Reilly (2005)	The marketing/ creativity interface: A case study of a visual artist	This paper aims to contribute to an understanding of the marketing/creativity interface in the visual arts at the level of the individual artist. The analysis highlights the significance of emotional, cognitive, spiritual and physical processes for the artist's positioning, process and products, as well as her difficulties with promotion and pricing issues. The study points out that 'at the level of an individual artist, her work may be not only product-oriented but self-oriented'. It therefore behoves artists and their agents to be able to offer appropriately distinguishing promotional accounts of the artist's artistic identity, process and work based on a deep, self-reflexive awareness and understanding by the artist of her own creative practice.
Lee (2005b)	Rethinking arts marketing in a changing cultural policy context	The paper raises the question of whether the arts marketing framework can reflect the new reality of arts management. It investigates recent changes in British cultural policy and their implications for arts marketing. It first points out the decisive role of the policy in shaping the environment of the non-profit arts and argues that arts marketing developed as an organisational strategy within the context of marketisation policy since the 1980s. This is followed by an analysis of the current cultural policy, where 'social impacts' of the arts are highly emphasised and state intervention intensifies. Through a case study, it is demonstrated that non-profit arts organisations are adapting to the new environment by rapidly expanding programmes for educational and social purposes while implicitly resisting top-down political pressure.

ART FORMS: PERFORMING ARTS

The domain of visual arts and film has been explored within the broader context of the performing arts, i.e. jazz, popular music, drama, opera and theatre (Fraser et al., 2004). In their study, for example, Fraser et al. (2004) described the wider context as one in which, for 'a variety of reasons, including space, many of the arts and crafts have been omitted'. On the question of whether there are any themes or issues common to all, the authors opine that, on the face of it, even the issue of profit does not seem particularly central. Most of the activities are not for profit, but by no means all. These authors isolated film based on its fluidity. According to them:

> Film could be considered a strong profit-making activity, yet there are plenty of filmmakers who try to work outside the Hollywood ethos where profit is considered first among equals. Even in the highest of high arts such as (arguably) sculpture or opera, there are private sector impresarios who even in today's competitive environment, present opera – admittedly under special conditions – free of any government or public-sector subsidy. In fact, several authors have pointed to the blurring of the boundaries between profit and non-profit activities. (Fraser et al., 2004: 188)

In their edited book, *Arts Marketing*, Kerrigan et al. (2004: 1) point out that 'although primarily focusing on the UK market, the subject has global relevance and appeal, and policy is evaluated on national, European and supranational levels', covering a 'range from the marketing of the theatre, opera, and museums, through to the film industry and popular music'. Three chapters from the edited book are worth highlighting for the purpose of this chapter: 'Museum marketing: understanding different types of audiences' by Ruth Rentschler; 'Societal arts marketing: a multi-sectoral, inter-disciplinary and international perspective' by Sismanyazici-Navaie; and 'Key issues in arts marketing' by Fraser, Kerrigan and Özbilgin.

Starting with the position of Rentschler (2004: 157), the 'positive word of mouth is most important to museums: it builds visitor numbers, visitor retention and social identity for visitor identification'. She goes on to highlight the 'consequences of museums becoming more oriented to their audiences, while at the same time recognising the importance of their product portfolio and organisational marketing culture'. As Rentschler (2004: 157) points out, 'the need for decreasing reliance upon government income has seen each museum move from an attitude of dependence – bemoaning the government's abandonment of the organisation – to an increasingly positive attitude in which innovative post-modern marketing has become central to museum operations'. She refers to the Art Gallery of New South Wales in Sydney, Australia, as a case in point – highlighting its ability to maintain effective publicity and harnessing its popular profile in attracting sponsorship. In the case of Canterbury Museum in Christchurch, New Zealand, she reported the adoption of the 'total visitor experience' as a whole new vision designed for reshaping the marketing operations of the museum. Sismanyazici-Navaie (2004), on her part (see pp. 159–63), takes a historical perspective on the development of the arts in 'marketing'. According to her (see p. 160), 'early art forms began as forms of communication, storytelling and record keeping, activities that are the fundamental tools of marketing'. Sismanyazici-Navaie (2004: 163) outlines the function of the arts as being 'a search for beauty and individuality, expression of internal and external worlds', being mainly about:

- communication, storytelling and record keeping
- architecture and engineering, resulting in commercial, residential and leisure artefacts
- consumer products (from furniture to light fixtures)
- household goods (decorative as well as functional appliances)
- personal items (the ornamental art of jewellery, toys, watches, fashion items)
- entertainment (movies, theatre plays, concerts, operas and ballets, computer games).

Terblanche (2003: 153) also points out that 'the performing arts are presently widely perceived as an industry in the economy, but one in a state of elaborate transformation'. According to him, 'one of the main challenges to any performing arts organisation is to be transparent and accountable because of the magnitude of private and public investments'. In other words, 'the challenge becomes somewhat more daunting because management is exercised in the absence of a bottom line'. Key arguments derived from the above are as follows:

- The role of marketing in enhancing the business of the performing arts ought not to be an issue of debate anymore; the question is rather: how might marketing be employed to the maximum benefit of a performing arts organisation?
- Marketing of the performing arts entails substantially more than introducing a marketing toolkit from the realm of consumer or business goods markets and applying it to the performing arts.
- Many performing arts organisations are not profit seeking and consequently it may be considered helpful to include a section on non-profit arts organisations to highlight some of their particular challenges to survive. (Terblanche, 2003: 153)

Such non-profit motives have been highlighted in the context of music such as hip-hop being embedded within the curriculum. For example, Madichie and Gbadamosi (2017) used the case illustration of a course launch at the University of Missouri to capture the relationship between hip-hop artistry and poetry. According to these scholars:

> [in] the value of hip-hop artistry in poetry, as epitomised by the University of Missouri's English department, there are lingering questions as to whether these should be considered fullblown courses in their own right rather than topics or case studies embedded within courses. (Madichie and Gbadamosi, 2017: 207)

Overall, Madichie and Gbadamosi (2017) capture the relationship between hip-hop artistry and poetry, as well as meeting the demands of society – societal impacts – not the least, bringing 'street cred' into the classroom (p. 196). Talking about hip-hop and poetry, dance also has its place in the arts. For example, Lee et al. (2016: 1043) 'examined the relationships among the variables that comprise the extended marketing mix and satisfaction, trust, commitment, and revisit intentions toward dance as a performing art in the context of Korean audiences'. These authors observed and reported that:

> Korea's performing arts market grew considerably during 2014, with the number of performing arts venues and industry workers, and total sales revenue having all increased … Despite its potential to grow into the cultural product most easily enjoyed by the public in daily life … the growth of the dance industry has lagged behind other performing arts categories. (Lee et al., 2016: 1044)

There are several possible reasons for this. First, in comparison to the more popular performing arts, the dance performance genre places an especially strong emphasis on the artistic values that are intrinsic to this art form. However, the artistic appeal of dance performances is often under-appreciated by the general public. Second, most dance companies are currently suffering from limited capital and a lack of systematised marketing strategies. Furthermore, Caldwell and Henry (2018) investigated the live and recorded performing arts in a large metropolitan city located in a Western country in which the dominant language was English. According to these authors (2018: 55), there is a need to benchmark consumption of the arts based on low cultural capital (LCC) and high cultural capital (HCC). According to them:

> Although research on the topic is scant, the literature suggests that systematic differences exist in the consumption values and consumption portfolios of LCCs and HCCs with respect to attending the performing arts […] LCCs are lesser-educated people who are employed in manual or semi-skilled jobs, while HCCs are typically formally educated professional/ managerial persons. (Caldwell and Henry, 2018: 55)

These authors go on to map their value against consumption portfolio along eight dimensions after undertaking a 'synthesis of the past research' (see Caldwell and Henry, 2018: 56), suggesting that consumption values linked to attending performing arts and associating with LCC and HCC types respectively are as follows:

- diversion versus affective intensity and/or cognitive complexity
- simple appreciation versus connoisseurship
- social integration versus social assertiveness
- imitation versus authenticity
- familiarity versus innovativeness and/or classicism
- luxury versus humanism

- parochialism versus cosmopolitanism
- self-reference versus critical detachment.

In recent times, low cultural capital (especially younger consumers) has been displaying a new type of consumption portfolio. As Peterson and Kern's (1996) research demonstrates, there has been an increase in the numbers of lower socioeconomic class consumers who consume 'highbrow culture'. This leads us into revisiting the relevance of arts marketing.

REVISITING ARTS MARKETING

Couched in the observation of Peterson and Kern (1996) on the changing demographics of highbrow cultural consumption, Lee (2005a: 289) provides something of an explanation for arts marketing as distinct from the generic marketing concept:

> Arts marketing theory is embedded in the existing context of the non-profit arts sector – i.e. romantic belief in the universal value of the arts and producer authority over the consumer. As 'a set of techniques' and 'a decision-making process', marketing was able to sit comfortably in the non-profit arts context during the 1970s and 1980s.

However, recent recognition of marketing as 'a management philosophy' has brought about incompatibilities between the customer orientation of the marketing notion and the Romantic view of artistic production. Lee (2005a), therefore, sets about demonstrating that arts marketing writing embraces *romanticism* through:

- a generic marketing concept
- a relationship marketing approach
- an extended definition of the customer
- an extended definition of the product
- a reduction of marketing to function.

He also argues that 'such findings suggest that persistence of the existing belief system and the embeddedness of the market be considered when marketisation in the arts sector is analysed' (2005a: 289). Furthermore, the arts needs to tell its own story as marketing praxis. For example, Lambert (2017: online) observed and pointed out that:

> through the centuries, society has sought to better understand artists and the meaning behind their legendary artworks ... Artists who identify and satisfy our ongoing search for meaning by describing art they create have already discovered this crucial truth: artists that

engage in storytelling create a compelling reason for collectors and admirers to invest in their work.[6]

What this means is that 'storytelling is a crucial part of the art-making process for the artist as much as the art viewer'.

Two articles explored in this chapter tend to support this view – those of Andy Warhol and Pablo Picasso. As artists' careers evolve, their professional journey is embedded within the work they create – when artists shift from one medium to another, there is a reason for that change. Artists who adopt unique viewpoints or processes in their practice have made specific choices in determining their art careers. Understanding and articulating how one's artistic practice has evolved can help artists better uncover parts of their own practice they may have overlooked. Storytelling for artists thus becomes a tool for developing both a better understanding of your practice, and engagement with new audiences. Thus, describing art and explaining the different facets of your practice in a unified narrative can hold interest for a wide audience if an artist knows how to tell their story effectively. As Brown and Patterson (2010: 541) point out, 'the rise of mass production, the emergence of mass consumption, and the technologies of mass communication have undermined humankind's ability to weave compelling yarns'. Key take-home points from the above are 'mass', whether in terms of production, consumption or communication – all three components highlight the Achille's heel in arts marketing.

Fillis (2006) once explored the debate surrounding the 'art for art's sake' versus 'art for business' sake' philosophies found within the industry, with a particular emphasis on the visual arts. According to him, the market orientation concept has received a large amount of attention in the marketing literature, but product-centred marketing has largely been ignored. Many studies have found that market orientation is positively linked with improved performance, but others have shown that the relationship is tentative at best. The arts have long been a domain where product- and artist-centred marketing have been practised successfully. He considered, therefore, the merits and implications of being prepared to ignore market demand and customer wishes.

In their closing chapter, Fraser et al. (2004: 195) provide a recap to the edited book and in so doing explore the notion of arts for business vis-à-vis arts for art's sake, as well as the relationship of artworks with their respective publics. The marketing concept, according to them, espouses the importance of understanding the needs and wants of the customer, but in the arts environment, the product is regarded as the brainchild of the producer, who, through a belief in its intrinsic value, seeks ways of bringing such value to an appreciative audience. This view resonates with another study by Muñiz et al. (2014), which develops the proposition that successful artists are powerful brands. It explores the branding acumen of Pablo Picasso and highlights how he maneouvered with consummate skill to assure his position in the art world. By mid-career, he had established his brand so successfully that he had the upper hand over the dealers who represented him, and his work was so sought after that he could count on selling whatever proportion of it he chose to allow to leave his studio. In order to achieve this level of success, however, Picasso had to read the culture in which he operated and manage the efforts of a complex system of different intermediaries and stakeholders that was not unlike an organisation. Based on an analysis of Picasso's career, the authors assert that in their management of these powerful brands, artists generate a complex, multifaceted public identity that is distinct from a product brand but shares important characteristics with corporate brands, luxury brands and cultural/iconic brands (Muñiz et al., 2014).

Furthermore, and building on observations from documentary accounts of the life and work of Andy Warhol, Kerrigan et al. (2011) interrogated the subject of 'celebrity and consumption' and the 'cultural logic' of the celebrity brand. They introduced the concept of celebritisation as the engine of celebrity culture, discussing ways in which celebrity brands operate as 'map-making' devices which situate consumers within networks of symbolic resources. Similarly, Schroeder (2005) points out that 'successful artists can be thought of as brand managers, actively engaged in developing, nurturing and promoting themselves as recognizable "products" in the competitive cultural sphere'. While all of these examples illustrate and/or justify the need to move away from a marketing orientation philosophy in the arts context, it is worth pointing out that this is only achievable in cases where artists have been successful and able to become brands in their own right.

Case Study 13.2

Chuck Gallery[7]

Historically, galleries have always needed to manage old relationships and cultivate new contacts in order to stay relevant. However, in today's branded culture this simple process takes a more complex approach that has proven to require greater multilateral thinking in order to develop strategies that promote conversations about the art as well as customer engagement. Marketing art and artists today requires an approach that fosters resonance and amplification of the art and artists in both online and offline media. A wholesome art-centred approach to marketing lies in the intersection between aesthetics, economics and emotive storytelling. For a gallery, it starts with the induction of a rich heritage and cultural significance unique to the gallery.

(Continued)

(Continued)

As an independent contemporary African art gallery, setting up in Manchester was deliberate – a city of creativity and diversity and a hotbed for radical ideas that influence political and social thinking. More so, the registered address of Chuck Gallery is on Plymouth Grove, a street that houses a rich history of local creatives like Elizabeth Gaskell and which is in close proximity to prominent landmarks like the Victoria Baths and the University of Manchester. Situating a modern and contemporary art gallery in such a progressive quarter is not only appropriate but also creates a connective link to the continued heritage of creativity. As a gallery, we have seen that this kind of storytelling and historically appropriate narrative lends to the prestige of the space, and ultimately to the artists we represent. This is of particular significance given the great and continued links between Africa and Manchester exemplified in the history of collaboration and support given by Manchester in ending colonial rule in Africa. Traditionally, galleries promote their services through different approaches, by direct mail or advertisements in newspapers, magazines or television. However, because of the increasing number of internet users engaging through online channels for a wide range of issues, products and services, it has become important for galleries like Chuck Gallery to adopt effective social media strategies. We have also realised that the costs of promoting our artists and services through social media are comparatively lower than traditional marketing methods. Although it is clear that creative social media marketing is an important way to draw attention to and raise demand for our artistic products among prospective and established clientele, the question of its effectiveness is still being answered. Essentially the gallery is adopting social media to influence sales, promote our artists, expand what is already known about our space and ensure continued allegiance from customers.

What has worked?

As already discussed, while increasing our engagement with new and old customers via social media channels has proved successful, traditional marketing strategies have also been beneficial. These include direct invitations to customers face to face or via telephone calls, personalised email invitations sent via marketing automation platforms like MailChimp or via the gallery's personal email address, word-of-mouth marketing by the gallery staff and customers, and signage outside the gallery premises. For social media strategies, building and growing our online presence on platforms like Facebook, Twitter and Instagram by posting regular and sponsored adverts of upcoming exhibitions and periodic blogs about the artists we represent, has also been successful. It appears that activities around these platforms have a greater impact than corporate advert representations and website statements. In essence, we have found commentary, recommendations of friends, and reviews to be persuasive.

What is working?

After a visit to the gallery in March 2018, a friend who is a business owner and an active user of LinkedIn, noticed the gallery's passive presence on the platform. He advised that we take advantage of the many available commercial opportunities inherent on the platform, especially as he was able to attribute the significant growth in his business directly to his LinkedIn connections. Following our useful chat with this friend, we realised the need to develop marketing plans that would be in consonance with the gallery's various online channels. LinkedIn was especially attractive to us as it has established itself as the preferred platform for individuals and businesses hoping to foster prospective relationships or cement growing entrepreneurial opportunities. Our connections on the site have since grown from 105 to 861 and counting. Similar to our activities on other social media platforms, we have increased posts and articles about the gallery and our services on our LinkedIn page, the only difference being that they are written to appeal more to business individuals and corporations. An important strategy has also been to promptly respond to comments on our page, helping to further cement relationships within our LinkedIn network.

What needs to work?

Although social media has proven to be a great propagator of our brand awareness, we cannot quantify the extent to which our adverts and other marketing efforts have impacted on customers and their purchasing of our art. We also face the uncertainty of the true marketing effectiveness of these social media platforms caused by the dissimilarity in the overarching promotional objectives of the gallery and the social networking purposes of these sites – is it suitable to upload content aimed at increasing sales to a social networking site where customers just want to connect socially? (This is less of an issue with business platforms like LinkedIn). We, at Chuck Gallery, are still convinced that Chuck Gallery needs to seize the opportunities that social media provides and design promotional advertisement strategies, however we need to develop and adopt tools that will help us objectively assess the effectiveness of these sites as suitable marketing channels. These could be via site statistical analyses or by carrying out surveys from our buying customers to understand whether our social media marketing strategies have influenced their purchase decisions. These surveys could also be useful in quantifying the effectiveness of our traditional marketing methods. The gallery also needs to identify elements of the posts on our site pages that will kindle customer engagement and popularise our content, such as understanding better what images and videos will attract engagement with our followers and connections. Additionally, the gallery needs to designate the duties of overseeing and monitoring our online activities to a social media-savvy staff member.

(Continued)

(Continued)

Questions for discussion

1. To what extent would you agree or disagree with the contention that 'A wholesome art-centred approach to marketing lies in the intersection between aesthetics, economics and emotive storytelling'?

2. Visit the website of Chuck Gallery and comment on the statement of the propriety that the gallery 'needs to identify elements of the posts on our site pages that will kindle customer engagement and popularise our content such as understanding better what images and videos will attract engagement with our followers and connections'.

3. Using the graphic illustrations in Figures 13.2 and 13.3, map these against the comment that 'LinkedIn was especially attractive to us as it has established itself as the preferred platform for individuals and businesses hoping to foster prospective relationships or cement growing entrepreneurial opportunities'.

SUMMARY OF KEY IDEAS

This chapter has explored and documented various dimensions of 'arts marketing' and the 'marketing of arts', as well as the debates in these areas. It started off with a discussion of the commonly confused discourse across diverse art forms (i.e. still art or drawing and painting) and the marketing approaches adopted across these. This was followed by an exploration of art forms such as poetry and literature, with a heavier accent on the former than the latter. The section on poetry and/or literature emphasised the intersections of creative writing and audience engagement, which paved the way for the next section on the enactment of the visual elements. In an attempt to further this discourse, visual and fine arts were interrogated along three key dimensions – notably credibility, visibility and desirability – with mini case illustrations cutting across a digital focus, the practitioner perspective of an artist in residence project, as well as an ethical focus of a DIY (do-it-yourself artist in a village in England). In the penultimate section, the chapter delved into the sub-field of performing arts, drawing on the works of leading scholars such as Fraser, Kerrigan and Ozbilgin (2004), Rentschler (2004), Terblanche (2003) and Madichie and Gbadamosi (2017) – covering aspects of jazz, popular music, drama, opera and theatre (Fraser et al., 2004). The chapter then wrapped up with the need to revisit arts marketing, and, by so doing, echoed Fillis (2006), who once explored the debate surrounding the 'art for art's sake' versus 'art for business' sake' philosophies found within the industry. Based on this latter debate, the distinction was between arts marketing and marketing of the arts resurfaces, especially in the studies by Lee (2005a and b) and Fillis (2006).

Chapter Discussion Questions

1. Research shows that 85 per cent of global art sales is realised only in three countries – namely the USA, China and the UK. To what extent would you agree with this statement? What other countries are renowned for arts consumption?
2. What should be the main focus of arts? Should it be 'art for art's sake' or 'art for business' sake'? Justify your answer.
3. This chapter seems to argue that 'storytelling is a crucial part of the art-making process for the artist as much as the art viewer'. Using real-life illustrations, debate the pros and cons of this viewpoint.
4. Discuss how the champions and gatekeepers highlighted in Figure 13.2 may facilitate or constrain marketing of the arts.

NOTES

1. Arts and the Market Special Issue on 'The culture and design of titles, teasers and trailers', edited by Daniel Hesford and Keith Johnston, 5(2), www.emeraldinsight.com/toc/aam/5/2
2. See the 2017 Arts and the Market Special Issue on 'Music, culture and heritage', edited by Sharon Schembri and Fuat Firat, 7(2), www.emeraldinsight.com/toc/aam/7/2
3. Another feature shows the creativity of the arts in regeneration projects related to converting a disused petrol station.
4. See, for example, 'Construction of the artistic brand' in Preece and Kerrigan (2015: 1225).
5. An artpreneur is defined as 'a resourceful person who merges their artistic skills and business expertise to establish a sustainable career. The artist should understand their value – how to emotionally and/or functionally offer value to their customers and associate a monetary value to their creative endeavour manifesting into a lucrative career'. See also Elliot et al. (2018: 392), who define artpreneurs as a subcategory who 'share similar traits with the category of entrepreneurs – creativity, proactiveness, alertness, and opportunistic behaviour' (Mañjon and Crum, 2017).
6. Audra Lambert is an independent curator and art critic, born in New Orleans, and based in New York. The founder of Antecedent Projects (2014), a sustainable urban curatorial consultancy investigating site-specific heritage and cultural regeneration, she has curated exhibits

with CoLab-Factory, White Roof Project, Flux Art Fair and, most recently, the New York City Parks Department's Arsenal Gallery (2017).

7. Chuck Art Gallery, 166 Plymouth Grove, Manchester, M13 0AF, UK. Website: www.chuckgallery. com/about-us

REFERENCES

Aldrich, H., Zimmer, C., Sexton, D. and Smilor, R. W. (1986) *The Art and Science of Entrepreneurship*. Cambridge, MA: Ballinger. pp. 3–23.

Anderson, A. R. and Jack, S. L. (2002) The articulation of social capital in entrepreneurial networks: A glue or a lubricant? *Entrepreneurship and Regional Development*, 14(3), 193–210.

Arora, P. and Vermeylen, F. (2013) The end of the art connoisseur? Experts and knowledge production in the visual arts in the digital age. *Information, Communication & Society*, 16(2), 194–214.

Barrere, C. and Santagata, W. (1999) Defining art: From the Brancusi trial to the economics of artistic semiotic goods. *International Journal of Arts Management*, 1(2), 28–38.

Bernstein, D. W. and Hatch, C. (eds) (2010) *Writings through John Cage's Music, Poetry, and Art*. Chicago, IL: University of Chicago Press.

Brown, S. (2007) Are we nearly there yet? On the retro-dominant logic of marketing. *Marketing Theory*, 7(3), 291–300.

Brown, S. (2015a) Selling poetry by the pound: T. S. Eliot and The Waste Land brand. *Consumption Markets & Culture*, 18(5), 411–26.

Brown, S. (2015b) Bow to Stern: Can literary theory plumb an unfathomable brand? *Marketing Theory*, 15(4), 445–64.

Brown, S. and Patterson, A. (2010) Selling stories: Harry Potter and the marketing plot. *Psychology & Marketing*, 27(6), 541–56.

Butler, P. (2000) By popular demand: Marketing the arts. *Journal of Marketing Management*, 16(4), 343–64.

Caldwell, M. and Henry, P. C. (2018) Deepening how cultural capital structures consumption of the performing arts. *Journal of Global Scholars of Marketing Science*, 28(1), 52–67.

Cellini, R. and Cuccia, T. (2014) The artist–art dealer relationship as a marketing channel. *Research in Economics*, 68(1), 57–69.

Currid, E. (2007) *The Warhol Economy: How Fashion, Art, and Music Drive New York City*. Princeton, NJ: Princeton University Press.

de Wal, A. (2012) What is Art Marketing, and Why Bother? Available at: http://emptyeasel. com/2012/10/15/what-is-art-marketing-and-why-bother (accessed 15 April 2018).

Drucker, P. (1985) *Innovation and Entrepreneurship*. Oxford: Butterworth Heineman.

Elliot, E. A., Jamal, A. and Cherian, J. (2018) Artrepreneurship and learning in ethnic markets. *Journal of Business Research*, 82, 391–9.

Fillis, I. (2004) The entrepreneurial artist as marketer: Drawing from the smaller-firm literature. *International Journal of Arts Management*, 7(1), 9–21.

Fillis, I. (2006) Art for art's sake or art for business sake: An exploration of artistic product orientation. *The Marketing Review*, 6(1), 29–40.

Fillis, I. (2011) The evolution and development of arts marketing research. *Arts Marketing: An International Journal*, 1(1), 11–25.

Foster, H. (2014) *The First Pop Age: Painting and Subjectivity in the Art of Hamilton, Lichtenstein, Warhol, Richter, and Ruscha*. Princeton, NJ: Princeton University Press.

Fraser, P., Kerrigan, F. and Özbilgin, M. (2004) Key issues in arts marketing. In F. Kerrigan, P. Fraser and M. Özbilgin (eds), *Arts Marketing*. London: Routledge, pp. 187–97.

Hagtvedt, H. and Patrick, V. M. (2008) Art infusion: The influence of visual art on the perception and evaluation of consumer products. *Journal of Marketing Research*, 45(3), 379–89.

Holt, D. B. (1998) Does cultural capital structure American consumption? *Journal of Consumer Research*, 25(June), 1–26.

Kerrigan, F., Brownlie, S., Hewer, P. and Daza-Le Touze, C. (2011) 'Spinning' Warhol: Celebrity brand theoretics and the logic of the celebrity brand. *Journal of Marketing Management*, 27(13–14), 1504–24.

Kerrigan, F., Fraser, P. and Özbilgin, M. (eds) (2004) *Arts Marketing*. London: Routledge.

Kim, M., Pandey, S. and Pandey, S. K. (2018) Why do nonprofit performing arts organizations offer free public access? *Public Administration Review*, 78(1), 139–50.

Lambert, A. (2017) Why storytelling is crucial for artists. *Artrepreneur*, 26 July. Available at: https://atp.orangenius.com/storytelling-for-artists (accessed 17 January 2018).

Langer, S. K. (1953) *Feeling and Form* (Vol. 3). London: Routledge and Kegan Paul.

Lee, H. K. (2005a) When arts met marketing. *International Journal of Cultural Policy*, 11(3), 289–305.

Lee, H. K. (2005b) Rethinking arts marketing in a changing cultural policy context. *International Journal of Nonprofit and Voluntary Sector Marketing*, 10(3), 151–64.

Lee, Y. G., Yim, B. H., Jones, C. W. and Kim, B. G. (2016) The extended marketing mix in the context of dance as a performing art. *Social Behavior and Personality: An International Journal*, 44(6), 1043–56.

Lehman, K. and Wickham, M. (2014) Marketing orientation and activities in the arts-marketing context: Introducing a visual artists' marketing trajectory model. *Journal of Marketing Management*, 30(7–8), 664–96.

Livesay, H. C. (1982) Entrepreneurial history, in C. A. Kent, D. L. Sexton and K. H. Vesper (eds), *Encyclopedia of Entrepreneurship*. Englewood Cliffs, NJ: Prentice Hall. pp. 7–14.

McAndrew, C. (2017) *The Art Market 2017*. Switzerland: Art Basel and UBS.

Madichie, N. and Gbadamosi, A. (2017) The entrepreneurial university: An exploration of 'value-creation' in a non-management department. *Journal of Management Development*, 36(2), 196–216.

Mañjon, S. B. and Crum, M. (2017) ARTrepreneurship: Shifting to a business mindset in a creative world. In J. M. Munoz and J. W. Shields (eds), *Arts and Entrepreneurship*. New York: Business Expert Press.

Martindale, C. (1990) *The Clockwork Muse: The Predictability of Artistic Change*. New York: Basic Books.

Masserman, J. H. (1986) Poetry as music. *The Arts in Psychotherapy*, 13(1), 61–67.

Muñiz Jr, M. A., Norris, T. and Fine, G. (2014) Marketing artistic careers: Pablo Picasso as brand manager. *European Journal of Marketing*, 48(1/2), 68–88.

O'Reilly, D. (2005) The marketing/creativity interface: A case study of a visual artist. *International Journal of Nonprofit and Voluntary Sector Marketing*, 10, 263–74.

O'Reilly, D. and Kerrigan, F. (2013) A view to a brand: Introducing the film brandscape. *European Journal of Marketing*, 47(5–6), 1–24.

Peterson, R. A. and Kern, R. M. (1996) Changing highbrow taste: From snob to omnivore. *American Sociological Review*, pp. 900–07.

Plattner, S. (1998) A most ingenious paradox: The market for contemporary fine art. *American Anthropologist*, 100(2), 482–93.

Preece, C. and Kerrigan, F. (2015) Multi-stakeholder brand narratives: An analysis of the construction of artistic brands. *Journal of Marketing Management*, 31(11–12), 1207–30.

Preece, C., Kerrigan, F. and O'Reilly, D. (2016) Framing the work: The composition of value in the visual arts. *European Journal of Marketing*, 50(7–8), 1377–98.

Pusa, S. and Uusitalo, L. (2014) Creating brand identity in art museums: A case study. *International Journal of Arts Management*, 17(1), 18–30.

Rentschler, R. (2004) Museum marketing: Understanding different types of audiences. In F. Kerrigan, P. Fraser and M. Ozbilgin (eds), *Arts Marketing*. London: Routledge, pp. 139–58.

Resch, M. (2016a) *The Global Art Gallery Report 2016*. London: Phaidon Press.

Resch, M. (2016b) *Management of Art Galleries*. London: Phaidon Press.

Rodner, L. and Kerrigan, F. (2014) The art of branding: Lessons from visual artists. *Arts Marketing: An International Journal*, 4(1–2), 101–18.

Rodner, L. and Preece, C. (2015) Tainted museums: 'Selling out' cultural institutions. *International Journal of Nonprofit and Voluntary Sector Marketing*, 20(2), 149–69.

Schroeder, J. E. (2005) The artist and the brand. *European Journal of Marketing*, 39(11/12), 1291–1305.

Sismanyazici-Navaie, N. (2004) Societal arts marketing: A multi-sectoral, inter-disciplinary and international perspective. In F. Kerrigan, P. Fraser and M. Ozbilgin (eds), *Arts Marketing*. London: Routledge, pp. 159–86.

Smith, R. (2015) Entrepreneurship and poetry: Analyzing an aesthetic dimension. *Journal of Small Business and Enterprise Development*, 22(3), 450–72.

Solkin, D. H. (1993) *Painting for Money: The Visual Arts and the Public Sphere in Eighteenth-Century England*. New Haven, CT and London: Yale University Press.

Sozuer, A. (2017) Exploring the emergence of contemporary art galleries in Istanbul: The effectuation perspective. In J. M. Munoz and J. W. Shields (eds), *Arts and Entrepreneurship*. New York: Business Expert Press, Chapter 6.

Terblanche, N. (2003) The performing arts and marketing: Concepts and challenges. *SATJ: South African Theatre Journal*, 17(1), 153–76.

Wiid, R. and Mora-Avila, P. (2018) Arts marketing framework: The arts organisation as a hub for participation. *Journal of Public Affairs*, 18(2), e1657.

14
RELIGION AND CONSUMER BEHAVIOUR

Richard Shambare and Gift Donga

Learning Objectives

After studying this chapter, you should be able to:

- Define the terms religion and religiosity within the context of consumer behaviour
- Explain the various elements of religion and their effect on consumer behaviour
- Explain how religion impacts on consumer behaviour
- Discuss how mainstream religions and religious beliefs shape consumer actions and behaviour

---

INTRODUCTION

Religion is primarily about people: their ambitions, desires and goals, behaviour, thoughts, and actions. The marketing literature affirms that religious faith constitutes an important determinant of consumers' attitudes and behaviours. Many authors describe religion as an institution that provides meaning and purpose to people's lives. At a practical level, religion sets the tone for people's behaviour by defining moral standards of right and wrong, which place significant restrictions on how people ought to conduct themselves both as individual persons and as part of a collective. Consequently, there is an increasing strength of arguments linking religion and consumption situations. Against this background, this chapter seeks to examine the influence of religion on consumer behaviour.

The balance of the chapter is structured as follows. We first provide an overview of religion and the various faiths, practised in the various parts of the world. The next section concerns itself with discussing some of the challenges experienced by marketers in deciphering the religion, followed by a look at religion and consumer behaviour. Religion and the marketing mix and branding are discussed in the following section, before we present the religion–business interface. In this section, some of the businesses associated with marketing religion are discussed. Lastly, a summary of the chapter is outlined.

AN OVERVIEW OF RELIGION: SOME PERSPECTIVES OF THE MAJOR AND MINOR RELIGIONS OF THE WORLD

Religion is as old as humanity. It is that single factor that shapes, influences and regulates human behaviour, including consumer behaviour. As such, many authors argue that religion acts as a framework for human behaviour (Delener, 1994; Mansori, 2012; Mathras et al., 2016; Tukamushaba and Musinguzi, 2018). More specifically, Delener (1994) argues that religion shapes people's attitudes and actions in six ways, as follows:

- Religion is a foundation of meaning and purpose for life.
- Religion defines the manner, tools and techniques for doing things.
- Religion helps people to cope with and understand life events.
- Religion is a means through which people deal with challenges in life.
- Religion acts as a motivator for human behaviour.
- Religion is stable and observable.

When conceptualising religion, many authors make reference to at least one of the above-mentioned criteria. Whereas researchers have endeavoured to advance a definition of religion that is universal to all religions and geographic regions, many consider this task impossible as the pursuit for a generally agreed definition faces numerous challenges (Mathras et al., 2016). As a corollary, a multiplicity of definitions is proffered in the literature; these definitions range from those clearly pronouncing the existence of God as the only deity (superbeing) to those simply acknowledging religion to be a social system.

In the case of the former, authors such as Sheth and Mittal (2004: 65) define religion as being 'a system of beliefs about the supernatural and spiritual world, about God, and about how humans, as God's creatures, are supposed to behave on this earth'. In agreement, McDaniel and Burnett (1990) articulate God's centrality to religion. These authors avow that 'religion is a belief in God accompanied by a commitment to follow principles believed to be set forth by God [himself]' (McDaniel and Burnett, 1990: 110).

Another school of thought believes that religion is less prescriptive on the centrality of deities in religion. This point of view is persuaded by the social principles of humanity and morality as the building blocks of religion. This school of thought is supported by the definition that religion is a 'social arrangement designed to provide a shared, collective way of dealing with the unknown and un-knowable aspects of human life, with the mysteries of life, death and the different dilemmas that arise in the process of making moral decisions' (Johnson, 2000: 259).

Despite the varying definitions, scholars from different disciplines including sociology, psychology, theology and marketing all seem to agree that religion has an important function in people's lives. In particular, Harper (2012) acknowledges that religion is so central to life that at least 80 per cent of the world's population is affiliated to one religion or another. By the end of 2010, as shown in Table 14.1, the Pew Research Center (2012) indicated that close to 88 per cent of the world's population belong to some religious group.

Table 14.1   Size of the religions of the world

Religion	Number of adherents	Percentage	Cumulative percentage
Christianity	2.2 billion	32%	32%
Islam	1.6 billion	23%	55%
Hinduism	1 billion	15%	70%
Buddhism	500 million	7%	77%
Chinese traditional	394 million	6%	83%
Ethnic religions	300 million	4%	87%
African traditional	100 million	1%	88%
Other religions	< 1 billion	12%	100%

Source: Pew Research Center (2012)

The latest evidence points towards a growth in affiliation among religions such as Christianity and Islam (Hackspirit, 2017; Lipka and Hacket, 2017). From the look of things, this rise in the number of the faithful, naturally, further asserts an even greater importance on scholars' understanding of religion and its implications for human behaviour. This is particularly true for marketing scholars, whose ambition, among others, is to understand consumer behaviour (Tukamushaba and Musinguzi, 2018).

For instance, lessons on religion and its impact on consumers' behaviour should never be under-valued; and they can never be too many. In fact, they actually are too few (Delener, 1994; Mansori, 2012; Mathras et al., 2016). It is against this background that some of the religions of the world deserve to be highlighted in this chapter. Major religions such as Islam and Hinduism tend to be much older and attract larger numbers of adherents than minor religions. The former are more easily recognisable, as their followers or adherents are spread across different parts of the world. While major religions tend to be few, they attract large numbers of parishioners; minor religions, in converse, attract relatively fewer numbers of adherents across many small religions. Despite their small size, minor religions' influence on people and behaviour is not diminished. They are no less important and have been observed to have the same influence on people as the major religions. As such, both major and minor religions are discussed in this chapter.

MAJOR RELIGIONS

In this section, the discussion turns to the four major religious practices – Christianity, Islam, Hinduism and Buddhism (Pew Research Center, 2012). Table 14.1 demonstrates that adherents to these four religions account for approximately 77 per cent of the world's population. The four major religions are discussed next.

Christianity

Christianity is a religion centred mainly on the existence, death and ideology of Jesus Christ. Understanding the beliefs and practices of Christians is challenging as the religion encompasses the widest assortment of denominations and faith groups and each subscribes to its own set of principles (Fairchild, 2017). However, for the purpose of this chapter we will mainly delineate those beliefs which are central to almost all Christian faith groups. Christianity teaches about the existence of one God who made the universe, the earth, and created man in His image. In Christianity, instead of observing a list of 'dos and don'ts', the objective of a Christian is to develop a closer walk with the Lord. That relationship is achieved because of the deeds of Jesus Christ as well as the ministry of the Holy Spirit.

Islam

Islam is one of the most modest and unambiguous religions. It is more than an organised religion; nevertheless, it is a pervasive conduct to life that directs all thought and action.

For example, Bailey and Sood (1993) posit that the word 'Islam' means submission (i.e. to God's will) and the term 'Moslem' means someone who submits. Thus, a genuine Moslem lives face to face with God at all times, convinced that God is a ubiquitous ruler and a well-informed judge. The numerous sects of the religion all control behaviour, activities and dress, as well as women's rights. This is evolving somewhat as Islam seeks to adjust to contemporary times and as women are gradually battling the old traditions.

Hinduism

Central to Hinduism is the law of Karma, which essentially means that one will reap what one sows. This 'law of the deed', as it is called, along with transmigration, has served to keep one persistently on the rebirth wheel (Bailey and Sood, 1993). In one sense, the Hindu religion is simple with no chain of command, no divine disclosure and no strict code of conduct. However, in contrast, Hinduism has a single real God, but it also has other numerous gods which contribute to its complex theology. Compassion toward all living creatures constitutes a major objective of Hinduism. One of the ways in which this objective is conveyed is in the taboo on meat consumption (Klostermaier, 1989); Hindus are vegetarians. Lastly, a critically significant feature of Hinduism is the caste system, which is the splitting up of society into higher and lower castes, which perhaps had its origins in the variety of skin colours.

Buddhism

Buddhism has its roots in the disapproval of purported corruption in the Hindu faith by Gautama Buddha around 530 BC (Bailey and Sood, 1993). Buddhism is not centred on divine writings, nor does it illustrate rigid ceremonies or a system of beliefs. Instead, it endeavours to direct its believers through a routine of individual discipline that will result in a life characterised by noble works as well as internal peace of mind. Salvation is not guaranteed by the religion, but instead comes from the individual's regime of purification. Buddhism is not materialistic and is more interested in the betterment of one's person than in raising general living standards. Furthermore, it advocates for a process of human conduct centred on wisdom, with little reliance on the supernatural (Kalupahana, 1987).

MINOR RELIGIONS

There has been great contestation in the literature regarding the classification of minor religions globally as it often leads to the notion that some religions are inferior to others. It is important to note that the standard employed for the classification of religions as minor in the context of this chapter is according to the global number of adherents to a particular religion (Pew Research Center, 2012). Consistent with that criteria, there are a number of minor religions comprising relatively few adherents, such as Judaism, African traditional religion, Taoism, Jainism, Shinto, Rastafari, Paganism, Santeria, among others. The first four of these are discussed next.

Judaism

The Jewish religion believes that God represents hope for the world, which he created for a purpose. It can be defined as an ethical religion because of the belief that man has the free will to decide continuously between good and evil alternatives, and the belief that circumstances are not due to nature. Jews believe that mankind can comprehend God and the law through education and that man is accountable for his actions and is responsible for his own position in life (Hirschman, 1981, cited in Bailey and Sood, 1993).

African traditional religion

In African traditional religion (ATR), society is the most significant aspect of a person's life. This society constitutes individuals who share the same customs (South African History Online, 2018). In ATR, a person only exists within society and departing from it is at times worse than death. The family still exerts some influence over the individual, even if they live far away. In addition, ATR adherents believe that their ancestors' spirits are those that always guide them. Although ATR acknowledges a Supreme God, believers do not directly worship him as they do not feel righteous enough. As a result, ancestors are the mediators who communicate on their behalf. However, in times of great hardship and need, such as drought, famine or an epidemic that may pose a threat to human existence, the Supreme Being is called upon (South African History Online, 2018).

Taoism

As proffered by Hays (2013), the main belief and doctrine of the Taoist religion is centred on 'Tao' which refers to the origin and law of everything in the universe. Taoists believe that individuals can become supreme beings or immortalised through the practice of specific rituals and discipline. The emphasis of Taoism is on the person in nature and not the person in society. Taoism holds that the life goal of each person is to find one's own individual rhythm in both the natural and supernatural worlds, and to adhere to the way (Tao) of nature (Hays, 2013). Taoism often disputes the actions of humans, saying it is preferable not to do anything and let nature take its course, rather than do something that could be harmful to life. Finally, Taoism promotes a life of simplicity and advocates that its believers perform good deeds and seek inner peace through cultivating inner calm, optimism and passivity.

Jainism

Jainism is an ancient Indian religion that demonstrates that the way to liberation and enjoyment is to live a life of innocence and renunciation (BBC, 2014). The purpose of Jainism is to achieve the emancipation of the soul. In addition, Jains are of the belief that plants and animals, as well as human beings, comprise of living souls. Each of these souls is regarded of equivalent value and should be treated with compassion and respect. Furthermore, believers strictly adhere to a vegetarian diet and live a life that reduces their consumption of natural resources. Lastly, in Jainism, there are no spiritual beings, neither are there gods that will help humans, and the three guiding principles of Jainism are right belief, right knowledge and right conduct (BBC, 2014).

MARKETERS' CHALLENGES IN DECODING RELIGION AND FAITH

In previous sections, several definitions of religion have been provided. But those definitions tend to be only adequate in providing understanding when referring to one religion at a time; they are limiting and render a generalisation of concepts across different religions difficult. This, naturally, presents challenges for the marketer. These challenges are least likely to be experienced by retailers operating in largely mono-cultural cities such as Tokyo, where the vast majority of consumers are Japanese and belong to one culture and/or religion. However, in multicultural metropolitan areas, for example New York, London, Johannesburg, Cape Town and Paris, the situation is quite different. Marketers there are most likely to feel pressure from trying to cater for the needs and wants of customers from diverse cultures and religions. Some of the challenges related to religion and marketing include:

- Are all consumers religious?
- Is there a mechanism to measure the level of religiosity among consumers?
- What is religion?
- How can religion be operationalised in a systematic way so as to inform marketing action?
- How does religion influence consumption?

- How can retailers operating in multicultural and multi-religious environments ensure that they keep all customers satisfied and do not offend one group at the expense of another? (For instance, how do you keep atheist, Jewish, Buddhist, Christian, Hindu and Muslim customers all happy under the same roof?)
- What specific religious nuances should retailers consider when marketing their products to appeal to certain religious groups?

These challenges are also experienced by retailers operating across different countries or within markets characterised by consumers from different faiths or cultures. At the crux of the marketer's challenges is understanding religion and translating it into marketing effort. It would seem that these challenges are exacerbated by the overly simplistic and almost religious-specific definitions of religion within the literature. Among the existing definitions of religion is that of Sheth and Mittal (2004: 65), who assert that 'religion is a system of beliefs about the supernatural and spiritual world, about God, and about how humans, as God's creatures, are supposed to behave on this earth'. Most of the definitions of religion in the mainstream consumer behaviour literature, such as the above, make two assumptions that render a generalisation of such definitions across religions difficult. First, religion is largely viewed from a Western orientation. Religion is almost always treated as a synonym of Christianity and Judaism. One exception to this is when reference is made to Islam. Second, the other assumption, which is very much related to the first, is that religion is only associated with one deity – Yahweh, God or Allah, as proclaimed by the Jews, Christians and Muslims, respectively. Thus, extending current definitions to non-Western and polytheistic religions such as Taoism, Buddhism and Hinduism is problematic.

As such, this chapter is persuaded that a fruitful way in which to unlock the definitional challenges of religion, at least within the consumer behaviour literature, is to first carve up the construct of religion into its constituent parts. Thereafter, a more holistic definition could be proffered. This approach was initiated by Meyers-Levy and Loken (2015) and later refined by Mathras et al. (2016), who focused on religion and consumer behaviour. Since the main focus of the chapter is centred on exploring the influence of religion on consumer behaviour, working with less generic (i.e. more specific) definitions of concepts is advantageous. Such operationalisation of concepts facilitates theory building and generalisation (Mathras et al., 2016; Meyers-Levy and Loken, 2015). As such, let us now attempt to revisit the definition of religion from a consumer behaviour point of view.

(RE)DEFINING RELIGION: SOME CONSUMER BEHAVIOUR CONSIDERATIONS

In keeping with the foregoing arguments, it can be established that religion, from a consumer behaviour perspective, is a function of four dimensions – beliefs, rituals, values and community

(Mathras et al., 2016). As such, we adopt Schimdt et al.'s (1999: 10) definition, which denotes religion to be a 'system of meaning embodied in a pattern of life, a community of faith, and a worldview that articulates a view of the sacred and of what ultimately matters' (Schimdt et al., 1999). We therefore define religion to mean 'a community of people unified by common beliefs, rituals, and values of life, life processes, and the supernatural'. To operationalise religion, we utilise four elements – beliefs, values, rituals and community (Mathras et al., 2016). The interplay of these four tenets describes how an individual experiences religion. Figure 14.1 shows how these four elements are linked.

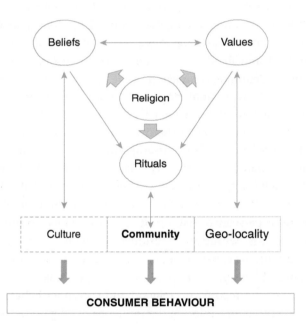

Figure 14.1   The four elements of religion

Religious beliefs

Religious beliefs are the sum total of all shared opinions or convictions relating to a particular religion (Park, 2005). Beliefs are those fundamental ideas that bind people or a community within a particular religion. For instance, Buddhists share the belief that reality is temporary and that the human tendency to cling and attach to worldly possessions is the main reason for the suffering of human beings. Likewise, the understanding that there exists a supreme, all-knowing and ever-present God is an example of a religious belief of the Christian faith. Overall, beliefs assist people in their quest for understanding and describing the world in which they live (Hood et al., 2009).

Religious values

Kraft (2017) explains that religious values delineate individuals' expectations of right and wrong. Values signify the core ideologies that inform people's everyday decision making. To illustrate this, the Ten Commandments are a crucial element of the Jewish faith; these teach how people ought to conduct themselves in an 'acceptable manner'. Essentially, religious values are mental images that reinforce accepted attitudes and behaviour.

Rituals

A ritual is some expressive symbolic activity that believers do in order to demonstrate their faith (Rook, 1985). In religion, rituals are actions performed as a means to express one's connection to religion. Rituals are often systematic and done repetitively, such as baptism in Christianity, the Hajj pilgrimage in Islam, the festival of lights (Diwali) in Hinduism, and Bhodhi in Buddhism. For many, the performance of and participation in rituals such as baptism are a rite of passage that symbolises one's commitment and affiliation to a religion (Mathras, 2016).

Community

Religion offers a system of values and beliefs through which individuals gather around specific beliefs and values. From time to time, people perform common religious rituals together (e.g. Diwali, Hajj and Bhodhi) in order to belong to and identify with a specific religious community. When people share a mutual religious doctrine, they develop a shared identity as well as a sense of companionship. Thus, religious affiliation to a specific group assists people in creating a sense of social as well as self-identity (Saroglou, 2011). Over time, shared identity and beliefs in turn develop into a unique culture. Figure 14.1 illustrates how religious beliefs and values further influence rituals, another element of religion which, in turn, determines culture. In the subsequent section, we discuss religion as culture and the expression of culture.

RELIGION AS CULTURE AND THE EXPRESSION OF CULTURE

Religion and culture are closely related. They are like the two sides to a coin; where you see one, the other is not too far off. To many people, their religion is a function or an extension of their culture, such that where you see religion, culture is also present. Thus, religion and culture are not opposites, but complementing social elements. Assael (1992: 319) defines culture as 'the norms, beliefs and customs that are learned from society and lead to common patterns of behaviour'. To illustrate this point, consider the practice of celebrating Thanksgiving in the USA. This tradition of eating turkey with family, on the last Thursday of November, finds its roots in the Christian ritual of offering a sacrifice to God as a sign of appreciation for his provision of good harvests (Tambini, 2017). It was, and still is, a physical demonstration of thanks to God; and that is where the name 'Thanksgiving' originates.

This example not only illustrates the link between culture and religion, it also demonstrates how the latter shapes the former. It is for this reason that marketers are continually trying to decipher religion, at least within the context of culture, consumption and consumer behaviour (Delener, 1994). Religion, thus, is that one constituent element of culture that has an immense impact on individuals' language, customs, attitudes and values (Mokhlis, 2006). In other words, religion defines culture.

As more people become affiliated with organised faiths, religious practices increasingly become deeply entrenched and are ultimately ingrained in mainstream culture. Such an example of this slow evolution of religious rituals into culture is Christmas (Bartunek and Do, 2011). For instance, Santa Claus and the practice of gift giving are contemporary symbols of Christmas. Santa Claus is a legendary figure that supposedly brings gifts on Christmas Eve (i.e. 24 December) to well-behaved children. According to Belk (1987), it is widely believed that the Santa legend grew out of the gift-giving traditions of Saint Nicholas, a 4th century Christian bishop who lived in Greece and was popularly known for his generosity. Meanwhile, Bartunek and Do (2011) trace the gift-giving traditions of Christmas to Calvinist theology brought to the Americas by Puritan settlers in the 17th century. Today, the prospect of buying and receiving gifts among family and friends has grown within mainstream Western culture. The extent of gift giving during the Christmas season is so big that winter holiday shopping in the USA is estimated to account for up to 40 per cent of total retail sales in the USA (Swilley and Goldsmith, 2013). Studying, for instance, the Santa Claus legend, a supposedly religious figure, is a testament to the link between culture, religion and marketing.

There are many religious rituals-turned-culture, such as Ramadan, Easter, Vesakha Puja and Hannukah. As demonstrated by the above-mentioned examples, religion is continually shaping and re-shaping people's lives, which ultimately redefines their consumption behaviour.

Over time, people who share similar religious doctrines develop a shared identity as well as a sense of companionship. This invariably develops into shared cultural practices and similar consumption habits, as observed in cultural festivities such as Diwali, Easter and Eid. The value which followers of a particular religion attach to certain cultural practices largely depends on religiosity.

Religiosity and culture

Religiosity refers to the extent to which people are devoted to a defined religious group. It is one of the paramount cultural forces and key stimulants in consumer behaviour (Patel, 2012). This is because buying decisions are, among other factors, influenced by the degree to which consumers abide by a certain faith. The degree to which religion influences one's beliefs and behaviour rests on an individual's level of religiosity and the significance one bestows on the religion itself. It has been a bone of contention that religion is extremely personal in nature, and, as a result, its influence on consumer behaviour is governed by an individual's religiosity or the significance placed on religion (Patel, 2012). This standpoint is that an individual who is highly religious will have a heightened understanding of the world through religious systems and, as a result, will incorporate their religion into the greater part of their life. For instance, research has found that while Islamic banking is the preferred mode of banking among Muslims, this call is sometimes ignored. Research has established that, on the one hand, Muslim consumers observed to have low levels of religiosity seem not to be sensitive about the banking brand they use. On the other hand, consumers with moderate levels of religiosity are quite sensitive about bank branding and prefer to only use Islamic banking products (Ahmad et al., 2011). Similar observations were made with regard to halal products. Preference for halal products was strongly correlated with Muslim consumers' level of religiosity (Mukthar and Butt, 2012).

The preceding discussion confirms that religiosity plays an important part in influencing several aspects related to consumer behaviour. In support, Mokhlis (2006) posits that religiosity affects consumers on a daily basis. It shapes their conduct in life, their search for information, a buying risk aversion, perceptions related to advertising, buying behaviour, and designated concepts of retail behaviour. Therefore, there is sufficient evidence confirming the utility of religiosity in determining the behaviour of consumers. The need for continual interaction among congregants might explain the rapid growth in community-based religions such as Islam and Christianity (Harper, 2012). The expectation, on the part of adherents, is that unlike individual-based religions, community-based religions offer adequate social networks, support, a sense of belonging and an opportunity for people to practise and express their culture (Mathras et al., 2016). In this way, religion affords people the opportunity to express both their personal and cultural beliefs, which is a public affirmation that they are not excluded from mainstream society. Religiosity, thus, acts as both a proxy for culture and a means through which it is expressed.

Religious beliefs and values, and their implications for consumer behaviour

Beliefs are shared opinions or convictions relating to a religion. These help religious communities by providing them with a frame of reference to explain fundamental aspects of life, reality and the world (Park, 2005). In the context of marketing, religious beliefs are part of the building blocks upon which ideas of consumption and the satisfaction of needs are based. In other words, to satisfy their everyday needs (food, clothing), consumers often turn to religious teachings, which, invariably, are embedded within religious beliefs. Therefore, from beliefs and values, consumers formulate ideas of what is and what should be considered right and wrong and what is permissible within the dictates of a religion. Consider Buddhism as an example; Buddhists believe that people should strive for tolerance, modesty and the middle path (Bailey and Sood, 1993). From these beliefs, Buddhists, therefore, develop a set of values that seek to govern, say, modesty. Accordingly, products that violate the value of modesty, for instance branded items, are generally undesirable to Buddhists. Thus, to fulfil these beliefs and values, it is likely that Buddhist consumers are not very materialistic. Consequently, Buddhist consumers are least likely to be motivated by product branding or by the consumption of high-quality products, since these violate their belief in modesty and the middle path.

RELIGION AND CONSUMER MISBEHAVIOUR

In consumption situations, consumers are expected to behave in certain ways. For instance, they are expected to pay for the products they purchase from the store; they are also expected to protect their own rights and those of other consumers. In reality though, it is not uncommon for consumers to exhibit actions (e.g. shoplifting, vandalism, abusing retail clerks and other consumers) that contradict generally accepted norms and behaviours. Collectively, such actions constitute a behavioural pattern known as consumer misbehaviour (Fullerton and Punj, 2004). As summarised in Table 14.2, there are five categories of acts of consumer misbehaviour (Shambare et al., 2018). These acts are classified according to the market players targeted by these actions; these are acts directed at: (1) marketers' employees, (2) marketers' merchandise, (3) marketers' financial assets, (4) marketers' premises, and (5) other consumers.

Having identified the various aspects of consumer misbehaviour, it is of particular interest for this chapter to ascertain what religion teaches about consumers' expected norms of behaviour. In other words, does religion stipulate acceptable standards of behaviour? If so, to what extent does religion promote or discourage acts of misbehaviour? These questions are briefly discussed next.

Does religion specify norms and standards of behaviour?

By definition, religious values prescribe ethical guidelines, in terms of ideal versus discouraged behaviour, and, therefore, what is permissible and forbidden. For instance, in Judeo-Christian teachings, the Ten Commandments, as contained in the Bible, establish guidelines for good behaviour. In Exodus, God himself decrees to 'his people' (i.e. children of Israel) how they ought to conduct themselves with: (a) their fellow men and (b) him (God). In Exodus (Chapter 20), a set of 10 rules guiding human interaction, which are now commonly known as the Ten Commandments, were set forth. Examples of these relate to prohibition against acts such as stealing, lying and killing, among others. Many of these prohibitions are those that are indicated in the marketing literature as acts of consumer misbehaviour (c.f. Fullerton and Punj, 2004; Milavec, 2012; Shambare et al., 2018). As such, the Christian and Jewish faiths require people to conduct themselves in a manner that is fair to others and the market. Therefore, various acts of misbehaviour are forbidden. Table 14.2 provides an overview of some religious teachings with respect to consumer misbehaviour.

Table 14.2   Consumer misbehaviour and religion

	Misbehaviour categories				
	Retailer's employees	Retailer's financial assets	Retailer's merchandise	Retailer's premises	Other consumers
Examples	Consumer rage	Insurance fraud	Fraudulent returns	Vandalism	Jumping queues
	Verbal, emotional and physical abuse directed at a retailer's or producer's employees	Credit card fraud	Shoplifting	Hacking	Intimidation and violence towards other consumers
		Defrauding cashiers	Price tag switching	Arson, database theft	Abusing express checkout tills

(Continued)

Table 14.2   (Continued)

	Misbehaviour categories				
	Retailer's employees	Retailer's financial assets	Retailer's merchandise	Retailer's premises	Other consumers
Christianity	A soft answer turns away wrath, but a harsh word stirs up anger	Better is a little with righteousness than great revenues with injustice	Thou shall not steal	A man without self-control is like a city broken into and left without walls	Do not envy a man of violence and do not choose any of his ways
Islam	Whoever believes in Allah should do good to others	And do not cloak (and confuse) the truth with falsehood	You shall mark their hands as a punishment for their crime	Whoever believes in Allah should do good to others and their property	And do not let the hatred of a people prevent you from being just
Hinduism	You need to show compassion to all living beings	Nothing is higher than the Law of Righteousness	*Asteya* (no desire to possess or steal)	Dharma demands that one should have a virtuous character	*Ahimsa* (non-violence)
Buddhism	With gentleness overcome anger	Tell no lies and deceive no one	Do not take what is not given you	Be gentle and sensitive to others and their property	Seeing the similarity to oneself, one should not use violence or have it used
Judaism	For the anger of man does not produce the righteousness of God	No man who practises deceit shall dwell in my house	Do not steal	Scoffers set a city aflame, but the wise turn away wrath	*Shalom* (promotes peace and submission)

Source: Adapted from Shambare et al. (2018)

Table 14.2 clearly demonstrates that religion does have an influence on consumer misbehaviour. Most major religions, as shown in Table 14.2, discourage and at times forbid acts of misbehaviour such as shoplifting (i.e. stealing) and not being courteous to others. For instance, within the context of Buddhism, unfairly treating other people, be they retailers, employees or fellow consumers, constitutes behaviour that removes one from the 'middle path'.

THE MARKETING MIX, BRANDING AND RELIGION

Many religions regulate consumption. Regulating consumption is important because it helps individuals achieve their personal objectives and also those of their religion. To illustrate this point, consider Hinduism as an example. Hindus believe in the principles of a caste system. The implication of this is the common understanding that people are born into a definite caste; and they ought to live and die by the dictates of that caste. Naturally, this introduces a certain level of fatalism or feelings of an inherent incapacity of consumers to change their personal circumstances. As such, there is very little need for individuals to make decisions outside the norms and expectations of their caste. It is for this reason that Bailey and Sood (1993) refer to Hindus as having passive consumer behaviours. Passive consumers, in other words, refers to individuals who exert very little, if any, effort in acquiring information about new products, brands, retailers or lower prices. As such, searching for alternative information on, say, new products, is likely to be viewed as contradictory to Hinduism. Naturally, within Hindu societies, there would be a great willingness to accept existing products, services and prices.

Shifting attention to food consumption practices, individuals tend to select to consume or avoid certain foods in accordance with their religious beliefs. It is also important to note that most of the religious restrictions on consumption relate to food. As such, this chapter pays special attention to diet requirements across religions. While not all religions have specific guidelines regarding diet, Table 14.3 summarises some of the regulations imposed on food consumption by some prolific religions.

Table 14.3   Influence of religious values on food consumption

Type of religion	Practice or restriction	Value rationale
Buddhism	<ul><li>Meat is not recommended; a vegetarian diet is desired</li><li>Moderation in all foods</li><li>Monks are required to fast</li></ul>	<ul><li>Earthly natural foods are regarded highly</li><li>Pure Monks refrain from all solid food after noon</li></ul>
Christianity	<ul><li>Meat is restricted on certain days</li><li>Fasting is selective</li></ul>	<ul><li>Holy Days are observed, including fasting and restrictions to intensify spiritual progress</li></ul>
Hinduism	<ul><li>Beef is forbidden</li><li>All other meat and fish restricted or avoided</li><li>Alcohol should not be consumed</li><li>Several fasting days</li></ul>	<ul><li>Cows cannot be eaten as they are sacred, however products of the 'sacred' cow are considered pure and preferred</li><li>Fasting stimulates spiritual development</li></ul>
Islam	<ul><li>Refrain from eating pork and certain birds</li><li>Alcohol is illegal</li><li>Coffee/tea/stimulants not recommended</li><li>Fasting during specific periods</li></ul>	<ul><li>Food consumption is for good health</li><li>Failure to eat appropriately reduces spiritual awareness</li><li>Evil elements are cleansed through fasting</li></ul>

As portrayed in Table 14.3, Buddhists adhere to vegetarian diets, as these are seen as instrumental in improving quality of life. The lack of meat among many Buddhists' diet is in line with their beliefs around preserving life, including the lives of animals. Christians appear to have the most liberal diet, save for a few denominations such as the Seventh Day Adventists who seem to promote the vegetarian lifetyle (Tukamushaba and Musinguzi, 2018).

In the case of Muslims, food consumption is highly aligned to the prescripts of the halal (permissible) dietary laws. Food, to Muslims, is a means to achieving and maintaining healthy lives. Accordingly, food is not supposed to be abused as a recreation tool, which means that excess indulgence of stimulants, for example tea, coffee or alcohol, is not recommended in Islam (Tukamushaba and Musinguzi, 2018). Another important consideration among Muslims over and above halal food is that the food must be prepared in an absolutely spotless environment, so much so that even halal ingredients can be considered to be *haram* (i.e. forbidden) if the food preparation environment is unsanitary or if it is contaminated with prohibited (*haram*) items. As a result, Muslim consumers could easily become unhappy and sometimes often call for a massive boycott of any food outlets they perceive to be lacking in hygiene because of the value they attach to cleanliness (see ethical focus 14.1).

Ethical Focus 14.1

Jakim revokes Secret Recipe halal certificate over sanitary issues

Restaurant chain Secret Recipe's halal certificate has been revoked due to sanitary issues. According to a post on Secret Recipe's Facebook page, this came in the midst of its expansion plans. The management of Secret Recipe told customers on social media that all their 'ingredients and preparation of products and food are in accordance with the Halal Certification Standards of Malaysia', and that the certificate was revoked due to its renovation and upgrading works. Still, news of the halal certificate being revoked sparked heated conversations on social media, particularly on Secret Recipe's Facebook page. A quick check by A+M showed that consumers were unhappy with the restaurant's lack of transparency, since it did not immediately update its customers when the halal certification was first revoked. The Secret Recipe had not responded to A+M's queries at the time of writing. Meanwhile, the Islamic Development Department (Jakim) confirmed Secret Recipe's statement. Jakim's Halal Hub director Hakimah Mohd Yusoff said the halal certificate was revoked on 7 May due to violations of Good Manufacturing Practice (GMP) and the Malaysia Halal Certification Procedures Manual that involved serious cleanliness issues. Hakimah said, 'The revocation, however, has nothing to do with haram ingredients in the processing of products', adding that, 'the restaurant can re-apply for a halal certificate once the requirements are met'.

Source

Ismail, N. (2015) Jakim revokes Secret Recipe halal certificate over sanitary issues. Available at: www.marketing-interactive.com/jakim-revokes-secret-recipe-halal-certification-sanitary-issues (accessed 9 August 2018).

Questions

1. What are the implications of cases such as the revocation of the halal certification of Secret Recipe for contemporary marketing practice?
2. Assuming you are the CEO of Secret Recipe, what actions would you take to address this issue?

The discussion in ethical focus 14.1 illustrates how religion affects individual consumption patterns. Having said that, however, the important issue to consider is the marketer's response. Put simply, how can retail managers design marketing interventions that are consistent with their customers' religious beliefs? From a retailer's point of view, understanding consumers and how they practise their religion and how religion impacts on consumption is important. It allows marketers to design offerings that satisfy customer needs. This involves the application of the marketing mix, consisting of the 4Ps of marketing – product, price, place and promotion.

As already shown, when selecting products, consumers often take into account several factors among which are religious considerations, product branding and price. As such, for each product, it is not uncommon for consumers to tend to ask questions such as:

*   How does this product and this particular brand help (or hinder) my faith?
*   Are the raw materials used to manufacture the product safe for human consumption?
*   To what extent is this product permissible by my religion?
*   Have the necessary religious considerations been taken into account?
*   Can I afford this product?
*   Are the distribution channels used to deliver the product appropriate?

Throughout the consumption process, consumers ask these questions several times a day. It should be noted that the above list of questions is not exhaustive; consumers may ask hundreds, if not thousands, of other potential questions before satisfying themselves on a particular product. It goes without saying that the entire product information gathering exercise can be a daunting task, which leads to much confusion. To cope with this potentially challenging situation, research findings seem to suggest that religiously affiliated consumers resort to branded products, as a strategy. For instance, halal-certified products provide Muslims with the necessary assurance that all Islamic food preparation guidelines have been adhered to. Similarly, Islamic banking products provide such assurances in the financial services sector.

The importance of branding within the context of religion is underscored by the influence of religiosity and product selection. A large volume of research confirms the positive correlation that exists between religiosity and religious certified products such as Islamic banking (Ahmad et al., 2011). Therefore, to provide consumers with the necessary disclosures on products, retailers resort to utilising both product certification and branding.

In terms of religion, product certification refers to the practice of ensuring that the features and qualities of products are in line with the requirements of a particular faith. Although many religions have set some sort of restriction on which products may or may not be consumed, only a handful have a formally written code that seeks to regulate consumption; examples being Christianity, Islam and Judaism. Of these, Islam and Judaism have product certification boards, whose seals of approval and certification, which are affixed to recommended brands or products, are indicated in Table 14.4. It is also important to note that the bulk of product regulations relate to food. Once these conditions have been met, a retailer is permitted to display a certification label on its product. The two main religions with strict product certifications are Judaism and Islam. The respective certifications are kosher and halal, respectively, as presented in Table 14.4.

Branding and management of the marketing mix

Within the ambit of the marketing mix, certification relates mostly to one of the 4Ps, product – its qualities and the minimum prescribed religious standards – for instance, the absence of interest on banking charges in the case of Islamic banking. The remaining 3Ps (price, place, and promotion) are all associated with the product's branding. A brand, therefore, encapsulates the bundle of benefits to be derived from the product. In other words, a brand consists of the 'product itself, the packaging, the brand name, the promotion, the advertising and the overall presentation' (Murphy, 1988: 4).

Table 14.4   Product certification by religion

	Judaism	Islam
Restrictions	Grape products made by non-Jews Pork and pork products, shellfish, meat and dairy products must not be prepared, stored or eaten together	All types of alcohol and other intoxicating substances, pork and pork products, products containing gelatine, and food prepared without following halal procedures
Certification		
Examples of brands	Keebler	Zahara

From the brand, customers, essentially, will be able to deduce price expectations, distribution channels and promotions for the product. To illustrate this point, consider two brands of watch: (1) a no-name brand and (2) a Seiko. The former will likely be available from a local grocery store with a price tag of say $20 and no guarantee, whereas the Seiko will cost a few hundred dollars and only be available at specialist stores such as jewellery shops. Furthermore, the Seiko brand comes with a substantial product warranty. This example shows that a brand is a representation of the package of expectations given to customers.

In summary, religion informs consumption. From the standpoint of the marketer, the first step is to identify themselves through their brand. Thereafter, it is to understand the core religious beliefs and values of their target market. Key to that is being able to enter the mind of the target consumer. This can be achieved by establishing what consumers affiliated to a particular religion truly value and then helping them connect with brands through revealing the intersection of the marketer's offerings and the consumer's values. Furthermore, marketing strategy should demonstrate sensitivity for the target group's beliefs and customs. The ITC Group of Hotels in case study 14.1 best exemplifies this.

Case Study 14.1

ITC Hotel Group

The ITC Group of Hotels operates in various Muslim countries. As with many hotels, male waiters and attendants serve food and beverages. However, for most Muslim women, having attendants of the opposite sex can be regarded as offensive. At one ITC hotel in India, there was an outcry from women hotel patrons about the male employees in the hotel. In response, the hotel established Eva floors – this is a service exclusively for female travellers. On these Eva Floors, all services are provided by female staff. Only women employees serve guests, providing everything from ancillary services to room service (Hoyer et al., 2016).

Questions for discussion

1. Which of the 4Ps of marketing did ITC change in its product offering at its hotel in India?
2. Discuss why it is important for retailers to consider their customers' religious beliefs.

Branding and promotion

The remaining element of the marketing mix which is closely linked to branding is promotion. Promotion refers to the establishment of a means of communication between the manufacturer/retailer and consumers. To this end, a brand establishes a communication channel between market actors. Within the context of religion, a brand fulfils the communication function in three ways:

1. The brand helps consumers to differentiate products or services. That way, consumers are able to more accurately specify their desired products and, at the same time, reject or recommend brands. In this way, marketers can advertise to specific religious affiliations and reach a particular group via specialised websites or social media interaction with carefully tailored offerings. For example, Judaica Webstore (www.judaicawebstore.com) offers deals on Jewish holiday foods, jewellery, artwork, garments, magazine subscriptions and other products.
2. The brand conveys vital product information to consumers. Contained within the brand and product packaging is crucial information about a product's ingredients and certification (e.g. halal or kosher).
3. The brand acts as a de facto contract of agreement that consumers can continue to expect the same quality and standard of the product or brand. Therefore, the brand establishes a certain level of trust between consumers and retailers.

THE RELIGION–BUSINESS INTERFACE: THE BUSINESS OF RELIGION

In this concluding section, the focus of the chapter turns to the intersection of business and religion or the business of religion. Preceding sections of the chapter identified numerous aspects of consumer behaviour associated with religion. But, it must be appreciated that, if considered from a different context, religion itself is big business. Processes involved in facilitating people to connect with their religion have evolved, over time, to become big business. In particular, we will discuss three topical issues, namely the marketing of religion, the marketing of religious artefacts, and religious tourism.

The marketing of religion

With the global world swamped by commercial chaos, religion has emerged as yet another product sold in the consumer marketplace (Einstein, 2007). Religion, which is manifest in beliefs, values and behavioural norms, each occurring at a different level of depth (religiosity), has profound influences on business. Under these circumstances, in what she termed 'brand of faith', Einstein (2007) proffers that religious groups, as a way of marketing fundamental principles and values which govern the behaviour and life of their adherents, are coming up with various religious products branded in much the same way as consumer products have been branded. Thus, various religious faiths have had to become brands with easily identifiable symbols and spokespeople, with whom prospective believers can make immediate connections.

A typical example of religious marketing among Christian believers is the proliferation of mega churches which are becoming increasingly popular, not only by bringing thousands of worshippers together, but also through millions of dollars in profit. Mega churches are extra-large churches that can accommodate over 15,000 people (Rainer, 2015) and are popular among members of the evangelical Christian faith. Ranging from self-help books to CDs and DVDs, mega churches are becoming big money-makers for various ministries. Einstein (2007) attributed the growth of religious marketing to two main factors. First, the freedom to choose religion in most nations has necessitated the *real* open market for religion. Second, the level of media saturation in general has reached a height never before imagined. The mere fact that there is more media means that there is more *religious* media (see digital focus 14.1) which can be viewed any time of the day or night. For instance, there is currently a surge in televangelists who conduct religious services on various profit-making media such as television and YouTube channels, or even on social media such as Facebook. Besides preaching, televangelists often devote time to fund-raising activities by marketing religious products to viewers.

Digital Focus 14.1

How people of faith are using the internet

As the internet pervades American life, its influence has carried over to the areas of faith and religion. According to the Pew Internet and American Life Project, 25 per cent of internet users have accessed religious or spiritual information online at one point or another. More than three million people a day get religious or spiritual material from the internet. What specifically do 'religious surfers' look for online? According to the Pew study, the top five activities of religious surfers on the internet are: (1) looking for information about their own faith (67%); (2) looking for information about another faith (50%); (3) emailing a prayer request (38%); (4) downloading religious music (38%); and (5) giving spiritual guidance via email (37%). Most who used the internet for religious experiences indicated that they were likely to use the internet even more in the future. Among the net-based religious endeavours deemed most appealing were listening to archived religious teaching, reading online 'devotionals' and buying religious products and resources online.

Source

Global Christ Centre (2003) How People of Faith Are Using the Internet. Available at: http://globalchristiancenter.com/church-resources/applying-technology/24541-how-people-of-faith-are-using-computers-and-the-internet (accessed 9 August 2018).

Questions

1. Besides the internet, can you name some of the channels in which media has been used for the purpose of religious marketing?
2. Assuming you are a marketing manager, what strategies could you implement to trigger religious surfers to search for products online?

The marketing of religious artefacts

A religious artefact may be described as an object that is of special religious interest and is treated with great respect. Each religious tradition has items of special significance. Common religious artefacts include the Buddhist prayer flag, Christian rosary beads, Hindu Puja tray, Islamic prayer mat and compass, and the Jewish Passover (Seder) plate. Consumers affiliated with these religions often need to pay a specific amount which is sometimes referred to as a *donation* in order to acquire the respective artefacts. Thus, this practice of selling religious artefacts also explains the relationship between religion and business. Religious artefacts are used in worship, festivals, rites of passage, or as daily reminders to followers of their beliefs, traditions and identity. Furthermore, religious artefacts are instrumental in fulfilling the expression of faith through various religious rituals. Religious artefacts thus can be mediatory devices in the ritual setting for the purpose of making contact with the divine world. As discussed above, you will recall that ritual is among the four underlying dimensions of religion and, as such, it is imperative to assess its influence on consumer behaviour.

Religious rituals include practices such as consistent public and private prayer. Examples of religious rituals are Easter in Christianity, the Hajj pilgrimage in Islam, the festival of lights (Diwali) in Hinduism, and Bhodhi in Buddhism. Religious rituals usually involve products and services such as food and drink, ornaments, jewellery, candles, or ceremonial garments and visits to sacred sites, which are consumed or employed in the ritual setting. When performing religious rituals, religious artefacts convey precise symbolic messages that are fundamental to the connotation of the whole ritual experience. At Easter, Easter eggs symbolise new life for Christians. For Hindus during Diwali, there is an increase in spending as the most innovative gifts find their way to the shelves – food and clothing as well as durable household goods. Diwali is the five-day festival of lights, which accompanies the Hindu new year when Hindus attend to prayer and celebrate fresh beginnings and the triumph of light over darkness and good over evil.

In Islam, the biggest ritual performed is the Hajj pilgrimage. Hajj is an important feast, where millions of Muslims from around the world gather together at their most sacred site, in the Saudi Arabian city of Mecca on a yearly basis. During the Hajj pilgrim, Muslims partake in a sequence of religious rituals aimed at bringing about greater unity and humility among themselves (Batrawy, 2016). For marketers and retailers, the occasion also represents a large commercial event for brands and consumers.

Religious tourism

According to Tourism & More (2014), religious tourism is not only about visiting a particular holy destination, but may also be done to acquire knowledge, for reasons of friendship or even as a form of leisure. In the Western world, for example, holy cities such as Jerusalem, Rome and Mecca continue to attract millions of visitors on a yearly basis (see practitioner's perspective 14.1). Even though the primary motivation for a trip may be religious, the experience is usually also an opportunity for businesses to provide additional attractions. For instance, a common mistake is assuming that a traveller must be of a particular religion in order to visit a specific religious site. For example, although Mecca holds special meaning for followers of the Muslim faith, especially during Hajj, millions of non-Muslims also visit Mecca both for its spirituality and for its architectural beauty. As a result, during religious belief-based tourism periods (Tourism & More, 2014), it is essential that businesses such as hotels and restaurants connect with religious communities (consumers) to develop an overall faith-based product rather than a mishmash of unrelated offerings.

Practitioner's Perspective 14.1

Mecca makeover: How the Hajj has become big business for Saudi Arabia

An estimated 2.5 million Muslims begin the annual Hajj pilgrimage today and the total number of tourists to Mecca and Medina is expected to rise from about 12 million to almost 17 million by 2025. Hadi Helal, a marketing agent for Abraj al-Bait, says that different nationalities seek different styles of hotels when they perform the pilgrimage, which is the fifth pillar of Islam and a once-in-a-lifetime obligation for Muslims who can afford it. The level of pampering offered by some hotels – Asprey toiletries, a 24-hour butler service, $270 chocolate selections – jars with the ethos of sacrifice, simplicity and humility of the Hajj but it is not a contradiction felt by those customers snapping up royal suites at $5,880 a night, eating gelato or milling around hangar-like lobbies of polished marble in their Hajj clothing of bed sheets, towels or burqas. Raffles is reporting 100% occupancy for its 211 rooms. Helal further said: 'As long as you do what you have to do for the Hajj, it does not mean you have to eat bread or lobster, or sleep on a bed or the floor. It is not for me to say how people should stay when they get here.' Business reports conclude that Saudi tourism, especially that of the religious variety, is recession-proof. The Saudi government's commission for tourism and antiquities said revenue from tourism this year would reach $17.6 billion, then almost double again by 2015. Business Monitor International forecasts that there will be 319,000 rooms, up from 218,000 in 2009, in Saudi Arabia.

Source

Butt, R. (2010) Mecca makeover: How the Hajj has become big business for Saudi Arabia. Available at: www.theguardian.com/world/2010/nov/14/mecca-hajj-saudi-arabia (accessed 9 August 2018).

Questions for discussion

1. Think of any popular religious event which is held within your country and elaborate on how it is benefiting local businesses.
2. In practitioner's perspective 14.1, it is evident that the Hajj holds a very significant meaning for followers of Islam. Taking advantage of the Hajj, what are the marketing strategies that might be used by businesses to promote their offerings?

Case Study 14.2

Religion and advertising: Competing to be the real thing

Two recent bits of news will be of interest to people who worry about the offence which advertising and other marketing tools can cause to religious believers. As it happens, both items concern Christians in Britain, but one could find many similar stories from other countries and faiths.

The Advertising Standards Authority (ASA), a self-regulatory body, rejected a complaint from 30 people who said they were upset by a Christmas commercial for KFC, a fast-food chain. The advert poked lightish fun at some secular aspects of the winter holiday celebration (like shoppers squabbling over an item they both wanted) and showed carol singers trying to soften the heart of a Scrooge-like figure with what they self-mockingly called 'stupid songs'. It was the latter two words which offended some but, as the ASA noted, the singers were just making a point about their grumpy listener's state of mind.

Meanwhile, a sandwich-shop chain, Pret A Manger, withdrew a brand of tomato-flavoured crisps called 'Virgin Mary' after receiving protests from Catholics. In a message to the complainers, the company said 'we are extremely sorry that the crisp name we had selected has offended you ... [the CEO] has taken your advice and decided to remove all of the crisps from our shops ... we will be donating all the unsold crisps to homeless charities that we support across the country'.

Advertising regulators across Europe face many such complaints and they use broadly similar guidelines to deal with them, recommending that marketers avoid material that will either cause widespread offence, or intense offence to a small group.

Questions for discussion

1. What strategies should marketers implement in order to avoid advertisements that are offensive to religious believers?
2. Explain why branding is an important marketing tool when targeting religious consumers.

SUMMARY OF KEY IDEAS

The purpose of this chapter was twofold. The first half attempted to provide a broad definition of religion and also to determine a more specific definition applicable to consumer behaviour. As such, religion, within the context of consumer behaviour, was conceptualised to be a 'system of meaning embodied in a pattern of life, a community of faith, and a worldview that articulates a view of the sacred and of what ultimately matters'. The chapter further demonstrated that, in practical terms, religion denotes the convergence point and the interaction of religious beliefs, religious values, religious rituals and religious community. These four main attributes, the chapter demonstrated, are directly linked to much observable consumer behaviour. The second half of the chapter concerned itself with consumer behaviour implications as related to the above-mentioned tenets of religion. Several examples, as they apply to some of the world's prominent religions, such as Hinduism, Buddhism, Judaism and Christianity, were presented. These related to how consumers ought to interact with each other, restrictions on diet and choice of products. Overall, the chapter confirmed the importance of religion in consumer behaviour. The chapter concluded by presenting some marketing implications as they relate to religion.

Chapter Discussion Questions

1. State, and briefly explain, various elements of religion which might affect consumer behaviour.
2. With reference to any religion mentioned in the chapter, what are the implications of its values for consumer behaviour?
3. With reference to religion and marketing, what are some of the challenges faced by marketers?
4. Provide three examples of actions which constitute a behavioural pattern known as consumer misbehaviour.
5. Can religion be considered a business? Explain your answer.

REFERENCES

Ahmad, K., Rustam, A. and Dent, M. M. (2011) Brand preference in Islamic banking. *Journal of Islamic Marketing*, 2(1), 74–82.

Assael, H. (1992) *Consumer Behaviour and Marketing Action*. Boston: PWS-KENT.

Bailey, J. M. and Sood, J. (1993) The effects of religious affiliation on consumer behaviour: A preliminary investigation. *Journal of Managerial Issues*, 5(3), 328–52.

Bartunek, J. M. and Do, B. (2011) The sacralization of Christmas commerce. *Organization*, 18(6), 795–806.

Batrawy, A. (2016) What is the Hajj? The significance of the pilgrimage in Islam. Available at: www.independent.co.uk/news/world/middle-east/what-is-the-hajj-islam-muslims-mecca-saudi-arabia-explainer-a7235961.html#gallery (accessed 26 April 2018).

BBC (2014) Religions. Available at: www.bbc.co.uk/religion/religions/jainism (accessed 11 July 2019).

Belk, R. W. (1987) A child's Christmas in America: Santa Claus as deity, consumption as religion. *Journal of American Culture*, 10(1), 87–100.

Delener, N. (1994) Religious contrasts in consumer decision behaviour patterns: Their dimensions and marketing implications. *European Journal of Marketing*, 28(5), 36–53.

Einstein, M. (2007) *Brands of Faith: Marketing Religion in a Commercial Age*. London: Routledge.

Fairchild, M. (2017) Get to Know the Basic Beliefs of Christianity. Available at: www.thoughtco.com/basic-christian-beliefs-700357 (accessed 21 April 2018).

Fullerton, R. A. and Punj, G. (2004) Repercussions of promoting an ideology of consumption: Consumer misbehaviour. *Journal of Business Research*, 57: 1239–49.

Hackspirit (2017) New Study Reveals the World's Fastest Growing Religion, and it's not Christianity or Islam. Available at: https://hackspirit.com/new-study-reveals-worlds-fastest-growing-religion-not-christianity-islam (accessed 14 April 2018).

Harper, J. (2012) 84 Percent of the World Population has Faith; a Third are Christian. Available at: www.washingtontimes.com/blog/watercooler/2012/dec/23/84-percent-world-population-has-faith-third-are-ch (accessed 12 April 2018).

Hays, J. (2013) Taoist Beliefs. Available at: http://factsanddetails.com/china/cat3/sub10/item91.html#chapter-12 (accessed 9 August 2018).

Hood, R. W., Jr., Hill, P. C. and Spilka, B. (2009) *The Psychology of Religion: An Empirical Approach*, 4th edn. New York: The Guilford Press.

Hoyer, W. D., Macinnis, D. J. and Pieters, R. (2016) *Consumer Behaviour*, 7th edn. Boston, MA: Cengage Learning.

Johnson, A. G. (2000) *The Blackwell Dictionary of Sociology*, 2nd edn. Oxford: Blackwell.

Kalupahana, D. J. (1987) *The Principles of Buddhist Psychology*. Albany, NY: State University of New York.

Klostermaier, K.K. (1989) *A survey of Hinduism*. Albany, NY: State University of New York Press.

Kraft, D. (2017) Examples of Religious Values. Available at: https://classroom.synonym.com/examples-of-religious-values-12087784.html (accessed 24 April 2018).

Lipka, M. and Hacket, C. (2017) Why Muslims are the World's Fastest-growing Religious Group. Available at: www.pewresearch.org/fact-tank/2017/04/06/why-muslims-are-the-worlds-fastest-growing-religious-group (accessed 14 April 2018).

Mansori, S. (2012) Impact of religion affiliation and religiosity on consumer innovativeness: The evidence of Malaysia. *World Applied Sciences Journal*, 7(3), 301–7.

Mathras, D., Cohen, A. B., Mandel, N. and Mick, D. G. (2016) The effects of religion on consumer behavior: A conceptual framework and research agenda. *Journal of Consumer Psychology*, 26(2), 298–311.

McDaniel, S.W. and Burnett, J.J. (1990) Consumer religiosity and retail store evaluative criteria. *Journal of the Academy of Marketing Science*, 18(2): 101–12.

Meyers-Levy, J. and Loken, B. (2015) Revisiting gender differences: What we know and what lies ahead. *Journal of Consumer Psychology*, 25(1), 129–49.

Milavec, B. (2012) An analysis of consumer misbehavior on Black Friday. BSc dissertation, University of Delaware.

Mokhlis, S. (2006) The influence of religion on retail patronage behaviour in Malaysia. PhD thesis, University of Stirling.

Mukthar, A. and Butt, M. (2012) Intention to choose Halal products: The role of religiosity. *Journal of Islamic Marketing*, 3(2), 108–20.

Murphy, J. (1988) "BRANDING". *Marketing Intelligence & Planning*, 6(4): 4–8.

Park, C. L. (2005) Religion as a meaning-making framework in coping with life stress. *Journal of Social Issues*, 61(4), 707–29.

Patel, M. (2012) Influence of religion on shopping behaviour of consumers: An exploratory study. *Abhinav National Monthly Refereed Journal of Research in Commerce & Management*, 1(5), 68–78.

Pew Research Center (2012) The Global Religious Landscape. Available at: www.pewforum.org/2012/12/18/global-religious-landscape-exec (accessed 7 August 2018).

Rainer, T. S. (2015) One Key Reason Most Churches Do Not Exceed 350 in Average Attendance. Available at: https://thomrainer.com/2015/03/one-key-reason-churches-exceed-350-average-attendance (accessed 7 August 2018).

Rook, D. W. (1985) The ritual dimension of consumer behaviour. *Journal of Consumer Research*, 12(3), 251–64.

Saroglou, V. (2011) Believing, bonding, behaving, and belonging: The big four religious dimensions and cultural variation. *Journal of Cross-Cultural Psychology*, 42, 1320–40.

Schmidt, R., Sager, G. C., Carney, G., Jackson, J. J., Zanca, K., Muller, A. and Jackson, J. (1999) *Patterns of Religion*. Belmont, CA: Wadsworth Publishing.

Shambare, R., Muswera, N. and Shambare, J. (2018) Children's consumer behaviour in developing countries. In A. Gbadamosi (ed.), *Young Consumer Behaviour*. London: Routledge/ Taylor and Francis.

Sheth, J.N. and Mittal, B. (2004) *Customer Behavior: A Managerial Perspective*, 2nd edn. Georgetown, TX: Southwestern University.

South African History Online (2018) African Traditional Religion. Available at: www.sahistory.org.za/article/african-traditional-religion (accessed 13 July 2018).

Swilley, E. and Goldsmith, R. E. (2013) Black Friday and Cyber Monday: Understanding consumer intentions on two major shopping days. *Journal of Retailing and Consumer Services*, 20(1), 43–50.

Tambini, J. (2017) What is Thanksgiving? What is happening today and why do Americans eat turkey? Available at: www.express.co.uk/news/world/883364/Thanksgiving-2017-what-is-holiday-America-US-turkey-traditions (accessed 25 July 2018).

Tourism & More (2014) The Importance of the Religious Tourism Market. Available at: www.tourismandmore.com/tidbits/the-importance-of-the-religious-tourism-market (accessed 8 August 2018).

Tukamushaba, R. K. and Musinguzi, D. (2018) Faith, religion and young consumer behaviour. In A. Gbadamosi (ed.), *Young Consumer Behaviour: A Research Companion*. New York: Routledge, pp. 334–6.

GLOSSARY

Affective neuroscience the science of interrelationships of the brain with emotions (consumer emotions).

Analytics metrics used to monitor and improve performance in marketing and advertising campaigns.

Artificial intelligence (AI) an area of computer science that emphasises the creation of intelligent machines that work and react like humans, including speech recognition, learning, planning and problem-solving.

Behavioural neuroscience the science of interrelationships of the brain with behaviour (consumer behaviour).

Biological neuroscience the science of individual molecules, genes, proteins and hormones in the brain and its functioning (hormonal affects in the consumer).

Blogging a practice where people write about products, services and experiences and share them online for the benefit of other users on a weblog.

Brand A symbol, design, name or logo that provides identification for the products or services of an individual, organisation or group and differentiates them from others.

Brand architecture a process in which managers build brands from symbolic and physical infrastructure in a similar way that an architect would construct a building.

Brand community A non-geographical community based on a shared set of social relations among admirers of a brand.

Branded house a company where a master brand acts as the dominant brand name across multiple product offerings or categories.

Clinical neuroscience the science of interrelationships of the brain with medical conditions (understanding customers with mental health issues or specific learning difficulties).

'Cloud' computing the practice of using a network of remote servers hosted on the internet to store, manage and process data, rather than a local server or a personal computer.

Cognitive neuroscience the science of interrelationships of the brain with thoughts (decision making).

Computational neuroscience the science of how the brain computes, including how it handles mathematics and physics (pricing).

Consumer co-creation a process where consumers are regarded as partners in the creation of value with companies.

Content management system (CMS) a web-based software application or set of related programs that provide capabilities for multiple users with different permission levels to manage marketing content, customer data and campaigns.

Contextual marketing a direct form of marketing that serves targeted advertising based on a potential client's likes and interests.

Cultural branding an approach which considers how brands utilise cultural meaning and ideologies to create resonant identity myths in the marketplace.

Cultural neuroscience the science of interrelationships of the brain with cultural issues (the consumer and culture).

Developmental neuroscience the science of how the brain and nervous system develop from conception through childhood, adolescence to adulthood and old age (marketing to children).

Direct to consumer advertising (DTC) direct-to-consumer advertising (DTC advertising) usually refers to the marketing of pharmaceutical products but also applies to the direct marketing of medical devices, consumer diagnostics and sometimes financial services. This form of advertising is directed toward patients, rather than health care professionals.

Entrepreneurial marketing 'the proactive identification and exploitation of opportunities for acquiring and retaining profitable customers through innovative approaches to risk management, resource leveraging and value creation'.

Foreign direct investment (FDI) an investment in the form of a controlling ownership in a business in one country by an entity based in another country.

Globalism the operation or planning of economic and foreign policy on a global basis.

Glocal reflecting or characterised by both local and global considerations.

House of brands a company which operates a number of independent brands under its stewardship but does not feature the parent company name prominently in its branding.

Internationalisation the process of firms adopting an international outlook and becoming involved in international operations.

Localism a preference for one's own area or region, especially when this results in a limitation of outlook.

Luxury brands brands which have an associated high price as well as exclusivity, prestige and social status.

Neuroimaging a branch of medical imaging that concentrates on the brain. It is used to study the brain, how it works and how different activities affect the brain, and to diagnose diseases. Some ways in which the brain can be imaged are by Electroencephalogram (EEG), Computerised Axial Tomography (CAT), Positron Emission Tomography (PET), Magnetic Resonance Imaging (MRI), Functional Magnetic Resonance Imaging (fMRI), Steady State Topography (SST) and Magnetoencephalography (MEG) (experimental marketing).

Neurolinguistics the science of how the brain enables the understanding and use of language (consumers' uses and understanding of their own and marketing language).

Neurophysiology the science of how the brain and its functions relate to other parts of the body (consumers' reactions to sensory stimulations).

Small and medium-sized enterprises (SMEs) the EU defines SMEs as firms with fewer than 250 employees and whose turnover must not exceed 50 million euros.

INDEX

Page numbers in *italics* indicate figures. Page numbers in **bold** indicate tables.